Digital Convergence in Intelligent Mobility Systems

Scrivener Publishing
100 Cummings Center, Suite 541J
Beverly, MA 01915-6106

Publishers at Scrivener
Martin Scrivener (martin@scrivenerpublishing.com)
Phillip Carmical (pcarmical@scrivenerpublishing.com)

Digital Convergence in Intelligent Mobility Systems

Edited by

Rathishchandra R. Gatti

and

Chandra Singh

Scrivener Publishing

WILEY

This edition first published 2025 by John Wiley & Sons, Inc., 111 River Street, Hoboken, NJ 07030, USA and Scrivener Publishing LLC, 100 Cummings Center, Suite 541J, Beverly, MA 01915, USA

For more information about Scrivener publications please visit www.scrivenerpublishing.com.

Wiley Global Headquarters
111 River Street, Hoboken, NJ 07030, USA

For details of our global editorial offices, customer services, and more information about Wiley products visit us at www.wiley.com.

The manufacturer's authorized representative according to the EU General Product Safety Regulation is Wiley-VCH GmbH, Boschstr. 12, 69469 Weinheim, Germany, e-mail: Product_Safety@wiley.com.

Library of Congress Cataloging-in-Publication Data

ISBN 9781394275243

Cover image: Generated with AI using Adobe Firefly
Cover design by Russell Richardson

Set in size of 11pt and Minion Pro by Manila Typesetting Company, Makati, Philippines

Printed in the USA

10 9 8 7 6 5 4 3 2 1

Contents

Preface

The purpose of this book *Digital Convergence in Intelligent Mobility Systems* is to explore the integration of cyber technologies within transportation systems, highlighting the importance of intelligent transport systems (ITS) in enhancing mobility. The book discusses how advancements in mobility systems, electronic communications, data analytics, and connectivity can transform traditional transport networks into smart mobility solutions that improve safety, efficiency, and sustainability. It will serve as a valuable resource for researchers, engineers, policymakers, and students interested in the field of intelligent mobility.

Chapter 1 discusses a comprehensive analysis of semi- and fully-automated seed-sowing machines for agricultural purposes. Some of the shortcomings of traditional machines and practices are also compiled in this chapter. The scope for further improvement in seed-sowing machines and features is highlighted in the chapter, which encourages researchers to carry forward this research.

In Chapter 2, we discuss the intelligent mobility of agricultural drones that conforms to international drone policy and regulation. Make the necessary flying preparations and put up a safe mission. Create a mission strategy using free and paid software. Examine how image product delivery can be used for various objectives.

In Chapter 3, a Simulink model is developed with a magic tire system to simulate traction and speed control systems. The proportional–integral–derivative (PID) controller is tested to be more robust and stable compared to sliding mode controls. The chapter comprises vehicle terrain interaction through mathematical modeling and controller, which generates the voltage applied to the wheel electric motor.

Chapter 4 discusses how electric vehicles (EVs) are gaining importance in creating ecofriendly intelligent transportation systems. Although the demand for EVs continues to rise in the consumer segment, the costs of deploying EV charging stations are still high. This has slowed down investment in EV charging infrastructure. People who currently own or are considering owning an EV may become worried about running out of charge before they get to a charging station or being unable to find a charging point near their destination; these fears are known as range anxiety. To address this concern, dynamic wireless charging (DWC) systems enable vehicles to be charged as they are in motion.

Chapter 5 provides insights into how the operation of 5G technology will revolutionize vehicle communication while ushering in a revolutionary epoch of instant communications. Evolution of communication systems in the automotive from primitive ones used earlier to the complex and intelligent networks that propel present-day intelligent vehicles.

Chapter 6 focuses on the transforming effect of machine learning (ML) algorithms in traffic control systems through the use of advanced technologies. Given the worsening situation in large-sized towns and cities where traffic congestion is increasing, rates of accidents are rising, and crises for the environment are growing, a new approach is necessary. Machine learning provides possible solutions that can deal with this problem by providing more accurate traffic flow predictions, handling real-time incident management, and implementing dynamic route optimizations.

In Chapter 7, we discuss the regulations and ethical concerns and solutions of cybersecurity in autonomous mobility. The chapter focuses on a combination of theoretical discussion, case studies, and simulations which are required to create, implement, and maintain the safety of autonomous systems.

Chapter 8 focuses on an intricate aspect of infrastructure development, viz., the influence of EVs that keeps accelerating. The ensuing impending switch toward electric vehicles will greatly make charging services very demanding. This chapter focuses on developing infrastructure for EV charging, spotting new technologies innovating to meet the rising needs of EV users while sustainably protecting the environment.

Chapter 9 presents the exploration of vehicular power line communication (VPLC), which has emerged as a promising way to counter the growing convolution and escalating costs associated with the automotive wiring harnesses, which have become increasingly burdened by the heavy electronic devices as well as sensors in modern automobiles.

The future of V2X communications is discussed in Chapter 10, providing the insights on how the advancements in communication technologies will drastically change the connected vehicles systems with the ITS and provide a safe mobility environment.

To substantially increase the benefits of ITS, it is important that R&D teams must address its critical challenges, such as privacy, cybersecurity, and sustainability. This is addressed in Chapter 11. The chapter discusses how ITS can be designed using V2X communications that enable new control strategies such as adaptive traffic control interventions and dynamic routing with vehicle and roadside units.

Chapter 12 discusses the technology used in these dispensers, the general regulations and infrastructure required for their deployment, and the possible barriers to their large-scale application. Additionally, the chapter examines how these systems affect citizens' access to health care, the efficiency of health economic systems, and the impact of social equity on the environment.

Chapter 13 suggests a better viable Mobility as a Service (MaaS) paradigm that utilizes 5G networks to support human-centric wireless networks in urban areas. The system integrates multiple modes of transport alternatives, real-time traffic management, and personalized transportation services to revolutionize urban mobility by utilizing ultra-fast interaction, minimal latency, and widespread device compatibility of 5G.

Chapter 14 discusses the foldable electric vehicle (FEV) market, which is an emerging segment in the automotive industry, driven by the necessity for sustainable transportation solutions and advancements in battery technology, motor power, and fold mechanisms. There are, in fact, multiple categories available in this industry, such as hoverboards and stand-up scooters, appealing to consumers of all ages for short trips, leisure, and transit requirements.

It has been found that 50% of the accidents involve two-wheel drivers. In Chapter 15, a two-wheeler-based project for safe driving is proposed. This project utilizes a long-range sensor, a motor controller, and the ECU to design a speed regulator of an electric two-wheeler.

Chapter 16 focuses on a voting classifier-based machine learning algorithm (ML) that combines many ML techniques, including random forest, naive Bayes, logistic regression, and SVM. The experimental findings demonstrate that, in comparison to the conventional methods, the suggested voting classifier achieved greater accuracy and precision rate.

Chapter 17 provides an experimental evaluation of feature selection techniques and their effectiveness in processing social media content in order to analyze the text feature selection technique.

Editing this book was an incredible opportunity, and much help was expected from many individuals. We had fine support from our family, friends, and fellow members; we especially thank the Chairman, Principal, faculty, and fraternity of Sahyadri College of Engineering and Management, Mangaluru, and NMAM Institute of Technology, Nitte (Deemed to be University).

Rathishchandra R. Gatti
Chandra Singh

1

Arduino-Based Battery-Operated Multi-Purpose Portable Seed-Sowing Machine

K. Raju[1], M. Ajay Kumar[1] and Canute Sherwin[2*]

[1]*Department of Mechanical Engineering, St. Joseph Engineering College, Mangaluru, India*
[2]*CoE - Energy Science and e-Mobility, Atria University, Karnataka, India*

Abstract

Agriculture plays a crucial role in contributing about 17% of the gross domestic production (GDP) in India. The zest of rural population in India relies on farming and associated activities for their income. The use of traditional tools for agricultural activities like plow, spade, sickle, thresher, etc., gives less yield. Even though a lot of developments related to mechanization and automation of activities related to agriculture and farming are introduced, most of them are suitable for large-scale agriculturalists and farmers. The large-scale farmers associated with mass production are equipped with machines for cropping, thereby making huge profits. There is a need to develop automated/semi-automated systems for medium- or small-scale agricultural activities which would be energy efficient, easy to use and maintain, and economical. The manufacturers of agricultural machineries introduce machines which are imported in design, expensive, and suitable for large-scale applications like tillers, tractors, etc. However, developing and utilizing machines for specific purposes have been a challenge. The seed-sowing machines assist farmers in utilizing time and money to sow seeds in the desired position. In this chapter, the design and development of an Arduino-based battery-operated seed-sowing machine is discussed. The machine uses Arduino-controlled servo motors for controlled spacing and sowing of seeds. The battery eliminates the need for electricity to power the device. The Arduino-controlled design provides farmers a great level of precision and control over the operation of the machine. The depth, speed of tiller blades, and other parameters can be adjusted for the optimal performance of different types of crops and soil. The machine was tested for sowing the different types of seeds at a speed of 75 rpm. The motor and the battery

**Corresponding author*: cscanutesherwin8@gmail.com

Rathishchandra R. Gatti and Chandra Singh (eds.) Digital Convergence in Intelligent Mobility Systems, (1–24) © 2025 Scrivener Publishing LLC

capacities are 250 W and 21 Ah, respectively, and the battery charge will last for 1.3 hours. Overall, the Arduino-controlled multi-purpose seed-sowing machine is a valuable addition to the modern agricultural sector that helps the farmers to increase productivity, efficiency, and profitability. The proposed design is simple to use; hence, even an unskilled farmer can handle it. The chapter also discusses a comprehensive analysis on semi- and fully automated seed-sowing machines for agricultural purposes. Some of the shortcomings of traditional machines and practices are also compiled in this chapter. The scope for further improvement in seed-sowing machines and features is highlighted in the chapter, which encourages researchers to carry forward this research.

Keywords: Agriculture, automation, farmers, battery, seed-sowing machine, gross domestic production, tilling, trenching

1.1 Introduction

In the Indian economy, agriculture plays a crucial role in contributing about 17% of the gross domestic production (GDP). The majority of rural population in India depends on the agriculture and associated activities for their income. The use of traditional tools for agricultural activities like plow, spade, sickle, thresher, etc., gives less yield. Even though a lot of developments related to mechanization and automation of activities related to agriculture and farming are introduced, most of them are suitable for large-scale agriculturalists and farmers. The large-scale farmers are now equipped with machines that help in mass production of crops and hence make the profits. There is a need to develop automated/semi-automated systems for medium- or small-scale agricultural activities which would be energy efficient, easy to use and maintain, and economical. The manufacturers of agricultural machineries introduce machines which are imported in design, expensive, and suitable for large-scale applications like tillers, tractors, etc. However, developing and utilizing machines for specific purposes have been a challenge. The seed-sowing machines assist farmers in utilizing time and money to sow seeds in the desired position. The basic objective of the sowing operation is to put the seed in rows at the desired depth and seed-to-seed spacing, cover the seeds with soil, and provide proper compaction over the seed [1].

The traditional seed-sowing process includes broadcasting manually, i.e., opening furrows manually by the plow and dropping the seeds through a funnel attached to the plow. Dibbling, i.e., sowing in a small area, consists of making slits or holes through a stick and dropping seeds by the hand. The multi-row seeding devices are quite popular with the traditional farmers. Some of the limitations associated with traditional farming include non-uniform distribution of seeds and high labor requirement [2]. The labor shortage is one of the major challenges faced by many agriculturalists today. The need to develop machines suitable for increasing the production rate is increasing today to meet the supply and the demand gap for food products. Sowing is an important activity in agriculture and is labor intensive. Although the seed-sowing machines are available, they are not affordable for small/medium-scale farmers [3]. The mechanization along with the automation leads to improving the efficiency of the farming processes. It helps the farmers to reduce the efforts put toward the seed-sowing functions. This study is a sincere effort to develop a low-cost, compact, and multi-crop semi-automatic seed-sowing machine. A detailed literature survey on already-available seed-sowing machines, associated technologies, and activities related to the seed sowing has been conducted in the present work to help in designing an efficient system. For automation in the field of agriculture, one needs to take care of the process and understand the behavior of the technology at the same time. Care is taken in designing a system which provides the required soil cover, maintaining moisture and PH level, etc. In this line, different automation technologies are being studied, including solar-powered systems, seed metering systems, sensors with Bluetooth modules, etc. [4].

This book chapter discusses the design, construction, and working of a semi-automatic seed-sowing machine which defines the specific needs it needs to fulfill. This provides the base for the design. After the design stage, the manufacturing stage leads to the development of a working prototype. The book chapter culminates with the testing of the prototype for real-world situations, and appropriate modifications to the design and troubleshooting are made. The design comprises of an Arduino-based battery-operated multi-purpose portable seed-sowing machine. The main components of the system are the battery, chain drive and sprocket assembly, wheel, servo motor, Arduino UNO, relay, hopper, shaft and bearing, and DC motor. The machine is powered by a rechargeable battery and controlled by an Arduino microcontroller to control servo motors and other electronic components. The main features of the machine are portability and accessibility in the regions where there is no electricity. The machine is also cost effective, making it an ideal choice for small- and medium-scale farmers and agriculturalists.

1.2 Background

This section discusses a few designs on semi-automated and fully automated seed-sowing machines designed by researchers for small- and medium-scale farmers. This literature has been surveyed to get few insights into the important specifications for the design of a semi-automated seed-sowing and tilling machine.

Ratnesh Kumar *et al.* (2022) developed an automatic seed-sowing machine that moves and sows seeds in the farmland in parallel rows. The machine is designed to carry different types of crop seeds, and the spacing required for different types of plant seed sowing is adjustable. The machine runs with the help of a DC motor connected to a battery [5]. Senthilnathan *et al.* (2018) designed an Internet of Things (IoT)-based seed-sowing machine, which helps the farmers to sow the seeds with less time and effort. The system design comprises a DC motor, seed distributor, cultivator, hopper, relays, microcontroller, and belt drives. The machine can be controlled using an Android phone or a laptop [6]. Vidya Yedave *et al.* (2019) proposed an automatic seed-sowing robot which performs the task of soil loosening and seed sowing at a fast rate. The robot can be controlled to move forward, backward, right, and left using a remote control and RF module. A 12V battery is used to power the system, and an Arduino UNO is used to control the motor drivers. A mechanical mechanism is used in this design for loosening of soil and seed-sowing purposes [7]. Kalash Singhal *et al.* (2018) proposed a solar-powered seed-sowing machine which is cost efficient and performs multiple operations associated with seed sowing like tilling, sowing, and watering. It makes use of a 40 W solar panel, 24V battery, and 24V DC motor for its functioning. The seed-sowing machine's design, apart from being simple, cost effective, and efficient, needs to take into consideration row spacing, seed rate, speed depth, and compaction force [8]. Efforts are made to achieve multiple operations simultaneously by Smitha *et al.* (2018) [9]. Mohan Kumar *et al.* (2023) have designed and fabricated an Arduino-enabled and battery-operated seed-sowing machine. The machine is easy to operate and sows seeds of different sizes. The machine has been incorporated with IR and timing sensors. The IR sensor is used for sensing any obstacle in its navigation path, and the timing sensor is used for feeding the seed in the ground. The machine also feeds fertilizer to the crops [10].

Dangat Shraddha *et al.* (2023) have designed and fabricated an Arduino-based agriculture robot that automatically sows the seed, spreads the fertilizer, and also reaps the crop. It is a Bluetooth technology-based battery-operated robot [11]. Anirban Kumar and Heshalini Rajagopal (2022) have proposed an Arduino-based automated seeding and irrigation system. The proposed system is equipped with Arduino MEGA and Arduino UNO, which act as the main control unit, while ultrasonic and soil moisture sensors are used to detect the obstacles and soil moisture level, respectively. The robot consists of a funnel-like arrangement to perform the seeding procedure. The field is equipped with moisture sensors placed at different areas that monitor the moisture level of the soil on a regular interval for irrigation purposes [12]. Meena Chavan *et al.* (2022) have designed and fabricated an automated seed-sowing robot. It is an Arduino-based robot used for sowing seeds, spraying fertilizers, and leveling the soil. This robot is specifically designed to sow edible seeds like soybean, maize, pigeon pea, Bengal gram, ground nut, etc. [13]. Somasundaram *et al.* (2022) have developed an automated seed-sowing and watering robot using a wireless sensor network. The robot is made by utilizing Arduino UNO, LCD board, PH sensor, water pump motor, four-relay board, and DC gear motor for seed planting [14]. Shubham *et al.* (2022) have developed a farmer-friendly agricultural robot that does the digging of soil and sowing of seeds. It is a microcontroller-based robot [15]. Bibi Ameena *et al.* (2022) have proposed an IoT-based robot for sowing seeds automatically [16]. Adarsh *et al.* (2022) have developed an Android-based agribot that can perform operations such as automatic plowing, seed dosing, fruit picking, and pesticide spraying [17]. Abhijit Khadatkar *et al.* (2022) have conducted a review on the application of robots in changing the future of agriculture [18]. Prakash and Ashwini (2021) have designed a smart agriculture robot for sowing seeds. It is an Arduino-based Bluetooth-controlled robot [19]. Dinesh *et al.* (2021) have designed a smart and automated seed-sowing and grass-cutting rover. It is a solar-powered battery-operated Arduino-based robot that does seed sowing as well as grass cutting [20]. Likhitha *et al.* (2020) have developed an IoT-based smart robot for sowing seeds and harvesting the crop. The robot can be specifically used for sowing soybean, maize, pigeon pea, Bengal gram, ground nut, etc. [21]. Rafega Beham *et al.* (2020) have developed a Bluetooth-embedded solar-powered robot for plowing, seed sowing, and grass cutting [22].

Cihan Yurtsever *et al.* (2020) have designed and developed a robot for row-type seed-sowing applications. The robot consists of four subsystems: a four-wheel mobile platform, a digger mechanism, a seed-dropping mechanism, and an irrigation mechanism. The robot is remotely operated via an Android application on a mobile phone, and all operation data can be monitored via this Android application. Additionally, the robot can perform the row-type seed-sowing operation in an autonomous mode [23].

Komuravelli Nithish Kumar *et al.* (2020) have proposed an automated seed-sowing machine that takes care of plowing the field, sowing the seeds, and covering the seeds. The proposed automated seed-sowing robot has two parts, namely, head and tail. To the head, the blades are attached so that it will plow the land, and the ultrasonic sensor is attached to detect the obstacles in the way. On the tail, the seeds container is placed, and the seeds are placed in a regular interval, and the bent rod is used to cover the seed [24]. Prasada Rao *et al.* (2020) have developed an IoT-based and Wi-Fi-controlled robot for plowing and for sowing seeds [25]. Mosam *et al.* (2020) have developed a semi-automatic Freeduino-based robot for sowing seeds [26]. Shikha Sharma *et al.* (2020) have designed and implemented an agribot using IoT. This autonomous multi-purpose robot is used for plowing, seed dispensing, harvesting, and also for spraying the fertilizers and irrigating the system using a microcontroller [27]. Devashis Debnath (2020) has developed an autonomous agriculture robot—Agrobot Srishti. This robot is used for detection and removal of weeds in the crops [28]. Paul *et al.* (2020) have reviewed the basics of robotics, including a special focus on agriculture, and also highlighted the areas of applications with the concern of issues and challenges in brief [29]. Sweety Dutta *et al.* (2019) have designed and developed an autonomous seed-sowing robot. The robot divides the field into a grid, with intersection points as places where the seeds are sown. The depth of the hole and the distance between points where the seeds are sown are calculated according to government data and are fed to the logic board of the robot. The robot goes to the starting points and makes a hole using a toothed wheel with teeth of increasing height. The delivery system makes sure that only one seed is dispensed per hole, and the back plate mechanism fills the hole after sowing is done. Sensors are used for obstacle detection, and the robot changes its path accordingly [30].

Phansopkar *et al.* (2019) have proposed a remote controlled agricultural robot with a sowing seed mechanism. The proposed robot design can perform agricultural operations such as seed sowing, and it is a remote controlled robot with the reciprocating action of a seeding mechanism [31]. Aravind Kumar *et al.* (2018) have designed and developed an Arduino-based solar-powered seed-sowing and irrigation agribot [32]. Shraddha and Warsha (2017) have designed an Arduino-based robotic vehicle for performing functions like plowing the field, sowing the seeds, and covering the seeds with soil. The robot is autonomous and provides the facility for optional switching of the weeding system when required. The designed system involves navigation of the robot to the destination successfully [33]. Gajendran *et al.* (2017) have designed a multi-purpose agricultural robot to implement precision irrigation, fertilizer addition, and de-weeding, apart from continuous monitoring of crop and soil conditions. This will involve an efficient utilization of water resources, intensive plant and soil monitoring, condition-based use of fertilizers, and the ability to work in unstructured environments [34]. Mohammad Behmanesh *et al.* (2017) have conducted a survey and reported the main advantages of robotics in agriculture. They have categorized the robots into 4 main types: path navigators, harvesting robots, crop disease detectors, and weed detectors [35]. Prajna (2017) has conducted a brief survey on various kinds of robotic technology used in farming, and an idea of multi-talented robots has been presented [36]. Brittadevi and Hemalatha (2017) have conducted a survey on robots that are based on Arduino, IoT, Bluetooth, and big data analytics [37]. Vamshidhar Reddy *et al.* (2016) have reviewed the success stories of robotic agriculture in different areas of agriculture. The work also throws light on the future scope of robotic agriculture especially in developing countries [38]. Sagar *et al.* (2015) have designed a solar-powered microcontroller-based agriculture robotic system for sowing seeds in the field [39]. Sonu Yadav *et al.* (2021) have designed and developed a portable battery-powered electric tiller machine which is light in weight and cost effective to replace that traditional power tiller machines which are typically heavy and bulky, making it difficult for farmers to maneuver and transport. The electric power tiller improves agricultural productivity and efficiency by cutting down on time and costs associated with tilling [40]. Sandesh *et al.* (2020) have developed a portable electric power tiller machine that is used for soil and seedbed preparation and weeding. The tiller machine can be used for a variety of crops, including rice, wheat, maize, and vegetables. The battery-operated machine is portable and light in weight [41].

There are a lot of limitations associated with traditional seed-sowing and plowing practices. The most common limitation is that most of the seeds don't end up in the furrows, leading to improper germination of seeds. They germinate prematurely or don't mature at all. Many of the seeds remain on the surface of the soil where they get eroded by wind or eaten by animals. The furrows form only a certain part of the field, leading to over-seeding (wastage of seeds). The crops require optimum crop densities to prosper depending on the weather condition and the soil quality. Planting crops above this density leads to a fall in yield. This has led to competition among the plants for available resources. The mineral content of the soil also keeps depleting. The advances in technology have led to the invention of the seed-sowing machines. The seed-sowing machines use a series of plows spaced equally apart as the furrows. These plows excavate the furrows to uniform depths prior to planting the seeds. This improves the rate of germination and production considerably. The use of seed-sowing machines enabled farmers to control the depth at which the seeds were sown. This resulted in effective utilization of seed and time, leading to larger yields. The aim of the project is to design and fabricate a semi-automatic machine which finds real-world application. The gaps in the previous works are identified, and an effort is made to overcome these gaps.

Even though a lot of work is done in developing technologies for seed sowing and associated functions, a lot of scope still remains in the region of developing a technology for small- and medium-scale farmers. A lot of advanced machineries and technologies are developed for large-scale farmers, who can afford the high cost associated with machinery. However, cost is a major constraint when it comes to small- and medium-scale farmers. There is also an issue of labor shortage being faced by many farmers. This semi-automatic seed-sowing machine aims to serve the purpose of seed-sowing functions in an effective manner. The design is cost effective and ecofriendly. It is easy to use and portable in nature.

1.3 Design Details of Seed-Sowing Machine

The specifications of seed-sowing machines like row spacing, operating speed, and ground clearance are taken into consideration in the design after the field visits and interaction with the farmers. The sowing operation of similar crops with minor adjustments is selected. The specifications developed by previous designs from the literature motivated the development of a semi-automated seed-sowing machine which is easy to operate and maintain, cost effective, and suitable for small- and medium-size land holders.

1.3.1 Selection of DC Motor

When selecting drive wheel motors for mobile vehicles, a number of factors must be taken into account to determine the maximum torque required. One method of computing the torque is as follows:

1.3.1.1 Rolling Resistance

Rolling Resistance (RR) is the force necessary to propel a vehicle over a particular surface.

$$\begin{aligned}\text{Rolling Resistance} &= \text{Coefficient of rolling resistance} \times \text{Gross vehicle weight}\\ &= 0.15 \times (32 \times 9.81)\end{aligned}$$

Where Coefficient of rolling resistance = 0.15

Gross vehicle weight = 32kg
Rolling Resistance = **47 N**

1.3.1.2 Grade Resistance

Grade Resistance (GR) is the amount of force necessary to move a vehicle at a slope or grade.

$$\text{Grade Resistance} = \text{Gross vehicle weight} \times \sin\theta$$

$$= (32 \times 9.81) \times \sin(3)$$

where $\theta = 3°$
Grade Resistance = **17 N**

1.3.1.3 Acceleration Force

Acceleration Force (FA) is the force necessary to accelerate from a stop to maximum speed in a desired time.

$$\text{Acceleration Force} = \text{Gross vehicle weight} \times \left(\frac{\text{Maximum speed}\left(\frac{m}{s}\right)}{\text{Time required to achieve maximum speed (s)}} \right)$$

$$= 32 \times \frac{4.62}{1}$$

where Maximum speed = 4.62 m/s
Time for maximum speed = 1s
Acceleration Force = **148 N**

1.3.1.4 Total Tractive Effort

Total Tractive Effort = Rolling Resistance + Grade Resistance + Acceleration Force

$$= 47 + 17 + 148$$

Total Tractive Effort = **212 N**

1.3.1.5 Torque

$$\text{Torque} = \text{Total Tractive Effort} \times \text{Radius of wheel}$$

$$= 212 \times 0.147$$

where radius of wheel = 0.147 m
Torque = **31.2 N-m**

1.3.1.6 Output Speed

Speed of output shaft

$$N_1 \times T_1 = N_2 \times T_2$$

$$N_2 = (N_1 \times T_1)/T_2$$

where N_1 is the input speed of motor = 300 rpm
T_1 is the number of teeth in input sprocket = 9
T_2 is the number of teeth in output sprocket = 36
$N_2 = (300 \times 9)/36$
= **75 rpm**

1.3.1.7 Power

$$\text{Power} = (2\pi N_2 T)/60$$

(Where 'N_2' = 75 rpm)
= $(2\pi \times 75 \times 31.2)/60$
Power = **245 W**
Hence, a motor of **250 W** is selected

1.3.1.8 Battery Capacity Calculation

- Power of DC Motor = 250 W
- Current/h is I = (P/V) x 1 h

$$I = (250/12) \times 1$$

$$I = \mathbf{20.83\ Ah}$$

Hence a battery of **12V and 21 Ah** has been selected.

1.3.1.9 Run Time of the Battery

- Current drawn by DC Motor

$$P = V \times I \times \eta_{motor}$$

$$250 = 12 \times I \times 0.8$$

where $\eta_{motor} = 80\%$

$$I = \mathbf{16.7\ A}$$

1.3.1.10 Battery Stand-By Time

Stand-by time (hour) = Battery Capacity (Ah) / total current drawn (A)

$$= 21/\ 16.7$$

Stand-by time (hour) = **1.3 h**

1.4 Details of Components of Seed-Sowing Machine

1.4.1 Mechanical Components

1.4.1.1 Hopper

It is a container that can hold a large quantity of seeds, and it is designed to feed the seeds into the dispensing mechanism in a controlled manner. The function of the hopper is to ensure a continuous supply of seeds to the dispensing mechanism, which helps to maintain a consistent seed distribution rate. It is shaped in the form of an inverted pyramid or conical container, which carries the seeds (Figure 1.1a).

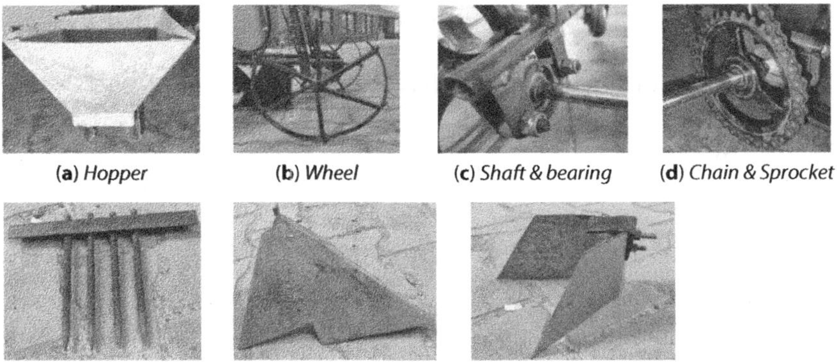

(a) *Hopper* (b) *Wheel* (c) *Shaft & bearing* (d) *Chain & Sprocket*

(e) *Tilling tool* (f) *Trenching tool* (g) *Levelling tool*

Figure 1.1 Mechanical components of seed-sowing machine.

1.4.1.2 Wheel

Two large wheels and two caster wheels are used in the design for easy mobility of the machine. The wheels are typically large and rugged, designed to handle rough terrain and uneven surfaces. A caster wheel is a type of wheel that is commonly used in carts and other objects that require easy mobility. It is typically made up of a wheel and a mounting bracket with a swivel mechanism that allows the wheel to rotate in any direction (Figure 1.1b).

1.4.1.3 Shaft and Bearing

A shaft is provided to transfer rotational motion from the motor to the dispensing mechanism. The function of the shaft in a seed-sowing machine is to transfer power and rotational motion from the motor to the dispensing mechanism in a precise and controlled manner (Figure 1.1c).

1.4.1.4 Chain Drive and Sprocket Assembly

It is used to transmit the power from motor to peg wheel and dispensing mechanism. The chain is made up of a number of rigid links which are hinged together by pin joints. The assembly comprises of two sprockets with a chain wrapped around them. They are useful in this case as they transfer mechanical power from one shaft to another which are placed quite a distance apart from each other. They are also rugged and not affected by temperature and environmental conditions. They also don't require any kind of initial tension. The sprockets used are mechanical wheels with teeth, having the same thickness and pitch (Figure 1.1d).

The chain drive and sprocket parameters used are provided in Table 1.1.

Table 1.1 Chain drive and sprocket parameters.

Parameter	Value
Sprocket	9 teeth fit #410 bicycle chains
For chain size	Pitch 0.5 inch
Roller diameter	0.3 inch
Roller width	0.16 inch

1.4.1.5 Tilling Tool

Tilling is the process of preparing the soil for planting by breaking up the ground and creating a loose, aerated soil bed that is ideal for seed sowing. The objective of tilling is to create an environment in which seeds can easily germinate, develop roots, and access nutrients. Figure 1.1e depicts the tilling tool which is used to break up the soil to a certain inch. The tool is made up of iron rods. Tilling also helps to mix organic matter and nutrients into the soil, which can help to improve soil fertility and support healthy plant growth. Additionally, tilling can help to remove weeds, rocks, and other debris from the soil, which can interfere with plant growth and development.

1.4.1.6 Trenching Tool

Trenching is a seed-sowing technique that involves digging a trench or furrow in the soil, sowing the seeds directly into the trench. This method is often used for planting crops like beans, peas, corn, etc. Soil conditions can affect the ease and effectiveness of trenching. Wet soil, for example, can be more difficult to work with and may require special equipment or techniques. The furrows should be deep enough to accommodate the seeds, but not so deep that they are buried too far underground. It creates furrows or rows in the tilled soil, using an attached trenching tool as shown in Figure 1.1f. It is made up of GI sheet metal.

1.4.1.7 Leveling Tool

After seed sowing, it is important to level the soil to create an even surface that will help to promote healthy plant growth. Leveling the soil can also help to prevent soil erosion and runoff and make it easier to irrigate the plants. Creating a level surface and ensuring that the soil is moist and well compacted help in promoting healthy plant growth and improve the overall health and productivity of the farm. The leveling tool used in the proposed seed-sowing machine is shown in Figure 1.1g, which is made up of GI sheet metal.

1.4.2 Electrical and Electronic Components

1.4.2.1 Battery

A 12V lead-acid battery is used in the seed-sowing machine to drive the motor. The 12V lead-acid battery is a crucial component of the seed-sowing machine, as it provides the power required to operate the machine's motor, dispensing mechanism, and other electronic components. The battery stores electrical energy that can be released as needed to power the various parts of the machine. The function of the 12V lead-acid battery in a seed-sowing machine is to provide a reliable and portable source of power that can operate the machine in areas where there is no access to electricity. The battery is typically rechargeable, allowing it to be used multiple times before it needs to be replaced. The battery's voltage and capacity will determine how long the machine can operate before needing a recharge. The 12V lead-acid battery is typically designed to be durable and long lasting and able to withstand rough handling and exposure to the elements. It is also designed to be easy to replace or recharge when necessary, ensuring that the seed-sowing machine can be quickly and easily brought back into operation (Figure 1.2a).

(**a**) *Battery*

(**b**) *DC Motor*

(**c**) *Servo Motor*

(**d**) *Relay*

(**e**) *Arduino*

Figure 1.2 Electrical and electronic components of seed-sowing machine.

1.4.2.2 DC Motor

A 250 W DC motor is used to provide the rotational motion to the planting mechanism. The motor is connected to a power source and a control circuit that regulates the motor speed and direction of rotation. In a DC motor, direct current electrical power is converted into mechanical power. They have internal mechanisms consisting of electronic or electromechanical elements to control the torque. The speed of the DC motor is controlled by varying the supply voltage or changing the strength of the current (Figure 1.2b). The specifications of the DC Motor are shown in Table 1.2.

Table 1.2 Specifications of DC motor.

Parameter	**Value**
Power	250 W
Speed	300 rpm
Torque	31.2 N-m
Full load current	16.7 A

1.4.2.3 Servo Motor

The servo motor is connected to the seed-dispensing mechanism and programmed to rotate to a specific angle, which controls the number of seeds being dispensed. The machine can be designed to sow a specific type of seed, and the servo motor can be adjusted to accommodate seeds of different sizes. The unique feature of a servo motor is that it produces precise rotation, making it ideal for many applications. The motor consists of a control circuit that provides feedback on the current position of the motor shaft. The servo motor used is rated at 3 kg/cm, representing the weight it can lift at a particular distance. It consists of three parts: a controlled device, an output sensor, and a feedback system. It works as a closed loop positive feedback system to control the final position of the shaft (Figure 1.2c).

1.4.2.4 Relay

In electronics and electrical engineering, a relay is an electrically operated switch. It consists of a coil and one or more contacts that open or close when an electrical current is applied to the coil. Relays are commonly used to control high-power devices or circuits using low-power signals, providing isolation and protection (Figure 1.2d).

1.4.2.5 Arduino

Arduino is a microcontroller platform that can be used in a seed-sowing machine to control and automate various functions of the machine. The Arduino board, along with its associated programming environment, offers functions like controlling servo motor (Figure 1.2e).

1.5 Methodology

1.5.1 Block Diagram of the Proposed Seed-Sowing Machine

The block diagram of the seed-sowing machine is depicted in Figure 1.3. The Arduino UNO controls both DC and stepper motors. The power necessary for the functioning of the system is provided by the battery. The DC motor is connected to the plowing tool to perform tilling, trenching, and leveling operations. The stepper motor is connected to the seed-dispensing mechanism to dispense seeds at right amounts. The mechanical components used for the design include the frame or chassis, seed distributor, hopper, wheel, and plow. The seed distributor uniformly distributes the seeds as it contains slots on the circumference of the disc. The slots are of equal dimensions. The chassis is designed trapezoidal in shape for load-bearing capacity.

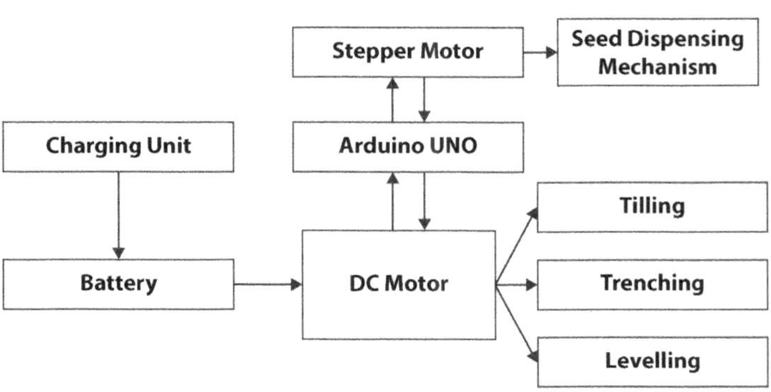

Figure 1.3 Block diagram of the proposed seed-sowing machine.

1.5.2 CAD Modeling of Seed-Sowing Machine

Figure 1.4 depicts the CAD modeling of the designed seed-sowing machine. Figure 1.4a–c shows the front, side, and top views of the machine, respectively, and Figure 1.5d shows the 3-D view of the machine.

1.5.3 The Working Principle of the Seed-Sowing Machine

The seed-sowing machine utilizes an Arduino microcontroller, which is programmed to control servo motors, and other electronic components. The machine is powered by a rechargeable battery, making it portable and ideal for use in areas where there is no access to electricity. The machine is equipped with a seed hopper and a servo-motor-driven mechanism to dispense the seeds into the soil (Figure 1.5). The machine is designed to operate in a controlled manner, ensuring that each seed is placed at the correct depth and spacing for optimal growth. The device can be programmed to sow a specific type of seed and can be adjusted to accommodate seeds of different sizes. The machine makes use of a wheel with welded angles to provide an efficient grip on soil. The wheel design is developed to provide a firm grip on soil strong enough to drag the cultivator forks during the tilling process. A switch provided on the handle is used to switch on or off the machine. The machine is driven by an electric motor which uses a sprocket chain arrangement to drive the pulling wheel. The battery is also used to power a DC motor to provide the force capable of pulling the tilling tool through soil. The cultivator tool allows for easy and narrow tilling exactly as needed for farming. The portable lightweight design makes it easy to control the direction of the machine while in use. Also, it can be easily carried around in vehicles or by hand for transporting the machine. Thus, the electric power tiller provides a smart innovative fuel free mechanism to farm and garden tilling.

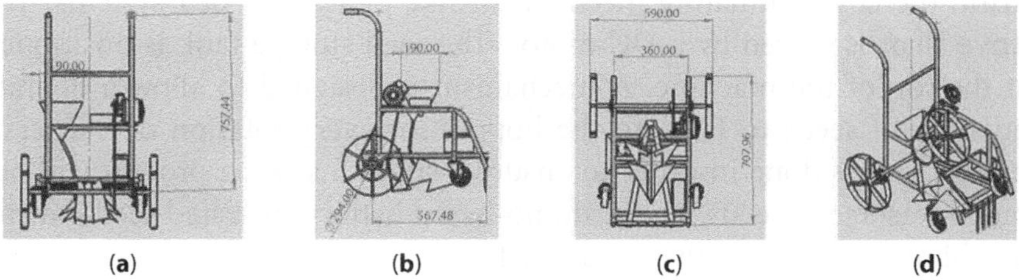

Figure 1.4 The CAD modeling of the designed seed-sowing machine: (a) front view, (b) side view, (c) top view, (d) 3D view (all dimensions are in 'mm').

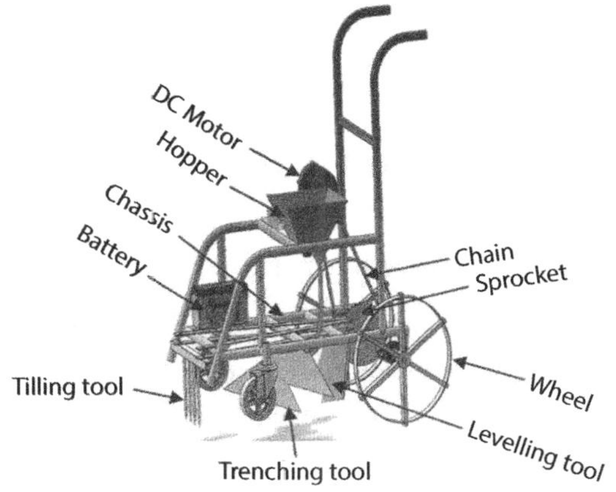

Figure 1.5 CAD model of seed-sowing machine.

The machine is designed to perform three functions: tilling, trenching, and leveling. The tilling component of the machine consists of tilling tools that till the soil to prepare it for planting. The tools associated with the three functions are attached to the chassis. A 250 W DC motor is used to drive the two large wheels in the back through the chain drive. Battery supplies the power necessary to run the motor. The tools are designed to dig into the ground with a blade digging into the soil, creating a new trench as the machine moves forward. The machine is also designed to move the loosened soil sideways. The seed-sowing component of the machine utilizes a hopper and a mechanism to drop seeds at specific intervals and depths. A leveling component made of a leveling blade is used to level the soil surface to obtain a level smooth surface for planting. The machine is guided over the field by an operator who maintains the speed and direction of the machine. The tilling and seed-sowing components are engaged by the operator as needed, depending on the specific requirements of the field.

In the present design, a drive shaft is connected to a metering mechanism, thereby eliminating mechanisms like pulley and belt systems. The drive shaft is driven by a DC motor. The seed storage tank is positioned at the top of the machine. A mechanism is designed to allow a definite quantity of seeds to fall into the hopper for every rotation of the servo motor. This is done in order to ensure a smooth sowing process without much wastage of seeds. The Arduino-based battery-operated seed-sowing machine is an innovative solution to help farmers and agriculturalists increase their efficiency and productivity at reduced labor costs.

The circuit connections of the model are displayed in Figure 1.6. Figure 1.6a depicts the real circuit whereas Figure 1.6b displays the pictorial

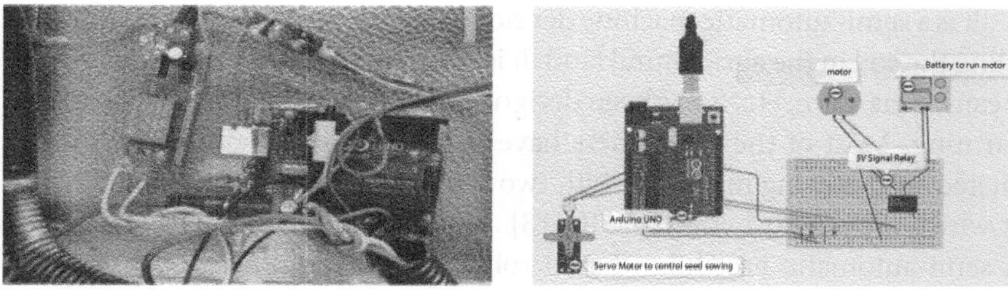

(a) (b)

Figure 1.6 Circuit connections to Arduino UNO: (a) real circuit, (b) pictorial circuit.

circuit. The main components include Arduino UNO, 9V battery for powering Arduino, servo motor, 5V relay, switch, 12V battery for motor, 250 W motor, jumper cables, etc. The Arduino is connected to a 9V battery. A 5V voltage is supplied from Arduino to the servo motor and relay. A 250 W motor turns on automatically when Arduino is turned on. It is turned on since the relay is supplied with a 5V voltage signal, and there is no need for using another switch to turn on the motor. One kill switch is provided to turn off the motor in case of any malfunction.

1.6 Results and Discussion

The designed and fabricated (manufactured) seed-sowing machine is shown in Figure 1.7.

Figure 1.7 Fabricated model of Arduino-based multi-purpose seed-sowing machine.

It is a semi-automatic machine developed for sowing seeds, tilling, and leveling the soil in the agricultural land. It is used for crops such as maize, wheat, beans, peas, corn, etc. It has been designed for small- as well as medium-scale farming. Most of the researchers have designed and developed fully automated seed-sowing machines with two or more functions incorporated into it which are not cost effective [10–18]. Mosam *et al.* (2020) have developed a semi-automatic Freeduino-based robot for sowing seeds which is not a multi-purpose machine [26]. The developed semi-automatic Arduino-based battery-operated portable seed-sowing machine is a multi-purpose machine which is cost effective and can help farmers to improve their efficiency and productivity while reducing the labor cost. This seed-sowing machine is very simple to use, and hence, even unskilled farmers can handle it with ease.

1.7 Scope for Future Work

For further improvement in the seed-sowing machine, the following features can be incorporated in the proposed multi-purpose seed-sowing machine:

- The machine can be fully automated with the help of a remote control or navigational sensors.
- For large farms, a multi-hopper can be incorporated instead of a single hopper.
- For precise seed spacing, spacing sensors can be incorporated.
- A watering system can be included for watering the soil or spraying the fertilizer.

1.8 Conclusions

Continuously reducing farm land holdings and non-availability of labor are going to increase the demand for simple and affordable farm machines suitable for small-scale farmers. The concept of a semi-automatic seed-sowing machine is designed and tested for working and found to be satisfactory. The semi-automatic seed-sowing machine is designed to reduce the overall seed sowing cost compared to manual sowing. This chapter presents a comprehensive analysis of semi-automated and fully automated seed-sowing machines for agricultural use. Limitations of traditional seed-sowing machines and practices are also compiled in this chapter. An innovative semi-automatic seed-sowing machine is designed, and the following conclusions may be drawn from the study:

- The machine is capable of performing the functions associated with seed sowing very effectively.
- The low cost of the seed-sowing machine is mainly beneficial for small- and medium-scale farmers.
- A variety of seeds can be sown, with no wastage of seeds.
- Traction power on the machine suggests that the design is safe.
- Benefits include improved productivity and reduced labor requirement.
- The seed-sowing machine is robust in design.
- The seed-sowing machine effectively reduces farming costs, animal use, and air pollution.

References

1. Balappa, B.U., Lokesh, A.C., Mahendra Babu, N.C., Development of semi-automated sowing machine for multiple crops. *J. Mater. Today Proc.*, 42, 1317–1320, 2021.
2. Thorat Swapnil, V., Kasturi, M.L., Patil Girish, V., Patil Rajkumar, N., Design and Fabrication of Seed Sowing Machine. *Int. Res. J. Eng. Technol.*, 4, 9, 704–707, 2017.
3. Adalinge Nagesh, B., Ghune Ganesh, P., Lavate Ganesh, B., Mane Rahul, R., Design and Manufacturing of Seed Sowing Machine. *Int. J. Adv. Res. Ideas Innov. Technol.*, 3, 2, 705–708, 2017.
4. Gowtham, J., Jahangir, H.K., Jayanth, B.R., Gajendra, K.A., Shreyas, P.S., Design and Fabrication of Automatic Seed Sowing Machine. *J. Emerg. Technol. Innov. Res.*, 6, 5, 42–45, 2019.
5. Kumar, R., Govil, A., Daga, P., Goel, S., Dewangan, S., Design of automatic seed sowing Machine for agriculture sector. *J. Mater. Today Proc.*, 63, 341–346, 2022.
6. Senthilnathan, N., Gupta, S., Pureha, K., Verma, S., Fabrication and Automation of Seed Sowing Machine Using IoT. *Int. J. Mech. Eng. Technol.*, 9, 4, 903–912, 2018.
7. Yedave, V., Bhosale, P., Shinde, J., Hallur, J., Automatic Seed Sowing Robot. *Int. Res. J. Eng. Technol. (IRJET)*, 6, 4, 2005–2007, 2019.
8. Singhal, K., Prajapati, G., Saxena, V., Solar Powered Seed Sowing Machine. *Int. J. Appl. Eng. Res.*, 13, 6, 259–262, 2018.
9. Solanki, S.N., Ramteke, R.T., Dhande, P.S., Agricultural Automatic Seed Sowing Machine: A Review. *Int. J. Res. Eng. Sci. Manage.*, 5, 2, 114–119, 2022.
10. Mohan Kumar, V., Navin, P., Hariharan, V., Manibharath, A., Sudarsanesan, S.D., Arduino enabled seed sowing machine. *Int. J. Eng. Res. Technol. (IJERT)*, 11, 3, 1–6, 2023.

11. Mhatu, D.S., Balasaheb, W.G., Balu, P.P., Arote, P.J., Arduino based agriculture robot. *Int. J. Res. Publ. Rev.*, 4, 4, 3181–3185, 2023.
12. Kumar, A. and Rajagopal, H., Automated Seeding and Irrigation System using Arduino. *J. Rob. Netw. Artif. Life*, 8, 4, 259–262, 2022.
13. Chavan, M., Tewari, D., Bawaskar, A., Rastog, S., Automated Seed Sowing Robot. *J. Electron. Commun. Eng. Res.*, 8, 7, 01–05, 2022, ISSN(Online): 2321-5941.
14. Somasundaram, M., Naveen Kumar, A., Nikhil Vamsi, B., Vishal Chowdary, B., Karthikeyan, S.P., Sarala, B., Automated Seed Sowing and Watering Robot using Wireless Sensor Network. *AIP Conf. Proc., 2519*, 050027, 2022.
15. Kosare, S., Dahane, P., Korke, M., Gajhbhiye, P., Kanhekar, K., Korde, S., Tibude, S., Farmer friendly agriculture robot with shovel control system using automatic seed dispensing. *Int. J. Res. Appl. Sci. Eng. Technol. (IJRASET)*, 10, 5, 3428–3433, 2022.
16. Ameena, B., Sania, A., Noorina, B., Fathima, H., AGROSMART - A Real-Time Cultivation Predication Robot System using Internet of Things (IoT). *Int. J. Sci. Res. Sci. Eng. Technol.*, 9, 2, 383–387, 2022.
17. Adarsh, A.K., Akash, R., Archana, B.H., Likitha, V., Chandru, A.S., Multifunctional Agribot using Android for Small Plantations. *Int. Res. J. Eng. Technol. (IRJET)*, 9, 7, 1151–1155, 2022.
18. Khadatkar, A., Mehta, C.R., Sawant, C.P., Application of robotics in changing the future of agriculture. *J. Eco-friendly Agric.*, 17, 1, 48–51, 2022.
19. Kanade1, P. and Ashwini, P., Smart Agriculture Robot for Sowing Seed. *Int. J. Eng. Sci. Comput. (IJESC)*, 11, 1, 27563–27565, 2021.
20. Dinesh, M.A., Aditya, Akshatha, J., Ankitha, D.M., Gowda, H.V., Design of Smart and Automated Seed Sowing and Grass Cutting Rover. *Int. Res. J. Eng. Technol. (IRJET)*, 8, 8, 1144–1148, 2021.
21. Likhitha, A., Anusha, D., Rajeshwari, N., Karthik, D., IoT based smart agriculture and automatic seed sowing robot. *Complex. Int. J. (CIJ)*, 24, 1, 371–389, 2020.
22. Beham, R., Asha, K., Sridevi, S., Samal, M., Bluetooth Embedded Robotic with Agriculture Ploughing, Seeding and Grass Cutting Powered by Solar Energy. *Int. J. Sci. Res. Comput. Sci. Eng. Inf. Technol.*, 6, 3, 477–483, 2020.
23. Yurtsever, C., Ertas, Y., Sustam, O., Ulu, C., Development of an agriculture robot for row-type seed sowing applications. *J. Selcuk-Technic*, 228–242, 2020.
24. Kumar, K.N., Balaji, R., Raviteja, S., Sakshi, K., Akhila, K., Automated seed sowing robot. *Int. J. Adv. Res. Ideas Innov. Technol.*, 6, 2, 460–464, 2020.
25. Bobbili, P.R., Tamiri, S.S.S., Naddimpalli, J.R., Manchu, J.S., Yempadapu, D., IoT based ploughing and seeding Robot for agricultural applications. *Int. J. Res. Appl. Sci. Eng. Technol. (IJRASET)*, 8, 12, 1040–1048, 2020.
26. Sangole, M.K., Patil, D.P., Dhamane, K.A., Jathar, R.K., Kardile, R.S., Semi-Automatic Seed Sowing Robot. *Int. J. Innov. Technol. Explor. Eng. (IJITEE)*, 9, 6, 1185–1188, 2020.

27. Sharma, S., Singh, P., Singh, V., Srivastava, P.K., Design and implementation of agrobot by using IoT. *Int. J. Eng. Appl. Sci. Technol.*, 5, 1, 319–325, 2020.
28. Debnath, D., Autonomous Agriculture robot - AGROBOT SRISHTI. *Int. J. Res. Appl. Sci. Eng. Technol. (IJRASET)*, 8, 6, 217–227, 2020.
29. Paul, P.K., Sinha, R.R., Aithal, P.S., Saavedra, R., Aremu, B., Mewada, S., Agricultural Robots: The Applications of Robotics in Smart Agriculture: towards More Advanced Agro Informatics Practice. *Asian Rev. Mech. Eng.*, 9, 1, 38–44, 2020.
30. Dutta, S., Shanker, U., Katiyar, S., Singh, V., Zafar, M.N., Mohanta, J.C., Development and Fabrication of an Autonomous Seed Sowing Robot. *IOP Conf. Ser. Mater. Sci. Eng.*, *691*, 012023, 2019.
31. Phansopkar, A., Waghmare, S.N., Gupta, R.G., Ughade, Y.S., Bavdhane, D.P., Remote Controlled Agricultural Robot with Sowing Seed Mechanism: A Proposed System. *Int. J. Res. Eng. Appl. Manage. (IJREAM)*, 40–43, 2019.
32. Aravind Kumar, M., Reddy, A.S., Saga Devan, K., Automatic Seed Sowing & Irrigation Agribot Using Arduino. *Int. J. Pure Appl. Math.*, 119, 14, 1089–1093, 2018.
33. Muley, S. and Kandlikar, W.S., Robotic Vehicle for Seed Planting & Weeding Applications. *Int. J. Innov. Res. Sci. Technol. (IJIRST)*, 3, 12, 213–216, 2017.
34. Gajendran, E., Vignesh, J., Boselin Prabhu, S.R., Real time application of robots for smart crop cultivation in rural community environments. *Int. J. Sci. Res. Publ.*, 7, 8, 83 - 88, 2017.
35. Behmanesh, M., Hong, T.S., Kassim, M.S.M., Azim, A., Dashtizadeh, Z., A Brief Survey on Agricultural Robots. *Int. J. Mech. Eng. Rob. Res.*, 6, 3, 178–182, 2017.
36. Prajna, K.B., Review of Robots in Agriculture. *Int. J. Sci. Technol. Eng.*, 4, 6, 50–54, 2017.
37. Brittadevi, V. and Hemalatha, P., Agricultural Robot: A Survey. *Int. J. Adv. Res. Sci. Eng.*, 6, 10, 1227–1232, 2017.
38. Vamshidhar Reddy, N., Vishnu Vardhan Reddy, A.V., Pranavadithya, S., Jagadesh Kumar, J., A critical review on agricultural robots. *Int. J. Mech. Eng. Technol. (IJMET)*, 7, 4, 183–188, 2016.
39. Chavan, S.R., Shelke, R.D., Zanwar, S.R., Enhanced Agriculture Robotic System. *Int. J. Eng. Sci. Res. Technol.*, 4, 2, 368–371, 2015.
40. Yadav, S., Deshmukh, H., Dhapodkar, C., Parihar, A.S., Verdi, G., Rahate, P., Portable Electric Tiller Machine. *Int. J. Adv. Res. Sci. Commun. Technol.*, 7, 1, 45–47, 2021.
41. Sawant, S., Gawade, A., Salgavkar, Y., Naik, K., Khumbhar, A., Rane, A.J., Review paper on Portable Electric Power Tiller Machine. *Int. J. Innov. Sci. Res. Technol.*, 7, 3, 1289–1291, 2022.

2

An Overview of Intelligent Mobility of Agricultural Drones

Prasad G.*, Sukumar Dhanapalan, Brandon Bernard Chiripanyanga, Trycene Tadiwanashe Tsabora and Felix Mwiya

Department of Aerospace Engineering, Chandigarh University, Punjab, India

Abstract

In this research, dive in and learn more about drones and drone technologies. Using an unmanned aerial vehicle (UAV) for a flight mission is the major objective, as is learning how to use and interpret drone data for your own applications (multipurpose). The agricultural multipurpose drone is what we'll be discussing here. Drones are becoming increasingly important in the age of precision farming, as they will elevate farming to entirely new heights. They're a low-cost technique to quickly gather information on a variety of crop conditions. Drones have also demonstrated enormous potential in the ability to provide sustainable farming, to boost yields, and to raise the overall profitability of farming operations. In agriculture, technological advancements are occurring all the time. Precision farming may maximize agricultural productivity and profitability by using remote sensing (drones), GPS coordinates, and automated steering systems to collect accurate and reliable geo-referenced data. Precision farming and related technology, while posing significant hazards and restrictions, have enormous potential for meeting the demands of modern farm productivity while also safeguarding natural resources.

***Keywords*:** Drones, spraying, unmanned aerial vehicle (UAV) aircraft, remote sensing, artificial intelligence (AI), crop monitoring, precision agriculture, sustainable agriculture

**Corresponding author*: prasad.e14018@cumail.in

Rathishchandra R. Gatti and Chandra Singh (eds.) Digital Convergence in Intelligent Mobility Systems, (25–38)

Introduction

The research aims to provide an overview of international drone policy and regulation, make the necessary flying preparations and put up a safe mission, create a mission strategy using free and paid software, and examine how image product delivery can be used for various objectives. Using unmanned aerial vehicles (UAVs) in sustainable agriculture has enormous promise. Farmers have the advantages of using agricultural drones instead of traditional methods like mapping, as evidenced by the market's estimated value of $32.4 billion.

Drones are more efficient in scanning large areas because they can collect high-resolution images for efficient design and analysis of data with artificial intelligence technology. Annual yield is especially useful in today's volatile market because it can aid decision making and expectations management. Aerial mapping with unmanned aerial vehicles (UAVs) is currently considered a safer alternative to terrestrial methods because they do not require workers to walk across potentially dangerous terrain, such as uneven or broad fields.

UAVs are fast replacing satellites and crewed planes as a more precise and cost-effective means of monitoring crops. Even on overcast days, studies demonstrate that UAV purpose has a higher resolution and accuracy than ground-based imagery. With UAVs, agricultural evaluations are done regardless of weather conditions, whereas previous terrestrial methods could cause delays of several days if used in bad weather [1].

Since satellites and manned aircraft cameras have not been able to map fields in the past, getting a good look at plants has been difficult. UAV technology overviews the agriculture through the various plant and can even help identify pests and illnesses early on. It used to take much longer to process these high-quality photos than ground mapping or satellite approaches, but now it only takes a few minutes, thanks to the development of new software solutions [2]. While still in the field, this allows for fast, evidence-based decision making and direct data input into high-precision farming.

Background of the Research

Using drones to aid farmers with various tasks such as seed sowing, crop health monitoring, chemical spraying, precision irrigation optimization, and threat assessment can be a precious resource for farmers. In traditional farming, these tasks were performed by farmers or specialized workers. Drones, on the other hand, have the potential to significantly cut farmers' operating and long-term costs by alleviating some of their current burdens [3]. Agricultural drone technology is still in its infancy, and there are many areas where it may be improved. The first concern is the price of the drones, which can reach $25,000 for the better models. For the average farmer, this can be a significant financial burden. Furthermore, even with flying time and range, most drones fall short of the needs of modern farmers. Drones could take over the bulk of farming tasks shortly if advancements are made in these fields.

Farmers need to think about several things before investing in drones for agricultural management [4]. There are rotary and fixed-wing UAVs, and each has specific advantages. It is also possible for the takeoff and landing space to be relatively small, which is more suited to cities. The take-off and landing space is unrestricted when mapping broad areas using a fixed-wing drone, such as farming. Its endurance and cruising speed enable up to 2.6x faster mapping for large open land mapping projects [5]. Farmers should consider that using the drones is more cost-effective than training a team. UAVs may now be smoothly linked with existing farm management information systems technological advancements, which save time both in the planning stage and on the farm.

The parameters between the drone and manual spraying are shown in Table 2.1. Ambitious plans have been implemented to balance feeding the planet and decreasing global emissions [6]. Regarding precision farming and sustainable farming methods, UAVs, unmanned aerial vehicles, or drones are playing an increasingly essential role. They assist agriculture experts in leading the way in sustainable farming techniques while safeguarding and improving revenue.

Precision agriculture practices include using GPS and GIS technologies to monitor and map yield and crop parameter data on a fine scale within fields [7]. GPS and GIS tools are integral to precision agriculture. Farmer decisions may now be made based on economic and environmental

Table 2.1 Drone versus manual operation.

	Manual spraying	**Drone spraying**
Efficiency	1 acre/hour	5 acre/hour
Cost	Increases	Decreases
Safety	Hazardous	Safe

variables [8]. This results in significant financial and environmental savings. Figure 2.1 shows the problems related to agricultural spraying in India.

Fixed-wing aircraft have been used to examine innovative information for agricultural UAVs while assessing control systems, infrastructure, and enhancement possibilities. Furthermore, this presentation encompasses the evolution of UAVs and their practical implementation in agricultural settings. The aircraft supports crop spraying processes within farming areas [9]. The quad-rotor the purpose of agricultural crop monitoring, a hierarchical arrangement was proposed, which is often based on the efficient cooperation between unmanned aerial vehicles (UAVs) and wireless sensor networks (WSNs). used for Checking on the crops.

An enforcement evaluation of four typical unmanned aerial vehicles (UAVs) used for pesticide applications in China was conducted, encompassing three single-rotor and one six-rotor configuration [10]. The octocopter the potential and challenges of using unmanned aerial vehicles (UAVs) to obtain multispectral ortho-mosaics at an ultra-high resolution, which is advantageous for monitoring a wide range of burnt areas. used for Checking on the crops. Fixed-wing aircraft and quadcopters used a UAV to get high-resolution photos of the fields where crops were grown. The allocation of areas was also accomplished through the use of software-based picture analysis. used for Checking on the crops, The nano-quadcopter constructed and carried out the implementation of a nano-quadcopter aviation system that is scientifically based on the ultra-wideband (UWB) indoor positioning high technology. Agriculture of livestock [11]. Micro-UAV an

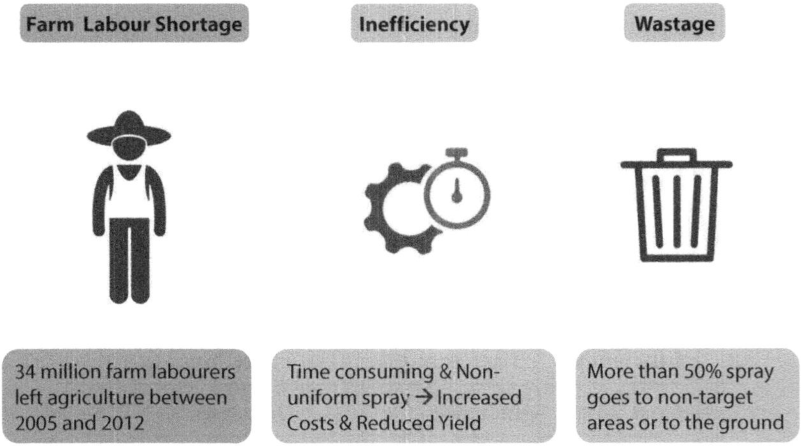

Figure 2.1 Agricultural challenges an overview.

approach that utilizes dictionary learning to facilitate the disclosure and arrangement of multiple micro unmanned aerial vehicles (UAVs) based on their micro-Doppler trademarks is proposed. The raising of livestock. UAV with six rotors the purpose of ensuring the safety of crops, a multi-rotor unmanned aerial vehicle (UAV) electrostatic sprinkling system was developed and tested. Use of sprays in agriculture [12].

Technology in Agriculture

Agricultural drones are gaining popularity as a cost-effective method for agricultural scientists, agricultural technologists, and producers to maximize their farm operations while also acquiring vital insights into the crops they grow through thorough data analytics [13]. This is one of the reasons why drones are becoming more prevalent in the agricultural sector. The data collected by drones can be utilized to achieve accurate planning and to make ongoing improvements, such as the utilization of ditches and the development of fertilizer applications to facilitate crop monitoring. By employing GPS coordinates, rather than the more conventional techniques of data collection, which require a significant amount of time and work, it is possible to reliably follow products from the farm to the consumer's plate [14]. From the farm to the consumer's plate, they can be traced.

Two of the most significant challenges that farming faces are the presence of large farm areas and ineffective crop monitoring methods. When weather conditions are unpredictable, monitoring becomes more difficult, which in turn increases the danger of field maintenance as well as the cost of doing so [15]. With the assistance of an agricultural unmanned aerial vehicle (UAV), some of these challenges can be alleviated. With the assistance of unmanned aerial vehicles (UAVs) that are fitted with thermal imaging sensors, the farmer is able to keep a close eye on his field [16]. In addition to identifying problem areas, the farmer is able to track the overall condition of the crops grown on the farm. There is a rise in profits as well as an improvement in yield as a consequence of this. Unmanned aerial vehicle (UAV) photographs have the potential to be utilized in the production of quantitative mapping products such as crop stress maps. Furthermore, the significance of utilizing UAV sensors in precision farming has been emphasized. The project involved the utilization of a single-rotor unmanned aerial vehicle (monocopter) that was outfitted with a number of different spectral cameras [17]. Additionally, a framework was developed in order to analyze the data collected by the UAV and produce composite images that could be matched with mappings for the purpose of future GIS integration.

Agricultural drones with thermal image cameras can provide a wealth of information on problem areas on the farm [18]. Soil moisture may be measured using thermal cameras so farmers can see which portions of the field have low moisture, which crops are parched, which regions are waterlogged, and so on. Traditional farming could not do such detailed and specialized monitoring since hiring experts and providing acceptable solutions was either impossible, inefficient, or too expensive. Farmers can now perform these tasks independently thanks to uncrewed aerial vehicles (UAVs) [19].

Agricultural emissions must increase because we need to modify farming practices to handle climate change and its potential impacts [20]. Agricultural cartography conducted with drones demonstrates environmental crop advantages which could lead to financial advantages for agriculturists and specialists in the coming years. The quick and efficient drone-based terrain surveying method outperformed traditional crewed airplanes and satellite image survey techniques. This advancement propels agriculture towards a data-centric paradigm. UAV technology has strong indications of developing into a sustainable tool for future applications. AI technology will allow the automated analysis of accumulated data after its initial application in the next period.

The implementation of more frequent health inspections would not only lead to operations that are more efficient, but it would also help the manufacturing sector as a whole become more environmentally friendly. Research was conducted to thoroughly analysis artificial intelligence (AI), unmanned aerial vehicles (UAVs), and AI-enhanced UAV vision systems used for precision agriculture. After performing extensive research, Srivastava and Prakash [21] suggested implementing an agricultural management system based on UAV imagery collection. The trajectory planning of agricultural UAVs was analyzed using a multi-mechanism enhanced grey wolf optimization algorithm by Stojcsics *et al.* [22]. Research was conducted by Su *et al.* [23] on methods, answers, and real-world applications of unmanned aerial vehicles (UAVs) for precision farming. A comprehensive evaluation of end-to-end precision farming UAV-based functions that were adapted to field characteristics was conducted [24]. Machine learning-based unmanned aerial vehicle (UAV) aided agriculture security architecture and detection of intrusions was the subject of research conducted [25]. Through the utilization of multi-agent reinforcement learning, Vayssade *et al.* [26] conducted an investigation into the robustness of unmanned aerial vehicle (UAV) agriculture field coverage.

The yield forecasting techniques of organic oil rose farming were examined by Xiongkui *et al.* [27] using photos captured by agricultural unmanned aerial vehicles, or UAVs, and machine learning algorithms. Comparative analysis of the restrictions that are now in place for agricultural unmanned aircraft that are used for spray purposes was the subject of research conducted [28]. Farming and the application of UAVs, current practices, and opportunities was the subject of a study project that was carried out by Singh and colleagues in the year 2024.

Using Unmanned Aerial Vehicles in Animal Farming

Raising livestock may be tedious and time-consuming, as with other elements of agriculture [29]. On the other hand, humans need to be better suited to such long-term work. Their design allows them to do recurring activities faster and maybe more efficiently (over time) than people, so that machines can find practical uses in agriculture. As a result, uncrewed aerial vehicles (UAVs) are no exception and have already been used in cattle farming.

It is essential to keep track of the height and density of your plants when searching for potential problems—soil analysis of the availability of nutrients for plant nutrition management. Water-stressed areas of the field/orchard need watering [30, 31]. Agriculture, particularly free-range cattle husbandry, has extensively used geo-fencing. Cattle, goats, and other livestock have sensors attached to their collars, which send the farmer location data. Geo-fencing technology efficiency has been the subject of recent research. Among geo-fencing sensors, low-cost GPS has an error range of 5 to 10 meters. This is especially true when many animals have wandered off the property's boundaries. Overall, drones assist farmers in making better use of inputs like seeds and fertilizers while reducing the amount of water and pesticides they must use. Thus, crops can be protected from pests promptly, saving time and money in crop scouting and ensuring high yields and quality harvests.

The drone uses a camera or sensor to capture high-resolution images while flying over the field. Images are taken in various wavelength bands, ranging from the visible (color) through the infrared spectrum, depending on the value of the measured parameter. The photographs gathered are unprocessed data that will need to be analyzed further. A prescription map can be developed for any operation a farmer wishes to carry out on the field based on the photographs captured immediately after they are taken.

Input (seeds, fertilizers, pesticides) applied to the field can be adjusted based on the maps uploaded to the farm equipment [32, 33].

Design Flow Process

The evaluation of each design is based on its payload capacity, data collection and analysis capabilities, and cost-effectiveness. First is the evaluation of a design concept with the highest payload capacity. This design has a maximum payload capacity of 5 kg, making it ideal for carrying heavy equipment such as crop sprayers, sensors, and cameras. It will soar for an impressive flight time of 40 minutes and can fly up to a range of 5 km, making it suitable for large farms. Several potential materials and equipment manufacturers could be used to build a UAV with a maximum payload of 5 kg, a flight time of 40 minutes, and a range of 5 km. One option for the frame could be carbon fiber, which is solid and lightweight. Potential manufacturers of carbon fiber frames include Toray Industries and Mitsubishi Chemical. Another option for the propulsion system could be brushless motors, which are efficient and powerful. Manufacturers of brushless motors include DJI and T-Motor. A lithium polymer battery could be used for the battery, which is lightweight and has a high energy density. Potential battery manufacturers include Turnigy and Tattu.

Finally, flight controllers such as those made by Pixhawk or DJI could be used for the control system. The overall cost of the materials and equipment will depend on the specific components chosen and the complexity of the design. However, building a UAV with these specifications for around $5,000 to $10,000 is possible. By carefully selecting the materials and equipment, it is possible to build a high-performance UAV that can effectively carry out agricultural tasks with a maximum payload, flight time, and range. However, the cost of this design is relatively high, at approximately $1,500, making it unaffordable for many low-income farmers. This design includes high-resolution cameras and sensors that collect temperature, humidity, and soil moisture data. It has a flight time of 30 minutes and can fly up to a range of 3 km. Several potential materials and equipment manufacturers could be used to build a UAV with a maximum payload of 2 kg, a flight time of 30 minutes, and a range of 3 km at a cheaper price point. One option for the frame could be PVC or foam board, which are lightweight and inexpensive. Potential manufacturers of PVC and foam board frames include Flyduino and Hobbyking. Another option for the propulsion system could be brushed motors, which are less efficient but less expensive than brushless motors. Manufacturers of brushed motors include E-flite and Axi. A lithium-ion battery could be used for the battery, which is less expensive than a lithium polymer battery but still has a decent energy density. Potential battery manufacturers include Zippy and Rhino. Finally, flight controllers such as those made by Beta Flight or Clean Flight could be used for the control system. The overall cost of the materials and equipment will depend on the specific components chosen and the complexity of the design. However, building a UAV with these specifications for around $500 to $1,000 is possible. By carefully selecting the materials and equipment, it is possible to build a cost-effective UAV that can effectively carry out agricultural tasks with a maximum payload, flight time, and range. However, the payload capacity is limited to only 2 kg, making it unsuitable for carrying heavy equipment. This design is also expensive, estimated at approximately $1,000. Finally, the design that has a payload capacity of 3 kg and a flight time of 35 minutes is the best and most effective. It can fly up to a range of 4 km and includes primary data collection capabilities such as GPS positioning.

Management Team, GTM Strategy, and Competitive Landscape

Similar to crop spraying, spot spraying focuses on weeds. Using high-resolution cameras on the UAV, weeds may be identified and a precise pesticide jet sprayed. Chemical herbicides can be reduced by up to 90% when spot spraying is used. UAVs for spot spraying have been the subject of numerous studies. Because of the technological nature of UAVs, the technology is seen as pricey. There is still much uncertainty surrounding unmanned aerial vehicles (UAVs). Regulating uncrewed aerial vehicles is difficult since regulations are nonexistent or loosely adapted from aviation laws. As a result, regulation governing the new possibilities and uses for uncrewed aerial vehicles (UAVs) is required.

These unmanned aerial vehicles, which have computers with artificial intelligence, present an innovative method to improve crop output forecasts and transform agricultural methods. Automation has brought about a new era of innovation in agricultural research, which is in line with the idea of a post-scarcity society. The researchers are at the forefront of this paradigm shift, having devised a primarily automated approach aimed at enhancing agricultural productivity. This technological progress is advantageous for farmers and establishes the foundation for strategies that enable direct harvesting of crops. Understanding the optimal timing for agricultural harvesting serves to reduce wastage, hence yielding advantages for consumers, farmers, and the environment. However, the process of anticipating optimal harvest periods requires a comprehensive understanding of each individual plant, which is not feasible for human beings.

The combination between computer science and farming provides a distinctive opportunity to investigate the potential synergies between advanced software and hardware in the field of agriculture. A significant advancement has been made in the field, showcasing the capability of cost-effective unmanned aerial vehicles (UAVs) loaded with specialized software to effectively catch and study juvenile plants, such as broccoli, thereby properly predicting their growth attributes. Surprisingly, these drones function independently, resulting in a substantial decrease in labor expenses. The economic ramifications of time on harvests are remarkable; even a slight deviation of one day from the ideal harvest period can lead to farmers experiencing a loss of 3.7% to an astonishing 20.4% of their prospective income.

Drones systematically and precisely detect and categorize each plant in the field, producing visually clear data that is easily understandable for farmers. As the cost of drones and computers decreases, farmers throughout the world are gaining greater access to a commercialized version of this system. One of the main obstacles pertains to the field of image analysis as well as deep learning. Although the process of obtaining image data is relatively simple, the task of accounting for variables such as wind-induced vegetation movement and fluctuations in lighting conditions presented significant challenges. To train the system, a significant amount of effort is needed to categorize different visual elements that drones may come across. In addition, the management of the substantial volume of data, which frequently reaches trillions of pixels, presented a significant challenge that surpassed the capabilities of even the most advanced smartphone cameras. AI drones have emerged as a promising solution for farmers globally in their unwavering endeavor to optimize crop productivity. Through the utilization of technology, the agricultural sector is making notable progress toward enhanced efficiency and sustainability, thereby advancing toward a future in which machines contribute to meeting human needs and ensuring the security of our food supply.

Design Constraints

The design constraints section of this research paper is essential as it addresses the various constraints that need to be considered when designing uncrewed aerial vehicles (UAVs) for agricultural use. The following are some constraints to consider when designing a UAV for agricultural use.

Regulatory constraints refer to the rules and regulations that must be followed when designing and operating UAVs. For instance, in some countries, UAVs are prohibited from flying over certain areas, including airports and military bases. Also, some countries have specific regulations regarding the weight and size of UAVs. Regulations to ensure that the UAVs are operated safely and legally should be followed. For example, in the United States, UAVs weighing more than 55 pounds must be registered with the Federal Aviation Administration (FAA) and follow specific rules. Economic and environmental constraints refer to the cost and environmental impact of the drone operation. The cost of the drone must be affordable to low-income farmers. UAVs with high operating costs are not practical for small-scale farmers.

The UAV's environmental impact must be minimized to ensure sustainable agriculture practices. Health and safety constraints refer to the potential risks associated with UAV operation. UAVs can cause physical harm to people and animals if not operated correctly. It is, therefore, essential to ensure that UAVs are designed and operated safely to minimize the risk of injury or harm. These issues refer to the ethical and social implications of UAVs' operation, including privacy concerns related to data collection. UAVs collect data, including images and other information, which may infringe on people's privacy. In conclusion, designing UAVs for agricultural use requires consideration of various constraints, including regulatory, economic, environmental, health and safety, and professional, ethical, social, and political issues. It is essential to adhere to these constraints to ensure that UAVs are designed and operated safely and legally, with minimal environmental impact and social implications.

Conclusion

The development of new technology to reduce their obligations is viewed as a wonderful boon, which explains the increasing popularity of drones. They can be used in a wide range of farming activities to reduce the workload of an important group in our population. Drones have the potential to change agriculture by alleviating the burden of numerous physical jobs and providing farmers with real-time information to aid in their decision making. The modern farming business is at relay with global supply at an all-time high and commodity prices at an all-time low due to rising food production and consumption demands. The duty of the agriculture business to ensure the safety of the supply chain is made more difficult by the fact that climate change is also causing new complications. These difficulties are made even more difficult by the rapid changes that are occurring in the environment. According to the most recent predictions, climate change will result in a loss of 16% in agricultural production around the world by the year 2050. The optimization of sustainable credentials in order to lessen the impact on accessible health and well-being as well as the planet will continue to be a priority. This is especially true in light of the fact that enhanced sustainability measures may also provide additional financial advantages by enabling farming professionals to focus their time and resources more efficiently on agriculture. A significant result of human and agricultural activity can be achieved through drones. As stated in the research, "cost-effective, immediate, and long-term advantages" could result from this implementation. With this in mind, it is critical that farms adapt their business models to combat climate change while also protecting themselves from financial harm.

References

1. Chamoso, P., González-Briones, A., Rivas, A., Bueno, F.D.M., Corchado, J., The use of drones in Spain: Towards a platform for controlling UAVs in urban environments. *Sensors*, 18, 14–16, 2018.
2. Chamoso, P., Raveane, W., Parra, V., González, A., UAVs applied to the counting and monitoring of animals, in: *Ambient Intelligence-Software and Applications*, pp. 71–80, Springer, Cham, Switzerland, 2014.
3. Czyba, R., Lemanowicz, M., Gorol, Z., Kudala, T., Construction Prototyping, Flight Dynamics Modeling, and Aerodynamic Analysis of Hybrid VTOL Unmanned Aircraft. *J. Adv. Transp.*, 7040531, 2018/01/01, John Wiley & Sons, Ltd. 2025/02/22, https://doi.org/10.1155/2018/7040531.
4. Demir, S., Dedeoğlu, M., Başayiğit, L., Yield prediction models of organic oil rose farming with agricultural unmanned aerial vehicles (UAVs) images and machine learnaing algorithms. *Remote Sens. Appl.: Soc. Environ.*, 33, 101131, 2024.
5. Fu, R., Ren, X., Li, Y., Wu, Y., Sun, H., Al-Absi, M.A., Machine-Learning-Based UAV-Assisted Agricultural Information Security Architecture and Intrusion Detection. *IEEE Int. Things J.*, 10, 21, 18589–18598, 1 Nov.1, 2023, doi: 10.1109/JIOT.2023.3236322.
6. Garcia-Nieto, S., Velasco-Carrau, J., Paredes-Valles, F., Salcedo, J.V., Fernandez, R.S., Motion Equations and Attitude Control in the Vertical Flight of a VTOL Bi-Rotor UAV. *Electronics*, 8, 208, 2019.
7. Hentschke, M., de Freitas, E.P., Hennig, C.H., da Veiga, I.C.G., Evaluation of Altitude Sensors for a Crop Spraying Drone. *Drones*, 2, 3, 25, 2018, https://doi.org/10.3390/drones2030025.

8. Istiak, M.A., Syeed, M.M., Hossain, M.S., Uddin, M.F., Hasan, M., Khan, R.H., Azad, N.S., Adoption of Unmanned Aerial Vehicle (UAV) imagery in agricultural management: A systematic literature review. *Ecol. Inf., 102305, Elsevier* BV, 2023, https://doi.org/10.1016/j.ecoinf.2023.102305.
9. Kim, D.-H., Go, Y.-G., Choi, S.-M., An Aerial Mixed-Reality Environment for First-Person-View Drone Flying. *Appl. Sci.*, 10, 5436, 2020.
10. Lomax, S., Colusso, P., Clark, C., Does virtual fencing work for grazing dairy cattle? *Animals*, MDPI, 9, 7, 429, 2019, DOI: 10.3390/ani9070429.
11. Li, B., Zhou, W., Sun, J., Wen, C.-Y., Chen, C.-K., Development of Model Predictive Controller for a Tail-Sitter VTOL UAV in Hover Flight. *Sensors*, 18, 2859, 2018.
12. Liu, X., Li, G., Yang, H., Zhang, N., Wang, L., Shao, P., Agricultural UAV trajectory planning by incorporating multi-mechanism improved grey wolf optimization algorithm. *Expert Syst. Appl.*, 233, 120946, 2023.
13. Lv, M., Xiao, S., Tang, Y., He, Y., Influence of UAV flight speed on droplet deposition characteristics with the application of infrared thermal imaging. *Int. J. Agric. Biol. Eng.*, 12, 3, 10–17, 2019.
14. Marwah, N., Singh, V.K., Kashyap, G.S., Wazir, S., An analysis of the robustness of UAV agriculture field coverage using multi-agent reinforcement learning. *Int. J. Inf. Technol.*, 15, 4, 2317–2327, 2023.
15. Oliveira, H.C., Guizilini, V.C., Nunes, I.P., Souza, J.R., Failure Detection in Row Crops from UAV Images Using Morphological Operators. *IEEE Geosci. Remote Sens. Lett.*, 15, 991–995, 2018.
16. Olejnik, A., Kiszkowiak, L., Rogólski, R., Chmaj, G., Radomski, M., Majcher, M., Omen, L., The Use of Unmanned Aerial Vehicles in Remote Sensing Systems. *Sensors*, 20, 7, 2003, 2020, https://doi.org/10.3390/s20072003.
17. Pfeifer, C., Barbosa, A., Mustafaa, O., Peter, H.-U., Brenning, A., Rümmler, M., Using Fixed-Wing UAV for Detecting and Mapping the Distribution and Abundance of Penguins on the South Shetlands Islands, Antarctica. *Drones*, 3, 39, 2019.
18. Raptis, E.K., Krestenitis, M., Egglezos, K., Kypris, O., Ioannidis, K., Doitsidis, L., Kosmatopoulos, E.B., End-to-end precision agriculture UAV-based functionalities tailored to field characteristics. *J. Intell. Rob. Syst.*, 107, 2, 23, 2023.
19. Savas, T., Comparative evaluation of current regulations regarding agricultural unmanned aerial vehicles used for spraying purposes in Türkiye. *Int. J. Sustain. Aviat.*, 10, 1, Inderscience Publishers, 2024/01/01,10.1504/IJSA.2024.136519.
20. Singh, A.K. and Gupta, S., Agriculture and the Use of Unmanned Aerial Vehicles (UAVs) Current Practices and Prospects, in: *Advances in Aerial Sensing and Imaging*, pp. 87–108, 2024.
21. Srivastava, A. and Prakash, J., Techniques, answers, and real-world UAV implementations for precision farming. *Wireless Pers. Commun.*, 131, 4, 2715–2746, 2023.

22. Stojcsics, D., Domozii, Z., Molnár, A., Automated evaluation of agricultural damage using UAV survey. *Acta Univ. Sapientiae Agric. Environ.*, 10, 20–30, 2018.
23. Su, J., Zhu, X., Li, S., Chen, W.H., AI meets UAVs: A survey on AI empowered UAV perception systems for precision agriculture. *Neurocomputing*, 518, 242–270, 2023.
24. Torres-Sanchez, J., Lopez-Granados, F., De Castro, A., Pena-Barragan, J., Configuration and Specifications of an Unmanned Aerial Vehicle (UAV) for Early Site Specific Weed Management. *PLoS One*, 8, 3, e58210, 2013, https://doi.org/10.1371/journal.pone.0058210.
25. Thu, K.M. and Gavrilov, A., Designing and Modeling of Quad -copter Control System Using L1 Adaptive Control. *Procedia Comput. Sci.*, 103, 528–535, 2017.
26. Vayssade, J., Arquet, R., Bonneau, M., Automatic activity tracking of goats using drone camera. *Comput. Electron. Agric.*, Elsevier, 162, 767–772, 2019.
27. Xiongkui, H., Bonds, J., Herbst, A., Langenakens, J., Recent development for unmanned aerial vehicle for plant protection in East Asia. *Int. J. Agric. Biol. Eng.*, 10, 3, 18–30, 2017.
28. Yallappa, D., Veerngouda, M., Maski, D., Palled, V., Bheemanna, M., Development and evaluation of drone mounted sprayer for pesticide applications to crops. *IEEE Global Humanitarian Technology Conference*, pp. 1–7, 2017, DOI: 10.1109/GHTC.2017.8239330.
29. Yamamoto, K., Togami, T., Yamaguchi, N., Super-Resolution of Plant Disease Images for the Acceleration of Image-based Phenotyping and Vigo Diagnosis in Agriculture. *Sensors*, 17, 2557, 2017.
30. Yinka-Banjo, C.O., Owolabi, W.A., Akala, A.O., Birds control in farmland using swarm of UAVs: A behavioural model approach. *Science and Information Conference*, Springer, Cham, pp. 333–345, 2018.
31. Singh, C., Gatti, R.R., Sairam, K.V.S.S.S.S., Singh, A., *Modeling and Optimization of Optical Communication Networks*. John Wiley & Sons, p. 381, November 2023, ISBN: 978-1-119-83920-0.
32. Singh, C. and Gatti, R.R., *Drone Applications for Industry 5.0*. IGI Global, SCOPUS, June, 2024, DOI: 10.4018/979-8-3693-2093-8. ISBN 13: 97983693 20938.
33. Gatti, R.R. and Singh, C., Shaping the Future of Automation With Cloud-Enhanced Robotics, in: Part of the Advances in Computational Intelligence and Robotics Book Series, IGI Global, p. 340, April, 2024, ISBN: 9798369 319147.

3

Simulation of Proportional-Integral and Derivative (PID) Based Traction and Speed Control System for a Four-Wheel Electric Vehicle Using MATLAB Simulink

Canute Sherwin[1]*, Christina Sundari[1], Aryan Bakle[2] and Mahijit Dodiya[2]

[1]CoE- Energy Science and e-Mobility, Atria University, Karnataka, India
[2]Department of e-Mobility, Atria University, Karnataka, India

Abstract

Traction and speed control has been a crucial parameter for control in the automotive and robotics industry. Traction from tires is essential to move the vehicle forward while accelerating. The purpose of this study is to create a simulation to test the model based traction and speed control system for a four wheel electric vehicle. The longitudinal slip ratio control method is employed to regulate the traction in this chapter. Maintaining the slip ratio within optimum range, ensures maximizing driving force by strengthening the force of friction between the tire and the road. A vehicle speed and traction control system is developed using a proportional-integral and derivative (PID) controller for an electric four-wheel vehicle that uses MATLAB/Simulink simulation software. Lack of an effective vehicle traction control system leads to severe damage on wheels of the vehicle. The control systems role is to prevent wheel damage, avoid slip, and maintain longitudinal and lateral stability of the vehicle. Literatures represent works on sliding mode controls by many authors. However it lacked effectiveness in maintaining the vehicle's traction. A Simulink model is developed with a magic tire system to simulate traction and speed control systems. The proportional-integral and derivative (PID) controller is tested to be more robust and stable compared to sliding mode controls. The project comprises vehicle terrain interaction through mathematical modeling and controller, which generates the voltage applied to the wheel

**Corresponding author*: cscanutesherwin8@gmail.com

Rathishchandra R. Gatti and Chandra Singh (eds.) Digital Convergence in Intelligent Mobility Systems, (39–58) © 2025 Scrivener Publishing LLC

electric motor. The generated voltage forces the slip rate to approach a desired value. The vehicle model is developed to predict the vehicle response under different road conditions. This model considers longitudinal, lateral and yaw motions. The results suggest that the project can be applied to various applications of commercial vehicles, defense vehicles, robots, and rovers. Simulation and road test results conclude that the electric vehicle with four wheels' steadiness and acceleration can be improved by equipping it with a traction and speed control unit.

Keywords: Proportional-integral and derivative (PID) controller, MATLAB, simulink, motor, electric vehicle, robots, simulation

3.1 Introduction

Energy crisis and environmental concerns have led to a huge demand on electric vehicles (EVs) during the past few years. Improvements in electric motors and motor controllers have accelerated the demand for developing novel powertrain configurations [1]. Some of the factors being considered while designing the powertrain include easy force and revolutions per minute (RPM) monitoring, fast and precise torque response, and independent control for each motor. These features provide a broad perspective for vehicle dynamics improvement [2].

The role of the Traction Control System (TCS) is to maintain stability and provide optimum traction during acceleration. This is achieved by regulating the driven wheels' slip ratio to the targeted slip ratio during cornering maneuvers and asymmetric road surfaces. The targeted ratio at which the adhesion coefficient of the road is highest is called the slip ratio [3]. Electronic Differential with Traction and Stability Control (EDTSCs) is used to manage longitudinal and lateral vehicle dynamics. Electric vehicles are much safer and much more robust in operation with the application of EDTSC. EV's EDTSC is much more sophisticated and demanding than that of Internal Combustion (IC) engine vehicles. This however, leads to new options for improving nonlinear dynamics of the vehicle's control [4]. EV Manufacturers around the globe use technologies like torques vectoring, EDTSCs, and TSCs to enhance traction and stability in critical driving situations to represent optimal driving conditions [5–7].

Prototype performance by improving tire grip, which enhances vehicle's straight-line and lateral acceleration are developed. Different traction control systems are being developed that limit the torque from the motor to the wheels or/and apply brake force to one or more tires. Traction control system was initially developed as a completely mechanical system with limited slip differential for high torque and high power applications.

However, with the development of technology, the system is nowadays complemented with electronics [8].

Tires' effects on handling and riding quality are being studied by various researchers to determine the dynamics of the vehicle. The Pacejka tire model or magic tire model is frequently employed by researchers to create vehicle models to study longitudinal and lateral behavior. Different models were developed by considering the normal force, brake gain, maximum friction coefficient, and traction for acceleration and deceleration [9]. In some simple control systems like cruise control, it is not required to consider the impact between road and tire as the longitudinal slip is small. While considering other complex control problems like adaptive cruise control (ACC), brake system control, or traction control system a more dynamic and sophisticated dynamic model is required [10].

Often the dynamic model is presented without considering the tire model for simplification. However, the tire model is the main reason to propel the vehicle forward when accelerating and hold the vehicle during braking. Longitudinal performance is impacted by aerodynamic force, gravitational force and the forces developed between the road surface and tire contact. The major advantage EVs have over IC engine vehicles is the ability to calculate directly the torque and speed of motors in EVs. It is crucial to understand the dynamic status of a vehicle like speed, yaw rate, and acceleration.

The prime objective of this chapter is to understand the fundamentals of traction and the factors affecting it. By examining different parts of the control system and control methods, a sincere effort is made to develop a robust and innovative traction control system tailored for four wheel electric vehicles.

MATLAB/Simulink tool is used to achieve this objective. This tool allows to model and simulate different control strategies and performance scenarios. The simulations form the base for framing the control algorithm, tuning the parameters, and evaluating its effectiveness. The chapter also focuses on developing a motor control system as the traction of the vehicle depends on controlling the torque output to the wheels and optimizing the motor control strategy is crucial for achieving this.

3.2 Literature Review

The application of PID control systems has gained significant attention in recent times particularly for providing effective traction and speed control. This literature survey aims to explore relevant studies focusing on

MATLAB simulations for PID-based control strategies for four-wheel electric vehicles.

Åström, K. J. *et al.* provided an overview of PID controllers, their theoretical foundations, design principles, and tuning methodologies. It serves as a fundamental reference for understanding PID control. One of the distinctive features of Åström's work is its extensive coverage of tuning methodologies for PID controllers. The authors present various tuning methods, discussing their advantages, limitations, and applicability in different scenarios. This section of the book becomes particularly relevant in the context, as it provides insights into optimizing parameters desired for traction and speed control performance [11].

Cikanek, S. R. *et al.* delivered the dynamics and control aspects of electric vehicles, offering insights into the challenges and opportunities associated with PID-based control strategies. A distinctive feature of Cikanek's work is its emphasis on control systems tailored for electric vehicles, on-road testing. The book covers various control strategies relevant to EVs, including those aimed at enhancing performance, energy efficiency, and safety. Cikanek's insights into the practical application of these control systems during on-road testing contribute to bridging the gap between theoretical knowledge and real-world implementation [12].

Al-Hallaj, S., & Sabli, N. discussed simulink simulation for electric vehicle systems, providing a simulation environment for PID control. The main aspect of the paper involves the simulation of control strategies for electric vehicles. Al-Hallaj and Sabli demonstrate the capability of Simulink in implementing and testing various control algorithms within electric vehicle simulation. This includes traction and speed control strategies evaluation of electric vehicles in diverse operating conditions [13].

Lin *et al.* explored techniques for managing power in hybrid electric vehicles using MATLAB, contributing to simulation techniques applicable to control system development. The objective of the power management strategy proposed by Lin *et al.* is to enhance fuel efficiency and reduce emissions in a parallel hybrid electric truck. Through the dynamic programming approach, the authors demonstrate the ability to strike a balance between the engine and motor, optimizing power distribution for improved efficiency. This focus aligns with broader industry goals of achieving sustainable and environmentally friendly transportation solutions [14].

Kim J. *et al.* developed a robust traction control system. Strategies for enhancing traction performance in electric vehicles, a critical aspect for PID-based control systems is covered in this paper. The work represents a notable contribution to electric vehicle traction control. By concentrating on the distinctive characteristics of in-wheel motors and emphasizing robustness in their control strategy, the writers offer insightful analysis for researchers, engineers, and practitioners working towards advanced control systems [15].

Taeibi-Rahni M., *et al.* addressed optimal design considerations for intelligent traction control systems in electric vehicles. They emphasized the importance of a systematic and well-considered design methodology that considers various factors, including vehicle dynamics, tire-road interactions, and control algorithm efficiency. The authors delve into the intricacies of designing a traction mechanism guaranteeing optimal vehicle performance but also maximizing energy efficiency, a critical consideration in electric vehicle applications. They contribute to the literature by addressing optimal design considerations for intelligent traction control systems in electric vehicles [16].

Li Y., *et al.* focused on DC motor speed control. This different control strategies study, including PID, provides a framework for assessing how well PID is used for electric vehicle applications. Their paper stands as a literature on control systems, particularly for DC motor speed control. By conducting a comparative study the performance of these strategies under varying conditions are compared. The paper's systematic methodology, thorough analysis of results, and applicability to DC motor speed control enhance its relevance as a foundational reference for those involved in control system design and implementation [17].

Sun, Y., & Jia, L. *et al.* delves into shedding light on the advantages and limitations of PID control compared to other methodologies. The primary focus of the paper is on PID and LQR controllers to energy management of hybrid electric vehicles. Sun and Jia recognize the relevance of such systems in the automotive industry, where optimizing fuel efficiency and reducing emissions are critical objectives. The insights cover broader understanding of how PID and LQR controllers perform in the specific context [18].

H. Wang, *et al.* introduced a model predictive controller (MPC) for Hybrid Vehicles. The MPC is developed using a real-world scenario representing typical HETB operational conditions. The outcomes are contrasted with two alternative techniques: rule-based approach and a dynamic programming (DP) strategy, the latter serving as an optimization benchmark globally. The impact of various parameters of the MPC, such as the prediction horizon length, is also investigated. The comparative results reveal approximately 6% enhancement in fuel economy in comparison to rule-based strategy and attains maximum fuel optimality achieved by DP in typical operating conditions. The efficacy of the proposed MPC in the face of significant disturbances, a 40% white noise is introduced in operational conditions. Simulation results indicate substantial increase in fuel economy [19].

Machacek, D. T. *et al.* introduced a controller utilizing the hybrid electric vehicle's (HEV) dual electric motor energy management system. The primary objective is to minimize the vehicle's fuel consumption based on a predicted driving mission. When the sole focus is on minimizing fuel consumption, there is a tendency to extensively use the electric components, potentially leading to overheating. To address this, a maximum motor temperature is defined to prevent overheating, resulting in a drastic reduction in the motor's maximum capability, known as thermal derating [20].

3.3 Methodology

Direct Yaw moment management is used for stability control of a vehicle. The forces that drive and brake are adjusted independently to produce inverse yaw moments to counter yaw moments causing instability. This avoids the skidding or spinning of wheels caused by longitudinal forces. Usually direct torque control of motors is integrated together with a yaw moment control for stability [21].

Vehicle speed and traction control system for the present chapter is designed for a remote controlled (RC) car. A DC motor utilizes direct current to generate mechanical force. For our study we have used a brushed permanent magnet DC motor since they are easy to maintain and affordable. These are used for small scale applications. The working is because of the interplay between the magnetic fields created by the flow of electric current through the motors wires. Motor parameters considered are represented in Table 3.1.

When a vehicle is powered by a DC motor, the vehicle parameters also need to be considered. The vehicle parameters include:

μ = friction coefficient
S = slip ratio
Rw = wheel radius (Constant)
Q = weight balance factor (Constant)
GR = Gear Ratio (Constant)
M = total car mass
FN = mgQ = Normal Force
FT = μ (mgQ), Tire Force

The car parameters selected for the analysis are represented in Table 3.2.

Table 3.1 DC motor parameters.

Parameter	Value	Units
R	1.41e-1	Ω (ohms)
L	3.0e-3	H (henry)
K_b	5.74e-3	Volt. S/rad
K_m	5.74e-3	N.m/Amp
b	3.97e-6	-
J	1.0e-4	Kg.m
f_c	0.00	-

Table 3.2 Car parameters.

Parameter	Value	Units
GR	2.50	-
Q	0.37	-
r_w	3.2e-2	m
Tol	1.0e-10	-
m	1.14	Kg
g	9.81	m/s^2

Table 3.3 System constraints.

Description	Variable (units)	Constant
Servo Pulse Width	PW (ms)	$1000 \leq PW \leq 2000$
Motor Voltage Input	U_1 (V)	$-12 \leq U_1 \leq 12$
Motor Angular Speed	ω (rad/s)	$0 \leq \omega \leq 2055$
Motor Voltage Output	Y_1 (V)	$0 \leq Y_1 \leq 5.0$

System constraints considered for the study are represented in Table 3.3. In this chapter, slip ratio is estimated for reaction torque. This is an indirect method of estimating slip ratio.

Slip Ratio, $S = \frac{\omega_b - \omega_f}{\omega_f + Tol}, \; Tol \simeq 0$

The coefficient μ = μ(s). This is also called the magic formula.

Note: $\omega_b = \frac{\omega_m}{GR}$, the goal is to keep $s \simeq 0$.

Constraints are given to the system for the initial voltage, current, angular speed, and desired speed. Considering the constraints for the vehicle, the equations of motion and current of the vehicle are modeled and simulated accordingly.

Initial current, io = 0; initial speed, Wo = 0; initial velocity, Vo = 0; Maximum desired speed, Wdes = 275; Desired slow speed = 110 and input voltage, Vi = 12.

Equations of motion for DC motor is given by Equations 3.1–3.3;

$$\frac{di}{dt} = -\frac{R}{L}(i) - \frac{K_b}{L}(\omega_m) + \frac{1}{L}V \tag{3.1}$$

$$\frac{d\omega_m}{dt} = \frac{K_m}{J}(i) - \frac{b}{j}(\omega_m) - \frac{f_c}{J}Sin(\omega_m) - \frac{T_d}{J} \tag{3.2}$$

$$\frac{d\Theta}{dt} = \omega_m \tag{3.3}$$

where, R, i and ω_m, V, T_d, L and J represent current, motor angular velocity, input voltage, disturbance torque, inductance, and inertia respectively. K_m, K_b are motor constants for size and back emf. Viscous friction coefficient is represented as b.

Equation for DC motor and car combined is given by:

$$\frac{di}{dt} = -\frac{R}{L}(i) - \frac{K_b}{L}(\omega_m) + \frac{1}{L}V \tag{3.4}$$

The motor current remains the same.

$$\frac{d\omega_m}{dt} = \frac{K_m}{J}(i) - \frac{b}{j}(\omega_m) - \frac{r_\omega}{GR}\frac{F_T}{J} \tag{3.5}$$

$$\frac{d\Theta}{dt} = \omega_m \tag{3.6}$$

$$\frac{dv}{dt} = \frac{F_T}{m} \tag{3.7}$$

$$\frac{dX_P}{dt} = \mathrm{v} \tag{3.8}$$

A current sensor measures the current flowing to the motor, used for the measurement of torque and speed. The angular velocity of every wheel is measured via velocity sensors. Further, vehicle speed is determined from angular velocity measurement. A PID controller is used to decrease the slip ratio. The controller plays a role of matching the rear and front wheel to reduce the slip rate. Reference speed of the DC motor is set to 1750 RPM.

A two degree of freedom (2 DOF) simple linear vehicle model is applied for determining vehicles lateral state variables. The vehicle can be modeled equivalent to half a vehicle as shown in Figure 3.1. β is the body slip angle, γ is the yaw rate, u and v are vehicle's lateral and longitudinal velocities, δ is the steering angle, α_f and α_r and front and rear side slip angles, Y_f and Y_r are the lateral tyre forces on front and rear wheels, l_f and l_r are the distances between center of mass to the front and rear axles respectively [4].

The lateral motion of vehicle is represented by:

$$Mv\left(\frac{dB}{dt} + \gamma\right) = 2\left(y_f + y_r\right) \tag{3.9}$$

$$I\frac{dr}{dt} = N_z - N_t \tag{3.10}$$

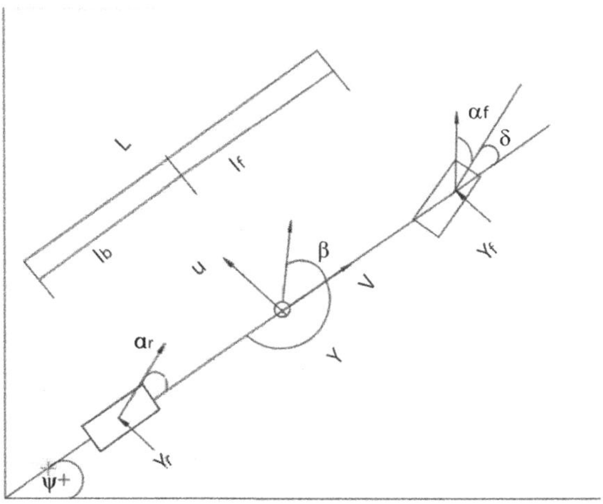

Figure 3.1 Geometric representation of the bicycle model.

where, I = vehicle's inertia

N_z = control moment generated by torque difference between left and right in wheel motors.

N_t = moment generated by lateral forces.

N_t is represented as:

$$N_t = 2C_f\left(\beta + \frac{l_f}{v}\gamma - \delta\right)l_f - 2C_r\left(\beta - \frac{l_r}{v}\gamma\right)l_r \tag{3.11}$$

where, C_f and C_r are cornering stiffnesses of wheels. Cornering stiffness usually rises linearly with slip angle up to a particular range. It is taken as a constant, assuming vehicles operating range of slip angle.

The yaw rate of the vehicle is represented as:

$$\gamma_{des} = \frac{v}{L + KV^2}\delta \tag{3.12}$$

where, L = Wheelbase

K = Stability factor

$$K = \frac{M}{2L}\left(\frac{l_r}{C_f} - \frac{l_f}{C_r}\right) \tag{3.13}$$

If K is negative, the vehicle overshoots and if K is positive, the vehicle will undershoot.

Simulation Models:
The model of a RC car was integrated to a non-linear transition state vehicle model with linear tire dynamics. Aerodynamic forces were also considered for modeling. Parameters of RC cars were used for the simulation as shown in Table 3.2. For our study, a brushless DC motor with an electronic speed controller was used. They are proven to be efficient, powerful, fast, and long lasting. The motor capacity was rated at 6000 kv 5.5 t brushless combo. LiPo batteries were used which are rated with c. The battery pack used for the analysis is of 20 c rating. The Pacejka tire model was used for the dynamics simulation. Time steps of 5 ms were used to solve the model.

Experiments:
A driver model with a predefined track was used for simulating the environment. Initial stage of testing was performed to observe that the slip ratio, response force, and cornering stiffness were appropriately estimated. The driver model was fed with a series of data. The initial velocity is considered zero.

Integrated Control Strategy:
An integrated control strategy is used for the present study to optimize and stabilize the driver's desired torque, road adhesion, and motor output. The integrated control approach that has been suggested is represented in Figure 3.2. It comprises two stages: control input and control case selection. Control input comprises procurement as well as incorporation. Driver's desired torque, motor RPM and wheel rotation speed signals are shared with the control case selection. The choice of control cases forms the basis of the suggested approach with two cases designed as follows:

Case 1: Efficiency Based
This case corresponds to a high adhesion road surface where no skidding takes place. For all $\omega i \leq \omega oi$, where the traction road has to offer is more than the motor output. The torque outputs for front and rear axles is given by:

$$T_f = p \times T_d \tag{3.14}$$

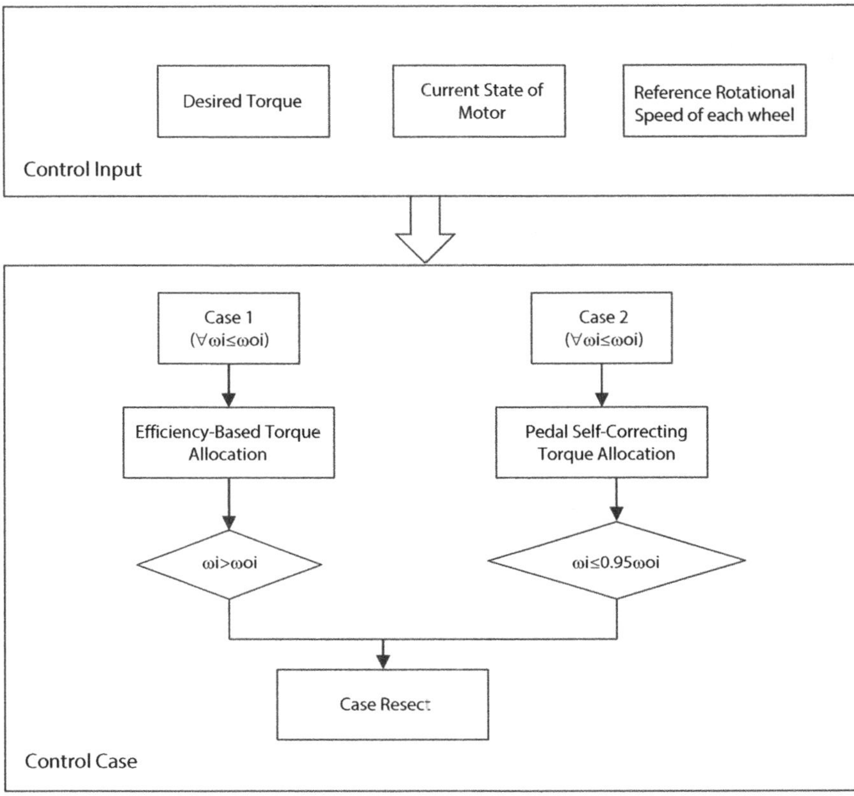

Figure 3.2 Structure of integrated control strategy.

$$T_r = (1 - p) \times T_d \tag{3.15}$$

Case 2: Pedal Self-Correcting

This case corresponds to poor adhesion roads like snow or cement roads, wherein the drivers torque requirement cannot be met by the state of road adhesion. To maintain vehicles stability under such circumstances the acceleration pedal coefficient is adjusted. For this case, the torque for front and rear axle is given by:

$$T_f = \frac{-\left[\varepsilon sgn(s) + ks + c\left(\omega f - \omega o\, f\right)\right] \cdot I + Ft\, f \cdot r}{beta} \tag{3.16}$$

$$T_r = \frac{-\left[\varepsilon sgn(s) + ks + c(\omega r - \omega or)\right] \cdot I + Ftr \cdot r}{beta} \tag{3.17}$$

3.4 Results and Analysis

MATLAB and its features are used to explore beyond theoretical calculations and investigate into the real world traction control system. A simulink model is built to simulate the behavior of RC vehicle and its interaction with the road, followed by virtually testing it in this computing environment.

Differential equation is modeled in simulink. The different block sets used for modeling the motor current includes gain block, integrator block, input block and adder block. The gain block multiplies the signal by a factor as determined from the original differential equation and the i value (current) is determined from the integrator.

For motor speed modeling, gain block is designed as per differential equation, integrator block is used to determine speed, w value. Angular position value tht (θ) is determined by integrating twice, i.e., by using the integrator twice. Terminator block is used for no result condition. A from block is used for routing a signal, gain block 1/m for car velocity and position (v and x). Initial conditions are copied for speed and position. A gain block is used for gear ratio (1/GR) and wheel size.

Adder with +, - condition is used for determining the slip. Output blocks are used to determine front wheel speed w_f and back wheel speed w_b. Slip ratio (s) is determined by combining divide block (×, ÷), adder block, constant blocks (tol and IuI, abs(v_f)), saturation block for friction $-1 < s < 1$. MATLAB function block is used to determine wheel force, FT.

Substitute all constants and determine friction value through the friction coefficient $y = mu$ and slip ratio. The DC motor + car model is represented in Figure 3.3 and the subsystem is represented in Figure 3.4.

A 12 V input signal is applied for a time period of 70 s to study the wheel speed results. This system is designed as an open loop system. The results wheel speeds and slip ratios are determined and compared. Figure 3.5 represents the comparison between the wheel speeds.

From the observations, the front wheel takes some time to speed up as there is slip and there is no control system integrated into the system. The slip ratio value is represented in Figure 3.6. It is seen that the slip ratio is about 4.1×10^7. It is a very high value of slip.

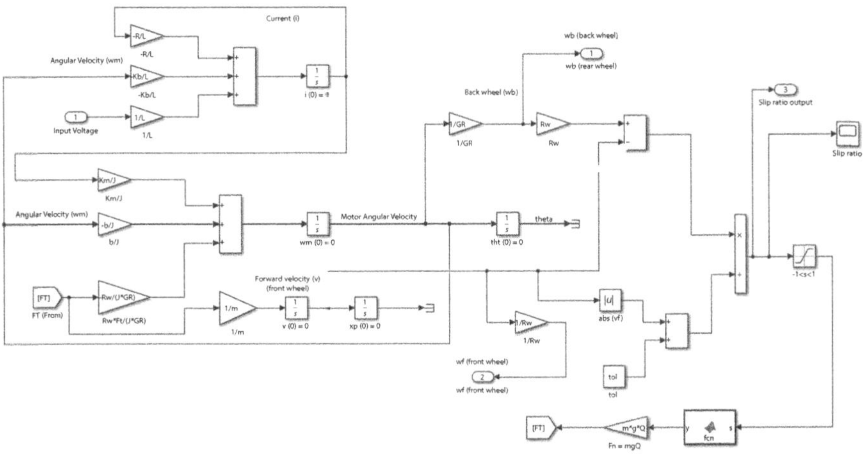

Figure 3.3 DC motor + car model.

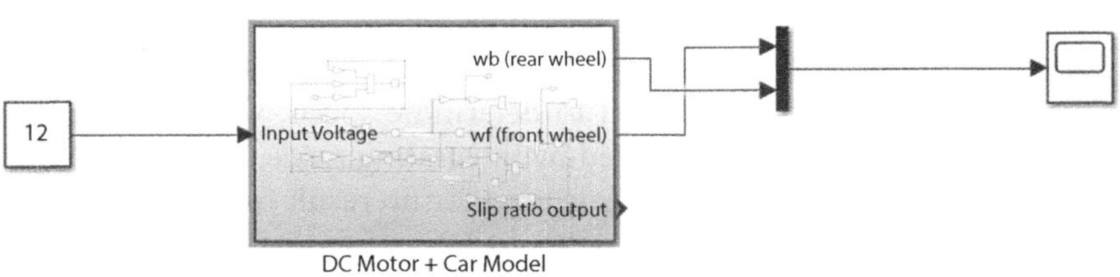

Figure 3.4 Subsystem of the model.

A PID controller is integrated to reduce the slip ratio and speed differences. Proportional gain block (K_p) is applied for speed control, saturated between 0 and 12 V. The maximum voltage being 12 V. The maximum acceleration, determined by the slope of the graph, is set as the desired value and saturated between 0 to maximum. Solver settings are fixed at fixed steps and ODE-1. Connect the scope and run the simulation. A multiplier is integrated to match the speeds and a gain block is further added as pre-compensation.

The PID controller is a two loop cascaded multiple feedback system. A switch is used for the sole purpose of turning off the slip controller when the speed of both front and rear wheel matches, i.e. the speed difference attains 0 (zero). Figure 3.7 displays the block diagram of the designed PID controller.

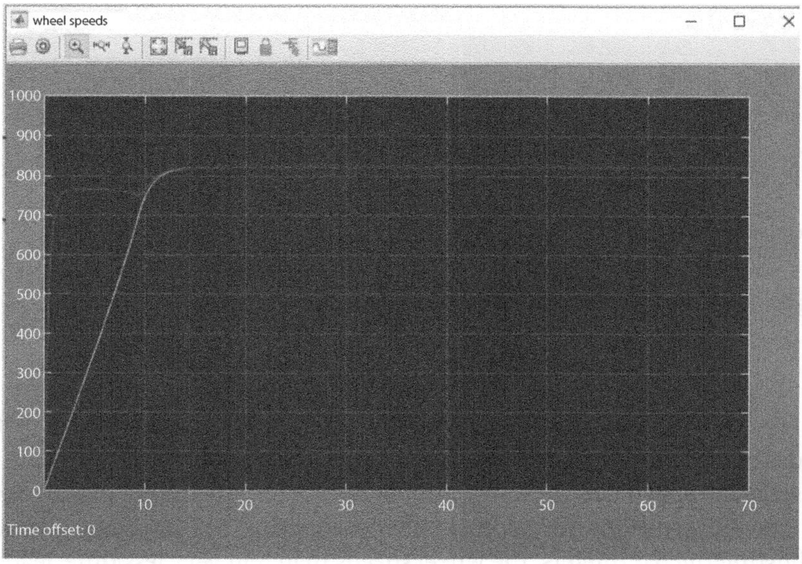

Figure 3.5 Front and rear wheel speed comparison.

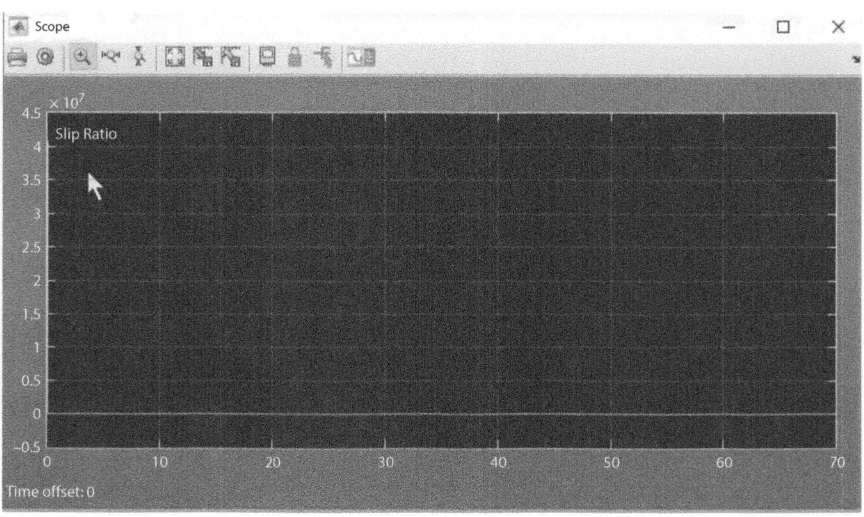

Figure 3.6 Slip ratio for the system without control system.

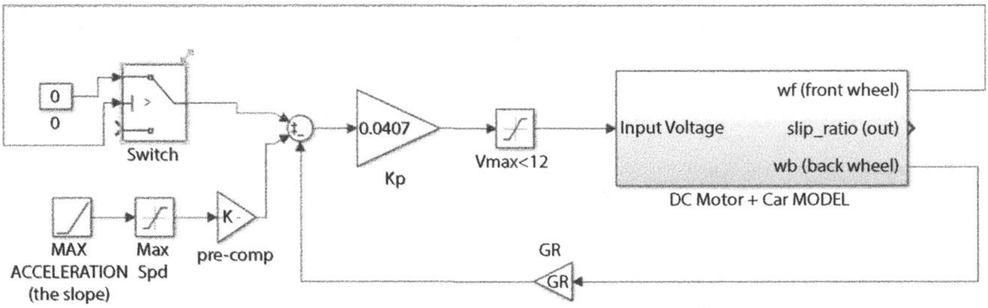

Figure 3.7 PID controller with two loop cascading.

The amount of time needed for the front and rear wheels to match reduces and slip ratio also reduces to a great extent. Figures 3.8 and 3.9 display the speed and slip ratio comparisons after integrating a controller.

The observations reveal that after integrating a PID controller and adjusting the parameters, the wheel speeds match in very less time, leading to very low slip with the integration of a slip control system. The slip ratio value is represented in Figure 3.9. It is seen that the slip ratio is about 257. There is a tremendous reduction in slip value in comparison with a system without a control system.

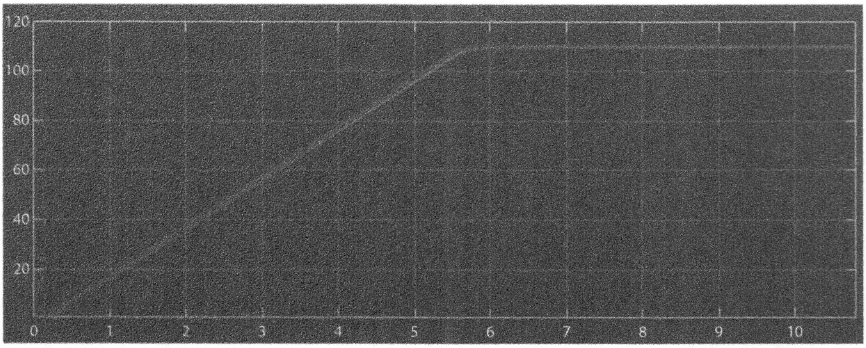

Figure 3.8 Front and rear wheel speed comparison after integrating PID controller.

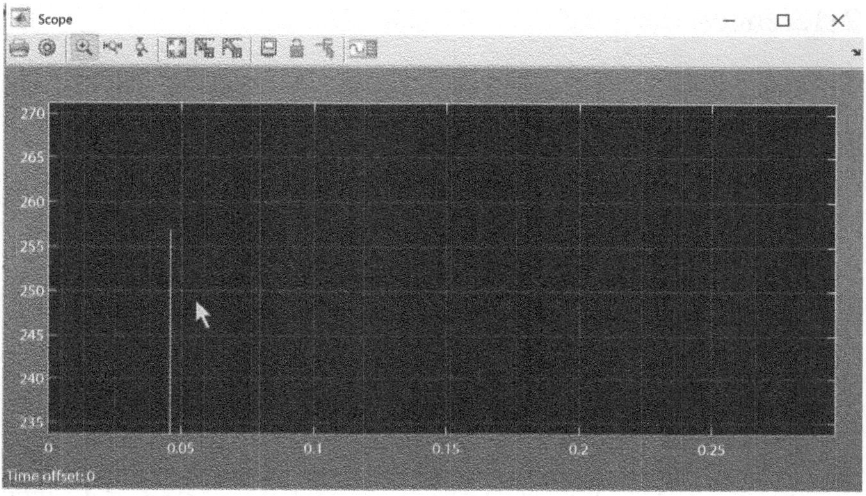

Figure 3.9 Slip ratio of the system with PID controller.

3.5 Conclusion

This chapter emphasizes the need for a vehicle speed and traction control system to maintain uniform speeds for front and rear wheels. An integrated control strategy presented in this study to optimize and stabilize the desired parameters of the driver by simulating the behavior of RC vehicle and its interaction with the road through MATLAB/Simulink model. The chapter focuses on a PID controller with a two loop cascaded multiple feedback system to stabilize the speed of wheels and reduce the slip. The controller also integrates a switch for turning off the slip controller when the speed of both front and rear wheel matches. A brief literature review of vehicle speed and traction control systems designed by different researchers around the globe is also covered in this chapter. Insights from the literature are taken to design the present control system. The designed speed and traction control system for a RC vehicle is efficient as the slip rate is observed to be very minimum and the front wheel attains the speed of the rear wheel in shortest time.

References

1. Esmailzadeh, E., Vossoughi, G.R., Goodarzi, A., Dynamic modeling and analysis of a four motorized wheels electric vehicle. *J. Int. J. Veh. Mech. Mobility*, 35, 163–194, 2001.
2. Hori, Y., Future vehicle driven by electricity and control-research on four-wheel-motored "UOT Electric March II". *J. IEEE Trans. Ind. Electron.*, 51, 5, 954–962, 2004.
3. Chu, L., Chao, L.B., Ou, Y., Lu, W.B., Hardware-in-the-loop simulation of traction control algorithm based on fuzzy PID. *Energy Procedia*, 16, 1685–1692, 2012.
4. Dasanayake, N. and Perera, S., Traction and Stability Control using Fuzzy-based Controller Integration for Electric Vehicles, arXiv preprint arXiv:2306.04782, 2023.
5. Geng, C., Uchida, T., Hori, Y., Body slip angle estimation and control for electric vehicle with in-wheel motors, in: *33rd Annual Conf. of the IEEE Industrial Electronics Society*, pp. 351–355, 2007.
6. Fujimoto, H., Fujii, K., Takahashi, N., Vehicle stability control of electric vehicle with slip-ratio and cornering stiffness estimation, in: *IEEE/ASME Int. Conf. on Advanced Intelligent Mechatronics*, pp. 1–6, 2007.
7. Nam, K., Fujimoto, H., Hori, Y., Lateral stability control of in-wheel-motor-driven electric vehicles based on sideslip angle estimation using lateral tire force sensors. *IEEE Trans. Veh. Technol.*, 61, 5, 1972–1985, 2012.
8. Fujimoto, H., Amada, J., Maeda, K., Review of traction and braking control for electric vehicles, in: *2012 IEEE Vehicle Power and Propulsion Conference*, IEEE, pp. 1292–1299, 2012.
9. Shakouri, P., Ordys, A., Askari, M., Laila, D.S., Longitudinal vehicle dynamics using Simulink/Matlab, *IET Seminar Digest*, 955–960, 2010.
10. Lee, C., Hendrick, K., Yi, K., Real-time slip-based estimation of maximum tire-road friction coefficient. *IEEE/ASME Trans. Mechatron.*, 9, 454–458, 2004.
11. Åström, K.J. and Hägglund, T., *PID Controllers: Theory, Design, and Tuning*, Instrument Society of America, North Carolina, United States of America, 1995.
12. Cikanek, S.R., *Electric Vehicle Dynamics and Control: An Application to On-Road Testing*, CRC Press, Boca Raton, Florida, USA, 2012.
13. Al-Hallaj, S. and Sabli, N., MATLAB/Simulink-based electric vehicle simulation. *J. Electr. Eng. Autom.*, 7, 6, 5–15, 2006.
14. Lin, K., Peng, H., Grizzle, J., Kang, J., Power Management Strategy for a Parallel Hybrid Electric Truck Using Dynamic Programming, SAE Technical Paper 2004-01-2472, 2004.
15. Kim, J., Cha, S., Rim, H., Robust Traction Control for Electric Vehicles with In-Wheel Motors. *IEEE Trans. Veh. Technol.*, 63, 9, 4434–4443, 2014.

16. Taeibi-Rahni, M. and Ghaffari, A., Optimal Design and Implementation of Intelligent Traction Control System for Electric Vehicles. *Electr. Power Compon. Syst.*, 46, 5, 468–481, 2018.
17. Li, Y., Sun, Z., Sun, F., Comparative study of PI, PID and fuzzy logic controllers for speed control of DC motor. *Procedia Eng.*, 52, 300–305, 2013.
18. Sun, Y. and Jia, L., A Comparative Study of PID and LQR Control for the Energy Management of Hybrid Electric Vehicles. *Energies*, 10, 10, 1465, 2017.
19. Wang, H., Huang, Y., Khajepour, A., Song, Q., Model predictive control-based energy management strategy for a series hybrid electric tracked vehicle. *Appl. Energy*, 182, 105–114, 15 November 2016.
20. Machacek, D.T., Barhoumi, K., Ritzmann, J.M., Huber, T., Onder, C.H., Multi-Level Model Predictive Control for the Energy Management of Hybrid Electric Vehicles Including Thermal Derating. *IEEE Trans. Veh. Technol.*, 71, 10, 10400–10414, 2022.
21. Nam, K., Oh, S., Fujimoto, H., Hori, Y., Design of adaptive sliding mode controller for robust yaw stabilization of in-wheel-motor-driven electric vehicles. *World Electr. Veh. J.*, 5, 2, 588–597, 2012.

4

A Case Study on Electric Vehicles (EV)

Sumiksha Shetty[1], Smitha A. B.[1], Manjunatha Badiger[2] and Chandra Singh[3*]

[1]Department of Electronics & Communication Engineering, Sahyadri College of Engineering & Management, Mangaluru, Karnataka, India
[1]Dept. of Electronics Engineering (VLSI Design & Technology) NMAM Institute of Technology, Nitte (Deemed to be University), Karnataka, India
[3]Department of Electronics and Communication Engineering, Nitte (Deemed to be University), NMAM Institute of Technology Nitte, Karnataka, India

Abstract

Electric vehicles (EV) are becoming more and more popular as people become interested in green, environmentally friendly transportation systems. However, the cost of deploying EV charging stations is still high, even though the number of EVs on the road is slowly increasing. This has slowed down investment in EV charging infrastructure. People who currently own or are considering owning an EV may become worried about running out of charge before they get to a charging station or being unable to find a charging point near their destination; these fears are known as range anxiety. To address this concern, dynamic wireless charging (DWC) systems enable vehicles to be charged as they are in motion, so people do not need to have their vehicles' service interrupted, thinking that the battery has run out of charge. This would help lessen range stress, which arise from the fact that cars have to be parked to get charged for an instance. Unfortunately, DWC infrastructure can be very expensive to implement and operate. Therefore, it is crucial to plan out where charging lanes should be located in order to minimize costs as much as possible. The number of inquiries and quandaries related to recharging facilities for electric vehicles has also grown with the surge in secondhand battery-powered cars. Data have been given about a number of criteria: electric vehicles per charging station numbers, charging stations per 100 km of motorway figures, and quantity of charging stations.

***Keywords*:** Autonomous and connected vehicles, charging infrastructure, battery technology, electric vehicle components

**Corresponding author*: chandrasingh146@gmail.com

Rathishchandra R. Gatti and Chandra Singh (eds.) Digital Convergence in Intelligent Mobility Systems, (59–78) © 2025 Scrivener Publishing LLC

4.1 Introduction

A charging station network for electric cars is a system that provides them with power to recharge. The term "electric vehicle infrastructure" refers to the number of individual places where you can charge your car, as well as their distribution throughout a given area or country. These networks may grow thanks to private enterprises setting up stations and government initiatives funding them; doing so is key in order to get people driving electric rather than traditional cars, which run on internal combustion engines. Originally, proprietary chargers were used by early networks which only worked with specific brands, but now, most suppliers offer universal systems compatible with different types of EVs. According to recent studies, failures occur in electric vehicles due primarily to inadequate charge stations rather than pricing or range issues. However, when comparing costs between gas-powered automobiles and those powered by electricity, it becomes irrelevant because all models had same price points at that particular time; therefore, both were priced equally. Because environmental problems related to vehicles with internal combustion engines (ICEs) have arisen, the electric vehicle (EV) industry has quickly grown. Electric cars are an essential part of the fight against climate change and air pollution. Nevertheless, there are many disadvantages associated with them such as limited driving range, expensive batteries, short battery life spans, long charging times, and scarcity of electricity for charging, which explains why they still have not taken off fully. Therefore, this remains true even though they continue gaining popularity day by day so much that their market share continues expanding, thereby necessitating an understanding on how these cars affect our electricity supply systems, including reserve margins, and reliability degradation, among other things, like power quality problems. The advantages of the new energy vehicles over traditional cars include reduced pollution, increased energy utilization, and lower operating cost. The introduction of smart charging into the grid system helps in showcasing the viability of this approach. The rapid development of electric cars contributes greatly toward industrial structure optimization design as well as sustainable industrialization. In view of these challenges facing electric vehicle technology today, governments are focusing more on charging-related research which majorly dwells on safety precautions taken during the charging process and power supply from charging stations, among others, with an aim of achieving safe sustainable rechargeable systems for electric automobiles. Electric car (EV) chargers are usually split into alternating current (AC) charging stations and direct current (DC) charging stations. EV batteries need DC electricity to charge, while most of the power from the grid comes as AC. To get around this, most electric vehicles have an onboard charger which converts it to DC in order to recharge the battery when using an AC charging station. On the other hand, DC charging stations achieve higher power by integrating larger AC-to-DC converters within the charging unit itself; therefore, they do not use onboard chargers that could limit size or weight. The DC charging station supplies DC power directly to the vehicle without passing through the onboard converter. Most modern electric vehicle models can be charged with either AC or DC power. Electric vehicle charging infrastructure is an essential component of the EV ecosystem. It needs to be built out rapidly and made accessible to all potential users, which requires investment in a diverse range of technologies and business models. A successful transition from fossil-fuel-based transportation systems will depend on continued innovation in this sector alongside supportive policies that encourage widespread adoption of electric vehicles and renewable energy integration into the grid.

4.2 Literature Survey

The literature survey conducted by Tianjin Chen *et al.* (2020) examines the construction of electric vehicle charging points across the United Kingdom. It looks closely at government initiatives, how to make them most useful, what needs thought about when designing them, and, finally, different models which could be implemented. The UK has set ambitious goals for reducing emissions by encouraging people to buy EVs. There are many incentives available, but this paper also talks about operational management, so that they become widely accepted as normal everyday objects. In the future, we need more electricity demand addressed; otherwise, there will not be enough power points available. Another issue is the grid infrastructure being able to handle such huge amounts of extra renewable energy being produced at peak times and sustainable commercial viability over the long term for public charging.

The study conducted by Till Bunsen *et al.* (2018) on global electric mobility uses "Global EV Outlook" as its yearly publication. This review provides historical trends up to 2030, together with future projections covering such areas as EV deployment, charging infrastructure, ownership costs, energy consumption, CO_2 emissions, and battery material demand. Moreover, policy recommendations are also given based on experiences learned from leading markets, so that policymakers can have a direction when promoting adoption of these types of vehicles among stakeholders, supported by members of the Electric Vehicles Initiative (EVI).

The literature survey conducted by C. Guo *et al.* (2015) investigates the intricacies of electric vehicle (EV) development, highlighting the necessity for holistic thinking about the whole system so as to optimize different areas of EVs, especially their relation with the power grid. It recognizes battery technology and development mechanisms as major blocks by recommending a stepwise optimization approach and franchising-based promotional strategy. The study puts more weight on system-level challenges that should be addressed alongside creating enabling policies which would hasten the adoption of EVs. In addition, it also suggests further research in battery technology and system analysis required to drive sustainable growth in the EV industry.

A study was conducted by Y. Saber and G. K. Venayagamoorthy *et al.* (2011) on the relationship between renewable generation integration into the electricity system via grid-connected energy storage units and smart grids in order to reduce greenhouse gases emitted from power plants. It suggests that there is a need for dynamic optimization methods, so that renewable resources can be effectively utilized while considering different types of grid-able vehicles, which include plug-in hybrid electric vehicles (PHEVs) or battery-powered EVs having v2g capability. This will enable them to serve as distributed storage devices throughout smart grid networks during peak load periods, thereby contributing significantly toward mitigating climate change impacts associated with global warming.

The literature survey conducted by C. Chen *et al.* (2007) examines electric, hybrid, and fuel cell cars in current use as well as the present state of knowledge regarding these vehicles. The study also underlines the significance of hybrid electric vehicles (HEVs) for achieving fuel efficiency and dealing with ecological issues. It talks about various key technologies such as electric drive trains, power electronics, and energy storage systems while pointing out modeling, simulation, and control theory as very important areas of focus in HEV design and development. Although still at their infancy stage in terms of market share, it is expected that due to the better performance they offer over other types of vehicles, HEVs will become more popular in years to come. This survey further underscores the criticality of advanced propulsion systems toward meeting strict energy demand side management strategies aimed at reducing carbon footprint related effects caused by human activities within our atmosphere.

4.3 Government Initiatives

4.3.1 Faster Adoption and Manufacturing of Hybrid and Electric Vehicles (FAME II) Scheme

The FAME II Scheme with a budget of Rs 10,000 is to boost the sale of electric and hybrid vehicles. The Faster Adoption and Manufacturing of Hybrid and Electric Vehicles scheme is in line with the government's bigger plans of rolling out better and environmentally friendly means of transport in the country. Quite a sizable proportion of the budget focuses on the establishment of an adequate charging network. The plan or strategy is to install nearly 2,700 charging points in metro cities, smart cities, and important highways across the country. Each charging station will have several charging spots, and they will be usable for charging a greater number of vehicles at once; thus, owning electric cars will be made easier for the users. This large number of charging stations should help to reduce range anxiety for owners of electric vehicles and promote the use of electric cars, buses, trucks, etc.

4.3.2 National Electric Mobility Mission Plan (NEMMP) 2020

The National Electric Mobility Mission Plan (NEMMP) 2020 is the key plan of the Indian government to encourage the production as well as the usage of electric vehicles in the country. Its main goal also includes creating a network of charging infrastructure that would be sufficient for the increasing amount of EV users. The plan envisages the participation of public sector partners to engage the private sector in establishing payment networks throughout the nation. The NEMMP 2020 in this connection aims at promoting the formation of partnerships and investment in charging infrastructure in order to reduce the dependency on fossil resources and make use of the potential that EVs have in transforming the future into a more environmentally friendly one. In this regard, this initiative is expected to solve one of the most significant challenges related to charging accessibility, which, in turn, will increase consumers' trust in electric vehicles and drive increased adoption of electric mobility.

4.3.3 Charging Infrastructure for Electric Vehicles—Guidelines and Standards of the Ministry of Power

The "Charging Infrastructure for Electric Vehicles—Guidelines and Standards" released by the Ministry of Power seeks to lay processes in the proper establishment of charging infrastructure in India. The above guidelines set out fairly specific specifications and design standards common to PCS while enhancing the safety of consumers. To support the affordability, the guidelines contain the provision for a special EV tariff so that charging becomes cheaper for the users. Further, regarding land allocation, they cover what to be done concerning the use of the land and the permits required to establish the charging stations. This broad structure helps in the general and sound development of the charging network so as to promote the use of electric cars and improve efficiency of the transport sector.

4.3.4 State Government Initiatives

For a while, different state governments of India are also coming up with their own policies and incentives pertaining to the construction of EV chargers. Memorable mentions include the Delhi EV Policy that entitles rebates for establishing charging structures and plans to set up 500 charging points by the year 2024. Maharashtra has set a bolder ground by aiming to set up 1,500 charging stations by 2025 and attracting private players by providing incentives for them to do so. The Karnataka EV Policy lays emphasis on the development of charging infrastructure—both the fast charging stations and the slow charging stations in the selected urban and semi-urban cities of the state. These state-level efforts work side by side with the national ones, thus providing a complex strategy in an effort to increase the usage of electric vehicles and charging infrastructure, which follows their growth in demand.

4.3.5 Public Sector Undertakings (PSUs) and Private Sector Collaboration

Major private companies and state-controlled companies or public sector undertakings (PSUs) are involved in the implementation of EV charging stations in India. Energy Efficiency Services Limited (EESL) is the joint venture of several PSUs under the Ministry of Power and is involved in the setting up of charging stations across the country. For example, companies like Tata Power, Indian Oil, and Bharat Petroleum are investing in or directly setting up the charging stations for electric vehicles as the number of electric vehicles being used is on the rise. Such cooperation with public institutions and private companies is crucial for the formation of a dense and inclusive network of stations that will enable people to switch to EVs and start the process of charging modern EVs' demand and increasing the speed of infrastructure growth.

4.3.6 Smart Cities Mission

The Smart Cities Mission unveiled to install EV charging infrastructure into the concept of 100 smart cities in India. This is centered at placing charging areas in strategic places like parking space, transport centers, and many more. Through integrating EV charging equipment in urbanization, the mission supports the application of electric automobiles, and utilizing electrical automobiles gets to be less complicated due to accessible charging services. They can all work to further the goal of achieving sustainable urban mobility in these smart cities, thus improving the quality standards in their view by diminishing urban pollution. This way, the Smart Cities Mission was designed to establish proper conditions for utilizing electric vehicles as the primary transport solution.

4.3.7 National Electric Mobility Infrastructure (NEMI) Guidelines

The NEMI Guidelines whose primary objective is to ensure that adequate guidelines are implemented for the deployment of charge point stations for EVs across India. These guidelines stress out the need to define and harmonize the kind of charging equipment so as to be compatible with different makes and models of EVs as well as EV charging stations. Because of these guidelines, a standard is set that ensures that users do not encounter any problems when charging their electric cars. Further, the guidelines focus on innovation on the charging; this helps to ensure that innovation in charging technologies is fostered in order to create proper solutions in the creation of charging networks for EV. This comprehensive strategy aims at developing a stable and effective charging network that would benefit the broad use of EVs and thus promote healthy advancement toward an environmentally friendly transportation system in the country.

4.4 Challenges

4.4.1 Capital Intensive Investments

Fixed charging stations for electric vehicles are capital intensive mainly because of the expensive hardware technology needed to support them and the extensive installation procedures that are needed. Fast chargers which are important for minimizing the duration of charging require costly hardware, and in most cases, the electrical infrastructure has to be upgraded to support the load requirements of the fast chargers. These are factors like land acquisition costs, installation of electrical systems, safety measures, and legal requirements in establishing the basic setup of a factory or a business enterprise, which go into the calculation of the working capital needed at the start of a business. This kind of huge expenditures can make it difficult for new and small investors to invest in the market due to the large initial capital and the complicated installation procedures.

However, as there are many fast charging stations out there, there should be many charging points, which again is costly. The second aspect of scalability is the problem of having to build large infrastructure to prevent what has been described as 'charging deserts' across the country while the demand for additional infrastructure increases in tandem with the growing number of electric vehicles. Due to unpredictable profitability of projects and possible market factors influencing durability of the infrastructure, small investors may not be able to obtain funds and wait for the long gestation periods. Therefore, the prospects are that a number of large players will dominate the market, thus restricting competitive environment and product development in this sphere.

4.4.2 Power Supply and Grid Stability

The deployment of charging stations of electric vehicles is closely related to problems of power supply and stability of the electrical circuits. The extent of charging performed at these stations magnifies with the uptake of EVs, and the utilization of electricity is significantly raised for fast charging points. The fast chargers consume a lot of power, usually in excess of what traditional systems can supply to the local grid that may not be ready for such loads. This increased demand may result in some areas experiencing overloads and therefore interrupt the supply of electricity, which may result to blackouts. Another major concern for maintaining the stability of electricity supply is how to ensure that the electrical power supply has the necessary capacity to meet these needs.

Furthermore, to level-connect a large number of EV chargers, it is necessary to coordinate for proper management in the process not to harm the grid stability. Characterized by alternating, for example, by the degree of consumption or by periods of maximum demand, these fluctuations can therefore also generate added pressure on the grid. It requires next-generation grid intelligence solutions like monitoring and control, smart grids, and energy storage solutions to manage the supply and demand. Further, there need to be coordination with the utility companies and investments in the grid framework to bear the increasing demand of the load owing to the EVs. Solving these challenges is rather important in order to provide a stable and balanced electricity supply as the market of EVs is developing.

4.4.3 The Issue of Uniformity in Charging Infrastructure

The question of standardization in secondary charging equipment is a problem when the station networks of electric vehicles grow more significantly. At the moment, there are nearly no unified interfaces of charging as well as communication and payment systems used by different manufacturers and service providers. They include compatibility problems wherein the EV owners may realize that their cars cannot be charged in some stations. For example, some of the stations may have different types of connectors or do not adhere to the charging standards. As a result, charging becomes even more of a problem and confusing to the users. This fragmentation can also be a problem with regard to increasing EV market share since prospective buyers may lack sufficient faith in the compatibility of their cars with regard to available charging points.

Besides, there is no common bar set by different industries regarding the charging networks, thereby posing some interference in the charging point network and the overall experience of the customers. If there is no standard, almost all the people could take multiple memberships. This means that in order to join different networks, people need to sign up for membership with different companies, which would mean that they would have to incur different payment systems when it comes to payment of membership fees to the said companies. It can also hinder in constructing a uniform, integrated system for charging across the country. As such, there exists a need for the development of best practices by all stakeholders in the sector to make appropriate and concrete recommendations when it comes to the charging connectors, communication, and payment systems.

4.4.4 Space and Land Constraints

One of the major issues affecting the establishment of electric vehicle (EV) charging stations is the issue of space/land, especially in urban areas where space is limited. Charging stanchions involve provision of a physical area for the charging stations, tools in charging, and, at times, the requirement for electrical infrastructure change. Cities mostly have restricted space, and the spaces that are available may be costly, thus the challenge of facing difficulty in identifying right places to install new charging points. On the other hand, upgrading old structures like parking lots into service stations to incorporate the EV chargers can be a sizable exercise. Such spatial constraints could mean less charging infrastructure and the creation of what has come to be known as "charging deserts," areas with limited access to charging stations.

In suburbs and rural areas especially, though the land resource could be abundant, the problem lies in how the structures can be situated to effectively impact a broad populace. In addition, incorporating the charging stations into the specified area takes considerable time if space is available; it takes additional time to negotiate with the property owners and local authority. The combination of the conflict between the use of land and the demand for EV charging stations implies that inventive measures similar to using multifunctional installations or vertical charging centers are becoming more essential. Solving these issues related to spatial and land availability is instrumental in increasing the number of EV charging stations and achieving their availability to every potential consumer.

4.4.5 Legal and Bureaucratic Obstacles

Regulatory and administrative factors pose some of the most pressing issues in planning for infrastructure of EV charging stations. Various installations and operation of the charging stations need different regulations, permits, and approvals; this makes the entire process very cumbersome. The laws of each location can be significantly different when it comes to codes and standards governing electrical works, zoning restrictions, and the use of land, which can slow down a project's progress and raise its expenses. Furthermore, the issuance of permits entails interacting with different ministries and departments that have different sets of requirement and procedures that can prove to be thorny and time-consuming gates that slow down the pace of undertaking the project.

Also, the regulations that cover the installation of EV charging equipment are fairly dynamic and could not necessarily pencil out the contemporary charging arrangements. Concerns like property rights, who is responsible for the electrical barring, how to manage the tariff, and setting the proper and reasonable price for using electrical energy may develop into additional problems. In some instances, specific or current regulation may even lack the ability to respond properly to the ever-changing nature and additional features that EV charging presents, meaning that existing policy or legislation will have to be altered or a new one drafted. These bureaucratic and legal issues would require policy-level interventions alongside reforming some of the existing procedures and, in some cases, the laws themselves, which may include lobbying for updates to the concerned laws due to the increased support to emerging technologies such as EV charging networks.

4.4.6 Technology and Maintenance

The key technological and maintenance problems are fundamental to the deployment of electric vehicle charging facilities. The innovation advancement of EVs and charging technology is constantly improving, making charging stations' need to be relevant a constant process. Every new line of EVs may have different charging standards or may call for a faster means to charge them, thus making the current infrastructure obsolete or unsuitable. The fact that charging technologies require regular upgrades and may require the integration of new features makes it a never-ending process and adds layers of complexity when dealing with multiple charging stations and different clients.

Besides technological enhancement, the management of charging infrastructure also raises certain issues. Charging stations therefore need to be maintained frequently for them to be in a good state and safe for use. It encompasses general checks, upgrades, or fixes to issues, which include but are not limited to mechanical breakdowns or even the normal tear and wear of the equipment. Maintenance is critical especially to minimize any form of downtime and enhance dependability; however, it can be time consuming and involves a lot of expense and planning, particularly when many stations are distributed over a vast region. Cohesive maintenance policies and structures must be put in place to guarantee the permanent stability of the charging stations and to meet the increasing needs of the EV consumers.

4.4.7 Adoption Rate of EVs

The use of electric cars affects the growth and feasibility of EV charging stations. A lower adoption rate means that the charging stations remain underutilized, hence making it difficult to recover the huge amount of money required to install and maintain the charging stations. When there are only a few cities with EV, demand for charging points remains low, hence preventing investors and stakeholders from investing on the infrastructure to make them available. This can lead to a slow expansion of charging stations; thus, the vicious cycle is created, where the scarcity of such infrastructure slows down the acceptance of electric vehicles because of the scarcity of charging points.

On the other hand, the factor of having a high adoption rate increases the rate in which there is a need for many and well-distributed charging stations. The increased quantity of EVs on road obsolescence of infrastructure comes with the prospect of lacking charging facilities and generating long queues for the users. This may form something like a 'charging desert' where some places will not be well equipped with charging stations, so owning an EV will prove inconvenient and unattractive. To solve these problems, a symbiotic and realistic solution is required that consists of systematic planning and preparation for the construction of charging stations for future consumption given the gradually improving usage of electric cars.

4.4.8 Integration with Renewable Energy

Charging most or all of an electric vehicle with electricity from renewable sources is a challenge and an opportunity rolled into one package of opportunities. On one hand, the use of renewable energy, including solar or wind, to power the chargers for EVs can greatly decrease the emission of carbon in transportation, which is one of the overarching goals concerning environmental conservation. However, there is the problem of credit availability and the intermittent nature of renewable energy sources, which can act as a challenge in charging frequency and reliability. Solar energy, for instance, is available in the day and is seasonal, while wind power is inconsistent and has fluctuating power outputs. This variation requires energy management techniques which will solve the problem of power supply to the charging stations by use of energy storage solutions.

In the same case, the inclusion of renewable energy in the already-existing grid system may present some challenges in terms of cost among other factors. One of them is increasing grid upgrade processes since the system deals with decentralized and rather randomly changing power inputs, which might be costly because of the need to install necessary smart grids and energy storage systems. These upgrades are needed in order to have a dynamic balance between the supply and demand sides and in order to really be able to obtain more renewable energy for the deployment of EV charging with relevant quality and efficiency. Additionally, the imperatives that remain to be addressed are policy factors that enhance the accommodation of the renewable energy in charging infrastructure, such as the subsidies toward the installation of renewable energy resources and the promotion of the technologies in the management of energy storage systems and the grid.

4.5 Important Factors

Design of Charging Equipment: When planning an electric vehicle charging system, one must determine what type of charging equipment to be used. There are a couple of different kinds, either floor mounted or wall mounted, with each having its own pros and cons. These usually consist of a power supply, communication systems, management systems, and a charger itself among others; safety should always be considered in their design along with efficiency and compatibility to various models as well as charging standards adopted worldwide, like the three-phase AC current connection commonly made using the type 2 AC connector. To make them more convenient for users, it is good if they can also be designed to be user friendly, durable, and attractive.

Charging Infrastructure Location: The location where one decides to put up charging facilities greatly affects how accessible or usable they become. For instance; residential areas could be a good idea because most people live there, while workplaces may work better since individuals spend much time at these places during weekdays. Then again, public parking spaces would also make sense considering that many motorists use them frequently, as do major transport routes where all vehicles travelling long distances pass through. In addition, visibility cannot be ignored together with safety; thus, proximity to power sources should not pose any threats, and convenience for drivers must also be looked into besides taking into account licensed areas by distribution network operators (DNOs) so that coverage does not become an issue.

Cost of Electric Vehicle Charging Infrastructure: The price of electric vehicle charging infrastructure is made up of many different things. These include capital costs, installation costs, and operation costs among others. What are capital costs? Well, they represent the initial investment that needs to be made in order for one to buy and install charging equipment. On the other hand, what do installation costs cover? Installation costs cover all the expenses incurred during site preparation, which includes electrical connections as well as infrastructure deployment among other related activities. Operation cost refers to any expense incurred after establishment, such as maintenance fee or warranty charges.

There are government grants available for people who want to install chargers at home or in the work place or even in public spaces like shopping malls, where many cars can park at once. This is done under the Office for Low Emission Vehicles (OLEV) scheme which helps subsidize these installations so that it becomes cheaper for everyone involved, including businesses that are mandated by law because they have a large number of employees.

Understanding how much money someone will need over time and looking into ways that funding could be provided should not only help them save their own but also assist authorities decide on the best places where this can be set up since once installed, new homes will come up around those areas, thereby increasing demand and hence ensuring its sustainability as a whole.

To sum up everything said earlier, the design considerations outlined suggest that some thought should go into where exactly each station should be located, taking into consideration factors such as proximity with other existing facilities like petrol stations or parking lots and along major roads/highways so that people don't have to make detours when going about their business. Also considered is what type (level) of power supply is needed depending on usage patterns, i.e., whether it's intended primarily for overnight charging while households are asleep, daytime use by businesses, etc. Another thing emphasized here is cost effectiveness—how one would achieve maximum coverage area within given budgetary constraints without compromising the quality of services rendered. Thus, stakeholders need to look at all these factors together; otherwise, they won't achieve much.

4.6 Infrastructure

4.6.1 Charging Stations

The signing up of electric vehicle charging points is an area that is determined by the public and private sectors by providing an expansion of the necessary infrastructure caused by the increasing number of electric cars. Several Indian driving forces, namely, Tata Power and Reliance, along with distinctive government-driven organizations are leaders in setting up many units of charging points at various offices such as shopping centers, executive associations, and dwelling complexes. This widespread deployment helps to satisfy the need to have very accessible charging points that will make EV ownership feasible for daily use. Such strategies of setting up charging points in popular and populated locations and apartments contribute significantly to fighting range anxiety and getting more consumers to make the switch to electric automobiles.

Moreover, the establishment of infrastructure, specifically charging centers, along the corridors is equally important especially for long-distance driving by the users of electric vehicles. Among them is the one that requires the creation of charging stations that can rapidly charge the batteries of the automobiles to allow longer travel and less charging time. Such cooperation of commercial organizations and governmental organizations in the development of this infrastructure demonstrates other organizations' responsibility behind the promotion of sustainable transportation and response to environmental obligations. Being aimed at improving the availability and quality of the charging facilities for EVs, these steps can be considered as highly effective in driving the demand for electric vehicles and generally promoting environmental improvements.

4.6.2 Grid Upgrades

Given that there has been a push behind EVs, it is currently vital that the electrical grid is given an upgrade in order to handle this upturn in power usage. With the increasing use of EVs, the supply of electricity needs far-reaching improvements to be stable as well as effective. This includes upgrades of the distribution lines, substations, and transformers in order to be able to handle the higher loads during peak hours and also to ensure stability of the system. Reacting to such possibilities, sophisticated infrastructure guarantees the non-occurrence of probable power blackouts while at the same time confirming the grid's ability to distribute electricity to EV charging stations located in both households and commercial stations without significantly impairing the standard delivery services.

Further, these grid upgrades also include smart grids and demand response systems among other complex technologies. Smart grids improve the possibilities of timely controlling the electricity flow and incorporation of the renewable electricity sources into the distribution system and the load. DR programs can help change the rates of charging EVs with reference to grid constraints and therefore help to manage peak stresses at such times. With such improvements of infrastructures, the utilities and grid operators can promote the proliferation of the EV market, so that the power of electricity can be stable and efficient while gradually transitioning to a sustainable energy system.

4.6.3 Battery Swapping Stations

Battery swapping stations are a very viable model especially for two- and three-wheeled electric vehicles because this model addresses major issues of conventional charging infrastructures. In heavily populated areas such as cities, battery swapping may be easier than establishing many charging stations each of which requires a huge space. These stations enable one to replace his exhausted batteries with fresh ones, and this does not take a long time compared to charging of batteries. This fast 'recharging' solves the problem of long charging times and contributes to the functionality of electric scooters and motorcycles used for first and last mile transportation as well as delivery purposes.

Moreover, battery swapping has potential benefits for energy generation, distribution, and usage resulting in a more sustainable and scalable future. Since batteries are swapped at these stations, operators of these stations can optimize or use technologies that are efficient in charging batteries. This process also creates easier control and possible recovery of batteries since they are returned and replaced during the swapping process. In summary, battery swapping stations are a viable solution to some of the problems related to charging for EVs, especially in well-populated areas of the country, and help in promoting the use of electric two- and three-wheel passenger vehicles.

4.6.4 Software Systems

Sophisticated software applications play a crucial role in addressing various challenges related to the EV charging stations and making it easy for the EV owners. Charging processes in these platforms can be done through secure payment systems that allow users to conveniently pay for charging sessions utilizing their mobile applications, contactless cards, and online accounts. Such systems are used to facilitate secure transactions in line with billing and payment history in real time. Also, the graphic interfaces of the applications, in the mobile applications, for example, or the in-car interfaces, encompass features such as the search of a charging point nearby, the possibility of making a check on the availability of the chargers, and the setting of the charging times, among others, that provide extra utility and optimize the charging processes for the users.

The management of the station is also important, as it is responsible for the operation of several charging points besides managing the load of the charge point and the grid. This program assists the managers of the charging stations in conducting remote monitoring of technical problems to address them as soon as possible and thus guarantee constant operation of the stations. It also entails features of dynamic price determination and demand management techniques which can vary rates based on time, the situation in the grid, or otherwise encouraging rational energy consumption and lower costs. Thus, the incorporation of these advanced software solutions leads to improvements in the reliability, utility, and flexibility of EV infrastructure from the technological and market perspectives.

4.7 Applications

The charging stations of electric vehicles (EV) are important in the migration from conventional combustion engines to lean electric automobiles. The main use case refers to the incorporation of the charging stations in public and private domains. Fast charging stations at highway rest stops, urban parking lots, and shopping centers as well as other public charging stations enable convenience, thus enabling the EV owners to charge their EVs. Here, these stations are diversified with charging rates and capacities of EVs and batteries that help support extended trips and minimize range anxiety.

Besides public stations, home charging is crucial for most users because most people drive their electric cars on short daily trips. Home charging is one of these methods that allow the owners of the EVs to plug their cars in a charging unit, and this normally happens at night, so that one is assured of a fully charged car the following morning. This infrastructure may comprise level 2 chargers that are generally a stepped-up affair when compared to basic household outlets. The charging technology evolves to smart home charging systems that could be connected with home energy management systems, and this enables the user to delay charging during expensive rates and when renewable energy sources are scarce, adding to the element of efficiency and affordability of electric vehicles.

Finally, even the deployment of charging infrastructure has a large impact on commercial and fleet activities. Many companies and public transportation providers are increasingly incorporating EV charging stations to power their corporate electric vehicles. Some of these are installing charging points at the companies' depots, distribution centers, and any other public transport terminal to ensure that the company's fleets are fully charged for use. Lastly, the development of the infrastructure for EVs may result in new businesses within the sector; these include a charging point network and related services within the sector, thus enhancing the process of stimulating economic development in the country and the improvement of the production of electric vehicles.

4.8 Conclusion

This review provides a comprehensive overview of the current state and future outlook for electric vehicle charging infrastructure in the UK. By exploring areas such as legislation, charging equipment standards, currently operational sites for charging points, site design considerations, management methods, and industry challenges, this study presents valuable insights which could help enhance the expansion and efficiency of the country's EV charge station network. In addition to underscoring the importance of managing and operating EV charging infrastructures using smart technologies, it also draws attention to factors like design, cost, or location that should be taken into account when setting up charging stations for electric vehicles. Moreover, what the evaluation further underlines is how crucial it is for governments' policies to create more electric car charging stations as well as lower carbon emissions from the transportation sector. The appraisal gives recommendations on how best to direct growths in relation with electric vehicle infrastructure within the United Kingdom, thus aiding toward development toward sustainable transportations and hence being seen as a key resource by various players in industries dealing with the automotive sector or those related with public service delivery involving transport.

References

Chen, T. and Yu, J., Cost-Benefit Analysis of Dynamic Wireless Charging Infrastructure for Electric Vehicles. *IEEE Access*, 8, 99901–99915, 2020.

Ding, Y. and Zhang, Y., Infrastructure Planning for Wireless Charging of Electric Vehicles: A Review of Models and Methods. *Energy*, 204, 117996, 2020.

Fang, W. and Zhang, J., Dynamic Wireless Charging and Battery-Swap System: A Comparative Study on Cost and Efficiency. *Energy Rep.*, 8, 78–90, 2022.

Gao, L. and Zhang, J., Dynamic Charging System Deployment for Electric Vehicles: A Stochastic Optimization Approach. *Math. Probl. Eng.*, 2019, 5127542, 2019.

Gatti, R. and Singh, C., *Shaping the Future of Automation With Cloud-Enhanced Robotics*, IGI Global, Pennsylvania, USA, 2024. https://www.igi-global.com/book/shaping-future-automation-cloud-enhanced/330967.

Gong, Y. and Liu, W., Economic and Environmental Impact of Dynamic Wireless Charging Systems for Electric Vehicles. *J. Clean. Prod.*, 278, 123548, 2021.

Huo, H. and Zhang, Q., A Cost-Effective Framework for Deploying Electric Vehicle Charging Stations: Case Study and Policy Recommendations. *Energy Policy*, 139, 111339, 2020.

Jin, H., Zhang, Y., Li, X., Optimal Deployment of Dynamic Wireless Charging Infrastructure for Electric Vehicles in Urban Road Networks. *Transp. Res. Part C Emerg. Technol.*, 117, 102743, 2020.

Li, Q. and Tang, X., Evaluating the Impact of Dynamic Wireless Charging on Electric Vehicle Charging Demand. *Transp. Res. Part C Emerg. Technol.*, 125, 103145, 2021.

Li, X. and Li, X., Optimal Location of EV Charging Stations Using GIS and Multi-Criteria Decision Analysis. *Appl. Energy*, 236, 1089–1104, 2019.

Liu, Z. and Wang, W., Modeling and Optimization of Dynamic Wireless Charging for Electric Vehicles on Highways. *IEEE Trans. Power Electron.*, 36, 7, 8162–8172, 2021.

Ouyang, Y. and Yu, Y., Evaluating the Impact of Dynamic Wireless Charging Systems on Electric Vehicle Adoption Rates. *Transp. Res. Part A Policy Pract.*, 155, 173–185, 2022.

Singh, C. and Gatti, R., *Drone applications for industry 5.0*, IGI Global, Pennsylvania, USA, 2024. https://www.igi-global.com/book/drone-applications-industry/331754.

Song, C. and Yang, W., A Review of Charging Infrastructure Planning for Electric Vehicles: Challenges and Solutions. *Sustain. Cities Soc.*, 54, 101956, 2020.

Wang, J. and Sun, C., Dynamic Wireless Charging for Electric Vehicles: A Review of Technology, Economics, and Policy. *Energy Rep.*, 8, 1–18, 2022.

Xie, L. and Wei, M., Assessing the Economic Viability of Dynamic Wireless Charging Systems for Electric Vehicles in Urban Environments. *J. Transp. Econ. Policy*, 55, 1, 81–99, 2021.

Yang, S. and Wu, X., Mitigating Range Anxiety with Dynamic Wireless Charging: A Simulation Study. *Transp. Res. Part D Transp. Environ.*, 92, 102730, 2021.

Zhang, H. and Geng, L., Dynamic Wireless Charging Technology for Electric Vehicles: A Review and Future Perspectives. *IEEE Trans. Veh. Technol.*, 70, 2, 1150–1162, 2021.

Zhao, H. and Xu, Y., Charging Infrastructure Planning for Electric Vehicles: A Review of Recent Advances and Future Directions. *Renew. Sustain. Energy Rev.*, 113, 109272, 2019.

Zhu, L. and Wang, X., The Role of Dynamic Wireless Charging in Reducing Range Anxiety for Electric Vehicle Users. *IEEE Trans. Intell. Transp. Syst.*, 23, 4, 2040–2049, 2022.

5

Accelerating Connections with 5G and Evolution of Vehicle Communication Technology

Dankan Gowda V.[1*], Chippy T.[2], V. Nuthan Prasad[3], Belsam Jeba Ananth M.[4] and K.D.V. Prasad[5]

[1]*Department of Electronics and Communication Engineering, BMS Institute of Technology and Management, Bangalore, Karnataka, India*
[2]*Department of Computer Science and Engineering, Mahaguru Institute of Technology, Kattachira, Kayamkulam, Alappuzha, India*
[3]*Department of Electronic and Communication, MSRIT, Bangalore, Karnataka, India*
[4]*Department of Mechatronics Engineering, SRM Institute of Science and Technology, Kattankulathur, Chengalpattu, Tamil Nadu, India*
[5]*Symbiosis Institute of Business Management, Hyderabad and Symbiosis International (Deemed University), Pune, India*

Abstract
This chapter provides insights on how operation of 5G technology will revolutionize vehicle communication while ushering in a revolutionary epoch of instant communications. Evolution of communication system in the automotive from, primitive used earlier to the complex and intelligent networks that propel present day intelligent vehicles. This chapter then moves on to understand the basics of 5G, depicting the technological developments that enable its unparalleled effectiveness. This chapter examines the challenges and viable options surrounding the incorporation of 5G into vehicle networks revolutionizing this process. Some of the major benefits that 5G introduces to vehicle communication include enhanced data transmission speed, reliability and high quality-of-service. So, in the following we provide deeper insights into how 5G and V2X communication technologies interact as mechanisms that optimize road safety and efficiency using these two technological principles. According to case studies, 5G may well be effective in

**Corresponding author*: dankan.v@bmsit.in

Rathishchandra R. Gatti and Chandra Singh (eds.) Digital Convergence in Intelligent Mobility Systems, (79–100) © 2025 Scrivener Publishing LLC

a wide range of cases where there is vehicle communication. Some of these examples demonstrate the immediate influences on IVS of 5G, and present insights into 5G's capabilities in terms of flexibility as well as adaptability.

***Keywords*:** 5G technology, vehicle communication, intelligent transportation systems, vehicular networks, wireless connectivity, V2X communication, massive MIMO, integration of 5G

5.1 Introduction

The development of 5G technology sets a critical change in the world of auto communication, which will bring forth a perfect blend of connectivity and performance that has never been witnessed before. This revolutionary technology leads the automotive industry in terms of innovativeness and innovation is about to change the concept of vehicle-to-vehicle interactions as well as vehicle-infrastructure interactions [1, 2]. Technically, 5G technology does not represent a gradual evolution from its predecessors but rather an almost complete revolution whereby the promised delivery is increased data rates tremendously reduced latency and greatly enhanced reliability. SKU: 101897 These improvements have become essential in terms of transportation communications [3], where quick decisions and data communication in real time are critical for safety, productivity; and the smooth operation.

Figure 5.1 shows a schematic representation of an Internet of Vehicles (IoV) network structure, illustrating the key components and their interactions within the network. 5G is a highly significant development that allows for improvements to vehicle communication, as it transforms the transport of goods and people [4, 5]. After its introduction, it is ready to open a broad range of new opportunities and features, including complex Vehicle-to-Everything (V2X) communication aspects as well as autonomous cars. 5G's ability to process tremendous data volumes while supporting various devices simultaneously makes it a perfect candidate to act as an infrastructure of the upcoming intelligent transportation systems [6]. This technological leap is not a mere evolutionary move but an absolute transformation that will define the future of mobility, creating the pathway for intelligent, secure and more efficient transportation systems.

The main purpose of the Internet of Vehicles (IoV) and Vehicle-to-Everything (V2X) technologies is to facilitate a close integration among vehicles, objects, and people in order to create an uninterrupted connection [7]. The current VANET works by considering each internet-enabled vehicle as a node. The system here has changed into IoV which includes

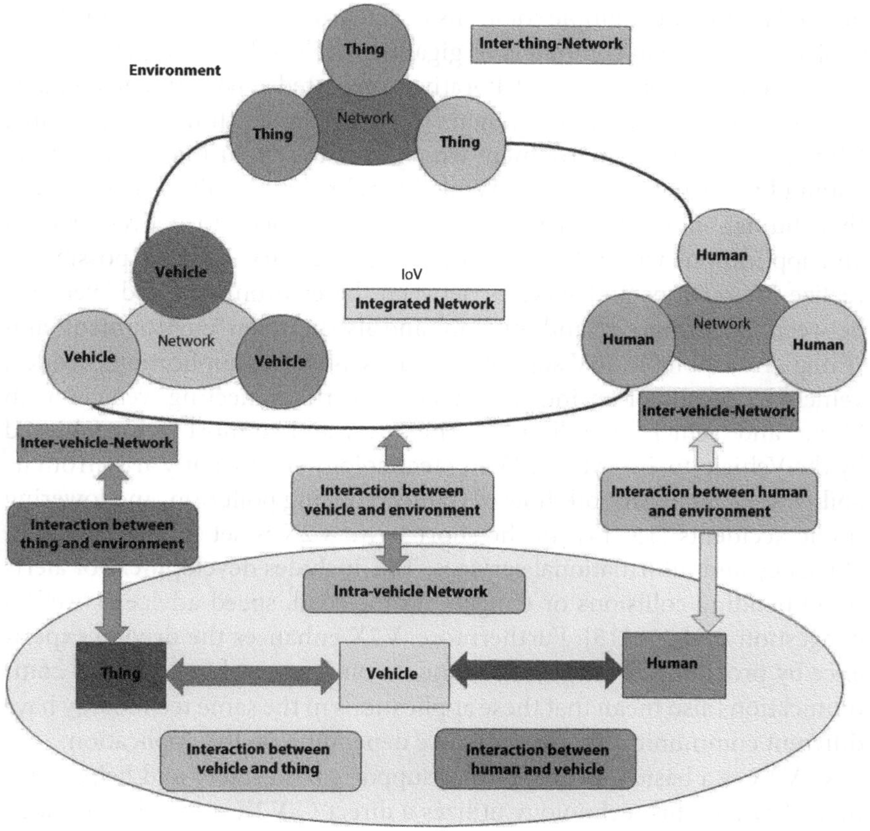

Figure 5.1 Schematic representation of an IoV (internet of vehicles) network structure.

the feature of integrating inside vehicles with IoT technology. This fusion enables data sharing and ensures a smoother flow of traffic, efficient fleet management, the prevention of occurrences and serves users with entertainment or location services around-the-clock. In IoV, sensors for distance, velocity differences as well as acceleration are fitted which enables much better driving assistants [8, 9]. For example, adaptive cruise control is based on the vehicle's AI system which reads other cars and their movements.

The recent developments towards IoT results in an evolutionary process of IoV. For example, the mentioned abilities include changing vehicle trajectories to fit into urban street patterns and traffic situation along with integrating humans and vehicles as complementary elements, building a connection between humans, vehicles, and advanced multi-layered systems by sensors and mobile devices in a vast scale [10, 11]. This convergence is devised to provide multiple solutions in and around the cars, making these vehicles into human computers or gigantic wireless devices on wheels.

The IoV network is a collaborative integrated environment containing three different groups: "human," "vehicle," and "thing" cooperating. 'Human' covers this environment which contains either individuals in the automobile or outside the car. While 'thing' refers to things that are neither 'human' nor cars but instead they can interact and deliver services and applications within these surroundings [12]. IoV makes it possible to realize interactions and services between the environment and "vehicle," between "environment" and "human", and also between "environment" and "thing". Additionally, IoV supports services as well as applications inside a vehicle by means of an intravehicular network connecting 'vehicle' with 'thing', and 'vehicle' with 'human'. The safety and comfort levels achieved by the Vehicle-to-Everything (V2X) technology significantly arise from its ability to facilitate smooth flow of traffic, reducing pollution, and lowering traffic accidents [13, 14]. In the short term, V2X is set to disrupt safety, efficiency and informational services. This includes development of alerts on impending collisions or dangers on the road, speed advice as well as congestion updates [15]. Furthermore, V2X enhances the driving experience by providing route guidance and automating parking. Various communications also mean that these applications in the same technology have different communication performance depending on the application.

C-V2X is a basic technology that supports road safety and helps automate driving. This technology utilizes a direct C-V2X transmission mode

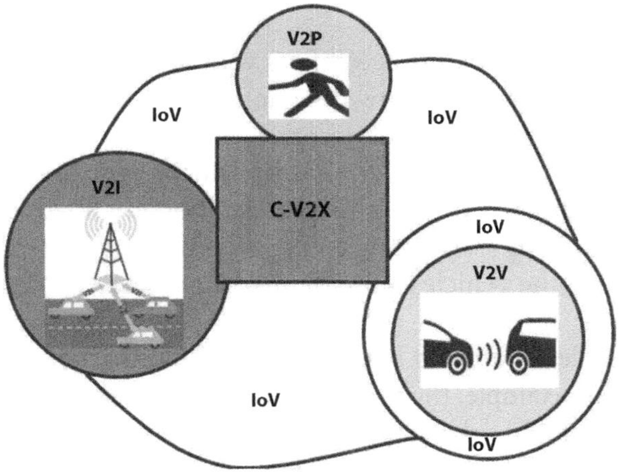

Figure 5.2 Schematic of internet of vehicles (IoV) on cellular vehicle-to-everything (C-V2X) technology.

that provides enhanced communication distance and reliability [16, 17], which supports links between "vehicles," "things," and "humans." The C-V2X chipset is designed to be integrated with 5G networks and ADAS sensors, being an integral part of the special platform for C-V2X direct communication.

This technology is intended to enable IoV connections under and without the cellular network. Figure 5.2 illustrates that it supports several different types of communications such as Vehicle-to-Infrastructure (V2I), Vehicle-to-Vehicle (V2V), and Vehicle to Pedestrian (V2P). IoV capability can be enhanced, then a more connected and efficient vehicular network will be achieved by the incorporation of C-V2X.

5.2 Historical Evolution of Vehicle Communication Technology

The development of vehicle communication technology has been a journey filled with innovations and developments over the years, which have largely contributed to its current state. At its early stages, the communication was basic in that it principally involved simple direct communicating systems, such as car radios and other vehicle signals. However these steps can be called the introductive scenario for yet more advanced means of communication. With the development of technology, the appearance of cellular technology and Internet paved the way for its introduction into vehicle communication systems during 1980s and 1990s. By integrating mobile communications and GPS technology into vehicles, a giant leap was taken that made it possible to support real-time navigational functions as well as rudimentary vehicle tracking [18, 19]. The early 2000s brought about an intensified advancement in automotive communication technology. Development of the dedicated short-range communications (DSRC) in the early 2000s was a significant milestone towards enabling cars to communicate with each other and roadside infrastructure. Such a time also saw the evolution of telematics, an interdisciplinary area that incorporates telecoms and infocomm in cars to achieve better safety systems, emergency assistance, and in-car entertainment.

With the introduction to IoT (Internet of Things) and the rapid proliferation of smartphones, a new era of connectivity dawned. Transport vehicles became much more than a mode of conveyance, they turned to be integrated devices interacting with an extended a set of devices and services. This is the time when ADAS was apparently born and it gradually shifted to semi-autonomous vehicles [20, 21]. IoV systems contain a number of networks that include Wireless Local Area Network (WLAN) used in accordance with the IEEE 802.11p standard, cellular networks (2G, 3G, LTE), and broadcasting transmission network. These standards and protocols play a major role in building the vehicle networking and communications [22]. But still, although these networks do not have perfect data processing and information exchange. 5G car networks are about to reintegrate these different networks, such that information interaction will be smooth while there will also be easy transition from communication [23].

The 5G mobile communication network is essentially a macro-layer network, comprised of a two-layer system with auxiliary layers. It has features in common with classical cellular networks such as the communication between base station and terminal devices via direct one-two-way points. In the case of IoVs, a device-to-device (D2D) communication protocol inside the 5G wireless network is especially important as is shown in Figure 5.3. The future direction of 5G car networking and its D2D technology is poised to redefine the ways in which communication architectures for IoVs take place [24]. For example, in the environment of in-car shift internet, On-Board Units (OBUs) could establish an efficient connection to the internet using 5G base stations or relays including neighboring OBU and mobile user terminals allowing a rapid exchange of information between vehicle and cloud servers. OBUs will thus be the medium through which in-car networks within the human user and vehicle interaction are improved.

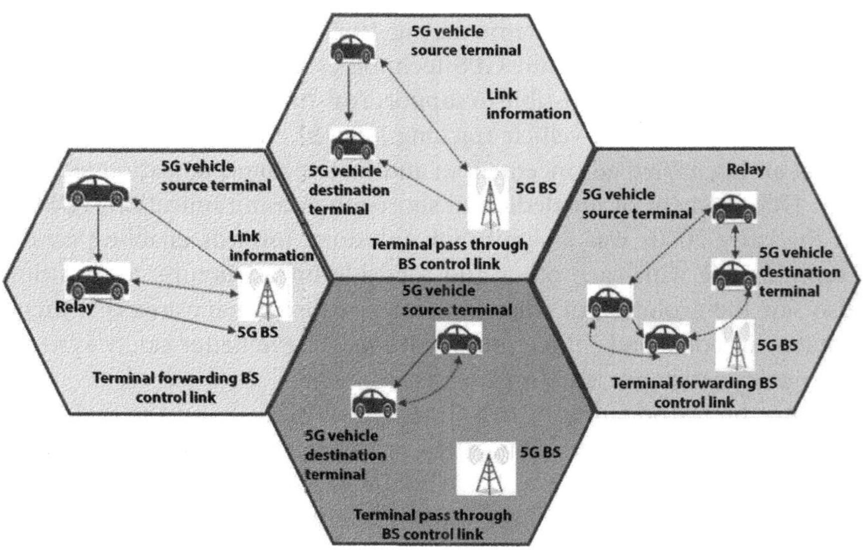

Figure 5.3 Schematic representation of device-to-device communication in 5G IoV.

Different from the configuration of traditional systems, there is no base station nor any other terminal that lies between the user and the 5G mobile terminal; short-range control addresses issues through a self-controlling link for independent vehicle data transmission [25]. As previous studies have shown, the integration of 5G technology significantly enhances the communication capabilities of IoV networks [26], leading to more efficient vehicle-to-vehicle and vehicle-to-infrastructure interactions [27]. This transformation is further supported by recent research on the evolution of network architectures, which emphasizes the scalability and low latency required for real-time communication in autonomous vehicles [28]. In 5G car units, D2Dbased communication networks can create an ad-hoc edge network or a situation where there are signal jams over the network communication. The result is through single- hop or multi-hop D2D vehicle self-organizing networks communication. As presented in Figure 5.3, this analysis of the various communication methods for 5G vehicle networking reveals that such a development will go beyond the current IEEE 802.11p standard. It will provide support for more advanced engagements and data share among many units that comprise OBUs, mobile terminals, pedestrians and the internet to attain a multiple network OBU connection.

Currently, the integration of 5G technology is in focus as it will transform the human communication system by delivering very high speed data rates, low latency and better connectivity. This integration should pave the way for developments such as V2X communication, which allows vehicles to communicate with each other and around them, setting a new milestone for autonomous driving. It does not change that vehicle communication technology is a resilient testimony of innovativeness role in the pursuit to the wiser, more secure and energy efficient transport systems.

5.3 Foundations of 5G Technology

A set of central ideas and new technologies that accompany the fifth generation of mobile networks 5G technology constitutes a revolutionary leap, which has fundamentally changed wireless communication. The issue is that the company's predecessors were modelled to respond to an explosion of data and connectivity in today's modern society, firstly Stemming from the growing Internet if things (IoT) and then increasing needs for fast internet.

Enhanced Mobile Broadband (eMBB): The bandwidth available to user is greatly increased which results in dramatic increases in achieved data rate. This is done with the help of high-tech antenna technologies such as

Massive MIMO (Multiple Input Multiple Output), which is based on large numbers of antennas at the base stations to serve multiple users simultaneously, increasing network effectiveness and capacity.

Ultra-Reliable Low Latency Communication (URLLC): What should be mentioned is that 5G reduces latency down to about one millisecond, which has been a highly desirable feature for applications requiring real-time feedback services like autonomous driving, telemedicine, and various versions of remote-controlled systems.

Massive Machine Type Communications (mMTC): It is due to this element of 5G that its functionality supports the mass implementation of IoT devices at their wider-scale deployment, allowing for connecting large numbers of sensors and devices with low power as well as bandwidth.

Architectural and Functional Aspects

Network Slicing: Network slicing is one of the most revolutionary enhancements that are brought with respect to 5G, as the operators can create a multiple sets of virtual networks within one physical network thus having various qualities of services. This adaptability allows fluidity to accommodate various needs, such as high data rates applications and low-latency operations.

Small Cells: Small cells, which are small-scale low-power base stations that further lessen the geographical boundaries of coverage area serve as a key feature of 5G networks. It is these beams that play a vital role in the provision of high-frequency millimeter-wave bandwidth which is used by 5G and which has a shorter range but higher capacity compared to what was previously employed.

Edge Computing Integration: It is the age of 5G, and its advanced networks are practically coupled with edge computing which processes information near the source rather than somewhere in a cloud-based system. The integration leads to a drastic improvement in latency, allowing faster response times for the applications associated with real-time. Spectrum Utilization: Now, 5G uses a frequency spectrum that is wider than what was used in the past and includes millimeter wave, which latently remained unused for years. This broad range of spectrum is very important for the aspect that allows achieving high data rates and capacity required by 5G.

The problem of disrupted connections is up against Vehicle-to-Vehicle (V2V) communication within Vehicular Ad-hoc Networks (VANETs), especially in traffic environments with few vehicles. This interruption affects timely communication of data. For example, it is shown in Figure 5.4, where one case stands out as the source node's output data packet sent to the destination node is blocked due to lack of intermediaries responsible for its transfer. As a result, the node at the receiving end does not get

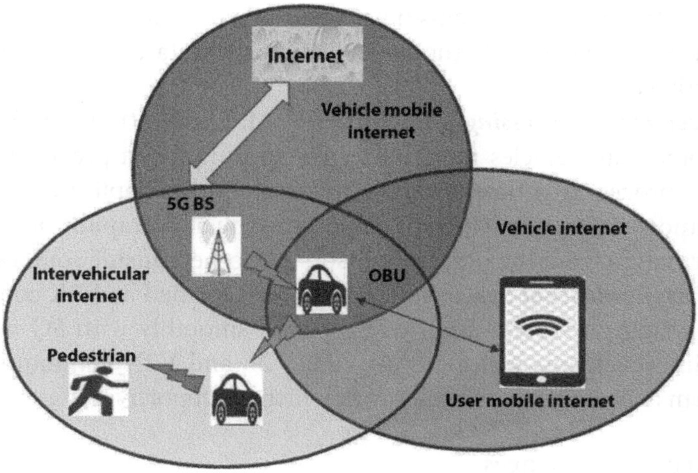

Figure 5.4 Schematic of the triple play system in 5G internet of vehicles.

the information in time. This requires boost in the speed of the pursuing car, relative to the lead vehicle, again for packet forwarding. It was already mentioned that 5G NR systems can be considered an efficient solution, providing a critical supplement to VANETs in the form of supporting communication. Apart from that, 5Th generation technology is not just expansion of 4th generation; it is full transformation of wireless network architecture to meet the growing needs of a world interconnected on every inch. Its architectural and functional innovations, therefore, are crucial in opening an ocean of new applications and services that would lead to unsurpassed interconnectedness and innovation.

5.4 Integration of 5G in Vehicular Networks

The introduction of the 5G technology into vehicular networks acts as a milestone in the development towards intelligent transportation systems. This integration will mean that vehicles will be able to communicate with each other and the transportation infrastructure in ways that could change very fundamentally. The process comprises a sequence of technical and infrastructural alterations to identify the awareness of the demands related to vehicular communication in 5G age.

Technical Changes

Upgraded Onboard Systems: It is becoming common for vehicles to incorporate high-tech communication modules that meet 5G standards. The infrastructure of these systems must ensure their capacity to transfer data at high speed and handle the larger volume of data associated with 5G connectivity.

Enhanced Data Processing Capabilities: For the realization of 5G's latency to become real, vehicles must have new and improved processing units that can process real-time analysis. This is critical to applications such as autonomous driving, in which decisions must be made rapidly on the basis of information from the different sensors and other outside sources.

V2X Communication Systems: A tension was formed as V2X communication systems are being improved to work smoothly with 5G network. These improvements will focus on V2V, V2I, and V2N communications that form a leading vehicular network which is supportive.

Infrastructural Changes

Deployment of Small Cells: 5G standards for vehicular networks, require a denser network of small cells because the range provided by shorter frequency bands is much smaller than that given by longer ones. The small cells have to be in the right location along roads, highways and all around urban areas because they ensure continuous connectivity for driving vehicles.

Upgrading Roadside Infrastructure: These elements are also being made ready to interact with 5G-compliant vehicles by other means such as the use of traffic signals, road signs and some of their other aspects on the roadside. Notably, this may involve mounting sensors and communication modules that provide instantaneous information on traffic statuses, risk areas, etc.

Network Slicing and Edge Computing: Network slicing enables the provisioning of dedicated virtual networks for different vehicular actions, making service quality and reliability. This is accompanied by edge computing, that processing data near its source thereby minimizing delay and rapid response time for critical communication necessities in vehicular network.

Backhaul Network Upgrades: For the data connectivity of more than 20 gigabits and less than one millisecond latency, it will be necessary for backhaul networks – the medium links between core network and small cell sites – to upgrade significantly. This encompasses laying fiber-optic cables or implementing improved backhaul wireless systems to meet the 5G bandwidth and speed needs.

Integration with Existing Communication Technologies: The process of transitioning to 5G entails combining it with established communication techniques, such as 4G LTE, Wi-Fi and Dedicated Short Range Communications (DSRC). This hybrid system is thus instrumental in ensuring a smooth communication and achieving the maximum coverage and reliability during the post-merger transition period.

Standardization and Regulation: It is necessary to update the standards and regulations, as policymakers routinely ensure stable and dependable 5G deployment samples for vehicular networks. This involves the hypothesis of international cooperation to establish standardized 5G protocols and spectral width for vehicular telecommunication, consistency, and safety in all areas and manufacturers.

The capabilities of processing are sure to revolutionize the 5G technology landscape, especially in multiple carrier systems such as Orthogonal Frequency Division Multiplexing (OFDM), which will bring a lot of flexibility improvement. This development can be ascribed to the fact that 5G allows a number of antennas in a single device. These antennas, namely micron and nano-sized ones, with shorter wavelengths are smaller in size enabling the formation of denser networks. This can then be achieved

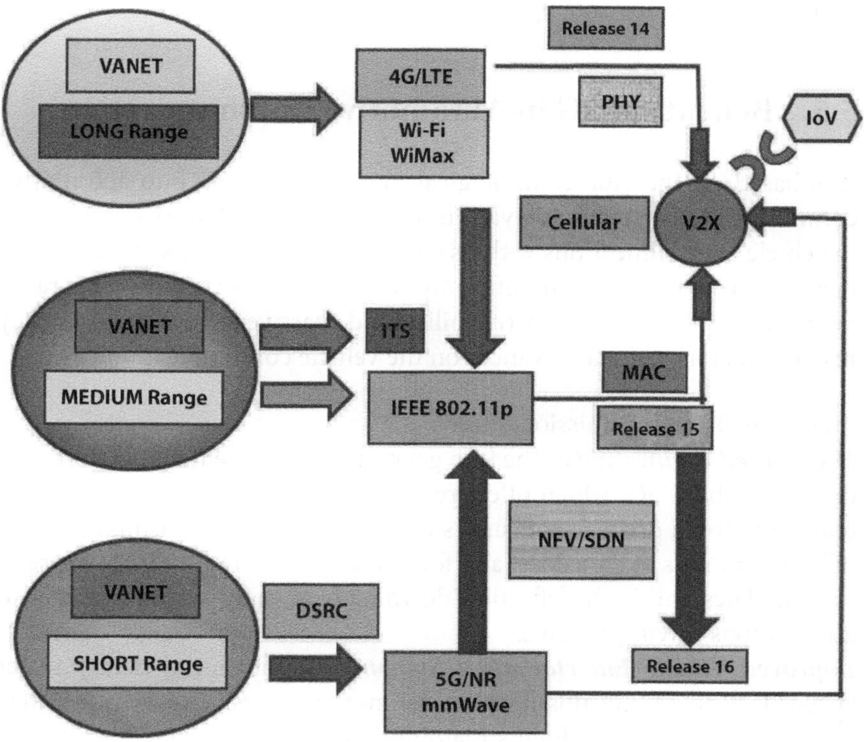

Figure 5.5 Schematic showing VANET communication ranges for C-V2X.

through a smaller cell size due to the density, resulting in an efficient use of the available spectrum.

Implementation of 5G will require the incorporating smart antennas. These antennas are crucial for two primary functions: developing radio positioning through switched beam technology and improving the capacity of wireless systems using adaptive array systems. Also, 5G software incorporates standard IP that partners other wireless networks. This integration spans a family of wireless technologies that include Wireless Access Technologies (WAT) and several others, providing service implementations, secure encryptions, and more flexibility in the systems. In the case of the IoV architecture, 5G has a crucial role to play; as V2X communications are concerned – this is especially true. Figure 5.5 is showing that not only does 5G provide a broader VANET but also makes all the integration components which allow IoV in C-V2X framework.

The introduction of 5G, the implementation and application within vehicular networks is a technical admix coupled with infrastructure knowledge to attain such efficiency. These developments are critical to making the most of 5G for vehicle communication, which will open doors to safer, more productive and intelligent transport.

5.5 Benefits of 5G in Automotive Communication

It is based on the vital technological integration of 5G into automotive communication systems, and various benefits are slated to pave a new path in vehicle communications with its own environment. The specific advantages of 5G - including significantly improved data transmission rates, appreciable improvement in reliability, and massive reduction in latency result in major practical advances on the vehicle communications front.

Increased Data Transmission Speeds

High-Speed Connectivity: The fifth generation in the cellular network revolution is about 5G, which offers remarkably higher data transfer speeds compared to its predecessors and significantly smaller transmission time of huge amounts of data. First and foremost, this is a requirement for real-time updates and high definition downloads of maps which are vital to autonomous driving systems.

Improved Vehicle Entertainment Systems: The advanced data transfer speeds lead to greater possibilities, the more immersive in-vehicle entertainment that could include streaming high definition videos and even augmented reality experiences.

Enhanced Reliability

Consistent Connection Quality: Reliable and stable connections are a matter of the greater safety aspect in automotive communication. Which is fairly provided by 5G. This reliability is crucial for preserving constant communication between cars, and the infrastructure even in high-density traffic sites or under unfavorable weather conditions.

Better Network Management: Massive Machine Type Communication technological capabilities of 5G networks allow simultaneous communications involving multiple devices which has ensured reliability of communications even in heavily crowded urban settings, this leading to an improved reliability aspect in terms of vehicular network efficiency.

Reduced Latency

Real-Time Data Processing: A great advantage of 5G is its ultra-low latency, which serves as a revolution for automotive communication. This gives virtually no delay in the transfer of messages, making it possible for real-time decisions to be made with self-driving and half autonomous vehicles.

Enhanced Safety Features: Low latency is vital for safety features such as collision avoidance systems and emergency braking, which can be just a matter of milliseconds. Instant reaction to the situation that requires quick adjustments in the traffic conditions or elimination of dangers is an amazing increase in vehicle safety.

Advanced Driver-Assistance Systems (ADAS): The performance of ADAS is also improved to some extent due to the high speed and low latency that comes with availability to 5G; thus, one can be more accurate and time sensitive in reposing road conditions thereby improving safety as well as driving efficiency.

Vehicle-to-Everything (V2X) Communication: With 5G, vehicles can more easily communicate and interact with other vehicles, people walking on the street as well as cables and sensors built into roads. This helps to ensure harmonious and well-organized traffic flow that will bring about efficient and effective road condition where congestion of the environment is mitigated while promoting safety.

Autonomous Vehicle Development: Such 5G features are more crucial for the design of self-driving cars. However, reliable and real-time communication provides the guided vehicles with the capability of processing high volumes of data produced from a variety of sensors, and able to make right decision at any given time.

Traffic Management and Environmental Benefits: Improved communication, coordination and cooperation help in effective management of traffic, thereby eliminating the problems of congestion and excessive emission.

The mobilization of effective traffic, thanks to the arrival of 5G connectivity, can make a huge difference from reducing fuel consumption and minimizing environmental impact in road transport.

All in all, the major 5G advantages for automotive communication - data speeds being much higher as well as reliability levels that are better, and latency response that is shorter - make it possible to achieve practical developmental steps gravitating towards increased safety, efficiency and user experience of contemporary transportation vehicles. These advancements are thus of key importance for the development of intelligent transport systems and the implementation of fully autonomous vehicles.

5.6 V2X Communication and 5G

V2X communication refers to a sharing of information between a vehicle and all the objects that have direct influence on it or can be affected by it.

Vehicle-to-Vehicle (V2V): The direct communication between vehicles carrying information about speed, place and direction to avoid collisions and optimal guidance of traffic flow.
Vehicle-to-Infrastructure (V2I): Vehicle communication with infrastructure components such as traffic lights, signs, and sensors to provide information on driving conditions, hazardous events in the roadways, and other related information.
Vehicle-to-Pedestrian (V2P): Vehicle pedestrian interaction comprising of smartphones or wearable devices, improving pedestrian safety through notification to drivers and by alerting them in case of an accident.
Vehicle-to-Network (V2N): Includes vehicle connection to the cellular network creating an opportunity for connecting with broader services such as traffic management systems and cloud services.

The Benefits of 5G to the Vehicle-to-X Communication Capabilities.
Increased Bandwidth and Data Transfer: The rapid V2X transmission requires large amounts of data, and 5G is capable of transmitting high-bandwidth which allows such large scale transfer. This allows the exchange and transfer of information, which is increasingly complex and can be detailed -- examples include high definition maps, sensor data from other vehicles, or infrastructure.
Ultra-Low Latency: The somewhat lessened delay in 5G is of great importance regarding V2X communication especially for processes that are part

of safety-critical applications. The quick reaction times promote real-time decision making, which means that vehicles can quickly respond to the changing situations in the road network and as a result no accidents would occur but adequate traffic flow.

Enhanced Reliability: The enhanced capabilities of 5G and heterogeneous networks ensure end-to-end integrity, enabling reliable V2X communications that are of particular importance in high density traffic areas or under challenging environments.

Support for a Large Number of Devices: In dense urban spaces, with high-speed railway networks, where large numbers of vehicles interact simultaneously with infrastructure elements and pedestrians require connectivity to amenities in the surrounding area, such as Energy suppliers or information services center; transportability is essential; 5G can support all this.

Facilitating Advanced Applications: 5G Rich capabilities enhance one of the V2X element i. e more advanced applications. For instance, in the case of autonomous vehicles live intercommunication of those is possible and complex maneuvers like passing intersection or merging to freeways by a heavy load can be easily done.

Improved Traffic Management and Environmental Impact: Through improving V2X communication, 5G may improve traffic management equitably as wells reduce congestion and greenhouse gas emission. This also includes working on improving traffic flow, reducing some of the time idles spent in the traffic lights and making better routing possible.

Enhanced Safety and Situational Awareness: As 5G-equipped V2X leads to prompt reaction from vehicles is the reason for better overall road safety and situational awareness, due to earlier detection of hazards that human drivers or other technologies can't afford. In conclusion, 5G technology integration significantly strengthens the status of V2X communication due to its provision of high speed, capacity, and reliability in line with the vastly changing environment for vehicular networks. This improvement is very important for the development of safety, efficiency, and application capabilities in intelligent transportation systems.

5.7 Case Studies

Case Study 1: This is in addition to the fact that Autonomous Vehicle Testing has been a gateway done in a smart city.

Scenario: A city seeks a partnership with technology company for test driving vans which are driven by autonomous vehicles entangled in 5G

communication circuits. The proposed project involves 5 G- based vehicles with onboard equipped devices to communicate between each other, the infrastructure and a centralized traffic management system.
Successes: 5G with its high bandwidth and low latency provides real time data sharing features which allow autonomous vehicles to take immediate decisions based on surrounding traffic, pedestrian movements etc. This reduces the danger of very much traffic congestion and accidents.
Challenges: However, a significant hurdle can be seen as the desperate need for massive infrastructure improvement, with 5G small cells built all around town. Lessons Learned: Firstly, the project shows that a reliable 5G network and an expansion of these networks across cities are crucial for proper traffic management.

Case Study 2: illustrates how with 5G technologies cities will be able to increase safety on roads.
Scenario: A five-generation (5G) emergency medical service (EMS) uses the connected ambulances transmitting signals to hospital systems and traffic control mechanisms of road lanes during transportation. This integration enables the dissemination of patient information in real-time, towards a hospital system and an adjustment of traffic signaling to minimize travel time.
Successes: The adoption of 5G greatly reduces the response times which are meant for emergency services and enhances patient results that follow with prompt medical intervention.
Challenges: Key challenges associated with this include the need to know that users will have unrestricted network access and also preserve data privacy.
Lessons Learned: This case highlights the necessity of sustainable and persistent 5G connection in lifesaving cases along with sufficient safety regulations for data protection.

Case Study 3: Enhanced Fleet Management for Logistics.
Scenario: An 5G technology-equipped logistics enterprise incorporates a fleet management platform. It provides just-in time monitoring, proactive resource management and responsive navigation based on traffic conditions.
Successes: The company's fleet operations become more efficient, fuel consumption is reduced, and there is a significant decrease in vehicle downtime due to autonomous resources guided by predictive maintenance features.

Challenges: The initial capital turnover for updating the fleet and training of personnel on a new system is enormous.
Lessons Learned: The case study highlights high long-term savings and operational efficiencies of incorporating the 5G in fleet managements despite draining upfront investment and training.

Case Study 4: Smart Traffic Management System.
Scenario: To reduce congestion. A city employs 5G-based smart traffic management which utilizes the technology that connects various elements such as computer vision, sensors to govern traffic volumes and improve flow.
Successes: This system is instrumental in reducing traffic congestion, decreasing current emission levels, and overall optimizing as a whole.
Challenges: Such issues are to which of the problems communication between different types of devices and systems and handling a huge amount of information generated can be number.
Lessons Learned: The Project demonstrates the possible scope of 5G in monitoring and decreasing city traffic congestion, as well as the requirement of standardization and solid data management strategies.

These case studies illustrate the revolutionary ways in which 5G technology influences communication about vehicles, as well as vehicle transportation management. They focus on the achievements in improvement of efficiency, safety, and times by referring to difficulties regarding infrastructure, investments, or data management. From each case, glean valuable lessons on the practical deployment of 5G in the field that should be instructive for upcoming implementations.

5.8 Challenges and Future Directions

Infrastructure Requirements: As one of the major obstacles to be addressed in implementing 5G networks on cars, significant growth and investments have to be made to ensure that the necessary infrastructure is developed. This applies to the use of small cell antennas, fiber-optic cables, as well as edge computing sites and other infrastructure. Infrastructure density required, especially in urban areas, leads to both logistical challenges and expenditure.
Standardization and Interoperability: The universal setting of standards for 5G implementation in vehicular communication is essential to enable conformity across the varying ensurging sectors through its heterogeneous

manufacturers and regions. With particular to devices, vehicles and infrastructure interoperability still requires an idea of one solution.

Security and Privacy Concerns: To address such concerns, researchers have developed new techniques to secure the 5G systems. Needless to say, cyber-attack and data breach prevention is best secured by applying solid cybersecurity measures as well as data privacy protocols.

Spectrum Management: It is a difficult job to effectively manage spectrum and prevent interference particularly in the higher band of frequencies, which will be utilized by 5G. They should therefore be approached carefully through regulations.

Cost Implications: The price of the 5G infrastructure development, both for providers and car builder, is staggering. These include purchase price of new hardware, software and ongoing maintenance.

Technological Integration: The technical challenges involved in the integration of 5G with technologies that are already preexisting, such as the 4GLT& e and WiLife, and in switching from these technologies offer a series of unique technological difficulties. Thus adjustments have to be done on this to ensure that there is smooth service provision during the transitional phase.

Future Directions and Developments

Advancements in Autonomous Vehicles: 5G will reach its gold standard with the amplification of the technology and thus, autonomous driving can attract its full capabilities. Further evolutions could entail more advanced and widespread autonomous vehicles, which operating with 5G would enable increasingly intricate decision-making and vehicle operation.

Smart City Integration: The fifth-generation cellular network is here to stay and will perform a critical task in the establishment of intelligent cities that work with IoT devices and sensors to facilitate management, alleviate congestion, improve community safety. In 2035, smart city of the future might be equipped sophisticated autonomous traffic management systems which are driven by bundled AI techniques riding upon the wave of 5G capabilities.

Vehicle-to-Grid (V2G) Systems: In the future, possible progress is in V2G systems where connected vehicles interact directly with the electricity grid and regulate demand/supply by making motion electric resources.

Enhanced Road Safety Features: Further safety innovations in vehicles may be implemented as future 5G develops to include real-time hazard detection and avoidance preemptive systems, and that better stabilize pedestrian safety conditions.

Expanded V2X Communication: Progress in V2X communication will make it possible to have vehicles interacting much better with everything in their surrounding and create a more integrated, coordinated transportation system.

AI and Machine Learning Integration: The integration of AI and machine learning with 5G could result to much smarter, smart networks for vehicular communication. At the onset, AI technology would be used in analyzing vehicle and infrastructure data which might lead to improved traffic flow, detection of maintenance requirement as well improvement while transportation efficiency.

Finally, despite the several issues that are associated with 5G implementation in vehicular networks, the opportunities and changes that can be realized through this challenge is endless. While this technology is still evolving, that being said it raised major changes in vehicular communication but also the wider field of urban transport and smart city structures.

5.9 Conclusion

To summarize, this chapter presents a complete overview of 5G persuasive power and development consequences in terms of vehicle connectivity systems. An evolution from its humble beginning to the present state of motor pile communication, the latter that has been established solid ground for implementation 5G. Unlike previous generations, the fifth generation of this particular technology is notable for its improved mobile broadband that is broader and faster, ultra-reliable low latency, and massive machine-type communication. The integration of 5G into the vehicles networks requires great technological and infrastructural changes, allowing for an array of opportunities that include high data transmission rates; improved feature protection, fastness diminished. To make these achievements noteworthy, advancements play a significant role in improving ADAS, turbo monitoring of traffic flow as well as enabling the coming era of autonomous cars.

The improvement of V2X communication by means of a 5G technology has become one development direction, allowing safer and more efficient intersections between vehicles, infrastructure, and pedestrians. Based on case studies drawn from real-world scenarios, the successes and challenges of 5G implementation have been demonstrated in practice, thus providing a rich source of information regarding its practical uses. But the road towards total embeddedness of 5G in vehicular networks is not without its challenges such as infrastructure development and implementation, standardization, security issues, as well as cost considerations. Although this presents significant challenges, the areas for future directions and possible developments in 5G vehicle communication are then promising to transform transportation networks.

The case with 5G does not end up being all about faster and more efficient communication; rather, it implies that we are in a process of transition to smart connected mobility systems. However, as this technology advances and grows up, it will open marvelous new capabilities in autonomous driving, smart temporary intake structure, and vehicular safety that establish automotive technologists. 5G integration into vehicular networks is not only a technological achievement but a means and an indicator of the state of affairs on the road towards realizing this smarter, safer, and better future in transportation envisioned by 5G.

References

1. Zhu, X., Yuan, S., Zhao, P., Research and Application on Key Technologies of 5G and C-V2X Intelligent Converged Network Based on MEC. *2021 IEEE International Conference on Power Electronics, Computer Applications (ICPECA)*, Shenyang, China, pp. 175–179, 2021, doi: 10.1109/ICPECA51329.2021.9362552.
2. Liu, J., *et al.*, Investigation of 5G and 4G V2V Communication Channel Performance Under Severe Weather. *2022 IEEE International Conference on Wireless for Space and Extreme Environments (WiSEE)*, Winnipeg, MB, Canada, pp. 12–17, 2022, doi: 10.1109/WiSEE49342.2022.9926867.
3. Garg, S., Guizani, M., Liang, Y.-C., Granelli, F., Prasad, N., Prasad, R.R.V., Guest Editorial Special Issue on Intent-Based Networking for 5G-Envisioned Internet of Connected Vehicles. *IEEE Trans. Intell. Transp. Syst.*, 22, 8, 5009–5017, Aug. 2021, doi: 10.1109/TITS.2021.3101259.
4. Hao, M., Ye, D., Wang, S., Tan, B., Yu, R., URLLC Resource Slicing and Scheduling in 5G Vehicular Edge Computing. *2021 IEEE 93rd Vehicular Technology Conference (VTC2021-Spring)*, Helsinki, Finland, pp. 1–5, 2021, doi: 10.1109/VTC2021-Spring51267.2021.9448805.
5. Kumar, Kalpana, V., Hariram, V., Artificial Intelligence based Health Monitoring System on IoTH platform. *2023 Second International Conference on Augmented Intelligence and Sustainable Systems (ICAISS)*, Trichy, India, pp. 1458–1463, 2023, doi: 10.1109/ICAISS58487.2023.10250460.
6. Pandya, P.M. and Gupta, A.K., Development of object identification model with deep reinforcement learning algorithm. *J. Inf. Optim. Sci.*, 44, 3, 355–367, 2023, DOI: 10.47974/JIOS-1346.

7. Kranthi, M. and Tanguturi, R.C., Design of Intelligent Medical Integrity Authentication and Secure Information for Public Cloud in Hospital Administration. *2023 2nd International Conference on Edge Computing and Applications (ICECAA)*, Namakkal, India, pp. 256–261, 2023, doi: 10.1109/ICECAA58104.2023.10212391.
8. Ranjan, A., Hegge, K.K., Agrawal, R., Wireless and Solar-Powered Multipurpose Robot for Industrial Automation: A Sustainable Solution. *2023 8th International Conference on Communication and Electronics Systems (ICCES)*, Coimbatore, India, pp. 146–151, 2023, doi: 10.1109/ICCES57224.2023.10192614.
9. Sarma, P., Hussain, N., Dixit, S.K., Gupta, A.K., A novel approach of unsupervised feature selection using iterative shrinking and expansion algorithm. *J. Interdiscip. Math.*, 26, 3, 519–530, 2023, DOI: 10.47974/JIM-1678.
10. Suryawanshi, V.A. and Chaturvedi, A., Novel Predictive Control and Monitoring System based on IoT for Evaluating Industrial Safety Measures. *IJEER*, 10, 4, 1050–1057, 2022, DOI: 10.37391/IJEER.100448.
11. Premkumar, S., Hussain, N., Chinamuttevi, V.S., A novel RF-SMOTE model to enhance the definite apprehensions for IoT security attacks. *J. Discrete Math. Sci. Cryptogr.*, 26, 3, 861–873, 2023, DOI: 10.47974/JDMSC-1766.
12. Singla, A. and Sharma, N., IoT Group Key Management using Incremental Gaussian Mixture Model. *2022 3rd International Conference on Electronics and Sustainable Communication Systems (ICESC)*, pp. 469–474, 2022, doi: 10.1109/ICESC54411.2022.9885644.
13. Latha, J., Selvakumar, C., Shekhar, R., Chaturvedi, A., Securing networked image transmission using public-key cryptography and identity authentication. *J. Discrete Math. Sci. Cryptogr.*, 26, 3, 779–791, 2023, DOI: 10.47974/JDMSC-1754.
14. Sharma, A., S, K., Arun, M.R., Priority Queueing Model-Based IoT Middleware for Load Balancing. *2022 6th International Conference on Intelligent Computing and Control Systems (ICICCS)*, pp. 425–430, 2022, doi: 10.1109/ICICCS53718.2022.9788218.
15. De, T., Tanguturi, R.C., Ashreetha, B., A Novel method of Improving Spectrum sensing Management system for CR-IoT Networks. *2023 4th International Conference for Emerging Technology (INCET)*, Belgaum, India, pp. 1–6, 2023, doi: 10.1109/INCET57972.2023.10170314.
16. Prasad, K.D.V., Kumar, P.S.V.V.S.R., R, S., Ashreetha, B., Performance Analysis of Energy Efficiency and Security Solutions of Internet of Things Protocols. *IJEER*, 11, 2, 442–450, 2023, DOI: 10.37391/IJEER.110226.
17. Mary, P.A. and Begum, A.Y., A Novel IoT Framework and Device Architecture for Efficient Smart city Implementation. *2023 7th International Conference on Trends in Electronics and Informatics (ICOEI)*, Tirunelveli, India, pp. 420–426, 2023, doi: 10.1109/ICOEI56765.2023.10125677.

18. M, S.P., Reddy, A.M., Tanguturi, R., Improved Secure Communication Mechanism for IoT Platform Devices. *2022 International Conference on Smart Generation Computing, Communication and Networking (SMART GENCON)*, Bangalore, India, pp. 1–6, 2022, doi: 10.1109/SMARTGENCON56628.2022.10083714.
19. Kumar, P. and Singh, P., IoT Enabled Smart Lighting System for Smart Cities. *J. Phys. Conf. Ser.*, 2089, 1, 012037, 2021, https://doi.org/10.1088/1742-6596/2089/1/012037.
20. He, R., Bai, F., Mao, G., Härri, J., Kyösti, P., Guest Editorial 5G Wireless Communications With High Mobility. *IEEE J. Sel. Areas Commun.*, 38, 12, 2717–2722, Dec. 2020, doi: 10.1109/JSAC.2020.3005498.
21. Boualouache, A. and Engel, T., A Survey on Machine Learning-Based Misbehavior Detection Systems for 5G and Beyond Vehicular Networks. *IEEE Commun. Surv. Tutor.*, 25, 2, 1128–1172, Secondquarter 2023, doi: 10.1109/COMST.2023.3236448.
22. Ullah, H., Gopalakrishnan Nair, N., Moore, A., Nugent, C., Muschamp, P., Cuevas, M., 5G Communication: An Overview of Vehicle-to-Everything, Drones, and Healthcare Use-Cases. *IEEE Access*, 7, 37251–37268, 2019, doi: 10.1109/ACCESS.2019.2905347.
23. Cheng, X., Zhang, R., Chen, S., Li, J., Yang, L., Zhang, H., 5G enabled vehicular communications and networking. *China Commun.*, 15, 7, iii–vi, July 2018, doi: 10.1109/CC.2018.8424577.
24. Kombate, D. and Wanglina, The Internet of Vehicles Based on 5G Communications. *2016 IEEE International Conference on Internet of Things (iThings) and IEEE Green Computing and Communications (GreenCom) and IEEE Cyber, Physical and Social Computing (CPSCom) and IEEE Smart Data (SmartData)*, Chengdu, China, pp. 445–448, 2016, doi: 10.1109/iThings-GreenCom-CPSCom-SmartData.2016.105.
25. Haryo Putri, K.S. and Kurniawan Usman, U., Analysis of Vehicle to Vehicle Communication Parameter on 5G Network. *2019 Symposium on Future Telecommunication Technologies (SOFTT)*, Kuala Lumpur, Malaysia, pp. 1–6, 2019, doi: 10.1109/SOFTT48120.2019.9068620.
26. Singh, C. and Gatti, R., *Drone applications for industry 5.0*, IGI Global, New York, USA, 2024.
27. Gatti, R. and Singh, C., *Shaping the Future of Automation With Cloud-Enhanced Robotics*, IGI Global, New York, USA, 2024.
28. Singh, C., Gatti, R.R., Sairam, K., Singh, A., *Modeling and Optimization of Optical Communication Networks*, John Wiley & Sons, Hoboken, New Jersey, U.S., 2023.

6

Predicting the Flow with Machine Learning Algorithms for Advanced Traffic Management

Dankan Gowda V.[1*], Rupali Suraskar[2], Ridhi Rani[3], K.D.V. Prasad[3] and Ved Srinivas[4]

[1]Department of Electronics and Communication Engineering, BMS Institute of Technology and Management, Bangalore, Karnataka, India
[2]Department of Electronic, Larsen and Toubro Edutech, Nagpur, Maharashtra, India
[3]Symbiosis Institute of Business Management, Hyderabad and Symbiosis International (Deemed University), Pune, India
[4]Department of Human Resources, Thiagarajar School of Management, Madurai, Tamil Nadu, India

Abstract

This chapter focuses on the transforming effect of machine learning (ML) algorithms in traffic control systems through the use of advanced technologies. Given the worsening situation in large-sized towns and cities where there is traffic congestion, rates of accidents are doing rise and crises for environment increase, new approach is very necessary. Machine learning provide possible solutions that can deal with this problem through provide more accurate traffic flow predictions, handle real-time incident management as well as implement dynamic route optimizations. This chapter delves in the structural analysis of different machine learning algorithms specifically intended for traffic data analysis, goes further to practically apply the algorithms he discusses different case studies drawn from cities that were able to integrate these technologies and fully use them. Information disclosure impends the full potential of ML in traffic management and gives rise to data quality, privacy, and real-time processing challenges. The next generation of the traffic systems, mobility aided by cutting-edge ML and, a home to new technologies like

**Corresponding author*: dankan.v@bmsit.in

Rathishchandra R. Gatti and Chandra Singh (eds.) Digital Convergence in Intelligent Mobility Systems, (101–124) © 2025 Scrivener Publishing LLC

the IoT and the autonomous vehicles, is presented to provide a holistic view of how an intelligent transportation system can be improvised for the future.

***Keywords*:** Machine learning, traffic management, traffic flow prediction, real-time incident detection, dynamic routing, urban mobility, traffic data analysis, smart transportation systems

6.1 Introduction

Efficient traffic management is a constituting element of city planning and mobility which are inextricably linked with the urban life quality and prosperity of an urban community. Comprehensive traffic management systems not only conserve petrol in vehicles and promote the safety of pedestrians and vehicles on the roads which altogether have an immense impact on the economic and social intermeshed structure of cities [1]. The rise of urbanization has made imperative the management of all the vehicular traffic in the urban areas, the link of vehicle ownership with the prevalent urbanization, and the tightness of the urban dwellings [2]. Traffic management is a crucial tool to shorten traveling time, to lower the high accident rate and to mitigate carbon emissions, thus to contribute to cleaner and greener environment and availability of jobs [3].

On the one hand, it is a high grown area for traffic management but as on the other hand encompasses manifold obstacles. One of the serious problems is traffic jams, they are happening due to more demand on the use of roads than they have available to handle the traffic. Congestion slows down the flow of traffic [4], more petrol is burned, and air quality deprives. In addition, this method used by many public transit operators has an undesirable psychological effect on its riders by increasing their tension or making their life lower in quality [5]. Besides that, congestion might lead to the severe economic consequence by raising transport costs and reducing the economic activities' efficiency [6].

Accidents and the number of them are one of the most significant items in the construction of urban transport. All over the world, many people are killed in traffic accidents on an annual basis [7]. This, in addition to the loss of revenue due to medical costs, workers' compensation, and damaged property results in global economic loss. This number of car accidents can be caused by roadway factors such as deuteriation, outdated traffic lights and inexistent traffic law enforcement [8]. Moreover, the multiple of different vehicle types inclining from vehicles to walking and biking in dense urban spaces causes collisions to a level that such an accident becomes unavoidable [9].

Significant environmental challenge needs to be addressed as well. In the world, the road transport is the leading sector in releasing the harmful greenhouse gas emissions with the bulk share coming from traffic [10]. Aside from fuelling climate change, vehicle pollution is damaging to land air quality and health, so it is causing the spread of chronic respiratory illness in cities [11]. The case of the traffic noise adding to the noise pollution in the cities is further sapping the quality of the urban community's living conditions.

The ML driven technologies incorporated into the traffic management systems may be an effective answer to the current challenges captured by this sentence [12]. With deep learning process, ML can tackle a huge amount of data coming from many sources, including traffic cameras, sensors, and GPS systems of the cars to develop more reliable patterns than traditional methods [13]. By working with historical and current data the ML algorithms can predict traffic situations, detect the places where the peak of congestion can occur and suggest traffic distribution that would work better.

Along with, thanks to Machine Learning, the platform may take an important part in the incident detection and response. Using ML algorithms to continuously analyze traffic data quickly gives an account on unusual patterns that may point at accidents or traffic jams [14]. These patterns can trigger alerts that reach emergency authorities and road users and therefore reduce the time of response and increase the effectiveness of the emergency services [15]. Another of the main benefits of ML industry algorithm optimization of a signal traffic in real time, a process that takes into account the traffic conditions to reduce waiting times and also unnecessary stops that cause congestions and higher amounts of fuel consumption.

ML-based traffic management also provides an instrument for environmental protection by regularly informing vehicles about the time ahead, which leads to less traffic jams, so less idle times and, as a result, lesser emissions [16]. The real time route planning capabilities promoted by cutting edge ML technologies can steer the vehicles through lesser crowded roads, thus balancing the whole network of traffic loads and resulting in a disrupted traffic which in turn contributes to decreased air pollution and energy use [17].

To sum up, the increase in the size of big towns and cities the traffic coordination challenges are becoming more complicated. Machine

Learning opens the doors of great-promise field that is the improvement of the efficiency and sustainability of traffic management systems [18]. Cities have the opportunity to adopt the latest ML algorithms to revolutionize their traffic management system, which aims at integrating peoples' needs with the city requirements [19]. By adopting such an approach, the safety concerns, environmental mutual degradation and the overall urban livelihood will be improved. In this chapter, we are going to discuss these aspects at length, creating awareness on how an ML system can be applied for smooth operation of a traffic management system [20].

Figure 6.1 illustrates the betterments in moving the traffic and the gridlock reduction respectively, in the graph before and after the implementing the machine learning technologies. The application uses bars and annual and seasonal anomalies shown as peaks and troughs to illustrate the improvements in average traffic speeds and decrease in congestion levels [21], providing stakeholders with the ultimate before-and-after comparison that clearly demonstrates the efficacy of ML in the optimization of traffic flows and the mitigation of bottlenecks.

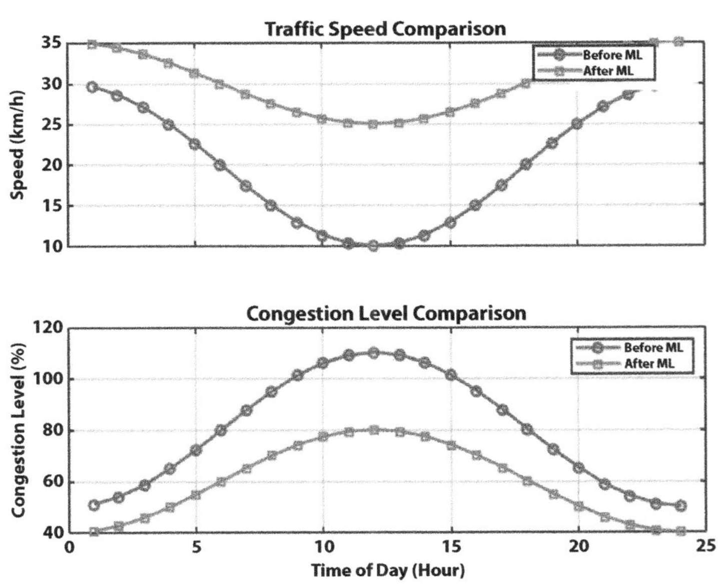

Figure 6.1 Comparative traffic speed and congestion levels graph.

6.2 Fundamentals of Machine Learning in Traffic Management

Machine learning (ML) is an important innovation in computational technology because it takes away the burdens of explicit programming, presenting learning, and developing merely from some simple experience. In the dynamics of traffic control [22], ML is functioning with the aim of dealing with complex data and then giving solutions or decisions based on the given data needed for reinforcement of traffic flow and security.

ML goes beyond generalization into several types; supervised and unsupervised learning forms the basics of it, with regard to traffic management. In the supervised training, the algorithm is being already taught on a dataset consisting of labeled data, which means that each training sample is with that output label as well [23]. In this method, traffic management tasks like traffic flow prediction containing input data as historical traffic data are extensively used. Unsupervised learning is totally different from supervised learning approach that involves data without any label attached [24]. This category of approach is applied for the detection of underlying regularities or hidden sides in the traffic data, such as finding the regions, where almost similar traffic patterns are present, and this effect can be observed without prior knowledge of the outcomes.

The more efficient traffic management through ML is data-driven, the higher the probability of the availability and quality of this data are. Several types of data are integral to traffic management systems:

Traffic Cameras: The sensors offer a live video, which can be transformed to the vehicles' number and type, congestion at set intersections, and traffic density [25].

Sensors: Four cases can be mentioned: 1) these are placed on roads or within vehicles and 2) there they monitor data like average speeds, vehicular counts, and weather conditions [26]. Traffic scenarios data help implementing up-to-date traffic control and insights for future traffic adaptation.

GPS Data from Vehicles: Nowadays, one can see the date on both the speed and position of a car, which are provided by the GPS in newer cars. In addition, this information aggregated can paint a picture of traffic conditions throughout various locations [27].

Social Media and Mobile Apps: The growing trend is to use data riding on social media platforms and traffic apps to identify information and reports of traffic jams and incidents. As such, they become a valuable latter layer on which to create a richer data framework.

When it comes to ML algorithms in traffic prediction and management [28], several are prominently used: When it comes to ML algorithms in traffic prediction and management, several are prominently used:

Regression Analysis: For this this simulated event is done predicting flows of traffic and travel times [29]. Linear regression can approximate a continuous variable value input by given time of vehicle registration.

Decision Trees: The models create a set of specific rules and thresholds for certain instances like traffic lights changing or traffic alerts being issued which are based on their input features such as streets' overcrowding and weather conditions.

Neural Networks: And as to deep learning models which are capable to process large sets of data and complex patterns [30], they are just instruments for predicting the situation on the roads and recognizing incidents. Peculiar network is a part of a dynamic traffic lights control systems and predictive traffic models of real time control.

Clustering: Clustering algorithms, such as K-means and DBSCAN, are used on a regular basis to classify similar traffic patterns and hotspots of accidents as distinct zones of the city to which traffic management measures can be channeled.

This is the way how traffic management systems shift from a reactive to a proactive way of making decisions, as they adjust to the existing situation of the moment and use forecasting, making future predictions based on current trends [31]. This is a 2 way traffic not only making the traffic flow efficient but also boosts safety by stopping mishaps such as traffic jams and accidents that may happen in future. As well it could be said that the melding of ML with traffic management is a continually developing project of improvement. Continuous learning is included as a function of the algorithm, so as new data comes up and the environment becomes challenging, due to changing in traffic, the algorithms improves their prediction over time thus leading to better environment [32]. The trait of the historical and real-time data added to the development of its optimization strategy which in turn provides a platform for continuous change in traffic management. Figure 6.2 analyzes thousands of data points collected from sensors and cameras by using the graphical illustrations like the scatter plots and histograms to fit and classify various traffic parameters across the study areas, like vehicle speeds, volumes, etc. [33]. The example tells you that machine learning algorithms deal with distributions and predictions considering traffic flows, which arises intelligent traffic systems theory concerns.

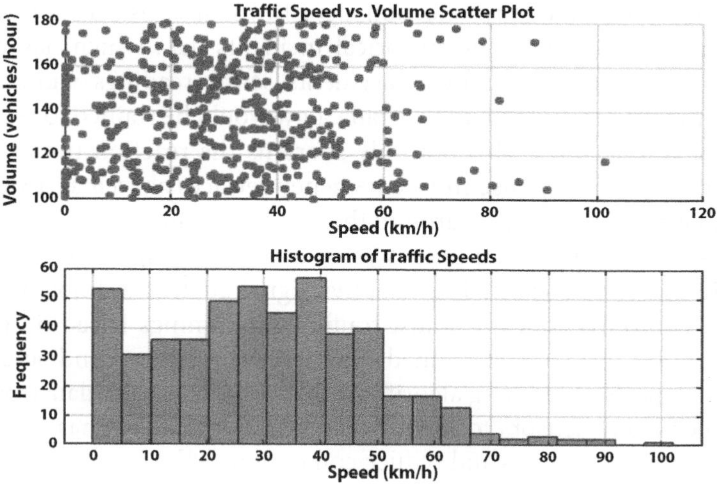

Figure 6.2 Distribution of traffic parameters: scatter plots and histograms.

6.3 Applications of ML in Traffic Prediction and Management

Machine Learning (ML) has revolutionized traffic prediction and management with exceptional technologies and breakthroughs that lead to higher responsiveness, better safety, and improving efficiency. One of the major usages of ML in this sector is predicting traffic flow. By means of sensors, cameras and historical traffic information, the ML models can be trained to predict the traffic volume and patterns [34]. Technologies like time series forecasting, neural networks or support vector machines are employed in the analysis of traffic data which has been collected in the past to find trends and patterns which ultimately help to make forecasts of traffic conditions in the future. Such models can grasp seasonal variations, daily deviations as well as the influence of special occasions, which enables the traffic management systems to anticipate eventual fluctuations in traffic volume and adjust their strategies [35]. Therefore, this function is developed to prevent congestion and achieve the better traffic flow of the city.

In addition to detection and management of the incidents, machine learning has also one of the main roles. Using recurrent traffic data analysis, a data-driven algorithm can find out any abnormal activities which may happen to be accident or exceptionally heavy traffic flows. An alarm is raised and the system informs the heads of traffic and drivers nearby that the anomaly has been detected and the response time is quicker [36].

ML models with anomaly detection algorithms and classification systems that have been exposing to historical incidents data which has various types of media such as pictures of accidents, sensor readings of unexpected stops or rapid deceleration in the traffic flow would be trained to recognize signs of conflict [37]. This not only shortens the reaction time but also ensure a quicker response from emergency services as well as a very efficient management of traffic around the incident scene.

Reason adjusting signal time is yet another very important area where the ML algorithms excel. This adaptive signal control technology makes use of ML to dynamically adjust traffic lights timings based on current traffic rather than predetermined time intervals. The second solution is using the machine learning algorithms that will analyze the data from traffic cameras and sensors to identify the best traffic light phase. That will help improve wait times and reduce congestion [38]. This adaptive nature results in responsive traffic lights that react directly to specific traffic demands, and more stopping times are not needed and indeed, the general traffic flow increases. Moreover, ML can be used to manage traffic lights for coordination of the signals at many intersections in order to create green waves that will allow traffic to flow uninterrupted over several intersections and thus significantly reduce total time of travel as well as lower emissions from vehicles.

ML enabled smart routing brings traffic management to an improved level of effectiveness by changing routes recommendations for drivers based on real-time traffic conditions, roads under reconstruction and accidents. These ML combined predictive analytics and real-time data can generate routes that are the most efficient for the drivers through alternative roads so as to avoid traffic jams or accident scenes. Learning algorithms, such as reinforcement learning, used for on-time route updates, periodically learn from the traffic conditions, as a way to optimize the route selection based on the traffic conditions. Also, it provides a shorter route and aids in the distribution of traffic in the town's roads efficiently. With intelligent routing apps coming as part of car GPS navigators and mobile applications, now routine commuters as well as professional drivers find that they are important add-ons to their daily lives, making their routes better and more predictable.

Employing ML in such an application illustrates large scale advantages of the advanced analytics and data processing in the real time which result in right traffic management. The implantation of these technologies can have a huge impact on the efficiency of transport systems, whereas environmental impact of road traffic, and life conditions of the society will be improved. The following chapter introduces you to using ML in a traffic management application with clear examples of how it helps to improve the current traffic management as well as opens new opportunities for innovations and improvement in urban transport.

In Figure 6.3, the plot will be a time-series graph showing the actual traffic volumes against that forecasted by the machine learning models for

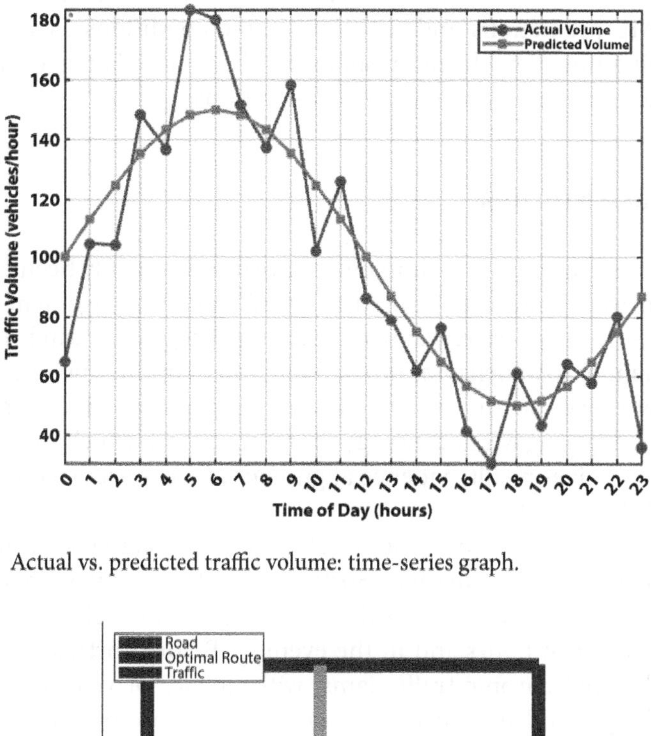

Figure 6.3 Actual vs. predicted traffic volume: time-series graph.

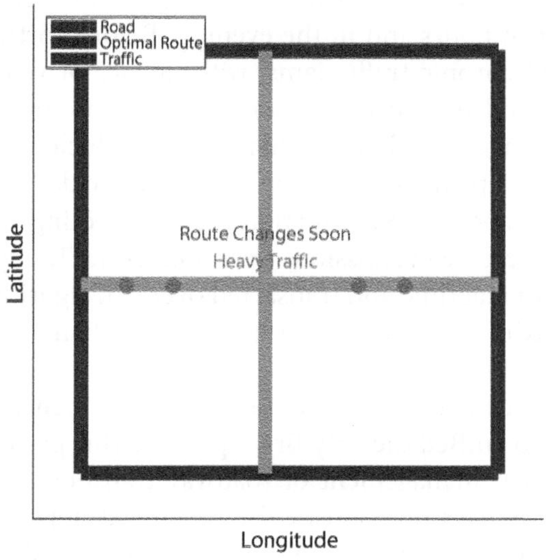

Figure 6.4 Dynamic routing interactive map.

24 hours' period. The comparison from the chart of ML predictions versus actual data shows the accuracy and precision of ML prediction of traffic, which is significant part of traffic management because it is a proactive element.

In Figure 6.4, the interactive map that demonstrates the possibility of route choice and brings real-world examples of ML implementation in traffic management. The map shows how traffic routes are adjusted in real-time by ML predictions and real-time traffic conditions as well, hence, emphasizing how flexible and responsible the system is regarding reduction of travel time and prevention of congestions.

6.4 Case Studies

Machines Learning (ML) technologies have omnipresently been embraced by several world cities, to boost the cities' traffic management systems. These real-life instances reveal what amazing changes ML can bring to the management of road behavior flows, reduction of traffic, and overall better security of every road in the city. This part examines various case studies illustrating applying ML technology in traffic control, which thus-comparative analysis gives result evidence alignment of what occurred before and after the ML integration.

There is Pittsburgh, Ohio whose traffic control system has been adapted in a way that it has a system called Sortras with adaptive rules. This machine learning- inspired system makes the traffic signals through the day to flow better during rush hours and in the evening. Before Sortras deployment, Pittsburgh faced chronic traffic jams, with queues of vehicles becoming growing longer and free-speed flows more and more frequent, thus also bringing about longer travel times and increased vehicle emissions. Sortras system was after implementing by the city and it yielded huge decrease in travel times with about 25%, reduction in vehicle idling with about 40%, and eventually decrease in emissions were noticeable. The system uses traffic data getting in real time and transacted over ML algorithms, thus making clear the way machine learning is applied in urban automated control systems.

The last instance is the Hangzhou city, China which worked with the Alibaba Group to emBed the City Brain project. This project employs ML for the touchdown management of roadway transport as well as public transportation vehicles. Previously, the intelligent application of ML in Hangzhou has been identified as a main reason for making the city one of the most congested cities in the country, resulting in the traffic jams that significantly affect the transport, the economy and the environmental conditions of the city. Smart City Brain system deploys data analytics and ML-tuning to work on adaptive traffic light signal timing and separate buses from other vehicles. After implementation, it was later observed that there is 15% improvement in speed and more precisely designed routes regarding public transportation, which undoubtedly leads to a better commute experiences and less traffic related pollution.

The Republic of Singapore is another significant study of the consequences of the application of an intelligent transportation system (ITS). Through the use of a Deep Neural Networks in video footage to find incidents and predict when congestion will occur, ITS-ML system of Singapore integrates the various applications of machine learning. Firstly, prior to the implementation of ITS, Singapore encountered the biggest hurdle which was the rise in the volume of the vehicles which came up as a deciding factor in the availability of roads and better air quality. After ITS (Intelligent Transportation Systems) were put into operations in Singapore, the city experienced a smaller cutting of traffic jams at rush hours, a faster response time to road incidents which led to increased safety, and a better route optimization for its public transport. Another notable output of the transportation system's dynamic capability of routing is the equalization of road traffic loads across the city roadway system.

Also in Europe, by implementing the congestion charging system in a collaboration with ML technology, Stockholm shows one highly applicable example of a practical solution. The system applies ML to evaluate current traffic levels and to change the toll prices on the spur of the moment with a view to reduce staying in the city center. In the close past, driving was a major problem in Stockholm, the worst congestion was during key traffic periods. The study after implementation proved a 20–25% classic traffic reduction became the norm in the city center and this meant less air pollution and less travel time. The general applicability of the model highlighted the possibility of applying ML for the development of policies to manage the urban traffic through the smart use of the given data.

The examples below give clear evidence of how machine learning can contribute to an antirad management system tremendously. The comparison of the outcomes before and after adoption ML technologies shows that not only that ML addresses congestion problems but also it helps the city planners and environmental agenda policymakers. Taken together, those examples demonstrate faster travel times, more traffic flow with multiplied safety and environmental benefits. On the other hand, these case studies give practical insights into the scaling-up, flexibility, and the successful implementation of ML in the urban setup thus, underlining the strong

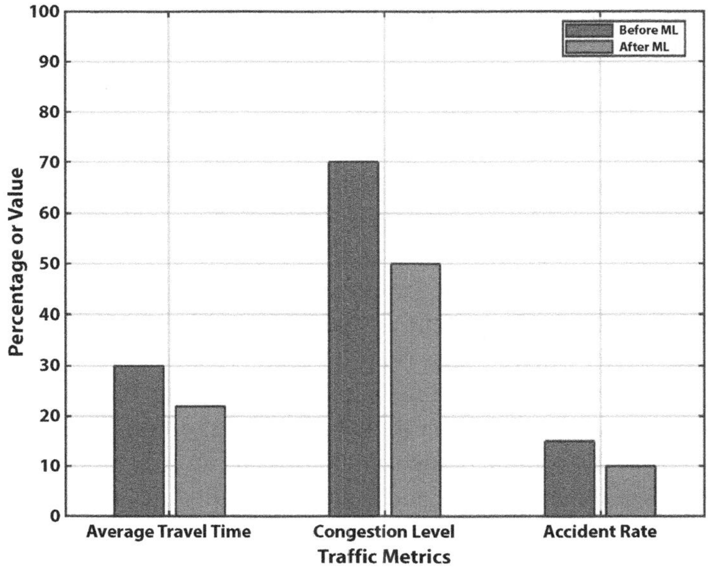

Figure 6.5 Before-and-after traffic metrics bar charts.

impact that these technologies can create consistent with the global traffic management issues. This comparison points out the fact that allocation of resources into the growth of ML algorithms and their comprehensive framework in urban planning programs is a desirable resolution in order to be able to build world-class, liveable and sustainable cities.

Figure 6.5 shows how bar charts indicate traffic metrics containing such elements as the average delay, vehicle throughput, and accident rates for the period before and after the introduction of ML into a transportation system. The graphic style helps to visualize the levels of improvements brought through ML, together with providing evidence to showcase the positive effect of assets and cost reductions along with upgrading the environment safety.

6.5 Challenges and Limitations

The integration of ML within the traffic management system has had an amazing impact in the sense that it has led to the reduction of congestion, improvement of traffic flow and also enhanced road safety. While it helps in giving us an insight into the activities and structures of our solar system, such a technological progress also has its issues and drawbacks. Critical problems such as data quality and privacy issues, integration gotchas and the difficulties with traditional data processing methods create a shortcoming for widespread use of ML in traffic management.

Issues such as data quality and privacy have to be very serious matters when machine learning oriented traffic systems would be enforced. It is true, that accuracy of machine learning will largely depend on the quality of data that is utilized for the purpose of training and analysis. Data accuracy i.e. data containing inaccuracies, missing values and a bias leading to inadequate prediction and ineffective traffic controls is so important due to these reasons. For instance, if the in-feed data of vehicles therein are continually wrong (faulty sensors), the ML algorithms can always estimate the lower volume of vehicles, which can end up as sub-optimal signal timing adjustments causing congestion. Concern of data quality along with the choice between data privacy is one of the generally faced problems. The number of heterogeneous data sources is being continuously expanded, such as footage from cameras, detailing the traffic from sensors and vehicles equipped with a GPS. This data may concern about secret data, which can expose people's exact location and how they can travel. While information on individuals is vital in finding the solutions to major health problems, the privacy of this data is of paramount importance. Regulations for example the General Data Protection Regulation (GDPR) in Europe have has set the standards for privacy for the data and require management authorities for traffic to implement strict measures to protect the personal data, may be much hard to follow and thus data collecting and using operations are complicated.

A different large challenge related to system integration occurs. It happens that traffic management systems are very much large in size and also complicated, and they consist of many parts made differently by various different companies at various different periods. Application of ML algorithms requires the implementation of a variety of technologies and logistics. Golfing for the legacy infrastructure to handle the many and varied intricacies of high-frequency data triggering and downloading may require extensive retrofit if not complete overhaul hinders ML deployment and this process entails huge input and output costs. In addition, the integration process should allow the new ML components to smoothly interact with already existing components of the traffic management system. This might require extensive levels of compatibility and interoperations work, thus, the key stakeholders should closely monitor and develop such collaboration. Scalability and flexibility are as much needed by integration efforts to suit for possible future technological advancements and peaks in volumes.

The real-time processing is one important part of ML traffic applications where the fast response to the data and decisions affect the traffic movement management in right way. In addition, operating massive data streams with instantaneity has technical engineering issues. Traffic measurement systems need, first and foremost, highly robust computational resources for processing the continuous incoming data, which is of a large volume and high-velocity, obtaining it from a variety of sources. The in-time processing of data must be well achieved to guarantee that the traffic management policies implemented present no delays at all. For example, failure to process real time data immediately that results into delayed detection of incidents will lead to slower emergency response times, which can actually worsen the traffic congestions and hence result in safety risks. Lastly, the reliability of real-time systems has to be made certain. Any scarcity of time or error puts the movement of traffic at a risk and makes it unsafe.

In the end, it is seen that ML can bring unprecedented changes in the traffic management systems, the problems of data quality and privacy, system integration, and real-time processing have to be overlooked first to fully get this from it. These problems should not just be resolved by technology solutions but a set of organizational and regulations too so traffic management systems could become efficient, secure and also with a high possibility of survival in the face of all the technological advancements. Overcoming these obstacles is a prerequisite for the seamless introduction

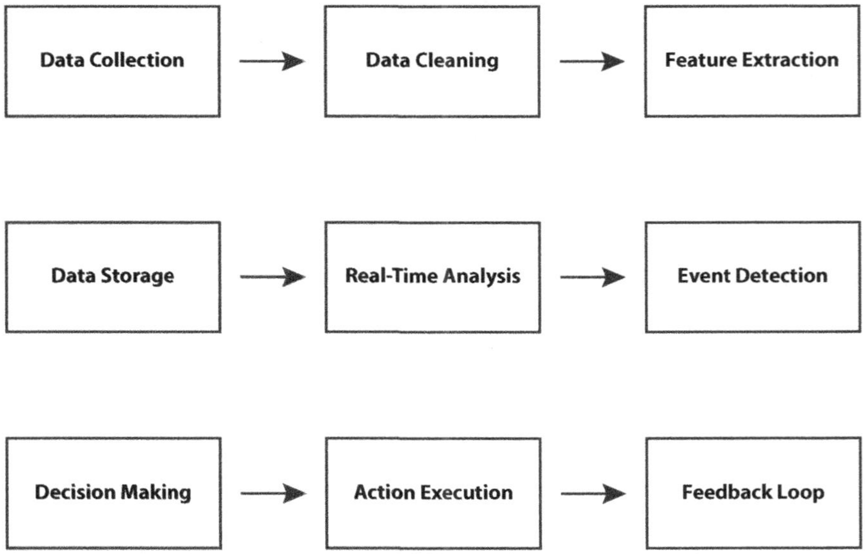

Figure 6.6 Real-time processing data pipeline flowchart.

of ML into traffic management, hence, the birth of the intelligent, safe, and thoroughly smoother and efficient transportation networks boosting urban livelihood.

Figure 6.6 here is an exquisite flowchart that carries a roadmap of a real-time processing data pipeline within the field of traffic management systems. It illustrates that information is continuously gathered, processed, and analyzed to adjust traffic signal patterns instantly, which serves to display operational requirements as well as arduousness of comprehending and managing real-time traffic data with ML.

6.6 Future Trends and Innovations

As urban authorities propagate, the role of machine learning (ML) in traffic control seems to be in the process of a major makeover. The future of ML in this area not only has the opportunities for better algorithms, it also creates platforms for innovation that will be applicable to other technologies and change the way people put policy and urban planning in place. This part talks about incoming trends and novelty and mentions, that we will see these innovations to get even fine-tuned with traffic management systems.

Advancements in Algorithms: The development of ML algorithms, however, is the most crucial element of second-wave improvements in the traffic management. ML popular-enough models today include neural networks, decision trees and support vector machines. Though, the road lies in elaborating on more sophisticated algorithms that can process larger sets of data, to make accurate forecasts, and to learn more efficient from less data. With techniques such as deep learning and reinforcement learning being the catalyst, AI has advanced rapidly in this domain. For instance, deep learning algorithms can perceive images from cameras or sensors to greater extent and help to improve the incident detection and the traffic density patterns. On the other hand, reinforcement learning is incredibly promising in the context of the optimization of traffic flow in a real-time fashion by means of dynamic changes in traffic signal demonstrations derived on the basis of traffic conditions. Such algorithms are now able to effectively adjust and react to the various and varying scenarios common to cities, bringing about a paradigm shift towards smarter, faster, and more efficient traffic control processes.

Integration with Other Technologies: Bridging Machine learning with breakthrough techs such as IoT, 5G, and autonomous vehicles will change the landscape of traffic control for good. IoT tech is the driving force of more interrelated traffic infrastructure with data from different sources (e.g. vehicles, traffic lights, road sensors) collected in real-time and analyzed based on traffic situation. This integration can enable better tracking and handling of traffic current affairs. One the other side, 5G technology, together with its high data throughput speed and low latency, provides particularly necessary feature for ML approach application in traffic management. It guarantees that information from all sensors and cameras is delivered at once and processed right away which results in quicker responses for traffic controlling systems that try to cope with changing circumstances. Besides that, driverless cars implement complications into the traffic control system. In addition, ML algorithms can be used to control and integrate the vehicles behaviors into the existing traffic grid, making use of vehicle-to-network technology in order to improve the traffic flow conditions as well as safety.

Policy and Governance: The rapid integration of ML in other technologies has a dynamic footprint on policy and governance, necessitating thoughtful questionnaires. While the cities are incorporating more technologically-advanced traffic management solutions, the privacy and security implications of data and ethical considerations of technology must be addressed through regulations. Policymakers should guarantee that all these emerging innovations are prioritized in terms of maximizing the pros while mitigating the cons. This also involves issuing data gathering, storage and processing standards to secure individual privacy while mitigate data breach. Also, we have to implement policies which promote progress and the adoption of new technologies while making sure that all the people can benefit from these new technologies. Operational urban planning will have to develop to perfectly fit these innovations. This refers to engineering traffic management operations and network aligning with a green transport plan and a goal to have reduced emissions and better performance of public transport.

In essence, the traffic management of the future depends heavily on the improvement of existing algorithms that will smoothly work with other fields including the Internet of Things, 5G networks, and driverless cars. These innovations will help to bring forth more effective, flexible, and adaptive traffic management systems to cater for the complex and ever-dynamic nature of modern urban areas. Although this possibility may be thoroughly exploited, it implies a combination of technological developments and suitable governing regulations that will stipulate innovation and public interests at the same time. Readers will find this chapter part engaging as it takes an in-depth look at these future trends. The trends may be the determining factor for how the next generation of traffic management systems may be established.

Figure 6.7 is a graph which estimates the overall efficiency gain in traffic shortly projection that could occur owing to the advanced technologies like ML, IoT, and autonomous vehicles. To clearly visualize the time frame

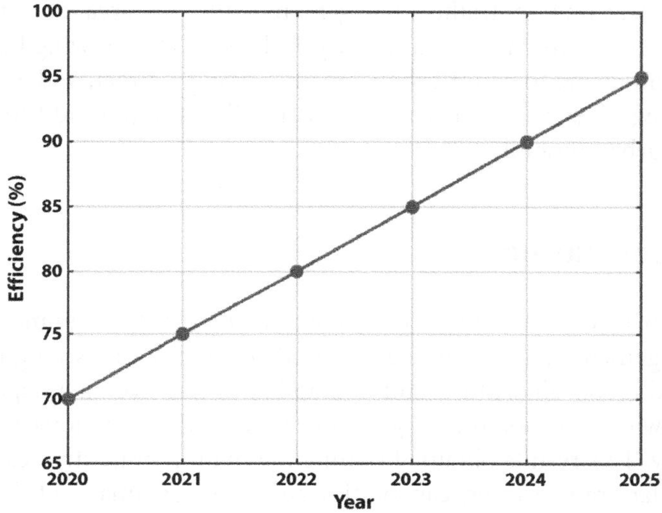

Figure 6.7 Traffic management efficiency forecast graph.

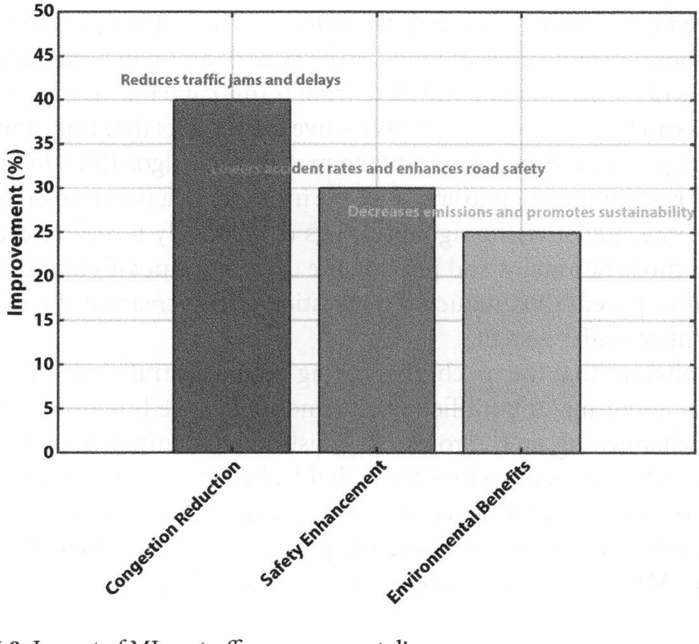

Figure 6.8 Impact of ML on traffic management diagram.

of improvements expected, this tool employs a timeline which provides stakeholders with a long-term view of the evolving role of technology in traffic systems.

Figure 6.8, in an impressive way, deals with the positive outcomes of machine learning in traffic management either in area of congestion, safety, or environmental sustainability. It does this by drawing bar graphs in different colors to count enhancements, giving a direct, and graphically compelling, illustration of what a new mobility solution add to the scenario of urban mobility.

6.7 Conclusion

Chapter will cover the idea of machine learning (ML) role in making traffic management systems more efficient. By exploiting the strength of programmed clever algorithms and availability of massive data depositories, ML has witnessed notable progress on urban traffic junctions' safety and efficiency. This results obtained outline the main points, stresses the ML's spectacular transforming capabilities and gives an image of future ML developments in a quickly changing sphere.

This chapter is a journey into ML applications in traffic management beginning with the basic ML notions, which are relevant in traffic, to advanced implementations that use different ML methods to allow better and smoother traffic flow and reduce the risks of accidents. ML algorithms by virtue of processing not only data from traffic cameras, sensors and GPS systems can but they come with predictive capabilities that traditional traffic management systems are unable to match. Such algorithms forecast the traffic flows, pay attention to and solve the incidents that occurred on the road in real time, adjust traffic signal settings dynamically to utilize the traffic streams more rationally, and provide the drivers the possibility to re-route traffic if required, thus reducing congestion and increasing the efficiency of the entire traffic system.

It is obvious that the machine learning policy for traffic management is not only about making traffic systems more effective but also adaptive to changes happening on the roads. To illustrate, this initiative makes use of learning algorithms to control traffic lights; hence, the wait times at crossroads are reduced, and hence, it is also possible to create smoother traffic that will really drop the idling car power emissions explainable. What is more, ML use in road safety systems brings about a quicker incident detection leading to a prompt reaction, which makes for safer roads as accidents are prevented or their consequences are lowered. They enable a greener urban environment that work towards making the city seem compact, with lower carbon emissions and better public safety.

On the other hand, the chapter emphasized the integrated ML technologies in the traffic management infrastructures and the challenges that emanate as a result of data quality, aware of privacy concerns, system compatibility, and the requirement of the systems that react in real time. Thus, these struggles show the necessity of further innovation and constant adapting of regulations for complete effectiveness of modern machine learning applications in traffic control.

Moving forward, ML tangled with traffic management will put its future feet on the sand which seem to be the deep waters of better applications of ML algorithm, and their harmony with other technologies such as the Internet of things, 5G and vehicles that are driving their selves. From these mergers, more integrated, as well as automatic and traffic systems will be born which allows for better traffic flow and safety at the same time. In a wider sense, the recent technical developments in the field of ML may open up new policy-making avenues and urban management practices for the existing technologies.

In addition to that, during the urban development urbanization never stays as it is and always develops. It is that why the scalable and flexible traffic management solutions become more and more important. ML opens up such opportunities by developing traffic management systems that suit the present-day traffic conditions as well as predict and plan for future expectations in the area. Research and development, joint activities of different departments and new policies will be going to be a key factor to utilize all aspects of ML in traffic management.

The path of incorporating ML into traffic control is still an evolving one. While the ML implementation may have some issues, the idea of creating efficient, safe, and environmentally friendly traffic systems is very obvious. The pace of evolvements in technology will only create much more possibilities, which in turn will make cities more intelligent and well-connected. By addressing the issues of data fusion, weaknesses of cognitive tools, and the dynamic nature of this fast-developing field, this chapter aspires to become an integral part of the ongoing discussion, and so provide a basis for any future developments and researches regarding this type of intelligent traffic management systems.

References

1. Jamshidi, M. and Chair, L.B.E., Leveraging Machine Learning Algorithms to Perform Online and Offline Highway Traffic Flow Predictions. *2014 13th International Conference on Machine Learning and Applications*, Detroit, MI, USA, pp. 419–423, 2014.
2. Lazar, H. and Jarir, Z., Predictive System of Traffic Congestion based on Machine Learning. *2022 9th International Conference on Wireless Networks and Mobile Communications (WINCOM)*, Rabat, Morocco, pp. 1–6, 2022.
3. Tian, Y. and Pan, L., Predicting Short-Term Traffic Flow by Long Short-Term Memory Recurrent Neural Network. *2015 IEEE International Conference on Smart City/SocialCom/SustainCom (SmartCity)*, Chengdu, China, pp. 153–158, 2015.
4. Gokasar, and Timurogullari, A., Real-Time Prediction of Traffic Density with Deep Learning Using Computer Vision and Traffic Event Information. *2021 International Conference on INnovations in Intelligent SysTems and Applications (INISTA)*, Kocaeli, Turkey, pp. 1–5, 2021.
5. Suneetha, S. and Patil, S.R., Advancements in Multi-Cloud Applications for Enhanced E-Healthcare Services. *2023 International Conference on Artificial Intelligence for Innovations in Healthcare Industries (ICAIIHI)*, Raipur, India, pp. 1–7, 2023.
6. Mallikarjun, S., D, S., Kawale, S.R., Cloud-Based Multi-Layer Security Framework for Protecting E-Health Records. *2023 International Conference on Artificial Intelligence for Innovations in Healthcare Industries (ICAIIHI)*, Raipur, India, pp. 1–7, 2023.
7. Mahindrakar, R.P. and Chandel, S., Advanced IoT-Enabled Warehouse Air Quality Monitoring and Live Security System for Medical Applications. *2023 International Conference on Artificial Intelligence for Innovations in Healthcare Industries (ICAIIHI)*, Raipur, India, pp. 1–6, 2023.
8. T, R.G., Simha, S.K., T, Y., Healthcare Energized by Motion Harnessing Piezoelectric Energy in Conjunction with IoT for Medical Innovations. *2023 International Conference on Artificial Intelligence for Innovations in Healthcare Industries (ICAIIHI)*, Raipur, India, pp. 1–7, 2023.
9. Kadam, K.R., Manivasagam, G., Prasad, K.D.V., Novel approaches to biometric security using enhanced session keys and elliptic curve cryptography. *J. Discrete Math. Sci. Cryptogr.*, 27, 2-A, 477–488, 2024.
10. Chandra, G., Kumar, R.S., Prasad, K.D.V., Securing digital authentication with cryptographic innovations in intrinsic verification systems. *J. Discrete Math. Sci. Cryptogr.*, 27, 2-A, 317–328, 2024.
11. Dekka, S., Thiruvenkadam, T., Prasad, K.D.V., Cryptographic image-based data security strategies in wireless sensor networks. *J. Discrete Math. Sci. Cryptogr.*, 27, 2-A, 293–304, 2024.

12. Prasad, K.D.V., Sarma, P., Rahman, M., Mathematical analysis of wavelet-based multi-image compression in medical diagnostics. *J. Discrete Math. Sci. Cryptogr.*, 27, 2-B, 675–687, 2024.
13. Barua, T. and Mohiuddin, K., Dynamic Disaster Management with Real-Time IoT Data Analysis and Response. *2024 International Conference on Automation and Computation (AUTOCOM)*, Dehradun, India, pp. 142–147, 2024.
14. Saxena, R., Barua, T., Mohiuddin, K., Innovative Urban Solutions with IoT-Driven Traffic and Pollution Control. *2024 International Conference on Automation and Computation (AUTOCOM)*, Dehradun, India, pp. 136–141, 2024.
15. Jadhav, M.R. and Kaur, M., Predictive Modeling of Dental Health Outcomes Based on Fluoride Concentrations using AI. *2023 3rd International Conference on Smart Generation Computing, Communication and Networking (SMART GENCON)*, Bangalore, India, pp. 1–7, 2023.
16. Uthaman, M., M, S.P., Prasad, V.S., Innovations in Voice Navigation Using Object Detection to Empower the Visually Impaired. *2023 3rd International Conference on Smart Generation Computing, Communication and Networking (SMART GENCON)*, Bangalore, India, pp. 1–6, 2023.
17. Prasad, K., Sethi, H.S., Prasanth, P.V., Optimizing Resource Allocation in Agriculture through IoT and AI. *2023 7th International Conference on Electronics, Communication and Aerospace Technology (ICECA)*, Coimbatore, India, pp. 1573–1578, 2023.
18. Hephzibah, K. and Aswani, T., Design and Implementation of an Android App for Real-Time Location Monitoring and Emergency Assistance. *2023 7th International Conference on Electronics, Communication and Aerospace Technology (ICECA)*, Coimbatore, India, pp. 1561–1567, 2023.
19. Srinivas, K.N.V. and Lakineni, P.K., Development of a Real-time Location Monitoring App with Emergency Alert Features for Android Devices. *2023 4th IEEE Global Conference for Advancement in Technology (GCAT)*, Bangalore, India, pp. 1–8, 2023.
20. Rupa Shiva Dharshini, M, P., Rahman, M., Jegadesan, S., Optimizing Book Recommendations through Machine Learning: A Collaborative Filtering and Popularity-Based Framework. *2023 4th IEEE Global Conference for Advancement in Technology (GCAT)*, Bangalore, India, pp. 1–8, 2023.
21. Parthasarathy, M.R., Rohith, A., Anil Kumar, N., Facial Expression-Driven Music Recommendation: A Novel Approach for Personalized Listening Experiences. *2023 4th IEEE Global Conference for Advancement in Technology (GCAT)*, Bangalore, India, pp. 1–8, 2023.
22. M N, and N, A.K., Smart Voice Navigation and Object Perception for Individuals with Visual Impairments. *2023 7th International Conference on I-SMAC (IoT in Social, Mobile, Analytics and Cloud) (I-SMAC)*, Kirtipur, Nepal, pp. 694–701, 2023.

23. Kalpana, V. and Hariram, V., Artificial Intelligence based Health Monitoring System on IoTH platform. *2023 Second International Conference on Augmented Intelligence and Sustainable Systems (ICAISS)*, Trichy, India, pp. 1458–1463, 2023.
24. M, U., K, S., K, A., A Novel Approach for Identification and Donation of Surplus Food using Machine Learning-based Replate App. *2023 Second International Conference on Augmented Intelligence and Sustainable Systems (ICAISS)*, Trichy, India, pp. 552–558, 2023.
25. Maheshwari, B. and Jeevitha Sai, G., A Novel Method of Identification of Delirium in Patients from Electronic Health Records Using Machine Learning. *2023 World Conference on Communication & Computing (WCONF)*, RAIPUR, India, pp. 1–6, 2023.
26. Kranthi, M. and Tanguturi, R.C., Design of Intelligent Medical Integrity Authentication and Secure Information for Public Cloud in Hospital Administration. *2023 2nd International Conference on Edge Computing and Applications (ICECAA)*, Namakkal, India, pp. 256–261, 2023.
27. L, L.S.V.S., K, S.R.C., H, V.C., Implementation of Machine Learning Approach for Detecting Cardiovascular Diseases. *2023 3rd International Conference on Intelligent Technologies (CONIT)*, Hubli, India, pp. 1–6, 2023.
28. Hegge, K.K. and Agrawal, R., Wireless and Solar-Powered Multipurpose Robot for Industrial Automation: A Sustainable Solution. *2023 8th International Conference on Communication and Electronics Systems (ICCES)*, Coimbatore, India, pp. 146–151, 2023.
29. Kishore Kumar, R., Pandidurai, M., Senthil Kamalesh, M.S.C., Design of IoT based Rural Health Helper using Natural Language Processing. *2023 4th International Conference on Electronics and Sustainable Communication Systems (ICESC)*, Coimbatore, India, pp. 328–333, 2023.
30. Hussain, N., Dixit, S.K., Gupta, A.K., A novel approach of unsupervised feature selection using iterative shrinking and expansion algorithm. *J. Interdiscip. Math.*, 26, 3, 519–530, 2023.
31. Premkumar, S., Hussain, N., Chinamuttevi, V.S., A novel RF-SMOTE model to enhance the definite apprehensions for IoT security attacks. *J. Discrete Math. Sci. Cryptogr.*, 26, 3, 861–873, 2023.
32. Selvakumar, C., Shekhar, R., Chaturvedi, A., Securing networked image transmission using public-key cryptography and identity authentication. *J. Discrete Math. Sci. Cryptogr.*, 26, 3, 779–791, 2023.
33. Hegge, K.K. and Agrawal, R., Industrial Automated Multipurpose Robot Using WIFI. *2023 4th International Conference for Emerging Technology (INCET)*, Belgaum, India, pp. 1–8, 2023.
34. De, T., Tanguturi, R.C., Ashreetha, B., A Novel method of Improving Spectrum sensing Management system for CR-IoT Networks. *2023 4th International Conference for Emerging Technology (INCET)*, Belgaum, India, pp. 1–6, 2023.

35. Srinivas, V. and De, T., Wi-Fi Router Signal Coverage Position Prediction System using Machine Learning Algorithms. *2023 International Conference on Sustainable Computing and Smart Systems (ICSCSS)*, Coimbatore, India, pp. 253–258, 2023.
36. Srinivas, V. and Anil Kumar, N., Approaches for Advanced Spectrum Sensing in Cognitive Radio Networks. *2023 7th International Conference on Intelligent Computing and Control Systems (ICICCS)*, Madurai, India, pp. 1485–1490, 2023.
37. Karimzadeh, M., *et al.*, Reinforcement Learning-designed LSTM for Trajectory and Traffic Flow Prediction. *2021 IEEE Wireless Communications and Networking Conference (WCNC)*, Nanjing, China, pp. 1–6, 2021.
38. Gao, S., Wang, Y., Gao, Y., Liu, Y., Understanding urban traffic-flow characteristics: a rethinking of betweenness centrality. *Environ. Plann. B Plann. Des.*, 40, 1, 135–153, 2013.

7

Secure Routes and Cybersecurity Challenges in Autonomous Mobility Systems

Dankan Gowda V.[1*], Ribhu Abhusan P.[2], V. Nuthan Prasad[3], K.D.V. Prasad[4] and P. Vishnu Prasanth[5]

[1]*Department of Electronics and Communication Engineering, BMS Institute of Technology and Management, Bangalore, Karnataka, India*
[2]*Department of Electronics and Communication Engineering, Centurion University of Technology and Management (CUTM), Paralakhemundi, Odisha, India*
[3]*Department of Electronic and Communication, MSRIT, Bangalore, Karnataka, India*
[4]*Symbiosis Institute of Business Management, Hyderabad and Symbiosis International (Deemed University), Pune, India*
[5]*Department of Physics, Mohan Babu University, Sree Sainath Nagar, Tirupati, India*

Abstract

Autonomous mobility systems, as they gradually become more and more ingrained in existing transportation structures, are increasingly exposed to highly specialized networked systems and therefore couple the issue of cybersecurity. In the coming paragraph, the core of autonomous systems and the cybersecurity vulnerabilities that have been identified to attack the operational integrity of these systems will be scrutinized. Through the presentation of diverse attack avenues such as flawed software and data breaching, this section serves as a reminder about the necessity of good cybersecurity practice to guarantee the safety of path planning and control systems. The defensive strategies including highly advanced encryption and intrusion detection systems are overviewed in the course. The chapter also talks about the responsibility of the regulation and ethical aspect of cybersecurity in the autonomous mobility. This work by the means of a specific combination of theoretical discussion, case studies, and simulations, will help in equipping

**Corresponding author*: dankan.v@bmsit.in

Rathishchandra R. Gatti and Chandra Singh (eds.) Digital Convergence in Intelligent Mobility Systems, (125–158) © 2025 Scrivener Publishing LLC

stakeholders with the skill to create, implement, and maintain the safety of the autonomous systems. The need is to provide for development of a safer operation of autonomous mobility by reducing cyber risks and enabling system resilience.

Keywords: Autonomous mobility, cybersecurity, encryption, intrusion detection systems, regulatory standards, ethical considerations, data privacy, secure communication

7.1 Introduction

Developing autonomy in the mobility systems provides a seminal change in the transport field, presenting opportunities for betterments of efficiency and personalized mobility, and along with this come intensified cybersecurity problems. The systems of autonomous mobility, as it is named, mean the applications of the technologies of self-driving, which are able to make the functioning of transportation without human control [1]. The range of resulting tech systems is broad and includes automated cars, drones, as well as unmanned rail systems. They are designed to operate on their own, staring at their surroundings with sensors, cameras, AI, and communication networks.

Autonomous vehicles, mostly known by cars but used in most autonomous systems, interpret the environment via a combination of LIDAR, GPS, odometry, and computer vision [2]. The utilization of such technology lets passenger cars, trucks, and buses to drive by themselves without the human role, dropping the number of accidents, speeding up the traffic flow, and decreasing human fatigue [3]. Unmanned aerial vehicles, shortened to drones, play multiple roles across a range of applications, from goods delivery and agricultural monitoring, among others, to surveillance and disaster management as well. Through the execution of real-time data communication, these machines have the ability to not only navigate but also finish their jobs successfully [4]. Unmanned trains are also a great gradual step into the future of rail transport, allowing somewhat safer and more efficient rail services through reducing human error and increasing efficiency.

It especially becomes relevant to the integration of these autonomous technologies into daily operations, due to the fact that such move might bear a cyber risk that could jeopardize people's security and public safety. Software systems are fundamental enough for cybersecurity in autonomous systems to be a vital issue, as these technologies rely on and are mainly controlled by cybernetic software systems [5]. Cybersecurity violation that finds its way into vehicles' control could also provide an intruder with access to vital infrastructure systems that could lead to examples of theft, hijacking, and even catastrophic consequences. An intruder might utilize software bugs in autonomous car systems to lead the vehicle to violate traffic rules [6], i.e. ignoring red lights or going the wrong way, which would in turn cause accidents and pose a danger to the public.

In addition, the data these systems collect and process are massive and extremely sensitive, such as users' real-time geographic track, users' behavior, and even personal identification information. Such provision is of great significance not only to safeguard personal information but also to keep intact the transport system security. Cybersecurity comprises of data breaches that cause the disclosure of sensitive information at a magnitude [7], which in turn may result in a decline of public confidence in these rapidly evolving technologies. While these risks may be a challenge, security measures in autonomous mobility are not only extras but a required function of their operation [8]. The cybersecurity protocols, which are quite robust, are the prerequisite to enable these technologies to live up to the expectations of quality improvement and safety while not exposing the users and the general public to new dangers [9]. The scope of this encompasses not only safeguarding from external threats but also mitigating the risks that could manifest in the hardware or software at different stages of their lifecycle—creation, production, or use. Ultimately, if autonomous system mobility becomes a common phenomenon, cybersecurity will become a more imperative role [10]. It is of enormous importance that the industry leaders, regulators, and technologists act in consonance to make these challenges alleviate. The implementing of comprehensive measures of cybersecurity will aid fostering risk mitigation, assurance of reliability of autonomous systems, and safeguarding them against attacks by malicious parties and technical problems [11]. The present chapter attempts to deal with all fundamental autonomous mobility technologies and associated cybersecurity problems. Therefore, it is designed to clarify the present state of the art in those fields. If we can successfully address these obstacles, we would therefore create conditions for such automation that would be as safe and efficient as it can get, maximizing the benevolent aspects of automation and minimizing the risks it poses [12].

Figure 7.1 expresses an informative pie chart depicting how autonomous mobility systems, including self-driving cars, drones, and unmanned trains, are being distributed by percentage. It is a visual presentation of the occurrence of each of the system types by making use of various colors to distinguish between segments [13]. Utilization of the chart plays a role of the instrument for the market composition perception and encourages or inhibits the rate of adoption or the development level of each type within the field of autonomous mobility.

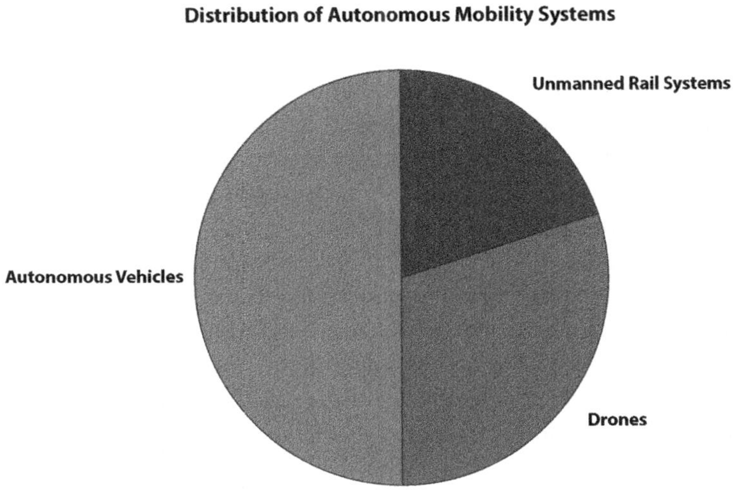

Figure 7.1 Pie chart showing the distribution of different types of autonomous mobility systems (cars, drones, trains).

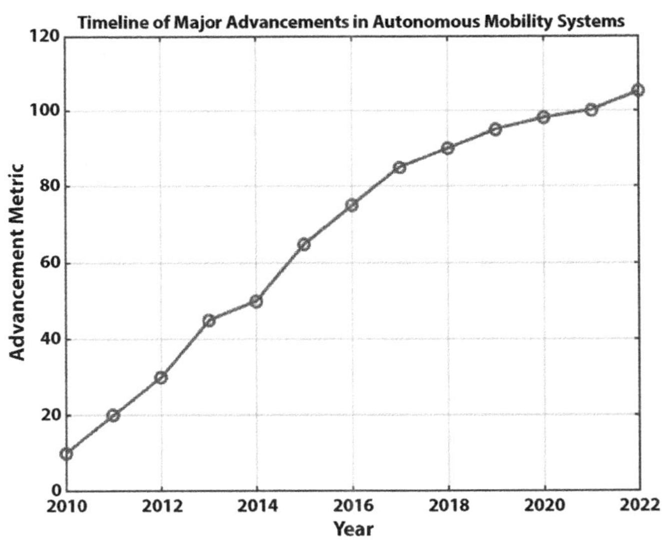

Figure 7.2 Timeline of major advancements in autonomous mobility systems over the last decade.

Figure 7.2 shows the time elapsed depicted with a line graph that shows the most major achievements in autonomous mobility status over the last decade [14]. Each graph point represents a major technical breakthrough or improvement in area of autonomous movement, like the use of advanced driver-assistance systems, authentication of autonomous driveways, or real operation of autonomous drones.

7.2 The Landscape of Autonomous Mobility

Autonomous mobility landscape is marked by quick technological advances; it is increasingly being adopted by many players, and both classical automakers along with innovative tech-focused companies are actively becoming involved. Currently, the domain of autonomous mobility is evolving at a rate close to the evolution of the state of technologies with deregulation in the process and changing consumers' feelings [15]. Autonomy and level during the World War league and after peace prevailed on the ground, air, and rail operations were used more. Autonomous cars may be the foremost distinguishing technology of the time. Significant car makers, namely, Tesla, Ford, and General Motors, and the society's heavyweights, like Waymo, Uber, and Baidu, are currently trying to perfect the mastermind of their autonomous driving technologies [16]. One of the most famous systems of autopilot version of Tesla and Waymo is the fully independent movement software. Both of them have the control at high level which covers most driving conditions. Utilizing such robotics in transportation creates an absolute need for an alliance of sensors, which are optimized, and the algorithm is of machine learning [17]. The last significant key needed is a powerful processor doing the real-time task, which makes it applicable in transportation.

Adoption rates of autonomous technologies span predictably everywhere while their applications show massive differences. The automotive industry of North America and Europe and a few Asian cities dominates in adopting autonomous vehicles because they are supported by the regulatory bodies and by the existence of the technology ecosystem. Regulatory-related framework was created in the U.S. and the EU (European Union), with a specific clause related to autonomous vehicle testing and deployment, which pushed along the adoption process [18]. The trend of drones in commercial operation for delivery and monitoring might have been located in regions like Australia and Rwanda, where they are widely welcome and where they also serve critical purposes like delivery services and healthcare.

Established companies who are recognized as the industry leaders in autonomous mobility are already players in the industry, but the innovative start-ups are the new entrants [19]. For instance, the famous Tesla and Waymo are known for their great contribution to the field of autonomous vehicles, and DJI is recognized as the leading player in consumer drone market [20]. Also, Hitachi and Siemens are able to promote automatic rail systems, and the example is Japan and Europe, where the role of public transport in urban life and transport is of paramount significance.

Nowadays, the next decade is going to be full of many fundamental shifts in the way automatic systems are assimilated into everyday life. Experts project that robotic algorithms will further develop, and it will not be just self-driving cars on the market but the expansion in commercial transportation as well [21]. For example, the use of truck drivers that are autonomous and delivery drones is anticipated to increase in logistics and delivery; their salary will be lowered as well as the cost of the entire services to customers while offering efficiency [22]. AI integration with autonomous systems is believed to add to the usefulness of these technologies. The applications will then become more complex and multi-environmental once AI and automation come together.

Besides that, technologies of smart cities are going to expand with it and make sure that more autonomous mobility system is applied to deal with more challenges by people and transportation growing [23]. Similar to this point, the interaction between 5G technologies that would improve vehicle-to-vehicle and vehicle-to-infrastructure dispersions, which are also key components to the proper conduct of self-driven systems, will be facilitated.

Self-driving powertrain, however, promises investments in energy efficiency and environment sustainability. Autonomous electric vehicles are anticipated to be the main players, with two types of supporting factors: batteries being developed to the extent that they no longer require fossil fuels and infrastructure for renewable energy being constructed; this, in turn, drops down the environmental impact of both public and individual transport [24]. Yet, the autonomous mobility landscape that has just been portrayed is the fact that transportation is progressing with technology, the use of which is growing and that different industry sectors are actively involved [25]. With this phenomenon likely to continue, we may expect that the next decade will be about the emergence of the autonomous transportation mechanism as a regular feature of the global mobility infrastructure, serving best efficiency, safety, and sustainability [26]. The constant technological development and integration will require maintaining vigilance over protective measures against cyber threats to actually achieve the idea of a smart city where the new solutions for mobility will be well coordinated with the protection of data and systems, and in this way, the transportation users' and the cities' systems will be safe [27].

In Figure 7.3 (the region-wise autonomous vehicles adoption rates bar graph), it is depicted that North America, Europe, Asia, South America,

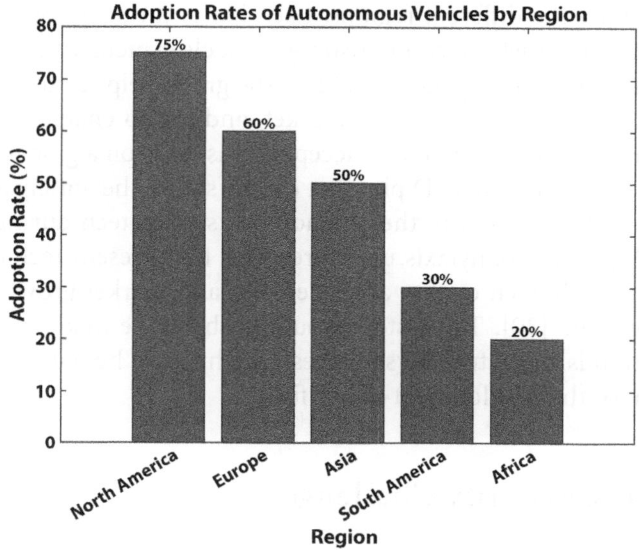

Figure 7.3 Bar graph depicting the adoption rates of autonomous vehicles in different regions.

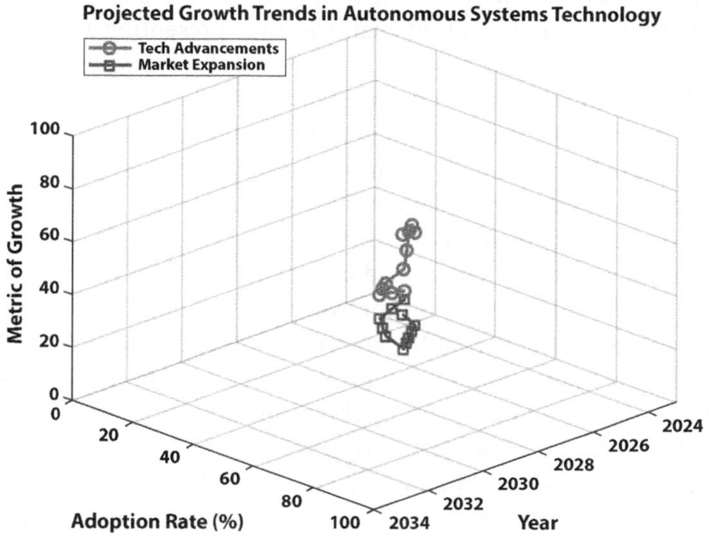

Figure 7.4 3D plot of projected growth trends in autonomous systems technology.

and Africa are the different regions. Each bar is the share of penetration within this region whose comparison gives a clear picture of the regional differences in technology outreach [28]. The graph helps us to evaluate the sector leaders and slackers in the market, and it also enables us to know how the autonomous technology acceptance is done on a global scale.

Figure 7.4 is built on a 3D plot that clearly shows the anticipated development or advancement in the autonomous system tech during the next decade [29]. The prophylaxis uses three axes that present tech consumption rate growth, tech quality advancement, and market growth over the upcoming years [30]. The system would probably be made by analyzing different trends and future perspectives, which would help us create a strategic plan for the development of our field.

7.3 Cybersecurity Challenges

As autonomous vehicles and systems in transit and broader sectors of service delivery become more commonplace, this brings about a new set of challenges on cybersecurity that must be addressed to mitigate the risks. The attacks of cybercriminals against autonomous systems can occur in a multitude of ways. These can range from software bugs and weak encryption to insecure communication channels, each presenting a unique threat that can be eventually broken into by malevolent forces. Identifying these vulnerabilities forms a key component in the cybersecurity roadmap of an organization [31]. A serious flaw of autonomous systems is embedded software bugs. Autonomous systems heavily depend on sophisticated software in order to execute, make the decisions, and communicate with the surrounding environment and with their users. Although, software bugs and flaws are a natural element and can be used by hackers as exploitable holes when left undiscovered or unresolved. These bugs might cause erroneous behavior on the part of the autonomous systems which could result in breakdown of the operational controls as well as improper processing of data. For instance, a fault in automobile software could be read as a misinterpretation of the sensor data, triggering wrong actions such as unexpected acceleration or braking, which could lead to crashes.

Inadequate encryption is another crucial weakness as well. Autonomous systems, including vehicles and drones, constantly communicate with external services, other devices, and infrastructure so as to achieve proper deployment in the surrounding [32]. Encryption is required for such communication to ensure that there is no unauthorized access or manipulation. The encryption plays a crucial role in the transfer of confidential information between the devices and the control centers; once encryption is weak, the interception of the data can occur, and subsequently, privacy breaches and manipulations can take place [33]. Further, an aggressor could tamper with the unencrypted data transmitted from a vehicle to track its movements or do the same with regard to its operational parameters.

Along with the non-secure communication channels, the major risk factor is also considered. Many unmanned systems sustain communication over the airwaves. If the connectivity lacks protection against foreign attacks, it is just like putting the key in the front door. Such networks, if disrupted, can permit attackers to both remotely access and control the car or another autonomous system [34]. Second, the rising popularity of Internet of Things (IoT) devices deployed in autonomous systems adds additional vulnerabilities, since many IoT devices do not have the best of the security features. The negativity of these cybersecurity vulnerabilities is not completely a hypothetical situation; rather, the incidents which have happened in real life sometime in the recent years have shown us the very real consequences. A careless case was when the researchers showed how it was feasible to exploit the entertainment system of the Jeep Cherokee through an unpatched vulnerability to gain access to the brakes and steering of a vehicle [35]. The incident had a dramatic effect, as 1.4 million vehicles were recalled to mend the software's vulnerability defect. Even more so, the security concerns about connected vehicles started to be raised. A very common use case concerned a well-established drone brand, which had their communication protocols revealed as insecure. Researchers were able to capture and re-route the information flow between the drone and its handler, resulting in a control handover. This vulnerability raises very serious security risks, especially in scenarios where drones are being used for surveillance and transportation of valuable items such as goods.

These cases highly underscore the vital importance of having many cybersecurity measures for the course of the development and deployment of autonomous systems [36]. They also show the danger of security gaps not only in economic consequences and lost trust but also looking at the physical harm and disrupting essential services. In order to be able to properly manage these hazards, the safety procedures have to be implemented for every phase of design, development, and operational work of autonomous technology [37]. This includes performing a detailed security audit and penetration test, using strong encryption algorithms, securing the communication pathways, and, of course, regularly updating and patching software systems to fix existing vulnerabilities. Furthermore, a constant monitoring and improving should be employed for any emerging risks as technology and hacking practices move forward. The integration of self-driving technology is full of promises, from increasing the level of automation to achieving better productivity in the transport and other industries [38]. Although those technologies can come with serious cybersecurity threats, the governance of which is paramount to the safe and secure adoption. Through understanding and identifying the vulnerabilities and lessons from previous events, the stakeholders can become more resilient to the cyber threats. This in turn will improve the security both of the systems themselves and of the public that depends on these systems.

Figure 7.5 shows a graph which elucidates the different areas of cybersecurity vulnerabilities in autonomous systems, such as software bugs, insufficient encryption, and weak transmission channels. Each weakness goes on to become one of the security threats involved in data breaches and system manipulations. The flowchart mode, which arranges and illustrates the cause–effect relations between the danger and its consequence, aids the risk evaluation and control.

The heat map in Figure 7.6 depicts a visual breakdown of cybersecurity incidents in the autonomous travel environment with the help of sectors such as autonomous vehicles, drones, and unmanned rails. The color intensity of the heat map relates to the number of incidents and thus shows right away which sectors are at risk of having many cybersecurity problems.

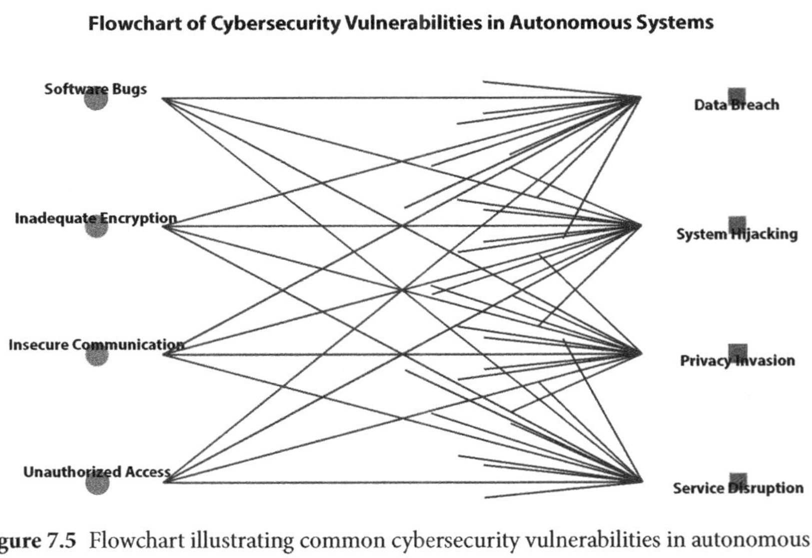

Figure 7.5 Flowchart illustrating common cybersecurity vulnerabilities in autonomous systems.

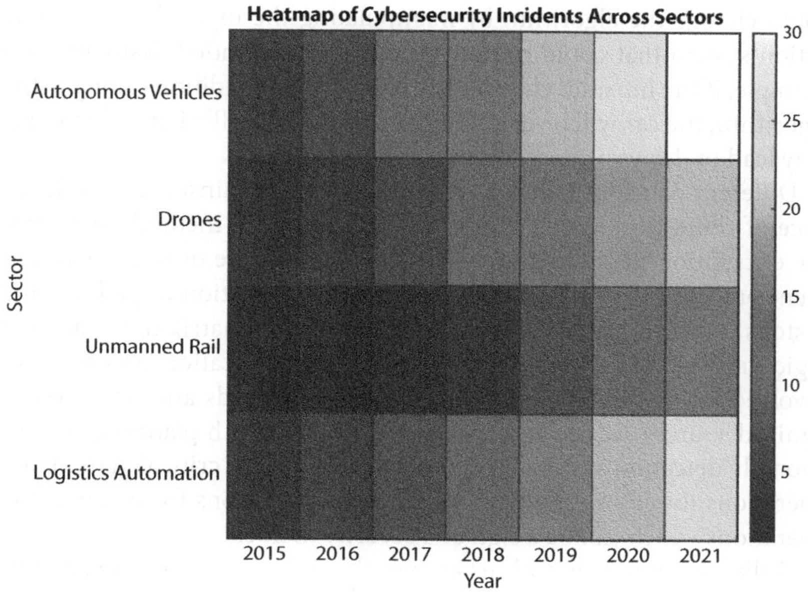

Figure 7.6 Heat map of cybersecurity incidents across different sectors of autonomous mobility.

7.4 Secure Routes: Ensuring Safety in Navigation and Control

Articulating route planning and shielding real-time data in autonomous systems make the system security equally important as the efficient operation of these technologies. Autonomous vehicles and systems use high-end algorithms to generate pathways while also utilizing real-time data to maneuver and perform their duties. The security of these items is a first priority to ensure that there is no interference from external forces to deal with the potentially disastrous consequences. Secondly, these components have to be inspected properly for the sake of credibility and reliability of the system.

The path planning in autonomous systems is performed by using tools such as algorithms and navigational sensors that computationally determine the vehicles' best and most secure routes around the system to avoid collisions. These algorithms analyze combinations of traffic patterns, types of roads, weather conditions, and other obstacles to create a unique, individualized route for every car. On the other hand, the security of these algorithms tends to be the main cause of the stress. In such case, hackers could change the algorithm by manipulating the input data to the navigation system that could reroute them to non-intended destinations. For example, if the intruder changes the given traffic conditions along with the algorithm, the car will be directed to the heaviest traffic jam, which in turn may lead to delays or possible accidents.

Different paths for controlling the algorithms against the outside influence of robot positioning are being designed. One method often used is the encryption of codes and safe cycling of software during the development process of the software devoted to the generation of path planning. It stops unauthorized persons from obtaining the matrix of the algorithm logic and its data inputs. Moreover, the authentication approaches are involved to confirm that only authorized commands and data from recognized sources are applied or responded to the path planning. Secondly, anomaly detection systems are employed to observe critical path planning operations for any sign of abnormalities or deviations from conventional operations which can be a sign of a security incident.

Offline planning algorithms are not the only thing which needed to be secured. The safeguarding of real-time data used for autonomous systems operation is just as crucial. Autonomous aircraft in fact have an advantage over using the original data from different sensors and digicam eras, which should be considered at the time of making autonomy decisions. This system allows it to get hold of such data that would include nearby vehicles, pedestrians, road conditions, and other factors that may surround the environment. Shielding this datum is essential since any altering or unauthorized access will give rise to dysfunctional decisions that may threaten the life of the passengers or anyone else.

Data security, at the time becoming a short-term principle, has several layers of defense. Next, it's really important that data transmission between the sensors and a vehicle's central processing unit is ciphered in order to precede unauthorized listening to the data and managing their data by third parties. Data integrity verification and alteration prove to be one of the most critical elements of the transmitted data not to be corrupted. Not only does this require strongly protected storage and processing systems against unauthorized access and cyberattacks, but it also necessitates data management and maintenance with streamlined and secure processes. For this purpose, organizations will most probably rely on such measures as firewalls, intrusion detection systems, and regular security audits to find out any actual weaknesses.

The difficulty of making sure the safety of both planning path and real-time data is double because of the dynamic element with autonomous vehicles and their system of environment of working. As the mechanisms of these systems grow in complexity and interact with a changing external environment, it becomes necessary for them to adjust themselves to new data and conditions that do not stay the same all the time. This implies a board security approach that can address new threats and a bay in the system's effectiveness in achieving its operational goals.

Hence, it is significant to build a security for route planning algorithms, along with real-time data, particularly while handling these systems. Through strong encryption, authentication, anomaly detection, and information protection, developers and operators use these platforms as the basis for preventing outside interferences that deter its reliability and integrity. Besides this, with the development of technologies and the appearance of new vulnerabilities, these processes to further investigate computer security will be necessary to develop these changes and to support the operation of autonomous systems in the world that is more connected and with different complexities.

Figure 7.7 depicts how data is being placed in layers of security during navigation using autonomous vehicles. It underscores the point that real-time data is used for processing, verification, and decision making, which is essential for maintaining the safety and integrity of the operations through the absence of costly delays.

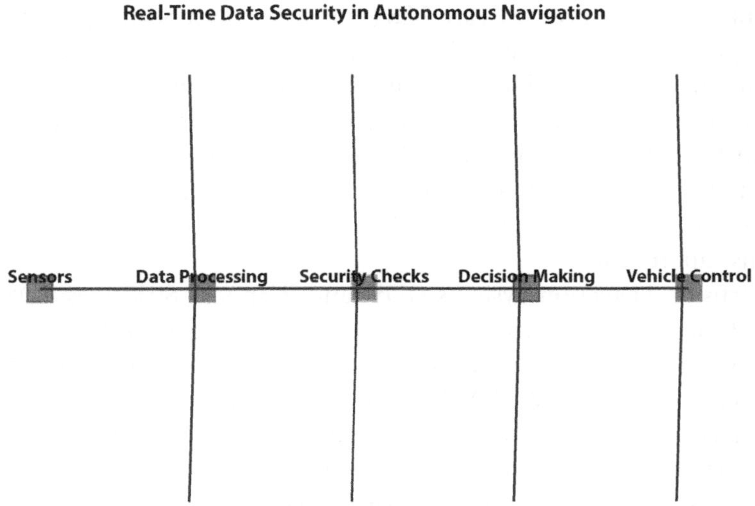

Figure 7.7 Real-time simulation of data flow and security checks during autonomous navigation.

7.5 Defensive Technologies and Strategies

In the case of security systems for autonomous transportation, the applicability of effective offense defenses and strategies could not be underestimated. In fact, these cyber systems, which are a very important part in various infrastructures, have some fundamental vulnerability to the wide variety of cyber threats because of their integrated communication networks with complex data exchange. So, having top encrypting, secure communication protocols, intrusion detection systems (IDS), and creating systems for redundancy and resilience are what provide essential steps toward ensuring the reliability and security of these technologies.

Encryption and Secure Communication Protocols: Secure communication between autonomous vehicles (AVs) and infrastructure would be the major factor. Vehicles are not only exchanging with center servers but also with each other and different components of the infrastructure (e.g. traffic light and street sensors); this needs to be secure, and ensuring that the information reaches the right destination should be addressed. The main task of encryption is to guard the data flow whose location is the starting point. The most effective approaches to encryptions these days feature the use of solid and well-established algorithms that conform to the industry standards like AES (Advanced Encryption Standard) which accounts for longer key lengths to resist any attacks of binary decryption by unauthorized users.

Similarly, when the data is transmitted from one system to another, the presence of a secure communication protocol is of equal importance. Examples of these protocols are TLS (Transport Layer Security) and DTLS (Datagram Transport Layer Security), which clarify how time-sensitive communications can be securely carried out in vehicular networks. Such a procedure will transform data into encoded format that cannot be altered by any third party that may be meddling or wandering in the middle of the communication. With that in mind, these guidelines require fine tuning and are subject to getting feedback in order to account for new threats and defense approaches.

Intrusion Detection Systems (IDS) and Response Strategies: IDS specially tuned for automotive systems (i.e., IDS tailored against autonomous vehicles) play an indispensable role, as they identify cyber threats in time and deal with the threats. IDS for autonomous cars are set up to ascertain unusual occurrences, subversions, or anomalies within Internet traffic and machine operations. They can use available known signature threats, signature systems, or anomalous behavior detection mechanism that utilizes machine learning to identify deviations from the normal operation.

After spotting the danger that's rising, the response mechanism is being triggered. Such an approach might consist in informing a central monitoring system, interrupting the operation of the vehicle, or isolating the lifted parts to prevent an outbreak. The performance of the IDS and the right strategies that follow can be determined by when the threats are detected completely and correctly, as that requires the frequent update of the IDS databases and algorithms so that they can quickly address the changing cyber threats.

Redundancy and Resilience: The attempt to back up and have the entire capacity within an autonomous system to stand the attack and resist the hard conditions without a failure that will lead to the crash is crucial for the safety of the devices. The situation where the reserve analogy or the secondary options of a system are duplicated to handle the critical components that can be switched to, in case the primary one gives way, was coined as redundancy. For example, an automated car could be composed of several separate systems like object detection and route navigation, so if one of the systems is ruined due to a cyberattack, the other system can manage to take control, and the vehicle will continue to operate safely.

Resilience in cyber defense means the existence of the system and its main functions after any interruptions. It releases a system back to a normal state, fast. Above all, the power to adapt and put right the mistakes that hackers will discover is its advantage. The array of protective procedures incorporates fault-tolerant design principles, regular exposure to stress tests by hacking system in emulation mode, and more efficient incident response that will prevent the worst consequences.

The way of effectively reducing risk and getting the resilient system is a very complex issue which involves not only the technical creation of the system but also the operational and organizational aspects. For this purpose, it could be arranging of the training sessions for employees on cybersecurity ethics, carrying out of routine security audits, and installation of appropriate policy foundations for the security reports.

In fact, risk reduction techniques and systems development become more important when autonomous motor system is the issue. Encryption and the conditions of secure communication convey the privacy and completeness of data in bites whereas the intrusion detections and the response tactics help in quickly recognizing and responding toward breaches. Moreover, the concepts of redundancy and resilience in the design and operation of these systems imply that they can survive and recover from attacks, thus working to adequately maintain its operation and safety at all times despite the cyber challenges. The technical necessity of these defense measures does not only contribute in establishing trust among the public and other stakeholders but also is one of the essential elements in the maturing world of automotive and mobility.

Figure 7.8 shows the network diagram implementation of the encryption that allows communication flow between the different autonomous

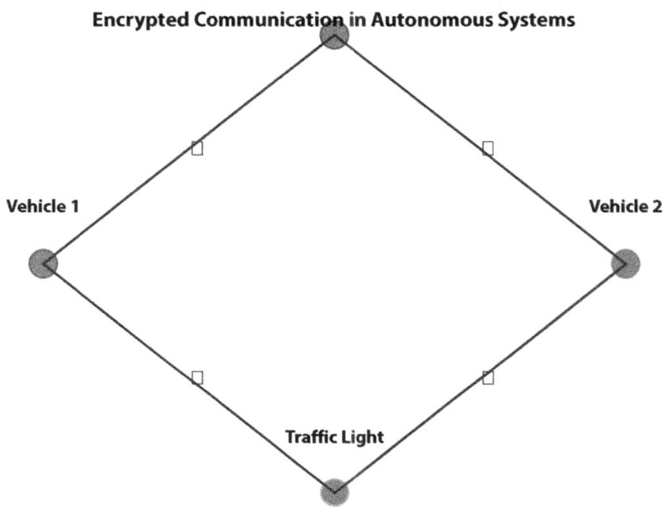

Figure 7.8 Network diagram illustrating encrypted communication between autonomous vehicles and infrastructure.

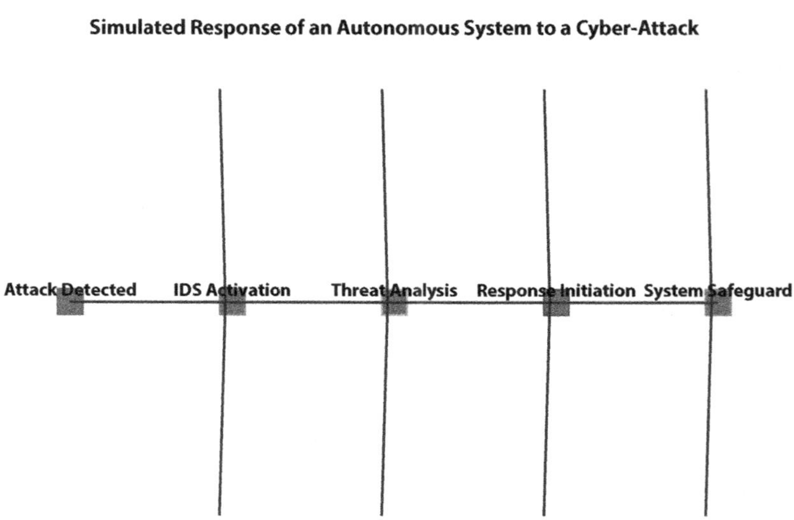

Figure 7.9 Simulated response of an autonomous system to a cyberattack using intrusion detection systems.

system nodes, such as the vehicles and control centers. It reflects the information traffic, and through encryption, the data transfer is secured without unauthorized access and meddling with the encryption; more emphasis on the confidence and integrity maintenance is given.

The sample graph confirms the actions of an autonomous system on detecting a cybersecurity attack (Figure 7.9). Following this structure, it presents five stages ranging from threat detection, system analysis, to triggering the application of response processes and system safeguards. This illustration gives the audience insights into the operant measures and sustainability of autonomous devices in case of cyber assaults.

7.6 Regulatory and Standardization Efforts

In the autonomous movement of cars and mobility, these conventional bodies play a fundamental role in establishing a guideline to help secure the operation and cybersafety of autonomous systems. The establishment of effective cybersecurity approaches by this way offers a basis for conducting research, developing, implementing, evaluating, and improving technology in a manner that curbs the risk of cyber threats. The following section contains information about the existing guidelines and regulations already in place regarding cybersecurity and the part the government plays in the formulation of these rules, as well as the role of international bodies in the shaping of this process.

The need for a regulatory and standardization environment cannot be ruled out given that ethical and safe use of autonomous mobility technology is expected to thrive in such an environment. Nowadays, there are some major standards and rules that are targeted specifically by various categories of cybersecurity in autonomous vehicles and other fare systems. For instance, the ISO/SAE 21434 standard, which is incontrovertibly the cybersecurity guideline for road vehicles, provide the standards for cybersecurity risk management for electrical and electronic parts in road vehicles, including the product development, production, operation, maintenance, and decommissioning of the devices. The statement about this standard not only allows manufacturers to determine dangerous factors and find solutions, but it also allows them to implement related mitigations from the beginning to the end of the vehicle.

There is a similar set of regulations from the UNECE WP.29 framework, which, besides being a guideline on vehicle cybersecurity, also stipulates the software update related domain. Thus, producers should ensure that those risks will be managed properly and cybersecurity measures are practiced in order to obtain an endorsement by the authorities. It requires the same measures as well for developers; hence, they should ensure vehicle security by controlling the software updates and protecting the vehicle data from illicit access.

Among these standards and regulations, there are country government institutions and many international bodies that are in charge of developing and promoting them. In the United States of America, the National Highway Traffic Safety Administration (NHTSA) is a key authority in developing regulations on automation security from cyber threats. NHTSA published a number of books for the manufacturers which covers the reasons to be cybersecurity conscious at the design and production stages and dealing with incidents during and post-launch, respectively. On the international platform, bodies like the International Organization for Standardization (ISO) and International Electrotechnical Commission (IEC) cooperate to create the global standards that will ensure safety, reliability, and interoperability of all electronic systems where these are included, such as autonomous vehicles. These institutions partner with leading industry and decision makers who set rules that become obsolete in line with the changing environment and new cybersecurity challenges.

The function of the government is not reduced to rule enforcement but also includes the stimulation of scientific research. In addition, the government should establish cooperation between the public and private sectors. As an example, the governments can launch programs of this type, which would cover investment in the technology's development and autonomous driving orientation. They still have the option to establish common platforms through which information exchange can be promoted between various entities such as car makers and infrastructure and cybersecurity providers, thus reinforcing collective protection.

In addition, international cooperation has recently been required from autonomous vehicles that are by nature worldwide due to practices and technology that have most likely spread across the globe. International agencies act as catalysts in bringing together various regional entities to align and assimilate their respective standards, rules, and regulations. This universal laying down of norms and principles is the essential requirement of multinational corporations and leads to a scenario where all cybersecurity measures are equally robust, irrespective of geographical borders.

As we wrap it up, the regulation and standardization that lies back is the cybersecurity practice framework in autonomous mobility. Besides merely positioning the ideal standard for companies' functions, they also catalyze change and improvement by boosting cybersecurity. Both national and international collegiality contributions are relevant in keeping pace with the fast development of technologies. Introducing these measures are one way of minimizing risks, protecting the users, and ensuring that the security posture of the autonomous mobility system is strong. Ultimately, fostering a high level of trust and an increase in the adoption of the advanced systems will triumph. As technology advances, it triggers a perpetual transformation of the regulatory framework. It brings on new challenges to be reckoned with and guarantees that friendly and useful autonomous mobility is achieved.

The line chart (Figure 7.10) shows a comparison between different international cybersecurity regulations like ISO/SAE 21434, UNECE WP.29, and NISTSsP 800-53 on the different scales of cybersecurity factors such as risk management and data confidentiality for instance. Every bar shows the numbers that express compliance with the criteria levels or the role that each standard could play in improving cybersecurity in autonomous systems. This gives a picture on which tools are strong and which ones are not fully prepared to handle the issue.

As can be seen in the flow diagram in Figure 7.11, the cyclic process of cybersecurity standardization, from the proposal level to the approval, goes through implementation and review. It shows the scheme of the standardization process that draws attention to the stages of what is being reviewed, the different types of feedback, and revision.

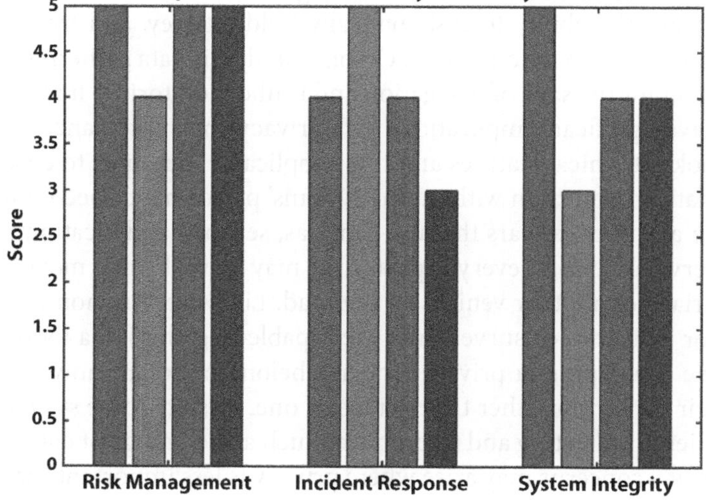

Figure 7.10 Comparison chart of different international cybersecurity standards for autonomous systems.

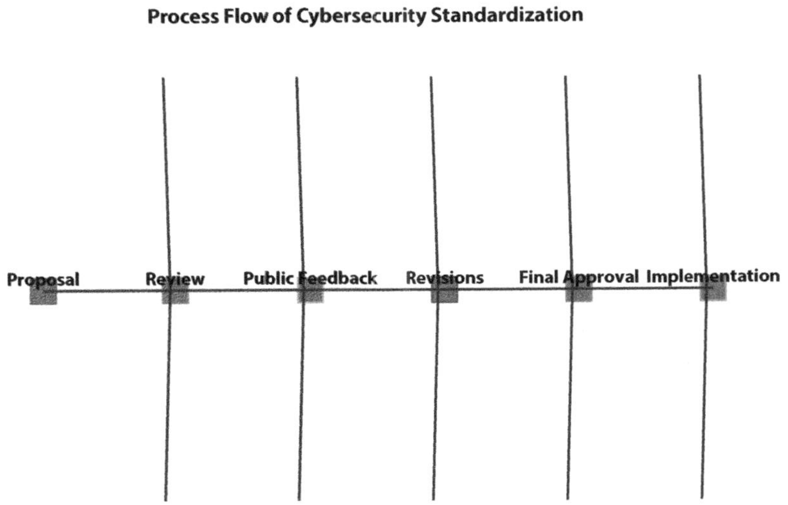

Figure 7.11 Process flow diagram detailing the standardization process for cybersecurity in autonomous mobility.

7.7 Ethical and Privacy Considerations

Autonomous systems have a tendency to be integrated into normal routine, and this may in turn result into certain ethical and privacy issues that mainly revolve around surveillance and data collection. An example of such systems would be the self-driving vehicles and unmanned aircraft which have the ability to systematically hold, convey, and transfer large amounts of data to function well. On one hand, this data gathering is vitally important for the sake of navigation and traffic monitoring. It might, however, have significant implications with privacy and surveillance. The third part looks at ethical features and finds applicable measures to ensure user information protection without the systems' performance becoming poor.

Such as driverless cars that use cameras, sensors, and location tracking to observe an area in every aspect, they may as well track movements of pedestrians or another vehicle on the road. Likewise, autonomous drones used for deliveries or surveillance are capable of gathering a lot of videos, and one can capture a private property belonging to an individual without their consent or other times video of one. Despite these systems' great capacities in collecting and interpreting such a wide range of data, individual privacy concerns may arise where privacy is less important than public safety and the two overlap one another.

The ethical dimensions of them are not simple, and the issues are patriated. We need to have moral obligation to use technology in a way that respects the individual privacy guidelines and the civil liberties. The prevalent data gathering of autonomics systems might apply as an intervention on these rights if to be tackled improperly. For instance, the problem could be data misuse involving system insecurity and intrusion from unauthorized personnel or the systems' controlling bodies. Say, data has the ability to track the person without their consent, to discriminate against some particular groups, or to influence behavior as it raises the problem of whether the person is free to give consent, to have autonomy, or to get manipulated.

Fixing these ethical challenges would likely require the deployment of extremely elaborate privacy protection mechanisms with the aim of finding a middle ground between the operational needs of autonomous systems and the privacy rights of individuals. One approach is data minimalization, where systems collect only the data that are derivatively required to provide the service. Therefore, for example, a driverless car can be made able to store and process information locally, instead of sending it to the server or a central place, thereby cutting down the data's quantity subjected to hacking or miscellaneous use. The other important technique of encryption provides a solid data protection for autonomous systems' collected data. Encryption will add a layer of protection to the data, not only when it is being transferred, but also when it is stored, making unauthorized individuals nothing but an obstacle on the path to this information, which even trying to intercept it they would have a hard time decrypting. Similarly, the system saves the privacy which is not only for the individuals but also for the information system. Beyond this, it should be highlighted that the imposition of anonymization practices are a significant step toward privacy limitation reduction. Data anonymization encompasses the conversion of identifiers into an untraceable form or the concealment of them from anyone. This is particularly suitable when working with great data sets received from automatic control sources where the specific identification of the individuals is not of much importance for the purpose already set. Another fundamental solution is using systematic access logs and audit spans. While individuals' access to data should be restricted to authorized only, and therefore, sophisticated auditing mechanisms for tracking who accesses what data and when should be in place to eliminate the possibility of unauthorized access or misuse, data security should be the top priority among policy areas.

Finally, transparency and accountability should be the key pillars of the ethical and privacy address. Data collection arenas should have clear guidance on the collected data, the reasons for which it is being used, and the protective mechanisms in place. Besides setting up the policies and procedures, users should have a defined way of expressing their concerns and the companies to respond to these concerns with the same policies. This transparency encourages a trust-building process between the users and the entities that provide these autonomous systems.

Eventually, making sure that autonomous systems advance with the provision of answers on ethical and privacy concerns is a must. The processes perfecting privacy protection—like data deletion, encryption, generalization, tough access system, and ensuring fairness and responsibility—are key challenges, which must be addressed in the quest of preserving user data and safeguarding the balance between rapid progress of technology on one hand and the basic human rights on the other. These endeavors are not just crucial in safeguarding people's lives, but also in creating an environment fertile for the acceptance and trust in these technologies, which in turn is paramount for advancing technology in our society.

Figure 7.12 is a risk matrix that shows the classification of the type of data, such as data collected by autonomous systems into privacy risk levels. The matrix of colors shows the gravity of risk radius for the given data type, and it can be used as an effective visual tool that will assess the privacy vulnerabilities in data handling by autonomy systems.

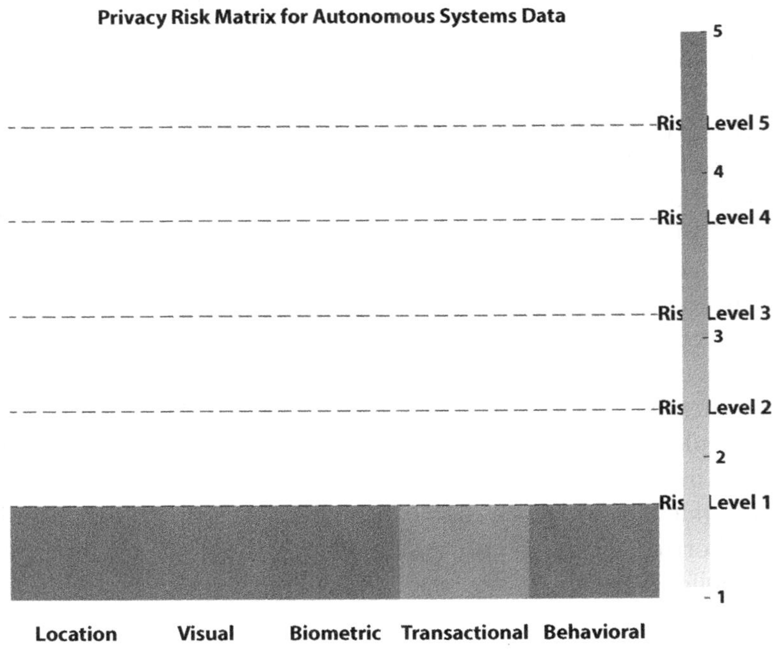

Figure 7.12 Privacy risk matrix for data collected by autonomous vehicles.

7.8 Case Studies of Secure Autonomous Mobility Implementations

Reviewing the successful cases of safe autonomous mobility applications strongly determines the optimal solutions within the cybersecurity discipline and identifies the lessons learnt from their stages. Through these case studies, both the practical benefits of safety technologies in autonomy systems and the ongoing challenges and how these troubles have chastened the current practices become evident. In this part, we will scrutinize several cases where these security autonomous mobility solutions were fully implemented. At the same time, we will closely examine the specific security measures used in these experiences and the broad lessons from these implementations.

Waymo's Autonomous Vehicles: Waymo, the undisputed front runner among autonomous vehicle technologies, has installed a whole array of security features to ensure the safety of their fleet of self-driving cars. The most important thing about Waymo's approach to security is the encryption protocols it has developed, which not only secure vehicle-to-vehicle and vehicle-to-infrastructure communications but also protect the whole system. Waymo uses a highly sophisticated cryptographic approach in order to ensure that any datum transmitted either between the vehicle and control centers is encrypted and authenticated, hence minimizing the risk of eavesdropping and any fraud.

Further, Waymo uses robust multi-layer security with IDS and data privacy measures, hence securing real-time data. IDS will keep monitoring the system in case of any sort of unusual activities that could indicate a cybersecurity threat, such as any attempt to get past the system fire walls. This procedure is supported by a strict policy of access controls that can prevent access of sensitive data to unauthorized personnel only, for assuring confidentiality of not just personal but also operational data.

From Waymo's experience, the lesson is clear: employing a multilayered security architecture, where a number of security measures provide coverage for various potential attack paths, leads to an increased resistance of autonomous systems to cyber threats. In this instance, too, the fact that the security measures should be constantly refined and be able to keep pace with the burgeoning threat of cyberattacks comes into play.

Tesla's Autopilot System: The second case of secure autonomous mobility is the Tesla's Autopilot System, which is more widely known and famous among consumers of electric vehicles. Through an iterative approach, Tesla conducts systemic security evaluation and modernization to identify and eliminate all security risks. OTA updates are an element of Tesla's security strategy used to make the car software always up to date. With the potential of upgrade, security patches, and feature updates to their vehicles as and when the vulnerabilities are spotted, Tesla makes swift deployment of these when needed. Therefore, when remaining reactive to cybersecurity risks, it is vital to adopt a proactive approach that is essential in keeping the security of vehicles during their operational life.

Apart from software-based security protocols, Tesla adopts hardware-based security measures as strong as a secure enclave within the electronic control unit (ECU). This secure hub minimizes the occurrence of a cryptographic key and other sensitive data theft by acting as the physical barrier isolating the remaining network systems away from such critical resources. This physical security layer will help the prevention of many different cyberattacks which try to pass the software protection systems with great skill.

By Tesla's way of thinking, we learn that there is always a need for preventative security measures apart from quick action. Prompt response capacity toward identifying loopholes and implementing countermeasures is a key component that adaptable defense strategies against the constantly changing cybersecurity risks are hinged on. The case of the Tesla is apparent that it becomes effective when the software and hardware security measures are combined to create a strong defense mechanism against multi-touch point cyberattacks.

Siemens' Unmanned Train Systems: Siemens was one of the innovators in the area of the public unmanned train transport's security, mostly in the European net. The trains which are running themselves use only secure communication channels and signaling systems which are fully encrypted. Siemens' security doctrine includes not only the safety of data traffic but also the soundness of signaling and dispositioning systems which are responsible for the trains' run.

Siemens builds not only in the extra redundancy and fail-safe measures but also inside the train system itself. They help to avoid the problem of the system going down even when there is a security breach, and these conditions can assure safe operation or that the system can be safely shut down. This is because the slightest problem in the production process may throw workers to the risk of facing major problems and hazards. When Siemens introduced the artificial intelligence-based technology of unmanned trains, a number of functions with redundant failure-proof mechanisms were integrated in the design of the autonomous systems. This is specially to show that security issues must be hard-coded into the system design to be later on added, and not vice versa.

Lastly, the complex autonomous solutions from Waymo, Tesla, and Siemens were used as case studies to extract necessary lessons for their implementation. It implies that the result is of layered security mechanisms, the need for speedy update abilities, and the necessity of embedding security into the system design process. The experience of these practices has led to the adoption of current ways of cybersecurity in autonomous vehicles. These approaches are proactive rather than reactive, comprehensive rather than piecemeal, and integrated rather than isolated in ensuring that neither the system nor its users are vulnerable.

Figure 7.13 demonstrates the number of cybersecurity breaches before and after the implementation of tight security measures. The timeline depicts how the mechanisms have impacted the occurrences of attacks by presenting how the different security solutions are modifying the state of the system, thus enhancing its security posture.

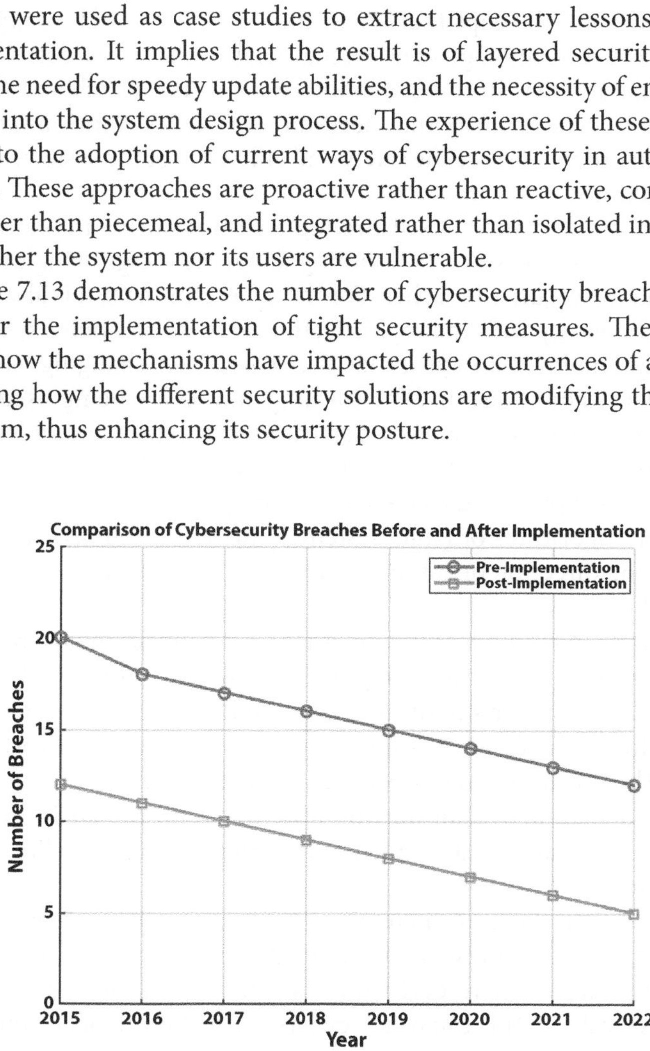

Figure 7.13 Line graph comparing pre- and post-implementation performance metrics concerning cybersecurity breaches.

7.9 Future Directions and Research Opportunities

As self-responsibility in activity traffic carries on developing, the dangers in cybersecurity follow suit. This dynamic waveform is the disease's main problem, as it can both complicate the scientific investigation process and give rise to other possibilities. Research into new technologies' security implications and the gaps that are in the existing research is expected to produce secure technologies and strengthen these systems' defense against novel vulnerabilities. In this section, we resume the search and investigation areas in cybersecurity that need more fresh and innovating ideas of research in order to assure the safety and efficiency of the systems of autonomous mobility.

The quick acceptance of self-driving tech transforms into a myriad of potential new dangers. A new looming danger is the growing complexity of information security breaches. For the cybercriminals, it is always a new level of complexity with the sophistication of these computer systems; the techniques employed in cyberattacks also keep on changing, sometimes rapidly. For example, as machine learning and AI are being used more in autonomous operations, adversarial AI attacks, where fraudulent inputs are in a process to fool machine learning models, can become a huge threat. One of the most profound challenges posed by cyberattacks is the ability to manipulate algorithms or faulty systems, which in turn may interpret data in the wrong direction or can make unsafe, hazardous decisions causing a catastrophe.

One more emerging terrific threat is the expanded linkage required in an autonomous system. Receiving the information via networks is a critical function for futuristic drones, cars, and other devices embedded in artificial intelligence, yet it is an entry point for many network-focused attacks. These can include DoS attacks that can prevent communication and an end-state of system making it defunct and a man-in-the-middle attack wherein data is intercepted and changed while travelling through the network.

Consequently, the implementation of self-governing systems into more significant infrastructures like the integrated ones can result in the suggestion of larger scale cybersecurity threats that can present extensive disruptions. A typical example can be the cybersecurity breach of an autonomous logistics network, which can bring about logistic delays, or an attack on the infrastructure of public transport systems, which can result in a serious threat to public safety and chaos in major urban areas.

Facing these challenges, the main focus of such research should be on multiple standing points of cybersecurity. One example of such is quite sophisticated and high-security cryptographic solutions that can be seamlessly embedded in the fast-paced and secure operational environments of autonomous systems in real time. The existing cryptographic methods, although effective against various attacks, can usually have a detrimental effect on system performance in terms of speed, limiting their use in applications where there is a need for real-time data and support rapid decision making. Investigation of lightweight cryptographic protocols can be an alternative means, improvising on security performance and with neural impact on the system.

Another area of research having the potential to cause gaps is in reliable AI and machine learning models that are necessary for autonomous systems to operate. This should include vulnerability mitigation techniques like developing products that can resist adversarial attacks, thus maintaining data integrity as well as private machine processes. Research is necessary to design AI systems that enable an auditing functionality so that decisions are not only made by machines but also the operators can monitor and understand them in order to raise the level of trust, safety, and security.

Apart from this, a continued development of more sophisticated intrusion detection systems that can robustly adapt to the highly dynamic surroundings of autonomous systems is indispensable. Those are defining mechanisms that are designed to detect and react promptly and uniformly even to new types of attacks and weird behaviors, which requires continuous education and updates. Maybe what are optimizing for research are those AI-based anticipation models that can detect potential threats before they come alive.

To sum up, while autonomous systems are being tightly connected to vital facilities, the threat of cyberattacks is real, and it is important for the researchers to study it from the security point of view in a systematic way. These frameworks must develop security concepts that span the entire life of the self-driving system, i.e., design, operation, decommissioning, etc. Besides, the creation of practices and standards for cybersecurity in this context can well contribute to a unified approach with the aim of securing such systems across different fields and regions. The future of cybersecurity based on self-driving systems will be to foresee upcoming threats and fill the holes in the current research on the topic. Through the concentration on aspects like nailing down lightweight cryptographic fixes, ensuring AI and machine learning, advancing intrusion detection technologies, and ultimately designing systemic security frameworks, scientists can assist the creation of the more secure and reliable, autonomous systems. These initiatives not only are aimed at overcoming the particular cybersecurity challenges of autonomous transportation but also stand for the advance of cybersecurity discipline as a whole, through the introduction of new-generation solutions to cybersecurity tackling current and imminent threats. The existing partnership between the academia, industry, and government will be imperative to bring the foreseeable progress to fruition as we go ahead with these grounds of secure autonomous technologies development.

Figure 7.14 should go straight to the point that the cyber threats will be going up against autonomous systems in the future compared to the current security status. Each point corresponds to a critical year that highlights the growing risks and severity of cybersecurity issues. It allows us to show how the risk grows and how serious cybersecurity is.

The chart of a radar in Figure 7.15 consists of levels of diversity of research areas in the cybersecurity of autonomy. Each coordinate corresponds to a different sector—one can be AI security and the other is data privacy; the values following a particular pattern mean niche areas. These niche areas are helpful in identifying high-priority sectors for further research and development.

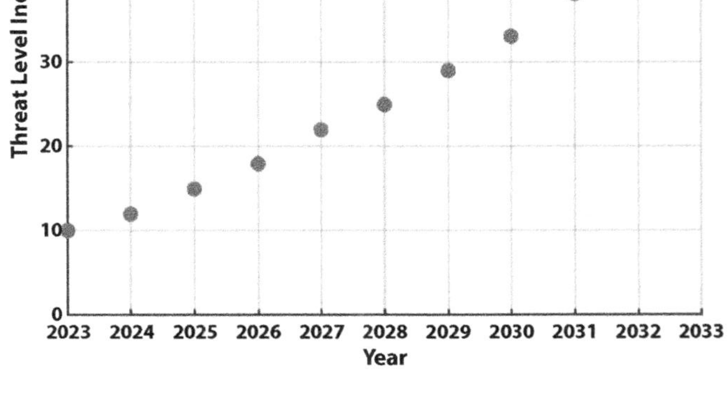

Figure 7.14 Scatter plot predicting the evolution of cybersecurity threats against autonomous systems.

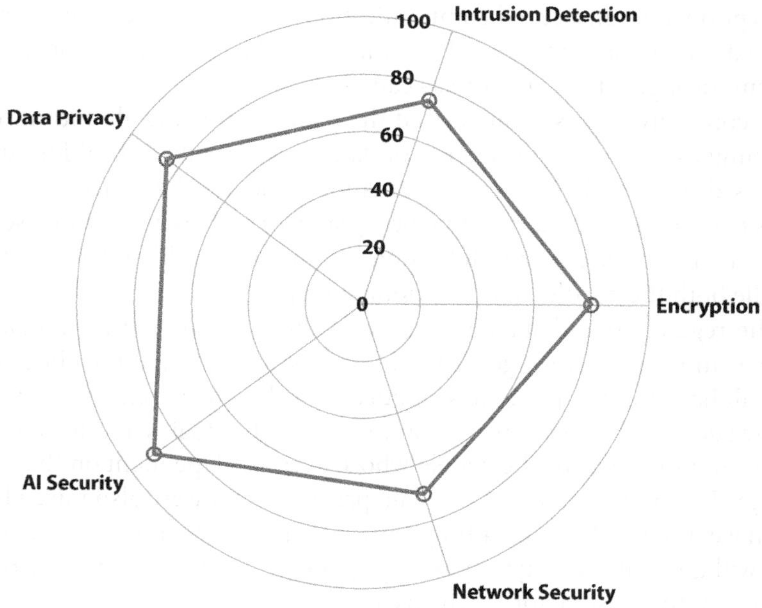

Figure 7.15 Radar chart highlighting key research areas in cybersecurity for autonomous mobility.

7.10 Conclusion

Autonomous mobility systems (AMS) are a newer innovation focusing on both daily operations and workload reduction while considering that cybersecurity is somehow the most vulnerable part of AMS. Autonomous cars, drones, and unmanned rail systems are the undeniable evidence that innovation has taken roots in transport and logistics and the name of traditional means of transport will never be the same again. However, with the risk of a large amount of data being used and interconnectivity being exposed, these systems are most vulnerable to attacks. Undoubtedly, a particular system's security must be accounted for from the technical point of view, considering that the activity and the service must be trusted by the users' community as well as the general public. Therefore, it is not just a technical requirement but rather a critical condition that must be maintained.

This dialogue steered us so that we would refer to the main parts only. We first brought a picture showing that the complexities of autonomous mobility and the major increase in use parallel the heightening of such incidents. These shortcomings include software vulnerabilities, poor encryption, and unsecured communication channels, which are the roots of the discussed security risks. Thus, they should have a competent security system through which any threats can be thwarted.

Accordingly, we also emphasized the issue of ensuring algorithm route planning as well as the protection of data operationally critical for autonomous driving and real-time information, among others. The organizations have to implement the same best practices such as encryption, secure transmission protocols, and intrusion systems and build systems that can handle both the hurdles and functioning issues.

The regulation and standards are also the domain of these regulators such as industry players, government bodies, and international bodies, as they all have roles to play. These regulatory rules are extremely significant in the successful development of autonomy technologies and for creating a safe circumstance for the people whose lives are dependent on that technology. Furthermore, moral and data privacy issues were also raised by us when we discussed them. Battling with such issues by arranging provisions that will guarantee anonymity is an imperative activity for the sake of the impact on the trust factor for the users.

The high determining factor of the case studies of the secure autonomous mobility interventions is that they have a real-life and practical effect to develop this area by sharing what is needed and what has been done and learnt already. With regard to our prioritized agenda, we first emphasized the strategic objectives for immediate harm reduction on cybersecurity. We also highlighted the fields that need deep research and improvements.

The only way to come up with sustainable solutions to the world's water resource management is through a cooperative effort that addresses the problems and makes use of the different opportunities. Union of the companies, research institutes, and the governmental organizations who have to be the main force to enhance the cybersecurity level of the autonomous systems is the purpose of this decision. Having the ability to keep industry experts will always be looking for breaking through vulnerabilities; hence, the demand for proactive research and development is a necessity. Education discipline should produce assessments in vital areas such as AI security, intrusion detections, and cryptography tools using scientific and innovative methods in order to solve AI-related problems. Regulators act as the main figures in this game that will make certain that relevant and up-to-date requirements are existent and obeyed. A balance between innovation and security will be realized in this scenario.

Moreover, major collaboration with all of the partners globally is least expected, so these problems related to cybersecurity tied with autonomous mobility are international and global as well. Research results, information, and best practices can be shared and communicated irrespective of geographical boundaries on a global scale, which can help uphold the standard of global security overall. The problems at hand could be understood better, and work could be done in this regard by combining efforts. When this is achieved, it makes sure that the benefits of autonomous mobility are reaped in a safe and secure way, creating a future society which is positively influenced by the technologies. This concerted effort (between involved authorities and parties) is not only required but plays the main role in the implementation of successful autonomous driving, where the technology and traffic merge together in one interaction.

References

1. Scalas, M. and Giacinto, G., Automotive Cybersecurity: Foundations for Next-Generation Vehicles. *2019 2nd International Conference on New Trends in Computing Sciences (ICTCS)*, Amman, Jordan, pp. 1–6, 2019, doi: 10.1109/ICTCS.2019.8923077.
2. McDowell, K., Nunez, P., Hutchins, S., Metcalfe, J.S., Secure Mobility and the Autonomous Driver. *IEEE Trans. Rob.*, 24, 3, 688–697, June 2008, doi: 10.1109/TRO.2008.924261.
3. Bello, Road context classifier and route mapping for Autonomous Vehicles. *2022 International Symposium on Electromobility (ISEM)*, Puebla, Mexico, pp. 1–6, 2022, doi: 10.1109/ISEM55847.2022.9976522.
4. Mahrez, Z., Sabir, E., Badidi, E., Saad, W., Sadik, M., Smart Urban Mobility: When Mobility Systems Meet Smart Data. *IEEE Trans. Intell. Transp. Syst.*, 23, 7, 6222–6239, July 2022, doi: 10.1109/TITS.2021.3084907.
5. Mali, U.S., Mallikarjun, S., D, S., Kawale, S.R., Cloud-Based Multi-Layer Security Framework for Protecting E-Health Records. *2023 International Conference on Artificial Intelligence for Innovations in Healthcare Industries (ICAIIHI)*, Raipur, India, pp. 1–7, 2023, doi: 10.1109/ICAIIHI57871.2023.10489781.
6. Mahindrakar, R.P. and Chandel, S., Advanced IoT-Enabled Warehouse Air Quality Monitoring and Live Security System for Medical Applications. *2023 International Conference on Artificial Intelligence for Innovations in Healthcare Industries (ICAIIHI)*, Raipur, India, pp. 1–6, 2023, doi: 10.1109/ICAIIHI57871.2023.10489747.
7. Kadam, K.R., Manivasagam, G., Prasad, K.D.V., Novel approaches to biometric security using enhanced session keys and elliptic curve cryptography. *J. Discrete Math. Sci. Cryptogr.*, 27, 2-A, 477–488, 2024.

8. Sarma, P., Arora, D., Suneetha, S., Patil, S.R., Advancements in Multi-Cloud Applications for Enhanced E-Healthcare Services. *2023 International Conference on Artificial Intelligence for Innovations in Healthcare Industries (ICAIIHI)*, Raipur, India, pp. 1–7, 2023.
9. Senthil Kumar, R. and Prasad, K.D.V., Securing digital authentication with cryptographic innovations in intrinsic verification systems. *J. Discrete Math. Sci. Cryptogr.*, 27, 2-A, 317–328, 2024.
10. Petrillo, and Santini, S., Editorial Special Section on Coordination, Cooperation, and Control of Autonomous Vehicles in Smart Connected Road Environments. *IEEE Open J. Intell. Transp. Syst.*, 5, 202–204, 2024, doi: 10.1109/OJITS.2024.3377216.
11. T. and Prasad, K.D.V., Cryptographic image-based data security strategies in wireless sensor networks. *J. Discrete Math. Sci. Cryptogr.*, 27, 2-A, 293–304, 2024.
12. Sarma, P. and Rahman, M., Mathematical analysis of wavelet-based multi-image compression in medical diagnostics. *J. Discrete Math. Sci. Cryptogr.*, 27, 2-B, 675–687, 2024.
13. Bagloee, S.A., Tavana, M., Asadi, M., *et al.*, Autonomous vehicles: challenges, opportunities, and future implications for transportation policies. *J. Mod. Transp.*, 24, 284–303, 2016.
14. Coutinho, B. and Ali Mirza, R., Autonomous Mobility Vehicle. *2020 IEEE International IOT, Electronics and Mechatronics Conference (IEMTRONICS)*, Vancouver, BC, Canada, pp. 1–7, 2020, doi: 10.1109/IEMTRONICS51293.2020.9216400.
15. Gangadharan, S. and N, S.C., Scalable and Reliable Cloud-Based UV Monitoring for Public Health Applications. *2023 4th IEEE Global Conference for Advancement in Technology (GCAT)*, Bangalore, India, pp. 1–8, 2023, doi: 10.1109/GCAT59970.2023.10353349.
16. Barua, T. and Mohiuddin, K., Dynamic Disaster Management with Real-Time IoT Data Analysis and Response. *2024 International Conference on Automation and Computation (AUTOCOM)*, Dehradun, India, pp. 142–147, 2024, doi: 10.1109/AUTOCOM60220.2024.10486101.
17. Shruthi, M. and Naveen K, B., Internet of Things: A Survey on Devices, Ecosystem, Components and Communication Protocols, *2020 4th International Conference on Electronics, Communication and Aerospace Technology (ICECA)*, pp. 611–616, 2020, doi: 10.1109/ICECA49313.2020.9297458.
18. Tan, X. and Leon-Garcia, A., Autonomous Mobility and Energy Service Management in Future Smart Cities: An Overview. *2018 4th International Conference on Universal Village (UV)*, Boston, MA, USA, pp. 1–6, 2018, doi: 10.1109/UV.2018.8642141.
19. Kalpana, V. and Hariram, V., Artificial Intelligence based Health Monitoring System on IoTH platform. *2023 Second International Conference on Augmented Intelligence and Sustainable Systems (ICAISS)*, Trichy, India, pp. 1458–1463, 2023, doi: 10.1109/ICAISS58487.2023.10250460.

20. Premkumar, S., Hussain, N., Chinamuttevi, V.S., A novel RF-SMOTE model to enhance the definite apprehensions for IoT security attacks. *J. Discrete Math. Sci. Cryptogr.*, 26, 3, 861–873, 2023.
21. Sagir, F. and Ukkusuri, S.V., Mobility Impacts of Autonomous Vehicle Systems. *2018 21st International Conference on Intelligent Transportation Systems (ITSC)*, Maui, HI, USA, pp. 485–490, 2018, doi: 10.1109/ITSC.2018.8569933.
22. Shekhar, R. and Chaturvedi, A., Securing networked image transmission using public-key cryptography and identity authentication. *J. Discrete Math. Sci. Cryptogr.*, 26, 3, 779–791, 2023.
23. De, T., Tanguturi, R.C., Ashreetha, B., A Novel method of Improving Spectrum sensing Management system for CR-IoT Networks. *2023 4th International Conference for Emerging Technology (INCET)*, Belgaum, India, pp. 1–6, 2023, doi: 10.1109/INCET57972.2023.10170314.
24. Shekhar, R. and Ashreetha, B., Performance Analysis of Energy Efficiency and Security Solutions of Internet of Things Protocols. *IJEER*, 11, 2, 442–450, 2023, DOI: 10.37391/IJEER.110226.
25. Begum, A.Y., A Novel IoT Framework and Device Architecture for Efficient Smart city Implementation. *2023 7th International Conference on Trends in Electronics and Informatics (ICOEI)*, Tirunelveli, India, pp. 420–426, 2023, doi: 10.1109/ICOEI56765.2023.10125677.
26. Sharma, A., S, K., Arun, M.R., Priority Queueing Model-Based IoT Middleware for Load Balancing. *2022 6th International Conference on Intelligent Computing and Control Systems (ICICCS)*, pp. 425–430, 2022, doi: 10.1109/ICICCS53718.2022.9788218.
27. Kumaraswamy, S., Sarma, P., Hussain, N., Dixit, S.K., Gupta, A.K., A novel approach of unsupervised feature selection using iterative shrinking and expansion algorithm. *J. Interdiscip. Math.*, 26, 3, 519–530, 2023.
28. Reddy, A.M. and Tanguturi, R., Improved Secure Communication Mechanism for IoT Platform Devices. *2022 International Conference on Smart Generation Computing, Communication and Networking (SMART GENCON)*, Bangalore, India, pp. 1–6, 2022, doi: 10.1109/SMARTGENCON56628.2022.10083714.
29. Ramesh Naidu, P. and Guruprasad, N., A High-Availability and Integrity Layer for Cloud Storage, Cloud Computing Security: From Single to Multi-Clouds. *J. Phys. Conf. Ser.*, 1921, 1, 012072, 2021.
30. Ramesh Naidu, P. and Guruprasad, N., Design and implementation of crypt-cloud system for securing files in cloud. *Adv. Math. Sci. J.*, 9, 7, 4485–4493, 2020, doi: 10.37418/amsj.9.7.17.
31. Shashidhara, K.S. and Gangadhara, Signal Analysis and Filtering using one Dimensional Hilbert Transform. *J. Phys. Conf. Ser.*, 1706, 1, 1–7, 2020.
32. Shivashankar, and Mehta, S., MANET topology for disaster management using wireless sensor network, in: *International Conference on Communication and Signal Processing, ICCSP 2016*, pp. 0736–0740, 2016, doi: 10.1109/ICCSP.2016.7754242.

33. Reddy, N.S. and Ashreetha, B., Technologies for Comprehensive Information Security in the IoT. *2023 International Conference for Advancement in Technology (ICONAT)*, Goa, India, pp. 1–5, 2023, doi: 10.1109/ICONAT57137.2023.10080332.
34. Reddy P, S. and Patwal, P.S., Data Analytics and Cloud-Based Platform for Internet of Things Applications in Smart Cities. *2022 International Conference on Industry 4.0 Technology (I4Tech)*, pp. 1–6, 2022, doi: 10.1109/I4Tech55392.2022.9952780.
35. Pavankumar, P. and Darwante, N.K., Performance Monitoring and Dynamic Scaling Algorithm for Queue Based Internet of Things. *2022 International Conference on Innovative Computing, Intelligent Communication and Smart Electrical Systems (ICSES)*, pp. 1–7, 2022, doi: 10.1109/ICSES55317.2022.9914108.
36. Singla, A. and Sharma, N., IoT Group Key Management using Incremental Gaussian Mixture Model. *2022 3rd International Conference on Electronics and Sustainable Communication Systems (ICESC)*, pp. 469–474, 2022, doi: 10.1109/ICESC54411.2022.9885644.
37. Alonso-Mora, J., Wallar, A., Rus, D., Predictive routing for autonomous mobility-on-demand systems with ride-sharing. *2017 IEEE/RSJ International Conference on Intelligent Robots and Systems (IROS)*, Vancouver, BC, Canada, pp. 3583–3590, 2017, doi: 10.1109/IROS.2017.8206203.
38. Kominami, D., Iwai, T., Shimonishi, H., Murata, M., A control method for autonomous mobility management systems toward 5G mobile networks. *2017 IEEE International Conference on Communications Workshops (ICC Workshops)*, Paris, France, pp. 498–503, 2017, doi: 10.1109/ICCW.2017.7962707.

8

Green Routes Building the Backbone for Electric Vehicle Charging

Dankan Gowda V.[1]*, Sadashiva V. Chakrasali[2], Ved Srinivas[3], K.D.V. Prasad[4] and Saptarshi Mukherjee[5]

[1]*Department of Electronics and Communication Engineering, BMS Institute of Technology and Management, Bangalore, Karnataka, India*
[2]*Department of Electronics and Communication, M S Ramaiah Institute of Technology, MSR Nagar, Bengaluru, India*
[3]*Department of Human Resources, Thiagarajar School of Management, Madurai, Tamil Nadu, India*
[4]*Symbiosis Institute of Business Management, Hyderabad and Symbiosis International (Deemed University), Pune, India*
[5]*Department of M.Tech Biotechnology, Sikkim Skill University, Namthang, Sikkim, India*

Abstract
This chapter delves into an intricate aspect of infrastructure development viz., the influence of EVs that keeps accelerating. The ensuing impending switch towards electric vehicles will greatly make charging services very demanding. This section tackles the present developing infrastructure of EV charging, spotting new innovative technologies to meet the rising needs of EV users while sustainably protecting the environment. The talk then carries on to the design of sustainable charging networks and their merger with renewable energy sources, which supports the notion that eco-friendly initiatives are the key to it. On top of this, it is assessing the economic impacts and business models of setting up and managing EV charging stations as well as their susceptibility to policies and public opinion which could further grow the charging infrastructure. By means of a combination of technical analysis, real case studies, and visionary views, this chapter proposes the strategies and teamwork that are required for building a green backbone for electric vehicle charging—a key component of the agendas for sustainable urban transportation.

**Corresponding author*: dankan.v@bmsit.in

Rathishchandra R. Gatti and Chandra Singh (eds.) Digital Convergence in Intelligent Mobility Systems, (159–192) © 2025 Scrivener Publishing LLC

Keywords: Electric vehicles (EVs), EV charging infrastructure, renewable energy integration, sustainable transportation, smart charging technologies, urban mobility, public–private partnerships, environmental impact

8.1 Introduction

Transportation ecology is experiencing a revolutionary change with growing popularity of electric cars. These changes are a result of several intertwining catalysts comprising of technological progress, environmental consciousness, the zeitgeist of society and to some extent extensive government support internationally. The global EV market the journey of exponential growth was remarkable indeed, being a blaze in about 10 years ago from a few thousands of units to few millions sold annually today [1]. This fast Alfa is likely to go on with the figures showing that vehicles those a third of sale of new cars by 2030.

The rapid increase in EV users is carrying multiple factors among which several play crucial role. Technological improvements have led to increased battery efficiency and a corresponding rise in driving range, making EVs a more viable option for everyday use [2]. Further, more and more detailed models in production had resulted in customers able to find models tailored exactly to their requirements [3]. Moreover, people are becoming more aware of the environmental impact of fossil fuels, so this is sparking the interest in cleaner substitutes which in turn is placing EV carrying the energy transportation future of our world on the menu.

Meanwhile, the main problem that we are confronted with is the increase in the demand for a grid system that can be used to charge the electric vehicles [4]. The fact that it is hard to underestimate the role that the creation of a powerful EV charging infrastructure plays clearly proves one's point [5]. If proper charging facilities are not built, EV market might not grow, as the existing and potential buyers might be afraid of the inconvenience of charging their vehicles by lacking of proper charging facilities [6]. Accordingly, setting up the smart grid to be user-friendly, fast-charging, and fully accessible charging stations are the keys to the increasing attractiveness of EVs in the eyes of the consumers.

At the moment, EV's charging infrastructure is not evenly automated, having many places for charging in urban areas–and none in rural places. It is this unevenness that is perhaps the most significant obstacle to EV adoption in towns with fewer people. Besides the strategy should be right so that EV infrastructure is distributed more thoughtfully [7]. The governments and the private sector businesses are having a growing recognition of the importance of charge station set up which should be both substantial and allow to serve the constantly growing demand for electric vehicles [8]. This means not only installing a larger number of the aforementioned outlets, but also considering the proper connection of the electrical grid, and using renewable energy sources to reinforce the environmental objectives.

For the same purpose, the environmental impacts connected with electric vehicles stands as an important topic when the discussions are being run around the topic of their adoption. EV models are a very visible means of reducing the GHG emission across the transportation sector, especially when charged from utility-scale renewable energy sources [9]. EVs help to drop the number of air pollution particles which are smog and low air quality producing agents in dense populated areas. In contrast with this, there are some greenhouse gas emissions contributing to the production of EVs, particularly during the battery mineral extraction stage [10]. Therefore, the EVs although place us on the sustainable way, still are not free form such a comprehensive environmental impact as the production and end-of-life stages need constant improvement to minimize environmental impact completely and give EVs a real chance of strengthening their sustainability all through the span of their life.

Last but not the least, buildup of the overall infrastructure for electric cars is now on a fast track, but the key to its completion lies in integration of the sustainable and systemic approach. This chapter would include the discussion of multiple aspects of the EV ecosystem, the main ones being technological innovations [11], business and economic models, integration with renewable energy, and the legislative framework applicable to the electric vehicles which help to cut down considerably on the transport business sector' environment impact. Under this infrastructure, it is not only addressing the current requirement with a mindset to forecasts developments in their technology [12], but also of the EV technology, which makes it one of the important elements in the path to sustainable urban mobility.

In Figure 8.1, the graph is composed of line graph representing dramatic increase of EV Sales on the global market since 2010 till 2020 with exponential rise. Sales we reported every year undergone rapid increase with EV generalization phenomenon. Figure 8.1 shows notable years when sales surges were observed, which is an evidence of the effect of factors, among which are technological advances, consumer awareness and government policies [13], all of which are in support of renewables. By means of this visualization the issues of speed-up of the sales of electric vehicles and an infrastructure are clearly seen understood by the stakeholders.

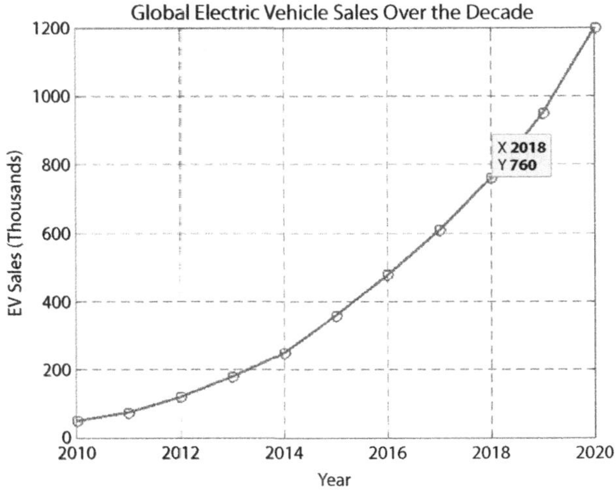

Figure 8.1 Growth trend of electric vehicles globally over the past decade.

Figure 8.2 shows a bar chart presenting the prediction of the fast-growing necessity for EV charging units related to the increment in the sales of EVs. It will display data from the year 2020 to the year 2030 showing projections that there should be a huge rise in stations that will charge electric vehicles as they rise in numbers [14]. The figure points to a medium-term

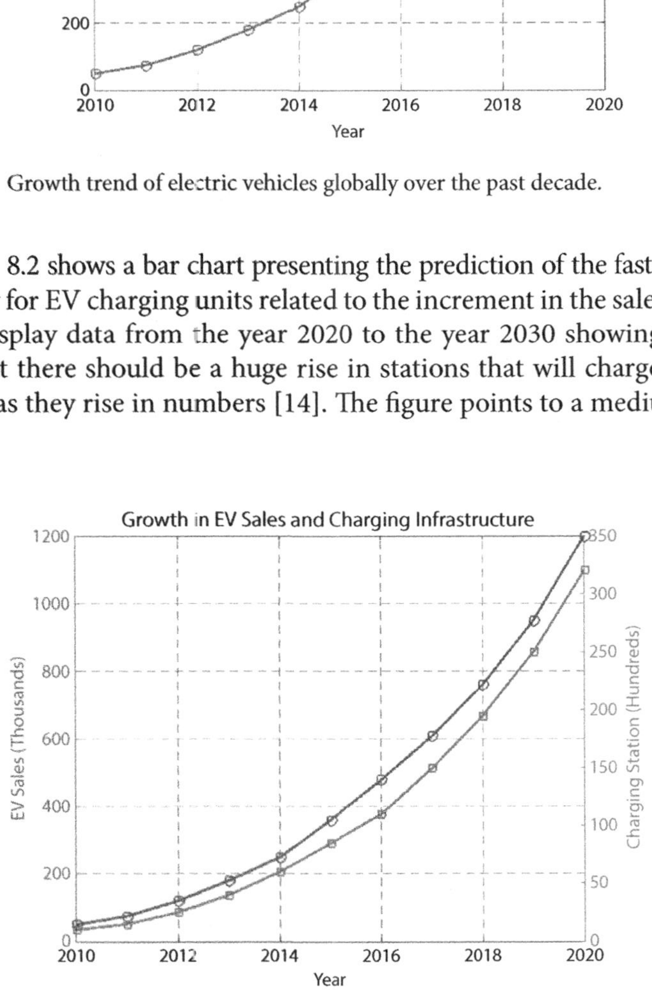

Figure 8.2 Projected increase in demand for EV charging infrastructure aligned with EV sales.

positive relationship existing between vehicle sales and the development needs of infrastructure, which confirms strategic planning and wise investing towards network charging enhancements.

8.2 Current State of EV Charging Infrastructure

The present condition of electric vehicle (EV) charging infrastructure across the globe has the picture of a landscape of different development and distribution which is an outcome of various scientific, economic and policy level factors. With electric vehicle (EV) demand growing at an ever-increasing rate, largely due to ongoing focus on increasing environmental consciousness and the government's commitment to establishing supportive policies [15], the establishment of charging points has taken center stage as one of the most important focal points for any country which is intent on facilitating the transition to electric mobility.

Generally, the EV charging technologies can be split into different categories based on their speed, price, and availability on a worldwide scale [16]. Level 1 charging is typically conducted by the use of a standard household outlet and is quite a slow form of charging. Level 2 charging requires the supply of a higher voltage system and thus a more rapid charging time while DC Fast charging system (DCFC) is an alternative very fast but relatively more expensive way of charging [17]. In terms of the charging technology users, a number of needs, purpose and strategy of national and local governments may come up [18]. Those may include air pollution reduction in urban areas and long distance travelling in places where the distance is large.

In urban arenas a high density of the infrastructure for EV charging versus the one with more diversity in terms of applied technology is typical [19]. In towns, first level and rapid chargers are often preferable for high use purposes in cities and they are also used for shopping places, business commercial areas, industry and office buildings [20]. Not only that but most cities consider EV charging solutions as part of a bigger strategy to electrify AC systems with charging stations located at bus depots and taxi stands.

On the flip side, for example, in the case of rural communities, EV charging infrastructure for electric vehicles have their own problems. Conversely, the smaller population size and the long distances travelled between different destinations discourage investors to start fast-charging points [21]. Therefore, often there are the less level 3 charging stations in the countryside and the existing one belongs to level 1 or level 2 standards.

The inequality among regions represents a serious hurdle in the widespread adoption of EVs in the countryside [22]. Customers can be reluctant to buy EVs if they are aware of the inconvenience and impracticability of charging their cars for a long time and the anxiety of not having a charging service while driving.

The obstacles in E-V charging infrastructure including, locations, technology, legal frameworks and physical resources, all vary significantly depending the geographical features and the economic condition, technology capabilities of regions. While in more developed countries problems are associated with electrification of the grid to withstand huge loads of chargers and integration of the clean energy resources [23]. There is also increasing demand for uniformity of charging systems for different motor models as well as charging networks to guarantee the systems are compatible which is of vital importance to allow for cross country traveling. The basic challenges of developing countries are more fundamental compared to their counterparts and they often include irregular infrastructure, inadequate capacity of energy distribution [24], and smaller amount of public and private investments in the upgrade of EV technology. These territories could rely on a great amount of international finance and funding for the infra-structural development and that will help in creating the workforce skilled with the installation and maintenance of that infrastructure [25]. However, a higher level of the policy framework could be asserted that can support the installation of EV charging equipment through benefits and regulatory mechanism.

In spite of challenges, prospective communities continue to make long stride towards progress. Several countries into recognizing strategic planning in infrastructure which future growth and current uptake considering [26]. Moreover perceived as the innovation in charging technologies, for example the battery swapping stations and the mobile-charging unit have been seen as solutions that fit into different conditions.

Summing up, the fact that the global roll-out of electric vehicle charging infrastructure has been unsteady undoubtedly shows some outstanding developments in the latter times [27]. Along with the progress of technology and consolidation of public authorities and companies which set the examples to the others, the EV charging infrastructure is headed for more development and improvements in the process [28]. This will enable the development of an infrastructure that would be equitable in terms of both urban and rural areas and regions that are developed and the ones that are yet to undergo the industrialization processes so as to enhance the smooth transition across the world towards sustainable transportation systems [29].

Figure 8.3 highlights an interactive world map, in which charging stations locations are shown with different colors according to their locations in various areas. The map shows high, medium, as well as low densities for the different regions accordingly, helping to compare which regions have more infrastructural development [30]. Such spatial distribution leads to

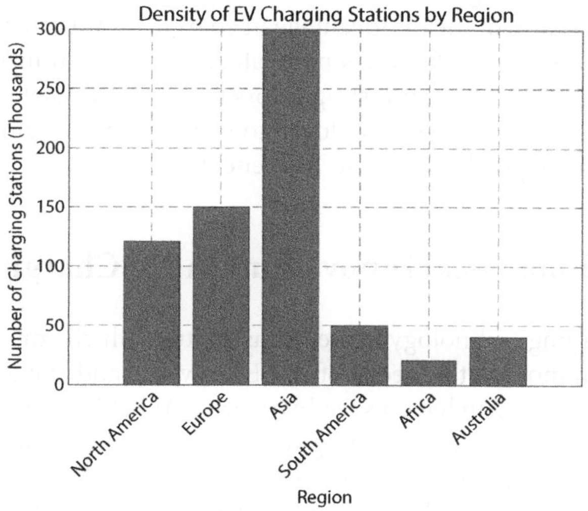

Figure 8.3 World map showing the density of EV charging stations by region.

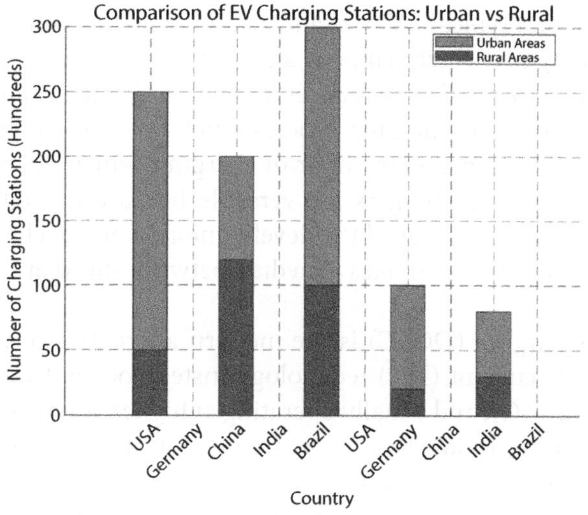

Figure 8.4 Comparison graph of urban vs. rural EV charging infrastructure availability.

the identification of the regions where EV infrastructure is more developed and where it progressed less. This information is key to policymakers and investors striving to resolve regional inequality and promote new investment prospects [31].

By means of the graph below that is figure four shows the comparison of the availability of electric vehicle (EV) charging infrastructure between local and rural settings in different countries (Figure 8.4). These numbers give a clear picture of the disadvantage in charging infrastructure between big cities and those in areas less populated. The graph utilizes two-color bars leads to paired but contrasting colors that truly stipulate specific policy measures that have to be employed to widen rural charging stations as well as amplify equitable access to EV benefits.

8.3 Technological Innovations in EV Charging

The EV charging technology is the infrastructure which constantly develops to accommodate the needs of the EV owners and the auto industry that is also expected to have a speedy progress. What is at the base of these innovations are numerous charging systems that have their unique characteristics which is defined by their specific functions [32]. The basic form, level 1 charging, takes place along standard household electrical outlets with a 120-volt AC plug, and the provided charging speed is the slowest. This overnight at home method is the best fit if you only need a slow one hour charging rate; it adds 4 to 5 miles of range per hour of charging. Hence it is practical for a typical EV user and a secondary charging method.

Level 2 charging, which happens after Level 1 charging, runs on 240-v AC, and it can be located in residences, public parking lots, and workplaces. This system makes the charging process much faster, with the distance of 12 to 80 miles recharged every hour of charging, which normally does in an overnight. Level 2 chargers are versatile because of higher charging speeds which have encouraged the development of public charging station infrastructure where one strikes a median between speed and energy conservation [33].

DC Fast Charging (DCFC) is the modern alternative to AC batteries, applying direct current (DC) technology instead of the traditional alternating current (AC), and usually operating at higher voltages of above 400 volts. Through this modality, EVs get tremendous filling power which can add 60–100 miles in as short a time as a 20-minute charge. With numerous DCFC stations along major highways as well as in places that need a rapid turnaround, such as fleet operations, the distance between charging stations becomes less of a concern for EV users, so they are able to travel long distances [34]. Although DC charging offers advantages, the fact that costly infrastructure accompanies it and the concern about grid and battery life are some essential matters which must be considered.

Besides those predominant modes of charging, the rapid evolution of charging technology is really the direction in which the EV infrastructure is heading nowadays. Inductive charging and wireless charging fall in a class of technologies that allow users to charge the EV without having a cable or a plug [35]. This system uses a wireless charging pad, which produces an inductive electric field to be transferred to a receiving unit on the vehicle through the air. Although at the moment wireless charging technology is just at the initial phase of the deployment, yet it can make the charging of EV easy by integrating with the public spaces such as streets and parking lots where instruments will be placed and whenever a vehicle parks beneath them, it is automatically charged.

Innovation in quick-charging tech is one of the key areas, which allows reaching the maximum of speed that EV batteries can be safely replenished. Innovations in battery chemistry and cooling technologies, giving the power to properly manage the amount of heat produced by fast charging cycles, are a must for this tech to work. These types of technologies aim to bring in line charging times with the time necessary to refill a standard internal combustion engine fuel tank, so as to address the major obstacle for EV adoption.

The smart grid technology is actually a new way of how we think about how EVs handle the energy grid. Smart charging stations can vary the charging speed in accordance with the grid load demand, cost of electricity, and status battery. This feature of the shifting load gives a relief to the grid in terms of demand and also enables EV owners to get advantage of the lower power rates during non-peak periods. Furthermore, smart charging in the coherence with renewable sources increases environmental favors of EVs. For instance, smart chargers can shift the timing of charging to coincide with the times when solar and wind energy are abundant which in turn will reduce the usage of fossil fuels, therefore, making the charging carbon footprints of EVs smaller in size. Integrating these technologies into the existing infrastructure is rather complicated because it involves the increased volume of hardware brands, software build-up, regulatory alterations, and market incentives. Similarly, V2G systems allow the electricity that is stored in EVs to be delivered to the grid at times of peak demand. This in turn can help to stabilize the grid and provide EV owners additional revenue streams. Besides enhanced charging facilities, legislation also needs to address the reciprocating technologies that help bidirectional energy flow.

On the one hand, the technology advances in EV charging are meant to improve the user's experience through their applications in faster more convenient charging options. On the other hand, the technology changes are aimed to integrate EVs into the energy systems which promote a sustainable and efficient ecosystem. The development of these technologies will have an increasing effect on transportation systems actors worldwide, and will greatly contribute to the drive to achieve a cleaner and more approachable future.

Figure 8.5 depicts a diagram that categorizes the different types of EV charging systems: Level (1), Level (2), and DC fast chargers. The name of each category is in a colored box, beside which is given specification data like voltage and usual charging time. The figure makes it possible to better understand the charging technologies and indeed serve as a learning tool for owners and other market players of EVs.

Figure 8.6 shows an EV smart charging system coupled with renewable power sources. It represents the associations between solar panel, smart grid, the charging station and EVs via the smart technology, which demonstrate how efficiently the energy flow is controlled. The shown diagram highlights the benefits of using renewable energy for clean charging as well as grid stability.

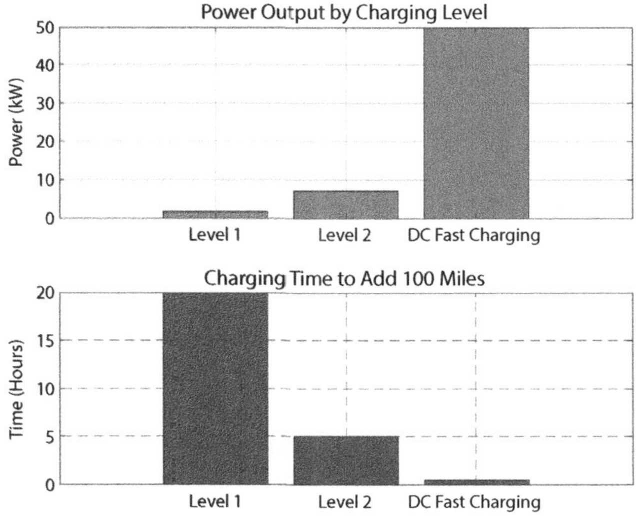

Figure 8.5 Diagram of different EV charging levels (Level 1, Level 2, DC Fast Charging) showing their power output and charging times.

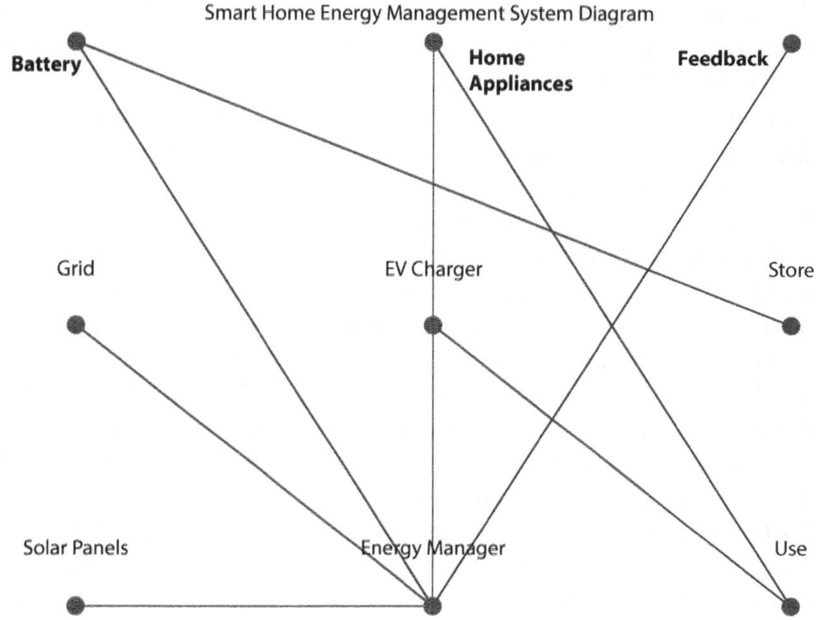

Figure 8.6 Conceptual diagram of a smart charging system integrated with a home energy management system.

8.4 Designing Sustainable Charging Networks

The infrastructure of the sustainable charging grids for electric vehicles (EVs) is one of the most important parts of the actual strategy to save the nature from the environmental challenges which come from the traffic. A sustainable charging networks' addresses not only immediate EVs needs about charging but is also designed with green principles in mind that aim at prolonged benefits such as lowering carbon footprint, improving power consumption efficiency, and increasing the use of clean energy. The following section defines the green infrastructure design peculiarities for EV technology and exemplifies their implementation in the form of some well-known examples. The role of government policy and incentives in the advancement of the green infrastructure for EV is also discussed.

The principles behind green infrastructure planning for EV charging networks include various initiatives that are meant to ensure durability of environment as well as efficiency of operations. The letter l and the topping of charging stations are the key factors in this aspect. Stations intended purposely to be in the right spots mean that an EV driver has to cover much less distance to charge and thus results in lower energy consumption and optimum convenience for the driver. Moreover, interweaving charging stations with already existing structures like car parks, commercial plots, and apartment blocks can maximize the efficiency of the current space allocation and reduce the need to create new facilities from scratch. Hence, in the long run, environmental pollution will be stopped hereby, the country will acquire old land, and people will have less bustle.

One of the concepts is to add of renewable energy sources into the charging platform. One area of efficiency improvement is clearly the solar power charging stations, which support the production of direct electricity through photovoltaic panels at the point of its use, which significantly decreases the demand of the conventional power sources and contributes to a reduction of greenhouse gas emissions. Moreover, eco-friendly design will incorporate energy storage systems that can keep the solar energy generated during peak sunlight hours and use it for vehicles charging when the skies are cloudy ensuring the steady and secure provision of energy.

Sustainable charging networks use of the innovative technical materials and technologies is also one of the factors improving their stability. For instance, letting recycled products replace non-recycled materials in construction at the same time as implementing technologies that have lower energy consumption and pollutant output can translate into great environmental benefits overall. Furthermore, the smart technologies including management systems can be used in the charging time distribution and power distribution through real-time data, and the grid demand. This, besides, improves the network performance and also proves to be quite helpful in that all loads are to be smoothened out to maintain the grid stability as the number of EVs increases.

Many states on the green design have managed to be successful, and this is due to the use of these green design principles. For example, a project which is being done in Norway within the area of hydroelectricity charges stations powered entirely by renewable and green power is an indicator of a perfect match of electric vehicle charging infrastructure and renewable energy resources. This project is going to help Norway to support its electric vehicles market which is an altogether big one and also it is in line with the country's commitments to sustainability, being that its hydroelectric resources are vast. Putting an example from California, which is the result of a blend of state subsidies and private financing leads to establishment of one of the most enormous and technically developed EV-charging networks in the US. This network comprises of features like solar energy stations powering chargers, energy storage systems, and smart meters which assist in avoiding the harmful impacts of EV.

In this regards, the role of government policies and incentives is to be the key to the introduction of sound architectures for EV charging infrastructure. Governments can use different ways to assist the growth of green charging networks and they may bring their services through the use of subsidies for the installation of charging stations, tax breaks for businesses which have the ability to incorporate renewable energy technologies and grants for investigations on advanced energy systems. Furthermore, regulations could require that sustainable principles be implemented in redevelopment projects whether they be new builds or renewal projects which can therefore hasten the spread of green infrastructure ideas.

Policies toward net-zero EVs charging is highly effective since many of them will only use renewable energy. For another thing, feed-in tariffs and net metering that may provide financial incentives for charging stations to generate renewable energy and direct it to the national grid by way of making such initiatives more cost effective for investors could be some of which. Government will require programs that properly outline the installation of EV charging through technical support for building codes and spatial planning to harmonize and simplify the process, hence more people will be willing to charge their vehicles.

Summarily, the designing of charging networks for electric vehicles calls for a nuanced and multi-dimensional approach that addresses green principles of designing, the integration of renewable energy, the adoption of sustainable materials and technologies, and the reinforcement of robust government policies and programs. Achieving the dissemination of such grids is crucial, not only for the supporting EV penetration but also for securing positive effects on environmental protection and rational energy use. Lessons learned from success cases can create a basis for action, and a systematic application of strategic policy tools may help building a sustainable charging infrastructure that is suitable for the transition from fossil fuel powered vehicles to another where the use of electricity is the norm on an international scale.

This line graph (Figure 8.7) is an example of a study done as a case study between a green designed EV charger and energy saving carried out. It plots a downward curve in a month-to-month comparison as carbon consumption decreases with the introduction of energy efficiency measures and increased use of the green energy sources. The figure clearly gives a data physical evidence on the advantage of green design to lessen operational expenses and environmental impact.

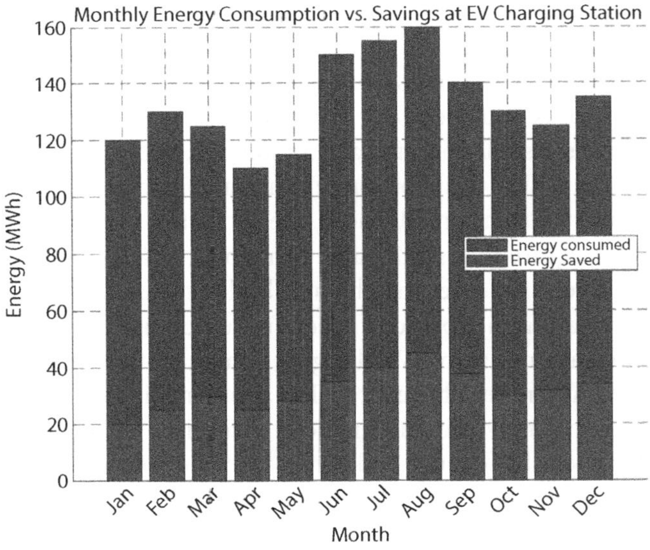

Figure 8.7 Case study results showing energy consumption and savings from a green-designed charging station.

8.5 Integration with Renewable Energy Sources

Renewable energy system integration into EV charging facilities is the top-most solution which will reduce transport sector carbon emissions and will subsequently be the building block of EV technology. The fusion of e-mobility with existing electricity grids not only facilitates the reduced pressure on conventional power networks but also leads to realization of the full benefits that is environmental advantage of electric mobility. Renewable-powered EV charging infrastructure is the subject of this section. Firstly, it helps to outline the different renewable energy sources that make this possible. Secondly, the benefits of renewable energy backed charging infrastructure are discussed. Lastly, it addresses challenges that exist and offers solutions.

One of the most frequently used renewable sources in the electric charging of EVs and with it all the energy savings that are coming from that is solar energy, which is available in big resources and whose decrease of costs reached even the development of solar panel technology. Connection to the grid may be necessary for the operation of one or two alternatives, but solar-powered charging stations can operate as standalone systems where the sunlight is converted directly to electricity on-site, or they can be grid-tied setups where solar power supplements traditional grid electricity. In a similar vein, both arrangements provide the same level of carbon emissions reduction and on the economic side, this is positively enhanced over time due to lower operational costs that are as a result of the solar energy harnessed.

Wind energy proves to be the best alternative as location is a key factor and wind streams are common in most places. Like in the case of solar, apart from the off-grid system of directly operating the charging stations, wind turbines are so efficient that they can also be fitted in the grid to contribute to the overall grid offset by the fossil fuel-generated electricity. Sometimes wind energy joins with solar energy; this hybrid renewable power system is one of the ways of multiplying their natural variability through the power output. This way, through their inconsistency, they can provide a more balanced and consistent outcome.

The impacts of this renewable resources application are exciting indeed. By contrast, they help significantly to shrink the carbon footprint while the vehicle is also taking charge. An EV would otherwise emit zero tailpipe emissions. However, by using green energy sources, EVs can reduce not only the immediate emissions but also the upstream electricity emissions. Accumulated, renewable energy can create a safe environment for the region it has in, discovering reliability of fuels that are volatile in price and supply. Furthermore, renewable energy also applies economic development. At an outset, the initial investment amount for setting up the solar panels or the wind turbines could be substantial; however, running these self-sufficient power generation systems will require less operational costs as compared to the traditional energy plants. However, it is also worth noting that many governments sometimes provide incentives for renewable energy projects like tax credit and feed-in tariffs and so this can assist in the financing of these projects at the initial capital cost while making the project development more economically feasible.

While EV charging infrastructure integration with renewable resources is not without obstacles, it is necessary for a reliable and affordable electricity system in the transition to clean energy. The principal problem is intermittency. In fact, solar and wind power sources cannot be relied upon always and might be insufficient to meet power needs in the grid. Power variability, both in terms of structure and quantity, can cause problems since it might result an inadequate amount of power to satisfy demand, especially during heavy demand periods or adverse weather conditions. As one of these issues, intermittency can be overcome by implementing several methods. One of the successful strategies is the use of energy storage systems for facilities, e.g., batteries, which aids in the reduction of energy wastage at peak production periods by storing excess power and releasing it when needed. This eliminates those surges and fill deficits hence stabilizing the grid and the power flow, which could be very helpful during periods when charge demand is very high. One of the solutions is to introduce so-called smart charging technologies, which include the ability to adapt the charging rate to the amount of renewables added to the power grid at a moment in time and how much power is used to fuel the grid. This may enable the preferential consumption of the EV power demand during the time of supply from renewable sources which would imply the best use of the green energy.

The other factor that makes this possible is using the most recent developments in grid infrastructure, including but not limited to power grids that are responsive and quickly adapt to changes in the grid, promoting the powering in of renewable energy. Upgrade the grid to allow power fluctuations in supply and making them capable of interacting with real-time monitoring and communication technologies enables the flexibility desired to efficiently replace fossil fuel-based power generators with renewable sources. In summary, the adoption of renewable energy into EV charging stations opens up a safe lane of efforts towards fighting the current environmental harm that the transportation sector caused and entrenching electric mobility for the sustainable future. Although uncertainties and cost issues may appear, renewable integration into the charging infrastructure has a great potential, as renewable source helps to decarbonize road transport, ensures energy security and beneficial economic development of the region. The future of renewables in sustaining global electric car fleet reliance lies in the solutions that entail energy storage, smart charging, and grid modernization which address these challenges and fully harness the potential of renewable energy sources.

Figure 8.8 demonstrates the flow chart of an energy supply of EV charging station which is backed by solar energy. It contains the system design in accordance with it, as it consists of solar panels, batteries with storage, and the user to charge, with their connection between them. This diagram helps in discussing the approach by which the solar power is effectively used as the source of energy in charging EVs, which means the energy solution of such type that is sustainable.

This line chart (Figure 8.9) reflects the activities with the results of a simulated escalation which are about the amount of energy exchanged at the solar-powered EV charging station in a daily basis. Expect also notifies about solar energy generation, charging, and energy accumulated during the day. Figure shows that the panels enable the accumulation and provision of energy in this kind of system which is evidence of preventiveness and efficiency of usage of solar power in EV charging applications.

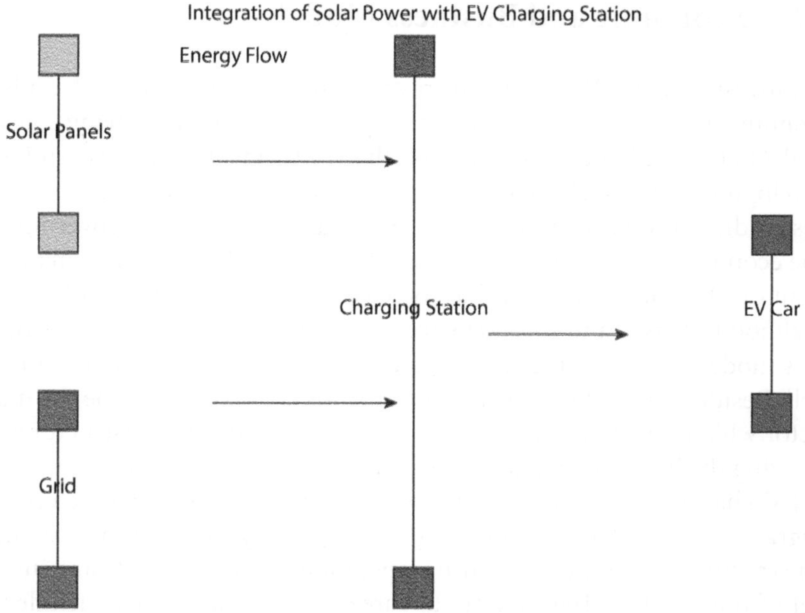

Figure 8.8 Schematic of an EV charging station powered by solar panels and connected to the grid.

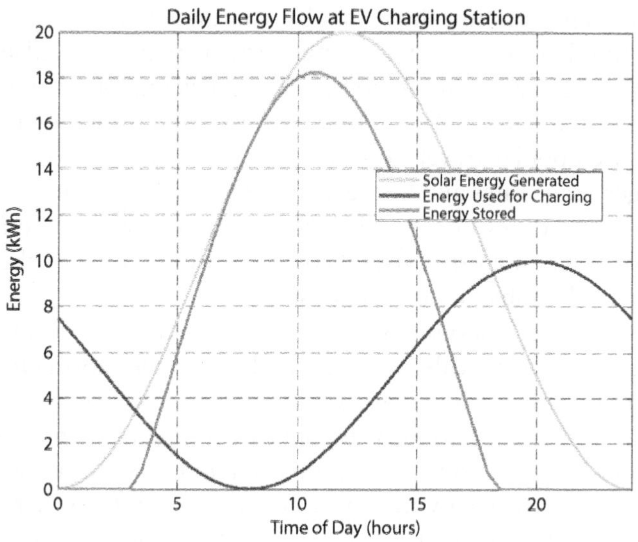

Figure 8.9 Simulation results of energy flow (input from renewable sources, output to EV charging) over a day.

8.6 Economic and Business Models

The investment in EV charging infrastructure is empirical with all kinds of economic implications and a multiplicity of business models being considered. On the one hand, this network is the one that will certainly permit the development of electric vehicle markets; however, it needs huge amounts of spending (both investments and operating costs) from the government. The economic implications assessment for the establishment and management of EV charging stations has forced participants to confront both the likelihood of risks and the existence of opportunities. Also, diverse business models may be utilized to enable network maintenance and profit as well. Besides this, public-private partnerships is considered to be the main factor which is responsible for increasing these kinds of infrastructures by allowing the blending of resource which are available at these sectors.

EV charging unit purchase, installation, which may include electrical upgrades costs and also engineering some buildings to accommodate new constructions or some retrofitting operations involve significant invest, right from the start. The continuous care of the stations, which include the tasks of software updates management, hardware repairing as well as customer service, causes also an operational expenses increase. Though, the economic impact, these investments can be really huge, by providing jobs in construction, technology and maintaining sectors as well as technological innovations and infrastructure basic developments.

Becoming an economically viable EV charging station largely depends on: where the charging station is located, pricing policy, as well as how distinct each time the charging station is used is. Pricing for charging stations can be measured with reference to areas that are busy with city traffic or those that are popular travel stops for consumers, as such locations ought to see bigger usage rates and hence be more profitable. Another side of the coin shows difficulties of something not too popular in stations of rural localities or places not often visited could be covered only by the supporting measures like subsidies or partnerships.

To resolve these economic issues different strategies were investigated. This charging model is widely popular and one of the most common ones is subscription which involves users paying a recurring fee for the charging stations network the sources of income for operators. The pay-per-use model is also another model, and in this system users are charged according to how much electricity they have consumed. On the other hand, this model can attract individuals who only use the service from time to time, but the ticket fee may have to be higher to cover the operational costs.

Besides these, businesses are making their mark by using EV charging services as an added-value service for their customers; hence shopping centers, hotels, and workplaces can be enumerated as such. The composite of these modes, where some services can be sold on subscription whereas others on per-use, is also making its way with the service providers, therefore, balancing the revenue streams and creating dynamic demand management is no longer a problem.

Public private partnership proves to be the battery of EV charging infrastructure, which is an essential component for its fast deployment. Such partnerships enable public officials to engage private investments as well as expertise whereas private companies get financial direction from the government through the provision of monetary incentives, tax breaks or rule consistency. The governments could, for instance, allocate the land for charging stations or provide easer route for the permits to be processed to speed up the whole process of development. On the other hand, private companies introduce the latest technologies and gain immediate traction due to their established operational processes. Simply, such collaborative efforts are very useful to reply for the high initial prices and operational risks connected with EV charging infrastructure Shared costs and risks of the parties serving as a common base enables both of them to cooperate achieving the desired goal of implementing EVs and cutting out greenhouse gas emissions. The equitable distribution of charging points is an objective that this partnership usually pursues to prevent vulnerability in access to charging as could be the case in areas which are poor or disadvantaged economically. Government policies are, without any doubt, pivotal in creating the economic scope of EV charging infrastructure. Examples of these incentives are electric power discounts for EV charging station operators, provision of grants and subsidies to owners who can secure institutional procurement of vehicles for their companies. To achieve this, the taxation and subsidies can be changed to generate a distribution that will benefit the larger community.

To sum up, a crucial role of installing and running EV charging stations in the economy is of great significance – initial setup amounts are offset by the possible later payoffs like job creation, technology innovation, and infrastructure improvement. The advancement of well-performing and sustainable business models as well as the strategic use of pivotal public-private partnerships are very critical for developing the charging infrastructures that are needed to support the introducing wave of electric vehicles. Such a complicated economic and business environment calls for skillful navigation aiming to mitigate prices, risks, and gains as

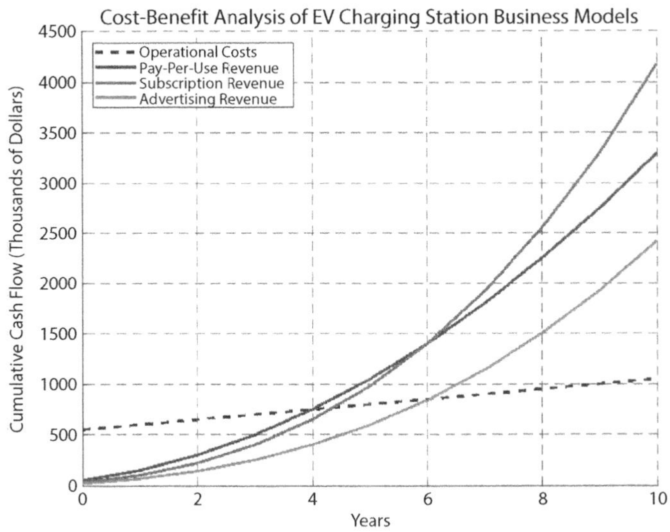

Figure 8.10 Cost–benefit analysis graph for different business models of EV charging stations.

extensively as possible, and achieve a productive environmentally sustainable development.

Figure 8.10 is an axis of pay per use that performs cost-benefit analysis for different types of business models of EV charging stations, ratio based, advertising funded, and so on. The graph portrays a combination of expenditures and earnings graph for a few years out, which gives the clues concerning the respective financial viability and sustainability each model. This analysis is a necessary preliminary work for the construction of EV charging infrastructure. It can play a vital role for stakeholders to decide on the most efficient business strategy.

8.7 Policy, Regulations, and Standards

Policy, regulation and standard are the ones that direct electric vehicle charging infrastructure's development in different jurisdictions, which present significant discrepancies. These legal systems help to promote the use and adoption of EVs, guarantee the stable and secure provision of charging services, and create competition for suppliers of electricity. In this section, the focus is on policy and regulations setting out for EV charging infrastructure and suggesting standardization of policies across jurisdictions, and the look at possible future trends in legislation and their consequences on industry.

Policies and regulations affecting EV charging infrastructure can be broadly categorized into three types: such as those promoting infrastructure investment, those which enforce technical standards and safety ones, and also those monitoring operations as well as tariffs. The government incentives, comprising tax relief and grants, as well subsidies are important because they help to reduce the expenditures related to installing the charging station. For instance, in the U.S. the government may offer a tax credit which would cover a certain part of the charging station installation costs by the owner. Similar sources of support can be found in European states, these are frequently supplemented by gratuities on a local and territorial level.

Technical standards and safety regulations become so important for the reason that they have to be in order to be sure that charging the equipment is highly reliable and compatible with all vehicle's variety. In the absence of such regulations we could experience the creation of obstacles to the usability of EV systems and furthermore their widespread adoption. Regulations mostly prescribe the precise connectors that are permitted, the least speed for a charger to have and the safety protocols that the charging stations are bound to meet. Likewise, the European Union settled CCS (Combined Charging System) as a rule, which helped to define uniform charging systems within Europe.

Operational requirements focus upon how charging stations are managed, how fees are set, and how users of these services can access them. Several authorities implement regulations to block price gouging and the fact of surging up prices over the normal price rates. Charging station operators can also be required by regulations to provide their clients with the opportunity to use their services without signing a subscription agreement, thus fostering better accessibility for users. The development of standardized solutions among different companies is now recognized the most important aspect for the rapid development of the international EV market. Standardization can facilitate journey over borders with EVs and lower producing costs for these. Also, this can make the charging process easy and simple. Though, the diversity of international regulatory regimes and a different pace of penetration of the EV market may result in the international standardization difficulties. The International bodies IEPC and WP.29 (e.g. World Forum for Harmonization of Vehicle Regulations) are working hard towards unified standards of the interfaces and safety regulations.

In the time to come, legislators might as well extend the system of EV adoption of charging infrastructure. Several governments have adopted very high goals for decarbonization and plug-in electric vehicles (EVs) are playing a central role in the plans of many governments. Consequently, future laws may include more severe mandates regarding the installation of charging stations in the construction of new residential and commercial properties, number of subsidies available for EV adoption and the development of charging infrastructure and regulations for the conventional gasoline vehicles to encourage the transition to the electric cars.

As well as, there has been an emerging phenomenon of smart and sustainable technology standards in the EV charging infrastructure. Future regulations might impose that charging stations should be outfitted with intelligent technologies that allow for several other functions, one of them being under system demand response that aids in managing peak hours of power delivery. This inclusion can elevate the pulchritude of the electrical grid as the share of EV ownership surges.

Finally, policy, regulation and standard development will become critical factors in EV infrastructure growth leadership. Today's framework serves as a growth catalyst for the industry through financial inducements, proper safety and compatibility, and consumer protection regulations. As the adoption of EVs is gathering momentum, standardized regulations and forward-looking laws would prove to be the ticket against any possible charging infrastructure demand issues in the future.

The course of events of EV infrastructure charging and the major policy influences (Figure 8.11) is graphically asserted. It showcases significant legal acts and regulations enacted to facilitate EV charging systems deployment and enhance EV incorporation, offering a historical overview of the governmental actions executed to impel electric mobility development.

Figure 8.12 shows a bar graph that demonstrates the degree of standardization of EV charging infrastructures' circumstances during different countries. Every bar shows whether a given country follows or not common international regulatory standards thus depicting the situation on a world scale where the struggle to achieve uniformity becomes apparent. The picture shows interconnection between the necessity of standard harmonization for smooth EV circulation within and cross-jurisdiction to grow EV industry.

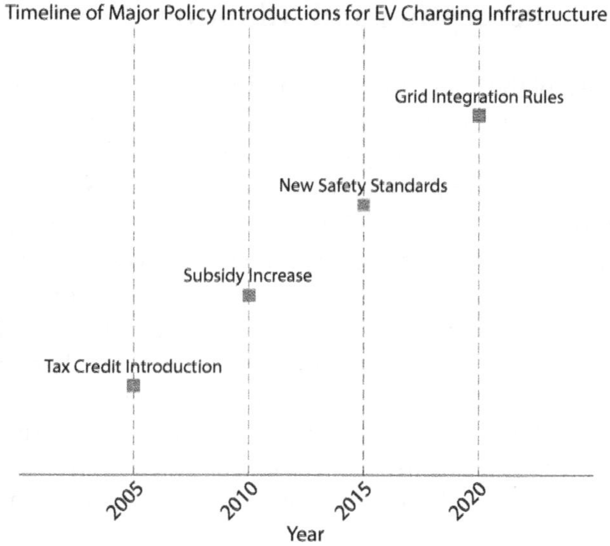

Figure 8.11 Timeline of major policy introductions affecting EV charging infrastructure development.

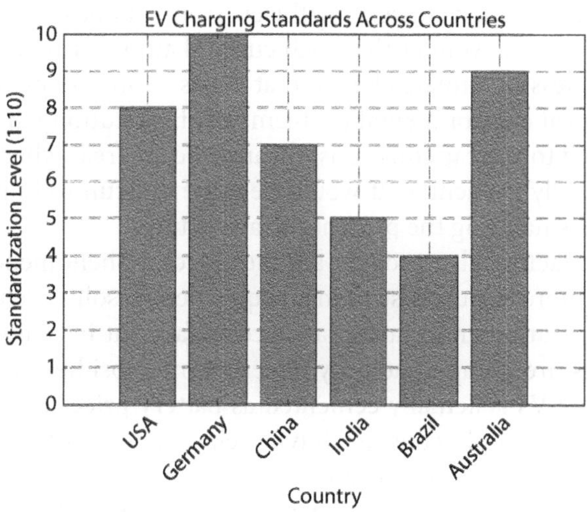

Figure 8.12 Map showing variation in EV infrastructure standards across different countries.

8.8 Public Perception and Adoption

The willingness of the public to take up and adhere to electric vehicles (EVs) follow both a complex and a varied mix of factors, with such as the availability and reliability of charging infrastructure, cultural attitudes to innovation and environmental protection as well as economic considerations and promotional and educational efforts being examples of these. Taking into consideration and solving these problems is necessary to increase EVs utilization technique and be able to make electric transition.

One of the many key issues considered in the public attitude toward the EVs is the level of availability and expandability of charging stations. Charging stations that are obvious to the sight relieve potential EV buyers and let them know that an abundance of convenient charging places is available to them, just like the places gasoline stations are perceived as by conventional drivers. Not only this transmission network reliance is critical but the velocity of charging stations and the area coverage is the other variable with a huge influence on consumer's decisions that EVs are worthy alternatives to traditional means of transport. Cultural inclination towards technologies and environmental concerns is where people differ from each other, thus, influencing the acceptance of EVs. Regions which has a strong cultural value laid upon conserving the environment has more prospect of EVs sales. It is not a wonder that such cultural attitudes are formed by the public awareness of climate change that exists at an ecosystem level, and also by the local environmental problems of air pollution which is almost directly linked to the car emissions. Meanwhile, in areas where oil and gas are economically influential, it would be quite difficult to implement EVs rather than dismantling the present infrastructure.

Economic factors also provide another pivotal phenomenon. The first EV will cost more to purchase than an equivalent gasoline vehicle, until or unless the operating and maintenance costs fall, but in many cases these shortcomings are compensated by government subsidies. The economic argument for EVs is actually cemented as battery prices are going down, more and more people consider buying electric vehicles, and long-term savings start to seem quite realistic.

Among the strategies used, many imperative and marketing campaigns have been put in place to attend to these factors and tap into broad public reception and support. Educational programs that deliver highly educated and accurate information concerning the advantages and feasibility of an EV transition are critically necessary. They may even include explanations of the whole-life costs, a tool to calculate individual usage and an explanation of how to use the EV charging infrastructure. The test-driving events or workshops which are initiated and conducted by auto manufacturers and government agencies are generally held to deepen the understanding of and support for the EV technology.

Advertising tools are also significant in creating the image of any business in the eyes of the public. Alkalise inositol dote marketing campaign often focus not only on environmental benefits of EVs, but also performance benefits, for instance, speed acceleration and noise reduction against gas powered vehicles, though marketing may respond to the misgivings comparing gasoline cars according to battery life, charging time, and range of the electric vehicles.

The improvement of long-distance travel capability without worrying of depleting battery power is comparatively one of the most challenging issues among all in increasing adoption of EV. In response to this challenge, however, the main focus has been grants to build the charging network and to design more effective chargers to make long-distance travel a real possibility. Contemporary EVs are fortified with more advanced battery tech whereas longer ranges and increased capacities are completed with in-vehicle navigation apps and apps that direct drivers to the charging stations, and help them manage their routes wisely based on their available battery life. Moreover, renaming consumer concerns like fitting the charging station in the building apartment and charging the EV in the long trips, calls for the efficient collaboration among the public authority, private sector, and the community. The local governments may choose to modify pre-existing building standards and zoning regulations, which in turn will mandate the installation of EV charging ports in new structures.

In sum, achieving widespread embrace EVs has to be a multifaceted undertaking that encompasses installation of infrastructural system beyond charging, resonance with societal values, and financial feasibility as well, and showcasing of robust marketing strategies. To a large extent overcoming range anxiety and the other resistance to the acquisition of electric vehicles that consumers may have through technology improvements as well as promoting the suitable policies is very important. Thus by implementing these tasks, stakeholders can contribute to speed up the shift to electric transportation, thus making it an inexpensive and easily adopted alternative for a wider market of users.

Below you can see the data (Figure 8.13) coming from the survey that shows alarming people fears about electric vehicles like range anxiety, availability charging infrastructure, cost, and maintenance. Each column will represent those groups of respondents who mentioned the related issues, depicting all the top obstacles for the EV adoption. The number is of critical importance for the manufacturers, state bodies, and all involved

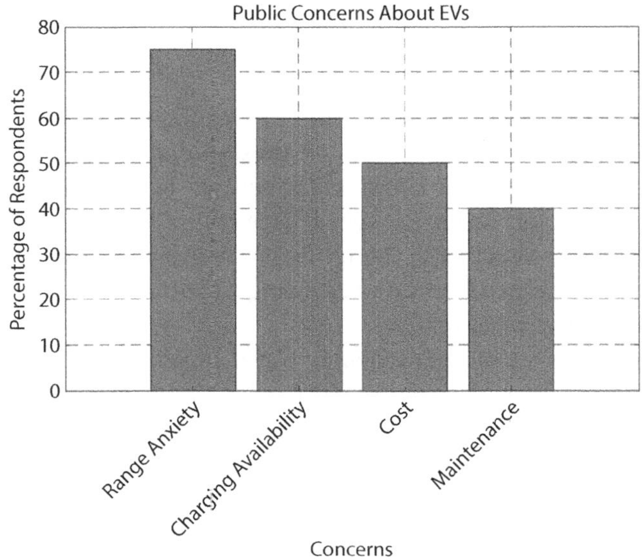

Figure 8.13 Bar graph of survey results showing public concerns about EVs (e.g., range anxiety, availability of charging points).

parties to take to the heart and eliminate the concerns of people to witness the popularity of EVs on the rise.

Figure 8.14 indicates a time-series graph tracing the rise of public awareness campaign effects on the increase of EV acceptance gear over some

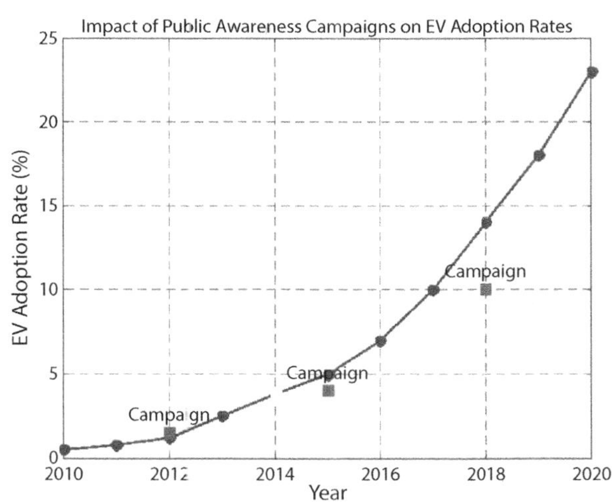

Figure 8.14 Time series analysis of EV adoption rates following public awareness campaigns.

time periods. Such details as showing the timing of campaigns and ensuing changes in the rate of adoption related to target outreach and education to help find out how efficiently electric vehicle uptake can be increased is contained here.

8.9 Future Directions and Innovations

The Electric Vehicles (EV) market is on the rise and with that also come the technology to support the market, particularly in the area of EV charging. This paragraph examines new EV charging technologies and trends, forecasts for the near future of charging infrastructure, as well as emerging technological advancements in automotive innovation and possible implications for infrastructure outlooks.

The trend in the EV charging technology development is a direct result of growing demand to manage an ever-increasing number of EVs on the road, make it easier for the users and thus a more natural convergence of charging infrastructure with the power grid and renewable energy sources. We can note the progress in the development of ultra-fast charging technology. It makes this process taking 80% of EV battery's charge within minutes possible, which is the same time as a gasoline car is being refueled. Companies such as Tesla and Porsche on top of others already eat the cake and foster these technologies by rolling the limits out on how fast the EV can be charged so the battery does not compromise to the heat stress.

Other than this, wireless charging is another trend of electrical vehicles that has increased their demand. This technology, developed on inductive charging, gives drivers the choice of simply placing their EVs on top of a charging pad instead of using plugs and cables. This could imply a great level of convenience when charging EVs as it would be as easy as parking in a designated area at your home garage, in public parking lots or while waiting at a traffic signal. Advances in this area include active wireless charging systems, where EVs charging while on the move through coils installed in the road. This makes it possible to continuously charge while the vehicle is in motion and thus eliminating range anxiety.

One of the significant innovation directions are EV charge infrastructure and smart grid integration. Smart grids employ computerized communications technology to find out and react to localized changes in electricity consumption. Introducing EV charging into the smart grid network increases the efficiency of the energy distribution, which results in better load management capabilities in the event of massive EV adoption which may end up overburdening the power grid. Intelligent charge stations may communicate with the grid in order to charge at the times of low demand or when oversupply electricity is available from renewables. This rather helps in balancing the grid and increasing the use of renewable energy sources. By extension, among future predictions for the evolution of charging technologies over the next ten years, widespread adoption of these advanced technologies is certain. Ultra-speedy and wireless stations are predicted to come more often, which make charging EVs easier and gives reasons to more people to switch to EVs. Furthermore, as the Renewable energy uptake increases, more charging stations will be linked to either direct connection or grid through the renewable power sources such as solar and wind power. The conversion of the grid to renewable sources will significantly contribute to EV charging carbon footprints reduction and help to combat global climate change.

Another consequence of the automotive industry's future technological advancement may be changes in how the power supply will be designed. This could be illustrated by the fact that the latest advances in battery technology will lead to higher densities and lower costs thus enabling EVs to be affordable and capable of greater distance. The latter may then lead to slowing down the rate of ultra-fast charging for daily commutes; however it will be still indispensable when it comes to long-distance traveling. Also, V2G technology, which enables EVs to contribute power to the grid during peak times of demand, most likely will spread. Besides this, it is the tool that allows balancing the grid and an opportunity to earn for EV owners, because EV batteries become mobile energy storages for the benefit of the energy system as a whole.

In general, the EV charging future is probably going to demonstrate a steady stream of latest technologies that significantly increase the convenience and efficiency of charging whilst also incorporate EVs in a broader sustainable environment. These innovations will play a very important role, such as helping the EVs to be kept up with growing number of automotive technologies, maintaining the charging infrastructure and keeping it match with these technologies and reduction of the greenhouse gas emissions. With the shifting patterns big on the horizon, they will determine the destiny of the transportation and energy sphere, thereby bringing about a more connected and eco-friendly future.

Figure 8.15 depicts EV charging infrastructure growth based on the present trends, and it projects more charging stations by the end of the decade. The chart blends the actual historical data with projections to highlight the projected growth mandating new capacity addition to support the increasing number of electric vehicles.

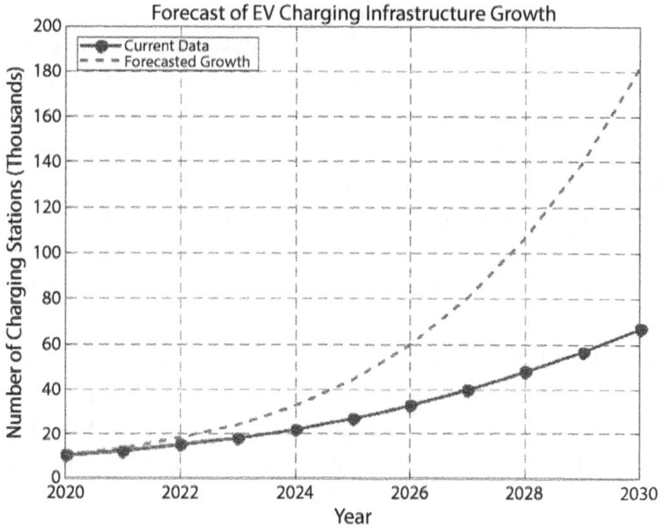

Figure 8.15 Forecast model of EV charging infrastructure growth based on current trends.

8.10 Conclusion

The chapter provides you with a deep understanding on the key features of EV implementation including the build-out of charging infrastructure. From the increasing use of EVs and the advancements in technology that has made them attractive while also performing numerous functions to the economic considerations that are fashioned to dictate if charging networks are worth employing, every aspect matters when it comes to the future of transportation. Besides, such subjects as policies, public opinion, and possible future implications were also pulled up, and these just added to what is important to know and how difficult it might be to make the shift to electric cars.

We conclude the current situation in the EV charging infrastructure which has been space that is evolving together with technological advancement and increasing demand from consumers. The different kinds of chargers, e.g. Level 1, Level 2 & DC Fast Charging, together with up-to-date technologies such as wireless and smart charging, built a very promising strategy for the future development of more user-friendly and effective EV charging stations. These technologies not only upgrade the mode of ride experience but also collaborate with renewable sources of energy making them the go to choice for electric vehicles.

The economic factors in the EV charging infrastructure models business have also played a crucial role. The fiscal analysis of costs, revenue streams, and profitability including the impact of public-private partnerships untangle the economic infrastructure that needs to be attained to developing sustainable charging networks. These economic facets are entangled with the policies (both the ones that enable and the ones that regulate the development of charging infrastructure). The paper saw that the government policies and incentives are very effective in ensuring a nurturing environment necessary for EV markets to grow as well as the development of the required infrastructure.

As urban mobility is one of the main contributors to emissions, EV charging systemizes to be a driver to reduce pollution and transform the urban environment. Efficient charging architectures remove the worries behind the adoption of EVs thus resulting into a greater rate of transition away from fossil fuel-reliant transportation. This transition not only works in the context of the international sustainability targets, but it provides a better quality of life in the city as the noise and air pollution are attenuated and, therefore, the cities become more liveable.

As we look into the future, the pace ahead relating EV charging infrastructure both have difficulties and capabilities. R&D of next-generation technologies, like intelligent electricity networks and electric vehicle-to-grid (V2G) systems, will be the need to keep developing and refining them. Furthermore, as the equation of personal and public transportation goes through change, the readiness and flexibility of infrastructure to new types of mobility and changes in the pattern of usage will be essential.

Togetherness of many sectors at various levels is a key element of success for the vision to be fulfilled. These key players - industry stakeholders, policymakers, planners of cities, and consumers - must be actively engaged to propose solutions that are not only innovative technologically but also affordable and equitable socially. Public education and public relations campaigns will be focused on re-educating society on EVs and empowering people to accept them. Lastly, although notable strides, there remains a lot to do in the regarding total and protracted EV charging infrastructure build-up. The collaborative efforts discussed here should not just be seen as important but rather as a matter of necessity if a green transportation system satisfying current and future generations is to be established. The constant increase in innovative technologies, together with smart partnerships formed and flexible policies that will help to propel the adoption of EV charging infrastructures. As underneath can be seen, indeed, the whole road to sustainable urban mobility by means of robust charging networks is quite complicated yet feasible, offering a "green" city with more connectivity and higher efficiency.

References

1. Hosseinzadeh, N., Hasan, K.N., Oo, A.M.T., Review of Electric Vehicle Charging Technologies, Standards, Architectures, and Converter Configurations. *IEEE Access,* 11, 41218–41255, 2023, doi: 10.1109/ACCESS.2023.3267164.
2. Rivera, S., Kouro, S., Vazquez, S., Goetz, S.M., Lizana, R., Romero-Cadaval, E., Electric Vehicle Charging Infrastructure: From Grid to Battery. *IEEE Ind. Electron. Mag.*, 15, 2, 37–51, June 2021, doi: 10.1109/MIE.2020.3039039.
3. Andersen, O., Krogh, B.B., Thomsen, C., Torp, K., Modeling and Analyzing Electric Vehicle Charging. *2016 17th IEEE International Conference on Mobile Data Management (MDM),* Porto, Portugal, pp. 302–309, 2016, doi: 10.1109/MDM.2016.52.
4. Vinoth Kumar, K., Radhakrishnan, P., Kalaivani, R., Devadoss, V., Vijay Anand, L.D., Vinodha, K., Implementation of Smart Electric Vehicle Charging Station Driven Using Experimental Investigation. *2021 2nd Global Conference for Advancement in Technology (GCAT),* Bangalore, India, pp. 1–5, 2021, doi: 10.1109/GCAT52182.2021.9587788.
5. Pant, D., Singh, N., Gupta, P., Charging System for Electric Vehicles. *2022 IEEE Delhi Section Conference (DELCON),* New Delhi, India, pp. 1–7, 2022, doi: 10.1109/DELCON54057.2022.9753117.
6. Senthil, R. and Prasad, K.D.V., Securing digital authentication with cryptographic innovations in intrinsic verification systems. *J. Discrete Math. Sci. Cryptogr.*, 27, 2-A, 317–328, 2024.
7. Prasad, K., Saxena, R., Barua, T., Mohiuddin, K., Dynamic Disaster Management with Real-Time IoT Data Analysis and Response. *2024 International Conference on Automation and Computation (AUTOCOM),* Dehradun, India, pp. 142–147, 2024.
8. Mali, P.S., Jagtap, B.K., *et al.*, Synergistic applications of nanostructured boron nitride in photocatalysis and targeted drug delivery. *Nanotechnol. Environ. Eng.*, 9, 179–188, 2024, https://doi.org/10.1007/s41204-024-00367-8.
9. Hephzibah, K. and Aswani, T., Design and Implementation of an Android App for Real-Time Location Monitoring and Emergency Assistance. *2023 7th International Conference on Electronics, Communication and Aerospace Technology (ICECA),* Coimbatore, India, pp. 1561–1567, 2023.
10. Srinivas, K.N.V. and Lakineni, P.K., Development of a Real-time Location Monitoring App with Emergency Alert Features for Android Devices.

2023 4th IEEE Global Conference for Advancement in Technology (GCAT), Bangalore, India, pp. 1–8, 2023.

11. Hussain, N. and Samal, A., Design and Implementation of Single to Multi-cloud Securities in Network, in: *Advances in Computing and Information, ERCICA 2023*, Lecture Notes in Electrical Engineering, N.R. Shetty, N.H. Prasad, N. Nalini (Eds.), vol. 1104, Springer, Singapore, 2024, https://doi.org/10.1007/978-981-99-7622-5_42.
12. Prasad, V.S., Mahajan, Y., Suneetha, S., A Cloud-Based UV Monitoring System for Remote Real-Time UV Exposure Tracking. *2023 4th International Conference on Smart Electronics and Communication (ICOSEC)*, Trichy, India, pp. 1764–1770, 2023.
13. Mouli, G.R.C., Venugopal, P., Bauer, P., Future of electric vehicle charging. *2017 International Symposium on Power Electronics (Ee)*, Novi Sad, Serbia, pp. 1–7, 2017, doi: 10.1109/PEE.2017.8171657.
14. Hegge, K.K. and Agrawal, R., Wireless and Solar-Powered Multipurpose Robot for Industrial Automation: A Sustainable Solution. *2023 8th International Conference on Communication and Electronics Systems (ICCES)*, Coimbatore, India, pp. 146–151, 2023.
15. Parismita, Hussain, N., Dixit, S.K., Gupta, A.K., A novel approach of unsupervised feature selection using iterative shrinking and expansion algorithm. *J. Interdiscip. Math.*, 26, 3, 519–530, 2023, DOI: 10.47974/JIM-1678.
16. Premkumar, S., Hussain, N., Chinamuttevi, V.S., A novel RF-SMOTE model to enhance the definite apprehensions for IoT security attacks. *J. Discrete Math. Sci. Cryptogr.*, 26, 3, 861–873, 2023.
17. Lobato, S.C., Pinto, J.H.D.G., Carneiro, R.N.M., Avelar, G.F., Valentim, J.A., Ferreira, A.A., Development of an electric vehicle charging station. *2018 Simposio Brasileiro de Sistemas Eletricos (SBSE)*, Niteroi, Brazil, pp. 1–6, 2018, doi: 10.1109/SBSE.2018.8395582.
18. Hegge, K.K. and Agrawal, R., Industrial Automated Multipurpose Robot Using WIFI. *2023 4th International Conference for Emerging Technology (INCET)*, Belgaum, India, pp. 1–8, 2023.
19. Prasad, K., Srinivas, V., De, T., Wi-Fi Router Signal Coverage Position Prediction System using Machine Learning Algorithms. *2023 International Conference on Sustainable Computing and Smart Systems (ICSCSS)*, Coimbatore, India, pp. 253–258, 2023.
20. M, S.P., Reddy, A.M., Tanguturi, R., Improved Secure Communication Mechanism for IoT Platform Devices. *2022 International Conference on Smart Generation Computing, Communication and Networking (SMART GENCON)*, Bangalore, India, pp. 1–6, 2022.
21. Premkumar, S., Prasad, K., V, D.G., Gugan, I., Enhancing Microcomputer Edge Computing for Autonomous IoT Motion Control. *IJRITCC*, 11, 3, 58–67, Apr. 2023.

22. Reddy, N.S. and Ashreetha, B., Technologies for Comprehensive Information Security in the IoT. *2023 International Conference for Advancement in Technology (ICONAT)*, Goa, India, pp. 1–5, 2023.
23. Suryawanshi, V.A. and Chaturvedi, A., Novel Predictive Control and Monitoring System based on IoT for Evaluating Industrial Safety Measures. *IJEER*, 10, 4, 1050–1057, 2022.
24. Patwal, P.S., Data Analytics and Cloud-Based Platform for Internet of Things Applications in Smart Cities. *2022 International Conference on Industry 4.0 Technology (I4Tech)*, pp. 1–6, 2022.
25. Pavankumar, P. and Darwante, N.K., Performance Monitoring and Dynamic Scaling Algorithm for Queue Based Internet of Things. *2022 International Conference on Innovative Computing, Intelligent Communication and Smart Electrical Systems (ICSES)*, pp. 1–7, 2022.
26. Meena, R.S., Kudari, J.M., Purushotham, S., Design and Implementation of a System for Vehicle Accident Reporting and Tracking. *2022 7th International Conference on Communication and Electronics Systems (ICCES)*, pp. 349–353, 2022.
27. Sharma, A., S, K., Arun, M.R., Priority Queueing Model-Based IoT Middleware for Load Balancing. *2022 6th International Conference on Intelligent Computing and Control Systems (ICICCS)*, pp. 425–430, 2022.
28. Ramesha, M. and Pai, G.N., Internet of things: Internet revolution, impact, technology road map and features. *Adv. Math. Sci. J.*, 9, 7, 4405–4414, 2020.
29. Puneeth Kumar, B.S. and Srinivasulu Raju, S., Smart Villages: IoT Technology Based Transformation. *J. Phys. Conf. Ser.*, 2070, 1, 012128, 2021.
30. Shashidhara, K.S. and Gangadhara, Signal Analysis and Filtering using one Dimensional Hilbert Transform. *J. Phys. Conf. Ser.*, 1706, 1, 1–7, 2020.
31. Ramachandra, A.C. and Pandurangappa, C., Optimization of motorcycle pitch with non linear control. *2016 IEEE International Conference on Recent Trends in Electronics, Information and Communication Technology, RTEICT 2016 - Proceedings*, pp. 1656–1660, 2017.
32. Mary, P.A. and Begum, A.Y., A Novel IoT Framework and Device Architecture for Efficient Smart city Implementation. *2023 7th International Conference on Trends in Electronics and Informatics (ICOEI)*, Tirunelveli, India, pp. 420–426, 2023.
33. Salavati, M., Driss, S., Farhangi, S., High Efficiency Electric Vehicle Fast Charging. *2019 10th International Power Electronics, Drive Systems and Technologies Conference (PEDSTC)*, Shiraz, Iran, pp. 689–694, 2019, doi: 10.1109/PEDSTC.2019.8697531.
34. Ferreira, J.C., Monteiro, V., Afonso, J.L., Silva, A., Smart electric vehicle charging system. *2011 IEEE Intelligent Vehicles Symposium (IV)*, Baden-Baden, Germany, pp. 758–763, 2011, doi: 10.1109/IVS.2011.5940579.
35. Naveen, G., Yip, T.H.-T., Xie, Y., Modeling and protection of electric vehicle charging station. *2014 6th IEEE Power India International Conference (PIICON)*, Delhi, India, pp. 1–6, 2014, doi: 10.1109/POWERI.2014.7117733.

9

Vehicular Power Line Communication

Smitha Gayathri D.[1]**, K.R. Usha Rani**[2*] **and Yasha Jyothi Shirur**[1]

[1]*Department of Electronics and Communication Engineering, BNM Institute of Technology, Bengaluru, India*
[2]*Department of Electronics and Communication Engineering, RVCE, Bengaluru, India*

Abstract

The exploration of vehicular power line communication (VPLC) has emerged as a promising way out to counter the growing convolution and escalating costs associated with the automotive wiring harnesses, which have become increasingly burdened by the heave of electronic devices as well as sensors in modern automobiles. VPLC uniquely leverages existing power cables for data transmission, thereby negating the necessity for extra wiring. Nonetheless, this method confronts significant hurdles, especially due to the dynamic nature of accessing the impedance, which differs with time, frequency, as well as geographical location. Such variability often leads to impedance mismatches that compromise the signal-to-noise-power ratios, undermining the reliability of data transmission. In response, we propose a novel adaptive impedance matching system designed to enhance the efficiency of signal transfer between the transmitter and receiver. Our approach involves conducting comprehensive simulations across a diverse spectrum of access impedance scenarios, applying S-parameters extracted from earlier VPLC network measurement campaigns. The results of our simulations are promising, showing that our adaptive matching system can align VPLC signal-power transmission in 30% of its theoretical maximum. This optimization interprets to a substantial power gain, potentially increasing by a portion of up to 10, a performance that outstrips other reported methods in the field.

Keywords: Optimization, passive elements, power gain, matching circuit, BPLC, VPLC

**Corresponding author*: usharani@rvce.edu.in

Rathishchandra R. Gatti and Chandra Singh (eds.) Digital Convergence in Intelligent Mobility Systems, (193–216) © 2025 Scrivener Publishing LLC

9.1 Introduction

Over the past several decades, the telecommunications sector has witnessed a significant increase in demand, driven by the constant need for innovative services and expanded transmission capacity. This sector offers substantial economic potential, prompting significant investment focused on developing extensive high-speed networks. These networks are designed to support an array of global telecommunications services, enabling connectivity across vast distances. Although a large portion of investment is channeled into transport networks that link nodes across various network providers, these networks often stop short of reaching the end user. Instead, the connection to individual customers is achieved through distribution and access networks. Distribution networks serve to bridge the gap between the more extensive transport networks and localized access networks, covering broad geographic areas. Access networks, on the other hand, are more localized, connecting subscribers within a neighborhood or a similar small radius. Despite their critical role, the infrastructure for access networks is notably expensive to deploy and maintain. It is estimated that around 50% of all telecommunications infrastructure investment is allocated to these access networks. Moreover, the high costs per subscriber mean that recovering these investments takes a considerable amount of time. With the telecommunications market becoming deregulated in numerous countries, control over access networks often remains in the hands of the incumbent network providers, which were once monopolistic telephone companies. This situation poses challenges for new network providers seeking to establish their own access networks without incurring prohibitive costs. One innovative solution that has emerged is the use of power line communications (PLC) technology, which leverages existing electrical grid infrastructure to deliver communication services. By utilizing the power supply grids, PLC technology bypasses the need to lay new communication cables, presenting a more cost-effective approach to building access networks. This solution not only reduces installation and maintenance costs but also accelerates the deployment of telecommunications services to a broader user base. Thus, utilizing PLC technology within low-voltage networks presents a financially viable strategy for addressing the "last mile" challenges in access networks. Today, users of these networks demand telecommunications services that offer not only higher data rates but also improved quality of service (QoS). As such, PLC provides an economical yet efficient solution to meet these modern telecommunications demands by leveraging existing infrastructure. This approach significantly cuts the

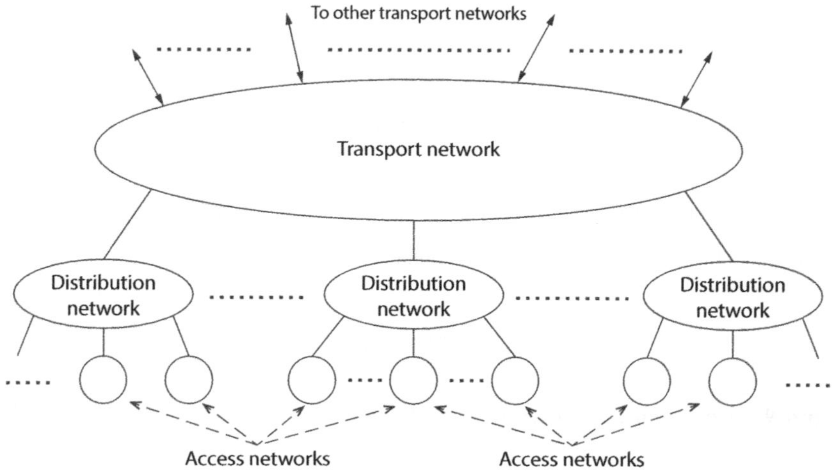

Figure 9.1 Telecommunications network structure [14].

costs associated with expanding new communications infrastructure while effectively catering to the evolving needs of network subscribers.

PLC systems used in the access sector, which provide telecommunications services meeting high quality of service (QoS) standards, are referred to as "broadband PLC access networks." The objective of this manuscript is to furnish vital details required for the development of broadband PLC systems and their associated network components (Figure 9.1). To facilitate communication over power supply networks, it's crucial to install devices known as PLC modems. These modems are responsible for converting data signals from standard communication devices like computers and telephones into a format suitable for transmission through power lines. Conversely, these modems also receive data signals from the power grid and convert them back, delivering them to the user's communication devices. This dual functionality ensures seamless data flow in both directions across the power infrastructure.

PLC modems, which are crucial components specific to PLC communications, serve as the essential interface linking various communication devices across power supply networks. These devices are specifically designed to enhance network efficiency, even amid the challenging transmission scenarios often encountered within power grid environments as shown in Figure 9.2. Although power networks were not initially devised for data communication, this has resulted in suboptimal conditions for such applications. To address these issues, PLC modems are crafted to mitigate these inherent limitations. The PLC transmission channel is characterized

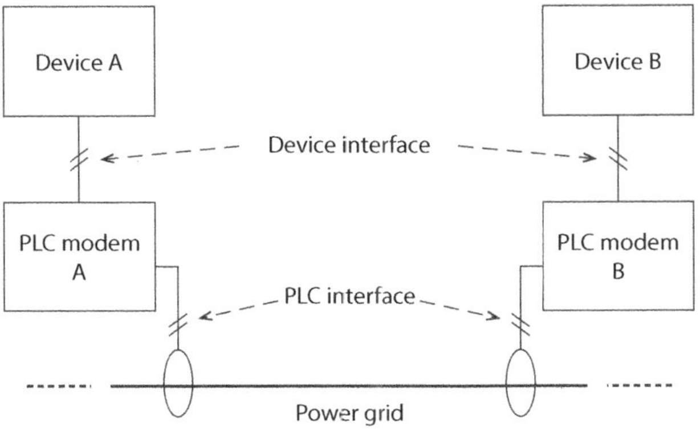

Figure 9.2 Communications over power grids [14].

by substantial signal loss that varies with frequency, fluctuating impedance, signal fading, and elevated noise levels. This noise originates both from various electrical devices connected to the network and from external environmental influences, which can significantly disrupt PLC system operations, thereby hampering consistent data flow. Furthermore, for PLC networks to support higher data transmission speeds, they must tap into a frequency spectrum extending up to 30 MHz. Unfortunately, this range coincides with frequencies utilized by numerous radio services. Such overlap can inadvertently lead to the emission of electromagnetic interference from PLC networks, potentially interfering with these radio services. As a result, regulatory bodies enforce stringent regulations on the electromagnetic outputs from PLC networks. These constraints compel the networks to operate at lower signal powers, which consequently diminishes their range and data transfer speeds and increases their susceptibility to interference. This decrease in data throughput poses a particular challenge in PLC access networks, where the transmission medium must be shared among multiple subscribers competing for the same network resources (Figure 9.3).

Vehicular power line communication (VPLC) utilizes existing power cables within vehicles, which helps in minimizing the costs and complexity associated with the vehicle's wiring harness by avoiding the installation of additional dedicated data communication wires. VPLC systems face multiple hurdles due to deficiencies in the transmission channel, including the presence of impulsive noise [17, 21], the frequency-dependent characteristics of the channel's transfer function [14, 16, 18–20], and the changeable nature of network access impedance which differs by both time and geographical position [22, 23]. These variations frequently result in impedance

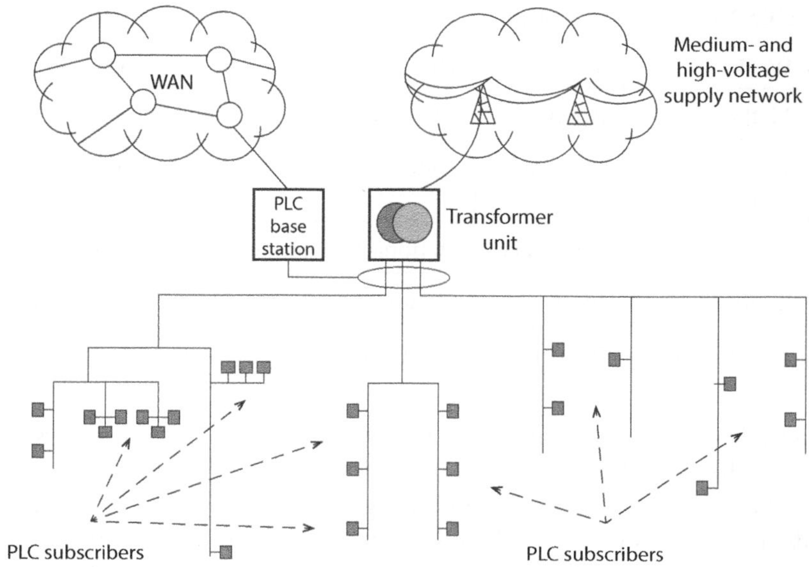

Figure 9.3 PLC access network [14].

mismatches at the VPLC transmitters and receivers, thereby reducing the efficiency of signal transfer across the network and consequently diminishing the overall effectiveness of signal propagation in the PLC system. Addressing these imperfections in the channel requires tailored solutions. Challenges such as channel frequency selectivity and noise can be managed through the creation of suitable transmission protocols and the use of advanced signal processing methods. However, the issue of impedance disparity requires the integration of adaptive impedance matching circuits at both the transmitter and the receiver ends to ensure effective communication. Traditional impedance matching circuits, which typically rely on fixed passive components, are often inadequate due to the dynamic changes in access impedance initiated by fluctuating network loads as well as signal reflections along with the power lines.

9.2 Review and Categorization of Impedance Matching Techniques in Existing Literature

The development of coupling circuits for effective data transmission via power lines has been a subject of significant research since the inception of power line communications [4, section 4]. In the context of vehicular

Table 9.1 Comparison of current research with other relevant studies.

Work	**9**	**10**	**11**	**12**
Method	Analytical	Analytical	Mathematical	Analytical
Type of impedance	Insertion loss	Solitary	Solitary	Solitary
Structure	Stationary	Stationary	Stretchy	Stretchy
Interpretation	Inert	Grouping	Inert	Grouping
Bandwidth	Narrowing	Narrowing	Widespread	Narrowing

power line communication (VPLC), which utilizes DC power systems, a basic theoretical configuration might include a single capacitor to manage the coupling and decoupling of high-frequency communication signals. Yet, this straightforward method often falls short of providing optimal signal transmission. To discourse this shortfall, a more complex coupler circuit is essential to accurately align the impedance between the network as well as VPLC modems. This segment provides an initial overview of the key concepts of impedance matching and then proceeds to examine various PLC impedance matching systems as detailed in the scholarly literature. Table 9.1 shows the comparison of the current research with related studies.

9.2.1 Impedance Matching: Concept and Classification

Impedance matching is a fundamental concept in electrical engineering, critical for optimizing power transfer in power line communications. This principle stipulates that maximum power transfer occurs when the load impedance is the complex conjugate of the source's internal impedance. In vehicular power line communication (VPLC), the vehicle's wiring harness acts as the load and is represented by its Thevenin/Norton equivalent, termed "access impedance." For ideal power transmission, the transmitter should match this access impedance with its complex-conjugate. Conversely, for efficient reception, it is crucial that the receiver's input impedance aligns with the access impedance as viewed from the receiver's side. In typical VPLC implementations [2], standard impedance values like [2] 50 ohms are used at both transmitter and receiver ends. However, these standard values may not always align perfectly due to the variable nature of access impedance, which can change based on different coupling points and may fluctuate over time. To ensure effective signal power transmission into and out of the network, it is essential to employ adaptive impedance matching circuits. These circuits must utilize lossless passive elements to avoid any power loss during impedance matching.

9.2.2 Related Works and Developments

Previous research in this domain, such as the studies conducted by Mavretic *et al.* [29], primarily addressed issues associated with resistive loads and sources, including challenges like insertion loss. Historically, conventional methods often utilized bulky and costly transformers to address these difficulties. In a shift toward more efficient solutions, Park *et al.* [22] pioneered the adoption of a voltage-controlled general impedance converter (VCGIC) [12] to develop compact active inductors, providing a more lightweight solution compared to traditional passive inductors. Despite this innovation, the inherent limitations of operational amplifiers, which cap the maximum allowable current and voltage, necessitated the use of a combination of static inert inductor with a smaller transformer, thereby diminishing some of the advantages of active inductors. Additionally, advancements in wide-band impedance equivalent structures have been made. For instance, Araneo *et al.* [30] implemented an LC-ladder configuration along with a mathematical strategy, specifically utilizing a meta-particle swarm optimization (M-PSO) algorithm, to enhance power transmission over an extended frequency spectrum. Despite its effectiveness, the need for a digital processor to perform rapid optimizations presents a challenge for integrating cost-effective, compact solutions. Our approach to narrowband matching, initially introduced in [1] and later adopted by Nisbet *et al.* [11], concentrates on eliminating the use of transformers for impedance identical at the transmitter side, covering a range of access impedances, and demonstrating its practicality. The increasing integration of electronic devices and sensors into vehicle DC power systems has expressively enhanced the complexity and weight of automotive wiring harnesses [12, 23]. VPLC reports these challenges by leveraging the existing wiring as a medium for data transmission, which helps reduce both the cost and complexity of installation. However, the dynamic and often unpredictable nature of VPLN which accesses the impedance, due to varying loads, frequently causes mismatches among the VPLC modem as well as the VPLN. This results in compromised signal power transfer and diminished reliability of communication [4, 8]. To overcome these issues, the development of new impedance matching circuits is crucial. For example, the method of selecting optimal winding ratios, as investigated in [9], utilizes a coupling transformer to achieve impedance matching by adjusting winding ratios. Moreover, a cost-efficient implementation of an impedance matching circuit was showcased in [10]. Additionally, alternative strategies involving L-C band-pass matching couplers [11, 13], which comprise a BPF circuit and an impedance equivalent circuit, offer solutions for environments where dynamic impedance adjustment is vital. This is particularly important as the fixed configurations of previous circuits were unable to accommodate the complex and evolving access impedance of the VPLN [6, 14].

9.3 Model of Vehicular Power Line Communication

In the VPLC system, the configuration consists of three critical components: the transmitter, the in-vehicle power line network (VPLN), and the receiver. Each of these elements is essential to the overall communication architecture.

Figure 9.4 shows the VPLC model, which includes three key elements: the transmitter, the receiver, and the in-vehicle power line network.

- Transmitter: The transmitter features a source voltage (Vs) and an internal impedance (Zs). These elements are crucial for initiating the transmission of power through the network efficiently.
- VPLN: Composed of wiring harnesses, including electronic devices, as well as lighting systems, the VPLN can effectively be represented as a dual-terminal network. The input impedance of this network, denoted as Zacc, can be accurately represented by the Thevenin/Norton equivalent impedance, facilitating a clear understanding of its electrical behavior.

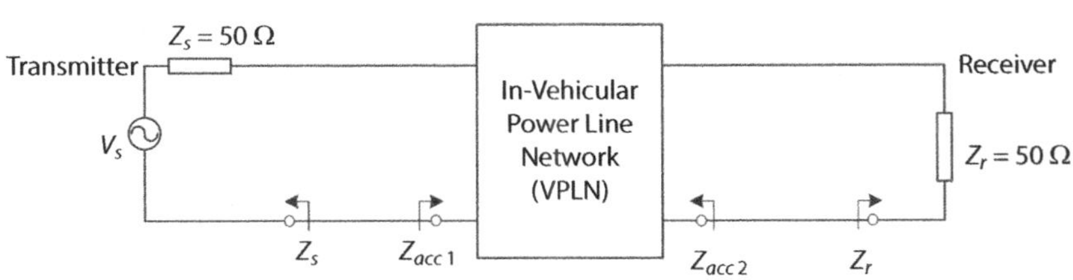

Figure 9.4 VPLC system model description [2].

- Receiver: At the receiver's end, the input impedance, noted as Zr, is a key determinant in the reception quality.

The VPLN's access impedance, represented as Zacc D Racc±jXacc, is a complex-valued parameter that fluctuates based on time as well as location. Standard impedance values such as 50Ω for transmitters or receivers may lead to impedance mismatches with the VPLC modem [2], potentially causing signal reflections and degradation. To enhance the efficacy of signal power transfer, it is essential to explore impedance matching among the VPLC modem as well as the VPLN [7, 15]. This exploration will include the implementation of a resonance as well as absorption-based complex impedance matching method tailored for T-shaped networks. Additionally, the process involves selecting appropriate load-Q and developing an adaptive impedance identical system structure. The detailed design and operational principles of the T-shaped adaptive matching system are further elaborated in the subsequent segment.

9.3.1 The Resonance and Absorption Technique for Advanced Impedance Matching

The impedance matching strategy for a T-shaped network based on real-to-real techniques. Nonetheless, the access impedance within the (VPLN) is characterized by both real and imaginary components, making it a complex quantity. To effectively match the impedance among the VPLC modem as well as the VPLN, a T-shaped matching network is devised, leveraging principles of circuit resonance and absorption.

9.3.1.1 Matching the Impedance to Access Inductive Impedance

Referencing Figure 9.5, the VPLC transmitter's voltage and output impedance are labeled as Vs and Rs, respectively. Notably, the output impedance Rs of the transmitter is set at 50Ω. This setup underscores the need for a nuanced approach to achieve impedance matching in scenarios where the network's inherent impedance includes inductive characteristics.

To simplify the complex impedance matching challenge into a straightforward real-to-real impedance matching problem, it's crucial to change the complex-valued VPLN access impedance into a real-valued format. As shown in Figure 9.5, the access impedance when displaying inductive properties (e.g., Zacc = Racc + jXacc) includes the imaginary component,

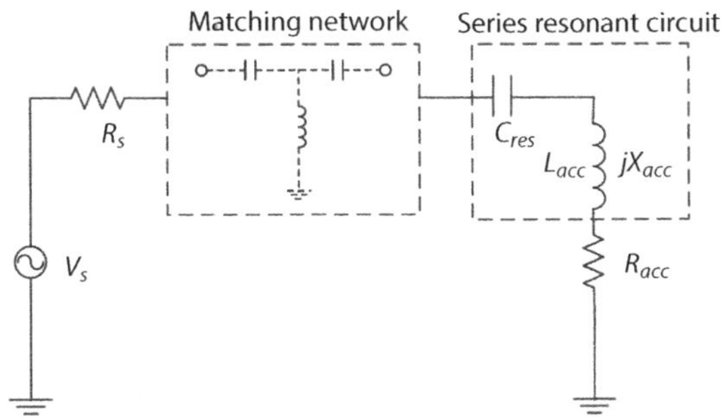

Figure 9.5 The series resonant circuit for managing inductive access impedance.

which is the reactance from inductance Lacc (ω_0Lacc = Xacc). Moreover, the VPLN access impedance is composed of both the resistance Racc and the inductance Lacc. In scenarios involving a series-resonant circuit, the inductance Lacc and the series resonant capacitance effectively neutralize each other. This interaction results in isolating the real component (Racc) of the VPLN access impedance.

$$C_{res} = \frac{1}{\omega_0 X_{acc}}, \tag{9.1}$$

where $\omega_0 = 2\pi f_0$ is the resonant frequency and Xacc is the imaginary part of the VPLN access impedance.

As shown in Figure 9.6, the shift from complex impedance matching to real-to-real impedance matching (between Racc and Rs) is achieved

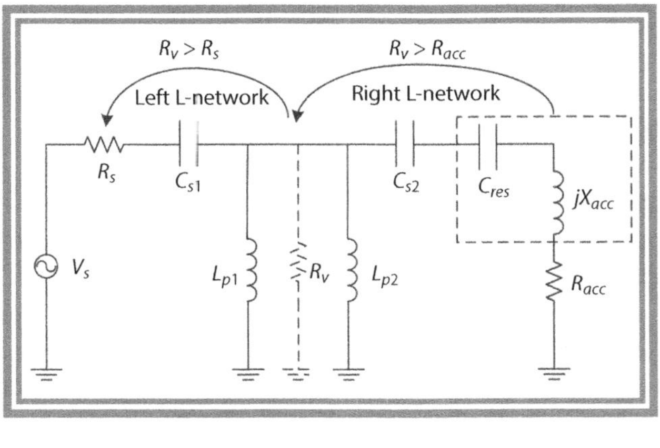

Figure 9.6 Impedance matching for inductive access impedance.

by eliminating the imaginary part of the VPLN access impedance. This adjustment paves the way for developing a T-shaped matching network. To optimize this network further, the series resonant capacitance Cres is incorporated into the design of the T-shaped matching network, thus streamlining and improving the impedance matching procedure. Because the Cres and Cs2 are connected in-series, the total series capacitance is

$$C_{eq} = \frac{C_{res} X C_{s2}}{C_{res} + C_{s2}} \tag{9.2}$$

The ultimate design of the T-shaped matching network, tailored for handling inductive access impedance, is depicted in Figure 9.6. To ascertain the correct values for the components in this network, a comprehensive system of equations is utilized. These calculations are crucial for ensuring the network efficiently matches the impedance characteristics of the VPLN, thereby optimizing the performance of the overall system. This methodical approach to calculating component values is key to achieving effective impedance matching, especially in environments characterized by inductive impedance.

$$C_{s1} = \frac{1}{\omega_0 R_s Q_{left}} \tag{9.3}$$

$$L_p = \frac{L_{p1} X L_{p2}}{L_{p1} + L_{p2}} \tag{9.4}$$

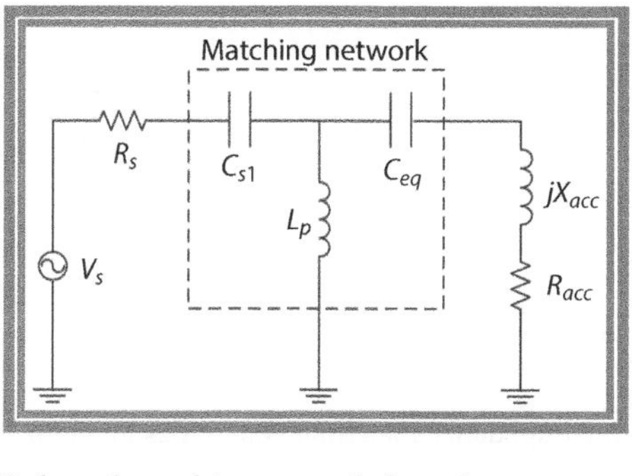

Figure 9.7 The final T-shaped matching network for inductive access impedance.

$$C_{eq} = \frac{C_{res} X \, C_{s2}}{C_{res} + C_{s2}} \tag{9.5}$$

When dealing with an inductive VPLN access impedance (Zacc = Racc + jXacc) as well as a specified anticipated load-Q, the T-shaped corresponding network is deliberated using Equations 9.1–9.5, as depicted in Figure 9.7.

9.3.1.2 *System Structure*

In this study, we develop a T-shaped adaptive impedance matching system that utilizes the complex impedance matching strategy characteristic of a T-shaped network. The architectural layout of this adaptive system is depicted in Figure 9.8. The system, implemented on both the transmitter and the receiver sides, consists of three primary components: the measurement unit, the control unit, and the impedance matching unit. This configuration mirrors the system structure described in [5, 8], underscoring its functional similarity and operational synergy with previously established designs.

The innovative T-shaped adaptive impedance identical system, the extent unit strategically positioned among the transmitter/receiver as well as the VPLN, precisely captures both the real and the imaginary impedance components of VPLN access point. The regulator unit interprets these data points and determines the optimal component values using a method that integrates resonance as well as absorption for complex impedance matching. Following this, it sends control signals to the impedance matching unit, commanding relay operations as well as modifying the configurations of digital potentiometers in both the tunable capacitor and the

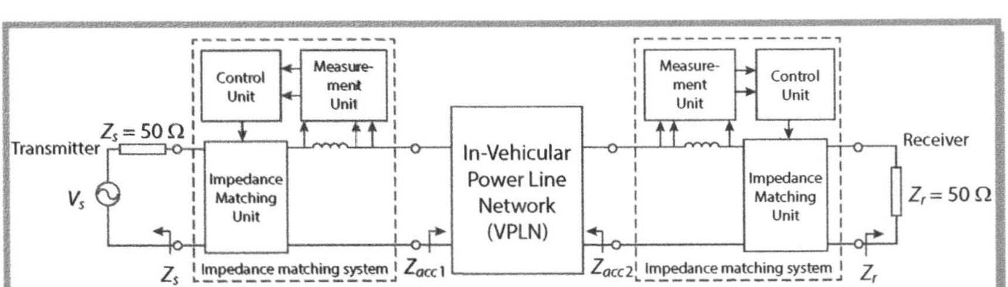

Figure 9.8 The dynamic impedance matching system designed for VPLC.

inductor's corresponding circuit headed for achieving the exact adaptive impedance matching.

The structural design of the system includes a dimension unit, a control unit, and an impedance matching unit. The measurement unit's role is to measure the access voltage as well as current, providing the control unit with the necessary real and imaginary components (Racc and Xacc) of the VPLN access impedance for detailed evaluation. Existing studies indicate that earlier designs have incorporated impedance measurement circuits featuring a sensing mechanism and a detection unit [19, 30]. These typically consist of a permanent inductor and dual operational amplifiers (Op-Amps) that effectively measure the VPLN's access voltage and current for the detection unit, which subsequently separates the real as well as imaginary impedance components.

A. Impedance Equivalent Unit

Illustrated in Figure 9.9, the impedance equivalent unit's layout is tailored for adaptive impedance matching. The calculations for component values appropriate for managing both inductive and capacitive access impedances are formulated in Equations 9.7 and 9.8. Although ideally, a T-shaped network would employ adjustable capacitors and inductors as shown in Figure 9.10, practical constraints limit this. Specifically, adjustable inductors are currently unviable [18], and the tuning scope of available adjustable capacitors does not meet the high capacitance demands of the matching network. To address this limitation, as depicted in Figure 9.10, arrays of capacitors with a scaling factor are utilized to effectively simulate the required adjustable capacitors.

In the dynamic impedance matching system, the microcontroller housed within the control module orchestrates the operation of digital relays (switches) to determine the appropriate capacitors from the capacitor bank

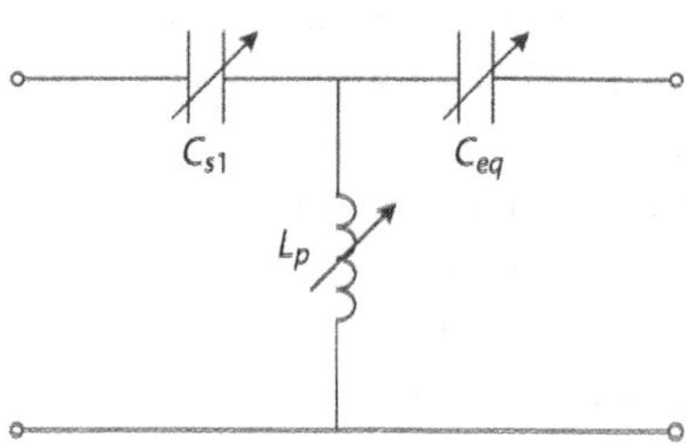

Figure 9.9 T-shaped impedance matching unit.

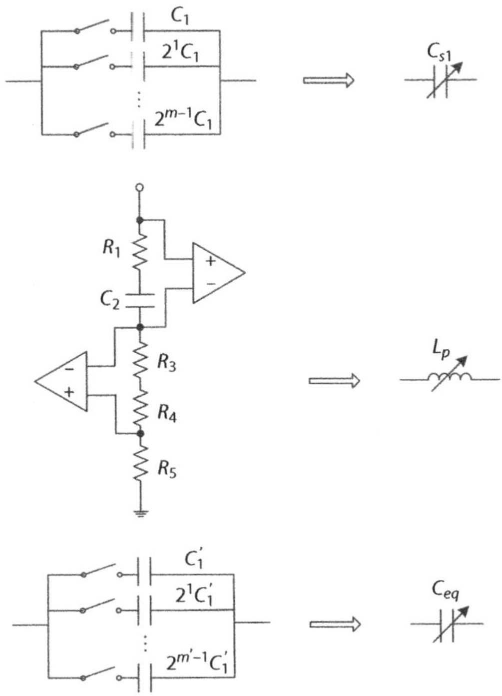

Figure 9.10 Equivalent tunable capacitor as well as inductor.

that will contribute to the total capacitance. This decision-making process employs a successive approximation algorithm to precisely gauge the active position of these digital relays. Choosing digital over analog relays offers benefits, as analog relays are known to add a conduction impedance that varies between quite a few ohms to dozens of ohms, potentially undermining the exactness of impedance matching in a T-type network. To elude using massive and cumbersome passive inductors, the system utilizes a dynamic inductor configuration. This system incorporates a general impedance converter (GIC [21]), equipped with two operational amplifiers (Op-Amps), three resistors (R1, R3, and R5), a digital potentiometer (R4), and a capacitor (C2), as depicted in Figure 9.10. The adjustability of the inductor is managed through the resistance setting of the digital potentiometer (R4), which determines the operational range of the active inductor. Such an arrangement ensures precise modulation of the equivalent capacitance and inductance values, critical for effective impedance matching. The equivalent capacitances as well as inductance are represented as

$$C_{s1} = \sum_{i=1}^{m} k_i C_i \quad k_i = 0 \text{ or } 1, \tag{9.6}$$

$$L_p = \frac{R_1 C_2 R_3 R_5}{R_4} \tag{9.7}$$

$$C_{eq} = \sum_{i'=1}^{m'} k'_{i'} C'_{i'} \quad k_{i'} = 0 \text{ or } 1, \tag{9.8}$$

where ki and ki′ signify the relay states; for example, ki=ki′ denotes the transmits in their exposed locations, while =ki′=1 specifies the transmits remain closed. The expression Ci=2i−1C1 and Ci″=2i′−1C1′ refer to the parallel capacitors in the tunable capacitor circuits as illustrated in Figure 9.10. The capacitance values Cs1 and Ceq can vary from 0 to (2m−1)C1 and 0 to (2m′−1)C1′, respectively.

B. Control Unit Operations

The central component of the control unit is a microcontroller, which processes input from the measurement unit to determine the component values for the T-shaped network and issues necessary control signals. These signals control the relay states and adjust the digital potentiometer settings for the tunable capacitor and the equivalent circuit of the inductor [15]. Initially, the microcontroller assesses both the real and imaginary components (Racc and Xacc) of the VPLN access impedance as provided by the measurement unit. It identifies the type of impedance by checking if Xacc is positive or negative, which helps determine if the impedance is predominantly inductive or capacitive. If Xacc is positive, indicative of inductive impedance, the microcontroller calculates Cres using Equation 9.6. It then compares Racc to Rs to decide the appropriate load-Q range, utilizing Equation 9.9 to opt for a lower load-Q to enhance the broadband equivalent capabilities. The standards for the T-shaped network in this scenario are established using Equation 9.7. Alternatively, if Xacc is negative, suggestive of capacitive impedance, Cacc is calculated with Equation 9.8. The standards for the T-shaped network in these conditions are figured out using Equation 9.8. The microcontroller concludes this process by dispatching control signals to the impedance-matching unit to refine the relay status as well as digital potentiometer adjustments, optimizing the T-shaped network's component settings [3].

9.4 Simulation Results besides Analysis

The performances as well as efficiency of the resonance- and absorption-based T-shaped impedance matching network were evaluated through three separate categories of simulations. Initially, two configurations of T-shaped matching network stayed simulated to test their transfer functions over a frequency range of 1 MHz to 100 MHz, aiming to assess broadband capabilities. The effect of the load-Q on the efficiency of impedance matching was also scrutinized [24]. Further simulations were carried out to validate the impedance-matching process within the adaptive T-shaped impedance-matching system. The final set of tests spanned four sub-frequency bands to provide a detailed analysis of the power transfer performance of the impedance-matching system. This advanced impedance matching system was modeled and tested using MatLab. The simulation settings were carefully adjusted to replicate typical access point impedance scenarios encountered during experiments. The simulation results were then meticulously analyzed and discussed, offering insights into the performance under three distinct constraints:

- Identical in the transmitter side
- Identical in the receiver side
- Simultaneously identical in both the transmitter and the receiver sides

This chart includes dashed lines representing scenarios without transmitter-side impedance matching and solid lines depicting scenarios

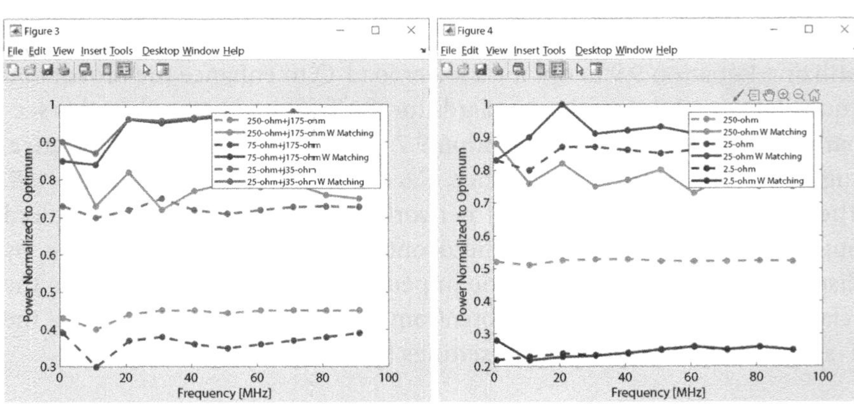

Figure 9.11 Graph of normalized real power transfer versus frequency.

with transmitter-side impedance matching. Figure 9.11 illustrates the identical real power transmitted to the transmission network across several frequencies as well as access impedances, comparing scenarios with and without impedance matching. Standardization refers to the optimal real power output achievable when an ideal impedance match is attained. The figure includes subfigures for access impedances of both inductive and purely resistive types. In these analyses, real power transmission shows significant improvement across a broad spectrum of frequencies and impedance values.

This graph displays efficiency across varying resistance levels, illustrating performance analysis at this specific frequency. The initial assessment sets the baseline for the effectiveness of the matching process, impacting the subsequent phases. In every scenario tested, real power transmission shows an enhancement, with increases exceeding 70%. In cases of optimal impedance matching, the improvement in real power transmission is even more pronounced.

This chart features hastened lines for scenarios without transmitter-side circuit impedance matching and solid lines for scenarios with impedance matching, clearly depicting the effects on power transfer. Additionally, the matching system ensures stable band behavior across the frequency spectrum. This consistency allows for high power transfer competence; still then, the frequency slightly diverges from the optimal corresponding frequency *fc*. Such performance demonstrates a clear advantage over systems lacking impedance matching, highlighting its effectiveness in maintaining efficiency across varied conditions.

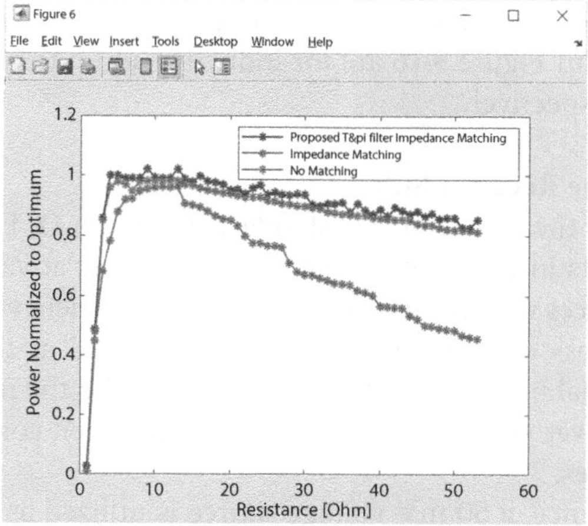

Figure 9.12 Graph of normalized real power transmission keen on the network designed for purely resistive impedance, through a cut-off frequency of 50 MHz.

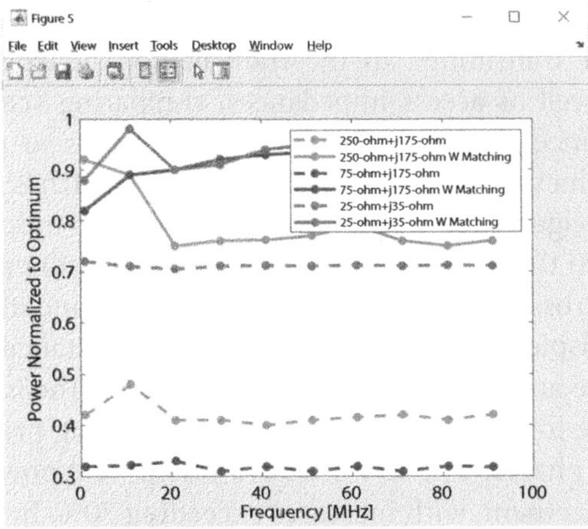

Figure 9.13 Graph of normalized actual power transmitted into the network over frequency.

Impedance matching solution is provided through Figure 9.12, which shows the normalized active power transfer as a function of the resistance of a purely resistive access impedance at a frequency of fc = 50 MHz. We observe that impedance matching consistently improves performance, but for the gap to the ideal matching increases drastically for access impedances below about 8. Figure 9.13 shows the normalized active power transmitted into the network with and without impedance matching, for different frequencies and access-impedance values. Normalization is with respect to the active power when optimal matching is applied, i.e., a normalized active power of one is the best possible performance. The top and bottom subfigures in Figure 9.16 are for inductive and purely resistive access impedances, respectively.

A. Matching the Receiver Side

At the receiver, the impedance is standardized to 50 Ω. Figure 9.14 illustrates the results in terms of normalized real power at various capacitive access impedances with resistance, observed at a frequency of 50 MHz (fc = 50 MHz). Across all scenarios, the power received at the receiver end shows substantial improvement. These findings echo the improvements in normalized power seen in the previous sections when compared to reference impedances.

In each instance, a 50 mV voltage source is utilized as the transmitter, and both the receiver and transmitter are configured with 50 Ω resistance.

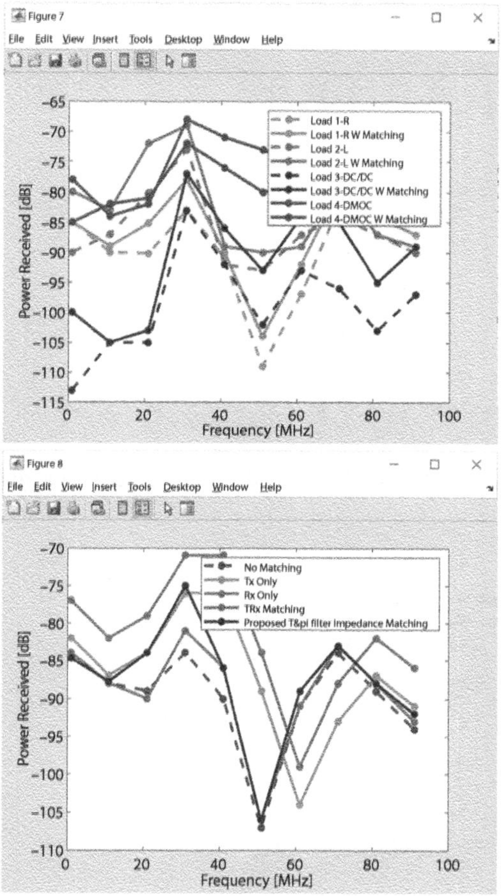

Figure 9.14 Real power at the receiver side by means of frequency aimed at entire cases.

B. Impedance Matching at BPLC's Two Ends

Implementing the adaptive impedance matching circuit at both the transmitter and receiver sides in the broadband power line communication (BPLC) system ensures effective power transmission. Using the S-parameters [11, 13], the system's behavior under authentic BPLC conditions is evaluated, providing an in-depth analysis of network dynamics. Illustrated in Figure 9.15 are the real power fluctuations at the receiver across varying frequencies, with and without all four links connected. These variations in frequency response curves stem from the channel attenuation sensitive to frequency, which impacts power levels at the receiver. Notable improvements in system efficiency, highlighted as "1 dB and 10 dB," reflect a tenfold increase due to impedance matching. Figure 9.16 displays the actual

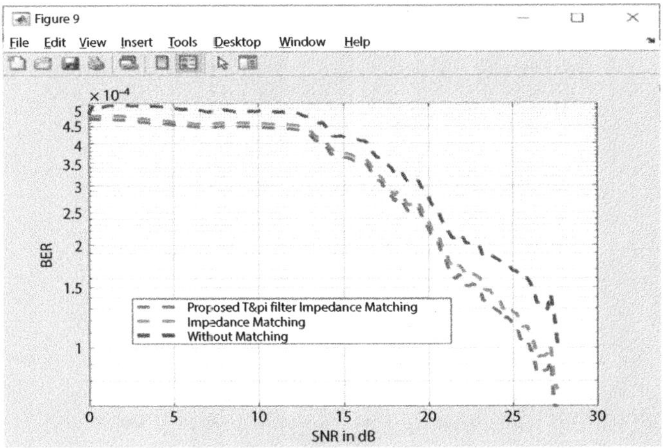

Figure 9.15 Graph of SNR versus BER at end of the data receiver with matching impedance.

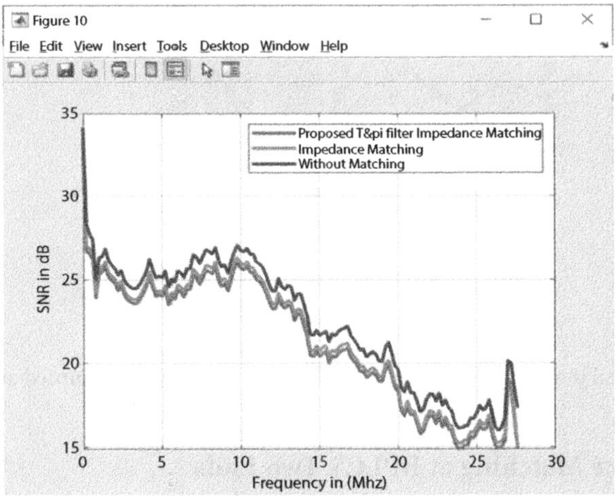

Figure 9.16 Graph of frequency versus SNR at the data receiver with matching impedance.

power received in various conditions, highlighting that peak performance matches the most advantageous frequency settings. However, variations in performance at each link endpoint arise from differing S-parameters and the variability of access point impedances at specific frequencies. In some instances, matching exclusively at the transmitter end yields more power than when both ends are matched, optimizing both the transmitter and receiver to enhance efficiency.

This visualization shows the relationship between signal quality and data integrity, highlighting how impedance matching affects communication performance at the receiver end.

This chart depicts how the signal-to-noise ratio varies with frequency, illustrating the effectiveness of impedance matching in enhancing signal clarity at the receiver end.

9.5 Conclusion

- This paper describes the development of a T-shaped adaptive impedance matching system, consisting of three principal components: a measurement unit, a control unit, and an impedance matching unit.
- Insights into the intricacies of the T-shaped adaptive matching system were elaborated upon, detailing how each component contributes to the overall functionality.
- Through rigorous simulations, the system was evaluated across various power line scenarios. These tests demonstrated a significant enhancement in signal power transfer attributable to the adaptive impedance matching system.
- The forthcoming research phase will examine the impact of inclusion loss on the impedance matching network, aiming to identify potential inefficiencies.
- Attention will be directed toward developing a parasitic-aware three-element impedance matching network, intending to optimize and refine system performance further.

References

1. Taherinejad, N., Rosales, R., Lampe, L., Mirabbasi, S., On the design of impedance matching circuits for vehicular power line communication systems, in: *IEEE International Symposium on Power Line Communications and Its Applications (ISPLC)*, pp. 322–327, 2012.
2. Taherinejad, N., Lampe, L., Mirabbasi, S., Adaptive impedance matching for vehicular power line communication systems, in: *IEEE International Symposium on Power Line Communications and its Applications (ISPLC)*, pp. 214–219, Mar. 2014.
3. Schwartz, M., Carrier-wave telephony over power lines: Early history [history of communications]. *IEEE Commun. Mag.*, 47, 1, 14–18, Jan. 2009.

4. Ferreira, H., Lampe, L., Newbury, J., Swart, T., *Power Line Communications: Theory and Applications for Narrowband and Broadband Communications over Power Lines*, Wiley, 2010.
5. Galli, S., Scaglione, A., Dostert, K., Broadband is power: internet access through the power line network. *IEEE Commun. Mag.*, 41, 5, 82–83, May 2003.
6. Leen, G. and Heffernan, D., Expanding automotive electronic systems. *Computer*, 35, 1, 88–93, Jan. 2002.
7. Navet, N., Song, Y., Simonot-Lion, F., Wilwert, C., Trends in automotive communication systems. *Proc. IEEE*, 93, 6, 1204–1223, Jun. 2005.
8. Strategy Analytics Automotive Electronics report, November 2007, Automotive Multiplexing Protocols: Cost/Performance Driving New Protocol Adoption, cited from http://www.businesswire.com/news/home/20071115006121/en/STRATEGY-ANALYTICS-Automotive-Electronics-Network-Market-Stretch, accessed on August 28, 2011.
9. van Rensburg, P. and Ferreira, H., Automotive power-line communications: favourable topology for future automotive electronic trends, in: *International Symposium on Power Line Communications and Its Applications (ISPLC)*, Kyoto, Japan, pp. 103–108, Mar. 2003.
10. Enders, T. and Schirmer, J., Automotive powerline communications – a new physical layer for CAN, in: *Int. CAN Conf.*, Munich, Germany, Oct. 2003.
11. Smitha Gayathri, D. and Usha Rani, K.R., Adaptive impedance matching system for broadband power line communication using RC-filters. *J. Ambient Intell. Hum. Comput.*, 14, 11823–11832, 2022, https://doi.org/10.1007/s12652-022-03738-8.
12. Huck, T., Schirmer, J., Hogenmuller, T., Dostert, K., Tutorial about the implementation of a vehicular high speed communication system, in: *International Symposium on Power Line Communications and Its Applications (ISPLC)*, Vancouver, Canada, pp. 162–166, Apr. 2005.
13. Smitha Gayathri, D. and Usha Rani, K.R., Analysis of Impedance Matching Technique on Broadband Powerline Communication Network Topologies, in: *ICT Analysis and Applications*, Lecture Notes in Networks and Systems, vol. 314, 2022, https://doi.org/10.1007/978-981-16-5655-2_85.
14. Hrasnica, H., Haidine, A., Lehnert, R., *Broadband Powerline Communications Networks Network Design*, All of Dresden University of Technology, Germany, 2005.
15. Gouret, W., Nouvel, F., El-Zein, G., Powerline communication on automotive network, in: *IEEE Vehicular Technology Conference (VTC)*, pp. 2545–2549, Apr. 2007.
16. Amrani, O. and Rubin, A., Contention detection and resolution for multiple-access power-line communications. *IEEE Trans. Veh. Technol.*, 56, 6, 3879–3887, 2007.

17. Ferreira, H.C., Lampe, L., Newbury, J., Swart, T.G., *Power Line Communications: Theory and Applications for Narrowband and Broadband Communications over Power Lines*, Wiley, Hoboken, NJ, USA, 2010.
18. Huck, T., Schirmer, J., Hogenmuller, T., Tutorial about the implementation of a vehicular high speed communication system, in: *Proc. Int. Symp. Power Line Commun. Appl.*, Vancouver, BC, Canada, pp. 162–166, Apr. 2005.
19. Taherinejad, N., Rosales, R., Lampe, L., Mirabbasi, S., Channel characterization for power line communication in a hybrid electric vehicle, in: *Proc. IEEE Int. Symp. Power Line Commun. Appl.*, pp. 328–333, Mar. 2012.
20. Mohammadi, M., Lampe, L., Lok, M., Mirabbasi, S., Mirvakili, M., Rosales, R., van Veen, P., Measurement study and transmission for in-vehicle power line communication, in: *Proc. IEEE Int. Symp. Power Line Commun. Appl.*, Dresden, Germany, pp. 73–78, Mar. 2009.
21. Barmada, S., Raugi, M., Tucci, M., Zheng, T., Power line communication in a full electric vehicle: Measurements, modelling and analysis, in: *Proc. ISPLC*, pp. 331–336, 2010.
22. Degardin, V., Lienard, M., Degauque, P., Simon, E., Laly, P., Impulsive noise characterization of in-vehicle power line. *IEEE Trans. Electromagn. Compat.*, 50, 4, 861–868, Nov. 2008.
23. Zhang, L., Ma, H., Shi, D., Wang, P., Cai, G., Liu, X., Reliability oriented modeling and analysis of vehicular power line communication for vehicle to grid (V2G) information exchange system. *IEEE Access*, 5, 12449–12457, 2017.
24. Taherinejad, N., Lampe, L., Mirabbasi, S., An adaptive impedance matching system for vehicular power line communication. *IEEE Trans. Veh. Technol.*, 66, 2, 927–940, Feb. 2017.

10

Future Trends in V2X Communication and Interoperability

Dankan Gowda V.[1]*, D. Palanikkumar[2], Satish Dekka[3], K.D.V. Prasad[4] and Shivoham Singh[4]

[1]Department of Electronics and Communication Engineering, BMS Institute of Technology and Management, Bangalore, Karnataka, India
[2]Department of Computer Science and Engineering, Dr. NGP Institute of Technology, Coimbatore, Tamil Nadu, India
[3]Department of Computer Science and Engineering, Lendi Institute of Engineering and Technology, Visakhapatnam, Andhra Pradesh, India
[4]Symbiosis Institute of Business Management, Hyderabad and Symbiosis International (Deemed University), Pune, India

Abstract
This chapter attempts to define the future of V2X communication wherein sure predictions can be made that by then trends will change and interoperability goes boggling. The scene is set in the introduction by emphasizing the need to look forward due to fast-paced technologies and their potential impact on connected car systems. We observe how 5G and other generations of wireless connection affect data speed, latency, and system performance as well as how it would determine V2X future communication. In the nearby future, linked systems will also increase functionality at autonomous fleets. The later part of the chapter elaborates the integration of V2X communication with autonomous cars. The article explains a possibility to improve the performance scalability, efficiency, and responsiveness for V2X system through moving toward decentralized topologies and edge intelligence. The complex and critical concept of achieving interoperability in a heterogeneous vendor ecosystem is studied, focusing on open standards and collaborative work. Finally, this chapter delves into the legal and regulatory issues that will shape the future of V2X communication going forward as well as changing user perception in connected cars. In a nutshell, the abstract paints a picture of a

**Corresponding author*: dankan.v@bmsit.in

Rathishchandra R. Gatti and Chandra Singh (eds.) Digital Convergence in Intelligent Mobility Systems, (217–240) © 2025 Scrivener Publishing LLC

world where V2X communication makes transport more efficient but also helps to create an intelligent, sustainable, and safe mobility ecosystem.

Keywords: V2X communication, interoperability, future trends, connected vehicles, wireless connectivity, 5G technology, autonomous vehicles, edge computing

10.1 Introduction

The current V2X communication space provides numerous technological advancements and focuses on interoperability. V2X communication incorporates vehicle-to-vehicle (V2V) and vehicle-to-infrastructure (V2I).

Technological Developments: Technological development in the wireless sector, especially the evolution of 4G LTE networks, has paved the way for successful V2X communication. All these advancements have facilitated the transfer of data at high speeds, reduced latency issues, and increased reliability that is crucial for communication in vehicular settings [1, 2]. Additionally, the arrival of DSRC and C-V2X technologies has led to such an advancement. The DSRC, in the 5.9 GHz band, has low latency and high reliability as a short-range communication application for vehicular transportation [3]. On the other hand, C-V2X, utilizing cellular networks, offers a more extensive range and supports direct (PC5 interface) and networked communications (Uu interface).

Challenges in Interoperability: In the context of V2X scenery, despite all these advancements, interoperability remains a key challenge. There are various communication standards such as DSRC and C-V2X, which have resulted in a fragmented market [4, 5]. Technology has not been the same across regions and manufacturers, making it difficult to set up a universal compatible V2X ecosystem [6]. This fragmentation does not allow the simple interaction between different vehicles, infrastructure entities, and networks that would be necessary for the full realization of V2X advantages.

Regulatory Landscape: The series of technological advancements have the regulatory environment playing catch up. Though some regions have begun to require V2X in new vehicles, such as the European Union moving toward C-V2X, others are still deciding on their next step. As a part of the interoperability challenge here, this regulatory unevenness plays the role because manufacturers find themselves facing up to different standards and norms often offered throughout various regions.

Cybersecurity and Privacy: Cybersecurity and privacy pose a lot of issues with the ever-increasing connectivity, exchanging data in V2X communication [7, 8]. However, ensuring the integrity of vehicular communications networks and respecting the privacy of user data is essential. Work is being done to create this and other measures providing effective protection against information dangers.

The application of vehicular communications has seen significant growth in the last decade. It is now one of the most widely used wireless applications. Its core objective is improving safety, security, as well as comfort in highway travel, while automating the system improves on human errors during transit [9, 10]. First, the efforts were mainly directed at enabling data exchange between mobile vehicles through communication networks addressing vehicle-to-vehicle interests. But with the development of this field, more and more researchers have focused on how to upgrade it to meet different needs of vehicular operation beyond manual control [11, 12]. However, as the development proceeded, a variety of features were incorporated such as "vehicle-to-vehicle (V2V)," "vehicle-to-infrastructure (V2I)," "vehicle-to-roadside unit (RSU)," and finally, also added on was "vehicle-to-pedestrian." Different technologies were integrated to help and control the communication techniques such as sensors, roadside units, Internet connectivity, intranet system, fog networks, cloud computing and also wireless support [13, 14]. The entire framework is called collectively vehicle-to-everything (V2X). The overall aim of vehicular communications is providing an integrated, convenient and safe driving; reducing the road accidents; increasing fuel efficiency; minimizing carbon emissions; saving time factor; and at the same time advanced level of comfortable drive. An example of an illustrative representation of the "vehicle-to-everything (V2X)" case in vehicular communications is shown in Figure 10.1.

Figure 10.2 offers comprehensive insights into two key applications within vehicular communications: To confine to vehicular-to-vehicular (V2V) and vehicular-to-infrastructure (V2I) communications, both coverages include various safeguardies [15, 16]. These apps are very technology-intensive with a huge bandwidth capacity. Importantly, it is worth mentioning that current tech does not provide the full range of vehicular technology applications [17]. This difficulty stems from the lack of secure and dependable, high coverage and necessary communication systems capable of providing continuous connectivity to offer a sufficient amount of bandwidth for the variety of HD applications needed to make autonomous vehicles reach their true potential [18, 19]. Ahead, the development of

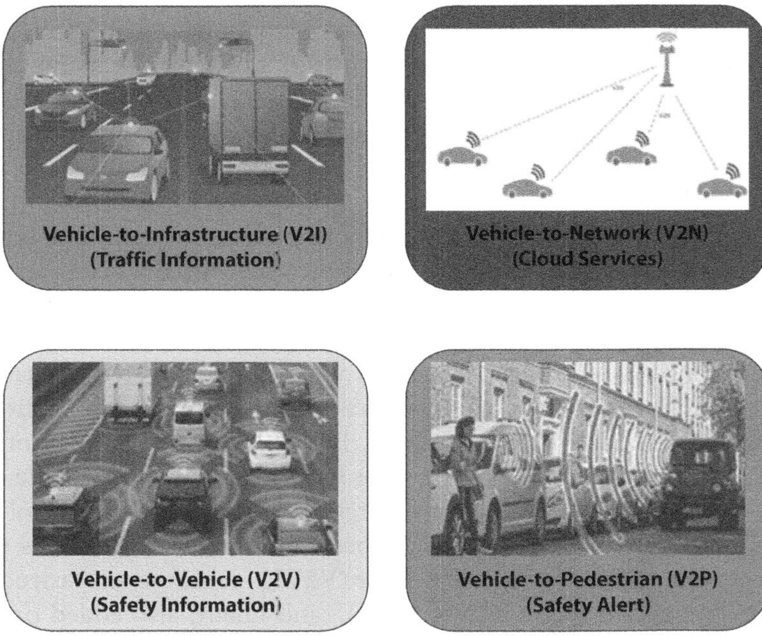

Figure 10.1 Illustrating V2X connectivity in the field of vehicular communications.

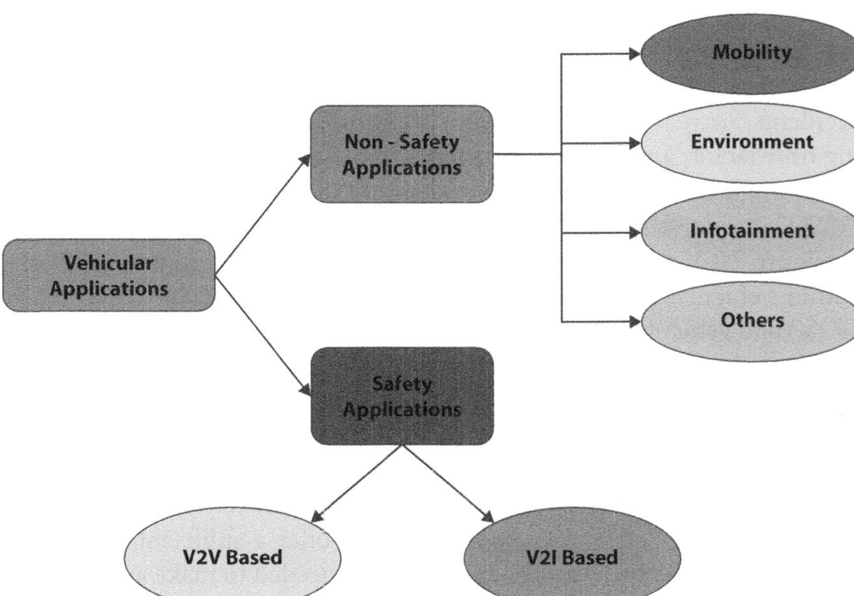

Figure 10.2 An overview of applications enabled by connected vehicles.

V2X communication is bound to largely benefit from the implementation of 5G networks, enabling faster speeds, reduced latency, and increased capacity [20]. Integration of new technologies, such as AI and ML, into V2X systems is likely to make decision-making processes even more efficient. Nevertheless, the road to a seamlessly merged and interoperable yet secure V2X environment would entail additional synchronization steps between stakeholders in industry, standard development bodies, as well as regulators.

This introductory section lays the groundwork toward a comprehensive analysis of future trends in V2X communication and interoperability, emphasizing how new technologies and participatory approaches can deal with present initiatives to deliver what V2X systems are capable of.

10.2 Emerging Technologies in V2X Communication

This section explores how 5G breaks the barriers placed by previous standards, presenting V2X with an opportunity for transformation beginning with the interdependence phase to the connectivity aspect.

5G Technology: A major leap in V2X communication is presented by 5G networks due to their high data rates, ultra-low latency, and massive device connectivity. Contrast and differences are 5G compared to its predecessors, which does not offer the bandwidth needed for dealing with the large amount of data that is required by modern cars: high-resolution maps, real-life traffic updates, and sensor information from a variety of sources [21, 22]. The low latency of 5G is essential for critical safety applications since the vehicles respond almost in real time to dynamic driving conditions.

Enhanced V2X Capabilities: In 5G, the domain of V2X communication increases considerably. It helps to enable more complex applications that include cooperative driving, platooning, and advanced pedestrian protection systems [23]. The huge-sized vehicles infrastructures and mobile equipment applications need real-time delivery of high-volume data structures between vehicles and infrastructure which 5G networks support reliably.

Integration with Advanced Technologies: In the long run, integration of 5G with other potential technologies such as edge computing and artificial intelligence is likely to improve immensely V2X communication [24, 25]. With edge computing, the transportation networks stakeholders can reduce the distance data travels and that lessens latency which in return results into faster response time. As opposed, the AI is able to analyze

and process an enormous amount of data produced by the V2X systems, thus allowing for more accurate decision making with predictive analytics involved in terms of traffic management as well as accident avoidance.
Beyond 5G—The Future of Connectivity: Going forward from 5G, the next stages in V2X communication lie with the advent of 6G and other advanced wireless technologies [26]. This makes way for future networks that are projected to provide even larger data rates, faster communication response times, and more reliable communication capabilities. Vanishingly particular technologies, including the terahertz (THz) frequencies and advanced network topologies associated with vehicle communications, are incredibly likely to complement their improvement in the future as well.
Challenges and Considerations: While these strides were made, the process of transitioning to 5G and beyond brought a number of challenges. 5G infrastructure deployment, especially for rural areas and communities that are not adequately served, poses a considerable challenge. Secondly, it is necessary to provide interoperability with the legacy V2X systems. Moreover, high prices of components in 5G could affect the cost-effectiveness, and hence, prevalence in driverless technologies is likely to be witnessed in automotive sector.

As part of the broad range of services in vehicular communications, autonomy is one of its most important features, allowing for smart transportation technologies like robots, drones, and teleportation to work. The key role of these services is to improve the capacities in which vehicular communications can operate [27, 28]. In Figure 10.3, we can see the

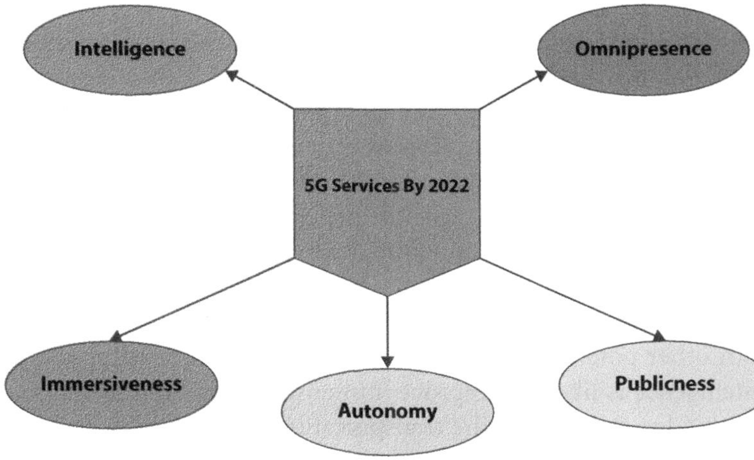

Figure 10.3 Envisioned landscape of 5G services.

development of 5G services that are expected to be implemented in 2025. The services are to have a leading function in the development and support of autonomous vehicles. It is a milestone in V2X communication with the coming out of 5G and the next-generation technologies. These improvements will not only improve the present V2X capabilities but also create new horizons for development in vehicular communications. Nevertheless, in order to achieve these gains, the infrastructure concerns, compatibility issues, as well as economic impacts arising from adoption of such fourth-generation connectivity solutions need to be dealt with.

10.3 Autonomous Vehicles and V2X Integration

This section reveals the importance of V2X communication in the realization and workings of autonomous vehicles which employ these technologies to enhance intelligent transport system.

Enhancing Autonomous Vehicle Capabilities: In addition to onboard sensors, V2X communication is a vital enabler for autonomous vehicles, making them aware of events outside their field of view. Through the use of V2X, AVs can obtain current knowledge on road surface condition, traffic signals status, walking movements, and static/dynamic intentions of other vehicles. This increased situational awareness is essential for AVs to be able to take intelligent and appropriate decision making on the road, but in particularly complex urban traffic situations.

Safety and Efficiency Improvements: The introduction of V2X into AVs provides notable improvement in road safety and traffic, which include efficiency. Vehicle-to-everything (V2X) allows for cooperative driving, initiating cooperation between vehicles to achieve an optimal degree of coordination in traffic flow, preventing or reducing congestion and subsequently improving travel times. As far as safety is considered, V2X communication enables AVs to avoid crashes preemptively through advanced warnings of impending potential hazards that sensors and cameras do not know in advance.

Infrastructure Interaction: V2X communication makes it possible for AVs to have a two-way connection with road infrastructure (V2I). The communication capacities of traffic lights, road signs, and other infrastructure elements are useful in transportation of information on routes and their optimization as well as management for the AVs. This type of interaction also promotes smart cities, for AVs can help formulate effective urban designs and environmental sustainability.

Data Exchange and Privacy Concerns: It is impossible to integrate AVs with V2X systems without sharing a huge amount of data. This poses numerous challenges related both to the privacy and protection of the information. The security of personal information while preserving the required flow is a key challenge. These challenges are inadequate and robust encryption on anonymization techniques, alongside a stringent data governance policy addressing these concerns.
Standardization and Interoperability: A sufficient and important condition for a successful V2X integration in AVs is the standardization of communication protocols and data formats. Interoperability between different vehicle brands, models, and infrastructure systems makes sure that all parties involved in the transportation ecosystem have smooth practice. The universal standards are being developed by the continued efforts made by a number of standardization organizations and industry consortia.
Future Prospects: Neglecting V2X communication has particularly affected AV products; as the technology progresses, they become of increased importance in improving the capabilities of these devices. Future improvements of wireless technologies—such as 5G and beyond—will additionally push the boundaries of what is possible with AVs to advance more mature levels of autonomy and a cleverer way forward in transportation. But the complete acceptance of these benefits is dependent on the overcoming of modern challenges regarding technology connectivity, standards, and protection.

Network slicing is a virtualized network infrastructure using technologies such as software-defined networking (SDN and NFV network function virtualization). It allows for the consolidation of several virtual networks on one shared physical network infrastructure. 3GPP defines a network slice simply as an entity that is a logical network with certain properties and characteristics. NGMN takes this concept further by arguing that network slicing is the ability of having multiple logically independent networks running on a single common physical infrastructure. Individual slices may have unique features such as the types of traffic, QoS factors, and security standards. Creation of network slice instances in realization of network slicing is made through compilation of NFs and related computing, storage, as well as specialized computing resources for each slice instance. Technologies such as SDN and NFV play a key role in the realization of network slicing. This approach helps to adopting the

NFs and resources, thus making them logical for various vertical markets within one common network infrastructure. It should be mentioned that the 5G network slicing covers various layers, which include 5G RAN, 5G core network, as well as end-user devices. Figure 10.4 provides an illustration of the network slicing concept, which comprises three layers: the service instance layer, network slice instance layer, and the resource layer. In other situations, network slicing is tied to the virtualization of base stations through which different organizations get a chance to share one spectrum. The word "network slice" implies a virtual network having a set of flows that are supported by one physical base station, which also supports many other virtual networks. Moreover, case studies have been conducted to analyze wireless network virtualization as a method for infrastructure providers (InPs) to separate wireless and physical resources. These slices are then assigned to service providers (SPs) serving their individual set of subscribers.

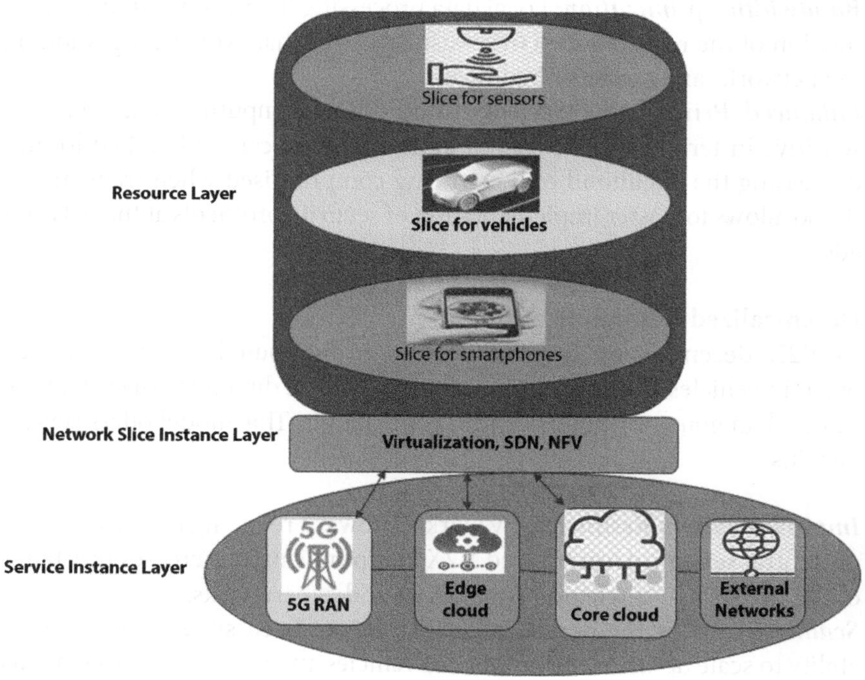

Figure 10.4 Illustration showing the concept of network slicing.

10.4 Edge Intelligence and Decentralized Communication

In this section, integration of edge intelligence and decentralized communication in V2X systems have been studied, knowing the importance of such solution for improving vehicular communication and data processing.

Edge Intelligence in V2X Systems

Edge intelligence is defined as the processing of data at the edge of the network near to where data is generated by vehicles and roadside units. This method provides a number of benefits in V2X communication.

Reduced Latency: Local data processing via edge intelligence results in considerably smaller transfer time when relaying information to the vehicle and central cloud. This is essential for real-time decision making in dynamic driving scenarios.
Bandwidth Optimization: Local data processing involves minimum transmission of the required data over vast distances that avoids congestion on the networks and conserve bandwidth.
Enhanced Privacy and Security: With edge computing, data that are sensitive in terms of privatization and protection can be handled locally, decreasing the likelihood of these being compromised when transmitted. It also allows for faster implementation of security protocols at the network edge.

Decentralized Communication

In V2X decentralized communication, a distributed strategy adopted wherein vehicles and infrastructure communicate directly with each other, rather than going through a central control unit. This model offers several benefits.

Improved System Resilience: By working toward reducing the dependency on central servers, decentralized V2X communication increases resistance of the network to single points of failure and cyberattacks.
Scalability: With the development of decentralized systems, there is an ability to scale up when the number of vehicles and infrastructure elements increases without huge overhauls in central infrastructure.
Adaptive and Responsive Network: In accordance with its entirety, decentralized communication is based on an adaptive and dynamic network that can monitor changes to traffic patterns in real time, as well as external factors influencing the connectivity it provides.

Figure 10.5 describes an event where there is an emergency vehicle, several cars moving on the road, and pedestrians trying to cross the street. Here's a description of the scenario: A medium lane is being driven on by an emergency vehicle toward its destination. Upon drawing closer to a traffic light, the vehicle transmits a message that causes the relevant adjacent traffic light turning green away from its path while those located along other crossroads turn red. At the same time, the emergency vehicle switches lanes by signaling cars in the middle lane to switch as well so that an unobstructed path is cleared. There are also a number of vehicles in the next lane, and one of them is yellow, which gets the signal from the emergency vehicle. The yellow car assesses the capacity of other lanes. When the other lanes are empty, the yellow car shifts to another lane. If other lanes are busy, the automobile computes the distances between vehicles in those lanes and decides which lane to shift into. After this calculation, the car makes changes of speed, announces to other cars in selected lane for safety reasons, and shifts to the desired right side. In one of the vehicles, a backseat passenger is watching an HD film, and a pedestrian who plans to walk

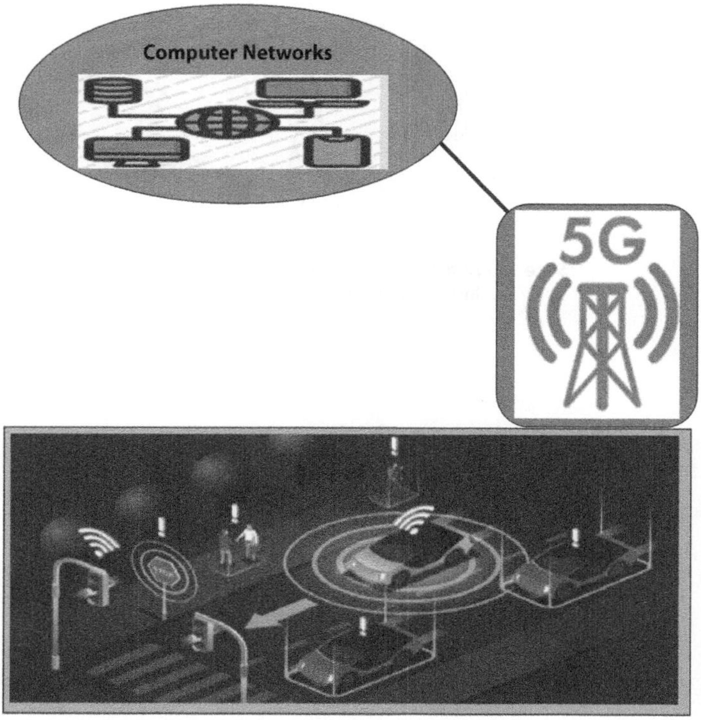

Figure 10.5 Sample instances of different V2X communications.

across the street is watching on YouTube via their smartphone. The emergency vehicle will send a warning signal related to an approaching pedestrian to their smartphone, preventing them from walking into the path of the approaching vehicle. The employment of edge intelligence and decentralized communication into V2X systems presents some major issues such as predicted in distinguishing computational capacities onboard vehicles and in the infrastructure, compatibility with other styles, as well as dealing with decentralized networks. Some such solutions of these challenges include the introduction of more efficient and less power-hungry edge computing equipment, proper standards-based communication protocols, and advanced network management tools that can dynamically tweak the performance parameters to gain optimal yields.

Slices described in this example are represented by Figure 10.6. All slices manage themselves independently from one another, given specific adaptation characteristics sufficiently satisfying the requirements of their users. Still, whereas some devices are privy to only one slice and thematic loading is limited by a scarcity in their numbers, either the pedestrian's smartphone

Figure 10.6 Exemplifying network slicing with two slices and varying needs.

or any other mobile device has access to both slices/channels. In the first scenario, all participants use an LTE Advance for communicating to find a match. In the latter scenario, participants on a 5G network have more advanced capabilities to meet the demands of various slices. It is an efficient way for managing the resources of a network that enables optimal allocation, addressing different requirements originating from various communication groups and leading to desirable user experience. Because its edge intelligence and decentralized communication are two complementary features that change the paradigm of V2X communication, this combination ensures more efficient security and scalability. The future of transport systems is vastly simplified with time elements, making it appear as if they are central in the growth of an intelligent, autonomous, and reliable transport system. But achieving the true potential remains dependent on continued efforts at innovation and collaboration by relevant automotive, technology, and infrastructural stakeholders.

10.5 Interoperability in a Multi-Vendor Ecosystem

Interoperability is a significant problem, and many V2X-related strategies are the subject of this section. It implies enabling connected vehicle operation within a multi-vendor ecosystem that will ensure proper functioning among the various connected vehicles. The multi-vendor environment is much more problematic.

In a multi-vendor world, cars have to talk to the stuff that is in them and with other infrastructure on the road as well as talk with other devices from different manufacturers. However, this interoperability is hindered by several factors:

Diverse Standards and Protocols: It is observed that different vendors may utilize diverse standards of communication and protocols resulting into a non-conducive flow of information. For example, the combination of DSRC and C-V2X technologies has resulted in a confusing landscape in V2X communication.

Software and Hardware Variability: Variances in software architectures and infrastructures, as developed by different providers, always interfere with the efficient interaction between systems.

Upgrading and Scalability Issues: It is logically problematic to make sure that systems support easy upgrades and vertical scaling along with the compatibility with legacy as well as future systems.

Strategies for Ensuring Interoperability

Standardization: It is also critical that global standards are developed and followed in order to achieve interoperability. Organizations such as IEEE, 3GPP and SAE International are participating to set up guidelines for V2X communications so that there is a uniform international code of practice. These standards should meet not only current but also future needs, and products that will be phased out due to technology demand to secure forward and backward compatibility of the technologies.

Open Platforms and Interfaces: The popularization of open platforms and uniform interfaces makes it possible to connect different systems despite the type of underlying hardware or software. Open-source platforms also allow for increased innovation and shorter development cycles.

Collaborative Testing and Certification: Following the joint effort of testing and certification programs, it will guarantee that items from different vendors are suited to interoperability standards. So programs that are designed in this way may support various types and arrangements of systems in real life in order to determine compatibility between a given number.

Industry Consortia and Alliances: It is possible to promote the cooperation between manufacturers, technology providers, and regulatory authorities to organize industry consortiums as well as alliances. These groups can cooperate to converge on standards, knowledge sharing, and promotion of the implementation of best practices for interoperability.

Regulatory Support: Interoperability standards can be enforced by government regulations to a great extent. Regulatory organizations can make these compliance requirements regarding interoperability principles a must by mandating all market players to adhere to the same in order to maintain comity.

The issue of interoperability is important in multi-vendor environments, and without addressing the needs for interoperability, V2X communication systems will not operate efficiently or effectively. This would require standardization, open platforms, collaborative feeding back verification to suture tightening at industry collaboration, and regulatory support. With the development of the V2X ecosystem, compatibility is a key factor, as combining telematics in vehicles offers a significant advantage in optimizing regulatory management, improving efficiency, and enhancing the overall travel experience.

10.6 Cybersecurity in Future V2X Systems

This section focuses on the cybersecurity needs that have to be satisfied in the new era of V2X communication systems as one of the cornerstones for safeguarding future automotive networks.

Evolving Cybersecurity Challenges

As V2X systems become more complex, interconnected, and reliant on time-dependent cycles, they are likely to become more vulnerable to a range of cybersecurity threats. These threats can be as innocent as a data breach or privacy violation or they may include more serious dangers, such as remote vehicle manipulation. The main challenges include the following:

Data Privacy: Providing user data security related to transmissions over V2X networks has a very important role. The personal data, the location information, and travel records are ultra-sensitive because they need to be guarded from other parties that have no business in interfering with them.
Network Security: Communication channels in V2X networks have to be protected from outside attacks that interfere with communication, such as DoS attacks, eavesdropping, or impersonation.
Software Integrity: The software housed in both in-vehicle and infrastructure V2X systems also has to be tamper-proof against injection of malicious code.
Hardware Security: The integrity of the V2X systems would be maintained by implementing measures that regulate tampering with its hardware components and that it is not compromised.

Strategies for Enhancing Cybersecurity

Advanced Encryption Techniques: Robust encryption is important for securing V2X networks in terms of data transmission. This encompasses secure and robust communication channel encryption mechanisms as well as measures for safe authentication standard protocols.
Regular Software Updates and Patch Management: The requirement of updating software with the latest security patches is therefore a necessity. Automated update mechanisms are capable of ensuring that patches for the vulnerabilities are rolled out quickly.
Intrusion Detection Systems: The use of advanced intrusion detection systems (IDS) for the monitoring of V2X networks will enable the detection multiple threats or strange behaviors that could potentially trigger security issues.

Secure Hardware Modules: In vehicles and infrastructure, making use of secure hardware modules can be an extra security in place. The modules are capable of performing cryptographic operations, and data can be stored safely as some of them require safekeeping.
Cross-Layer Security Approaches: By utilizing the defense layer policy, ensuring that security measures are implemented in all V2X communication layers the physical, network, and application levels contribute to developing a comprehensive antivirus plan.
Collaboration and Information Sharing: Stakeholders in the industry, cybersecurity professionals, and regulatory agencies must work together so that more knowledge can be generated about the new threats out there and practices to fight them.
Regulatory Compliance and Standards: Following the cybersecurity standards and regulations that have already been accepted is very important. Standards are crucial and have to be set by regulatory bodies that ensure adherence. Cybersecurity is one of the most important pillars in defining V2X systems in the future. And as these systems develop, so must the tactics to secure them. A multi-tiered approach that includes modern technology, coordinated actions, and adherence to regulatory requirements is necessary for the defense of the V2X system exposed to a wide range of cyber threats. However, meeting high standards of cybersecurity will ensure trust from the public and enable the optimal manifestation of V2X communication to improve road safety and efficiency.

10.7 Environmental and Sustainability Considerations

This section discusses the effects of V2X communication systems for nature and sustainability, stressing that it is important to include findings about ecological issues when developing new technology.

Reducing Carbon Footprint through Efficient Traffic Management: The possible reduction of vehicle emissions is an important environmental positive check on V2X communication. With more efficient traffic regulation, V2X systems can decrease waiting times at the traffic lights and thereby reduce congestion, which means lesser fuel consumption and subsequently lower emissions. Real-time traffic information and predictive analytics can tweak routes, which can help to reduce the additional traveling needed to cut down even more in unnecessary mileage and emission.

Facilitating Electrification of Transportation: V2X communication is crucial for switching to electric vehicles (EVs). It can help make the EV experience better through real-time data on charging station availability and optimal routes for energy efficiency purposes. Besides, the concept of V2X can provide smart charging infrastructure that has become essential for effective load balancing between grids as well as smart integration of renewable energy sources.
Promoting Sustainable Urban Planning: Urban area integrated V2X system can be viable toward helping in more sustainable city planning. Data obtained through V2X networks can be employed in the construction of urban cities that emphasize public transport, cycling, and walking, thereby reducing overall private vehicle dependence. This method not only minimizes impact on nature but also produces healthier environments in cities.
Lifecycle and Environmental Impact of Technology: V2X technologies should not be limited to their lifecycle environmental impact. This also includes the amount of resources and energy that is consumed in manufacturing V2X elements and, at the end of their lifecycle, are either disposed of or recycled. Considering eco-friendly manufacturing processes and sustainable materials for V2X components is a necessary step in minimizing the ecological footprint.
Energy-Efficient Communication Technologies: In order to mitigate the effects that V2X systems have on the environment, the installation of energy-efficient communication technologies is very important. This encompasses program code and hardware optimization to require less power as well as developing energy conserving protocols for communications.
Collaboration for Environmental Standards: Collaborative effort among technology providers, automotive firms, and ecological bodies is integral in setting and observing environmental standards for V2X technology. V2X standards should focus on lowering the level of ecological harm and yet harnessing the benefits of communication. One of the essential aspects associated with the future of V2X communication systems is environmental concerns and sustainability concerns. These technologies have shown great promise in the reduction of environmental implications of transportation, however, focused efforts must be made to address the ecological taboo associated with the technology itself. V2X communication has a vital role to play in ensuring the transformation of the transportation ecosystem into one that is more sustainable and environmentally friendly, through efficient traffic management, support for electrification, sustainable urban planning, and development of eco-friendly technologies. It is, therefore, proactive measures such as lifecycle analysis among other aspects related to

efficient energy designs and compliance with the environmental standards that need to be observed for V2X technologies to promote environmental sustainability. Here in this industry, the outside cooperation among different stakeholders will act as a driving force to establish how V2X improvements connect with ecological objectives, in order for mobility to serve a green and sustainable future.

10.8 User Experience and Human-Machine Interaction

This section discusses the changing nature of UX and HMI for implementation in V2X communication systems, highlighting their role in determining how users engage with and perceive the technology.

Enhancing Driver Awareness and Decision Making: The provision of information on road conditions, traffic, as well as potential hazards in real time by enhancement of the driver awareness (V2X communication systems) significantly increases. This improved situational awareness is integral to the process of decision making, making it possible for drivers to better react to their environment. The incorporation of visual, auditory, and haptic feedback mechanisms into the HMI architecture of a vehicle ensures that critical information is passed on to the driver in a clear and concise manner while not unnecessarily distracting him or her.

Interface Design for Usability and Accessibility: But in the case of V2X vehicles, it is crucial also to consider the design of user interfaces to ensure that they are user- and handicap-friendly. Intuitive interfaces that offer the user relevant information without a distraction are required. This ranges from the intelligent portrayal of information on dashboard systems, head-up displays, and infotainment system applications. Ease-of-use features, including voice recognition and personalized screens, ensure that diverse audiences are covered—persons with disabilities included.

Seamless Integration with Personal Devices: Since connectedness between individuals and such devices as smartphones or wearables takes place, the integration of V2X systems contributes to providing a better user experience. It enables a tailored user experience that includes acceptable navigation, infotainment, as well as comfort specifications. Mobile apps help to increase the capabilities of V2X systems, allowing users to use identified transport parameters and control features from a remote location.

User Trust and Acceptance: The trust of users is critical to the adoption of V2X technologies. One example of informational management that can create confidence is the provision of transparent communication with regard to the capabilities and limitations of the system, enhanced with strong privacy and security measures. Addressing the skepticism is also done by educating users about the benefits and workings of V2X communication; by using which, they are more encouraged to accept it.

Impact on Non-Motorists: The scope of V2X communication is wider than drivers because it covers pedestrians, cyclists, and other road users as well. The interaction of these non-motorists with V2X makes their safety and mobility experience better. For instance, V2P (vehicle-to-pedestrian) communications can notify pedestrians about approaching vehicles especially when visibility is low and give warnings of pedestrian movements to drivers. All of the wearable devices or smartphones can be built into the V2X format, which guarantees that non-motorists are being considered a key aspect in the communication network.

Adaptive and Context-Aware Systems: Further evolution in the V2X frameworks is expected to be on adaptive and context-aware features. These systems are able to format the accommodating prescriptive and descriptive content of such information based precisely on the driving situation at hand, driver behaviors enacted therein from moment to moment, and whatnots on emotional state. For example, while on high risk or difficult driving conditions, the system uses minimal non-urgent alerts to avoid cognitive overload and hence improve safety level and driver satisfaction.

Feedback Mechanisms and Continuous Improvement: Feedback from users when using V2X technologies should contribute to a development cycle, including the process of continuous perfection. User feedback, both positive and negative, must play a significant role in future development and application. This iterative approach assures that changes made to the V2X system take into consideration user requirements and preferences. Besides, the exchange of understanding human–machine interaction and user experience in V2X systems is an instrumental element in their effectiveness and society's acceptance. Through intuitive design, personalized interaction, user education, and inclusive technologies, V2X communication can lead to the significant improvement of how user perceives service provision. Continuing the work to perfect HMI and UX elements will be crucial, as these systems only continue to become more intelligent; the human interaction with it also must evolve into something more harmonious.

10.9 Conclusion

By predicting the future of V2X (vehicle-to-everything) communication, we are not simply forecasting predictions but establishing a transformative vision for transportation in urban life. This chapter discusses the expedition of emerging technologies such as 5G, AI, and edge computing integration into V2X systems, which fortifies vehicle communications in new epitomes. Undeniably, however, it will be at a rate never reached before in efficiency security and connectivity. All these improvements will result in a significant decrease in the number of road accidents and fatalities; this is achieved with the help of real-time data processing, which enhances our ability to cope and provides a clearer picture of the situation. Nevertheless, realizing this potential rests upon solving interoperability concerns in a heterogeneous multi-vendor environment. V2X interactions should be compliant internationally in terms of protocol standardization and collaborative efforts to ensure smooth, universal intercommunication. In addition to this, cybersecurity and so the privacy of data are that important as more complexities in these systems develop. V2X tech is undermined by the lack of transparency and safety seen as risks to human life if any hackers get into this system. If a monitoring system is in place with strong security, then it can make people believe more on technology.

Moreover, it is also a very vital point that the study about V2X systems should consider environmental concerns in three aspects of the process. The role of V2X in promoting environmental sustainability is also reflected from effective control over traffic, the support being provided to electric vehicles, and contributions toward green urban planning. Enhancements of user experience and even more concern with inclusiveness remain an essential focus area, with work on developing easily maneuvered human-machine interfaces and ensuring the well-being of all road users, not just motorized ones, being necessary for gaining wide acceptance and achieving success. It is an undeniable fact that V2X communication has become the driving force behind such radical changes, upon which we are at the cusp of witnessing an urban transportation revolution. The journey ahead is full of opportunities and challenges. This is a road that will entail an innovative spirit, healthy intersections with other sectors, and the consistent primal concern for society and its surroundings. The imagination here is a realized end goal—a transport environment that makes thing smarter, safer, and more sustainable through the latest endeavors in V2X communication. To sum up, the development of V2X is not only based on technology; it is shaping a better, improved, and more technological world in motion that will redefine mobility and space for future generations.

References

1. Shrestha, R., Nam, S.Y., Bajracharya, R., Kim, S., Evolution of V2X Communication and Integration of Blockchain for Security Enhancements. *Electronics*, 9, 9, 1338, 2020, https://doi.org/10.3390/electronics9091338.
2. Kunz, A., Nkenyereye, L., Song, J., 5G Evolution of Cellular IoT for V2X. *2018 IEEE Conference on Standards for Communications and Networking (CSCN)*, Paris, France, pp. 1–6, 2018, doi: 10.1109/CSCN.2018.8581830.
3. Aust, S., Vehicle API and Service Catalog for Next Generation Mobility. *2022 25th International Symposium on Wireless Personal Multimedia Communications (WPMC)*, Herning, Denmark, pp. 418–423, 2022, doi: 10.1109/WPMC55625.2022.10014905.
4. Joubert, N., Reid, T.G.R., Noble, F., Developments in Modern GNSS and Its Impact on Autonomous Vehicle Architectures. *2020 IEEE Intelligent Vehicles Symposium (IV)*, Las Vegas, NV, USA, pp. 2029–2036, 2020, doi: 10.1109/IV47402.2020.9304840.
5. Wang, J., Shao, Y., Ge, Y., Yu, R., A Survey of Vehicle to Everything (V2X) Testing. *Sensors*, 19, 2, 334, 2019, https://doi.org/10.3390/s19020334.
6. Casademont, J., *et al.*, Multi-Radio V2X Communications Interoperability Through a Multi-Access Edge Computing (MEC). *2020 22nd International Conference on Transparent Optical Networks (ICTON)*, Bari, Italy, pp. 1–4, 2020, doi: 10.1109/ICTON51198.2020.9203495.
7. Alalewi, A., Dayoub, I., Cherkaoui, S., On 5G-V2X Use Cases and Enabling Technologies: A Comprehensive Survey. *IEEE Access*, 9, 107710–107737, 2021, doi: 10.1109/ACCESS.2021.3100472.
8. Ranjan, A., Hegge, K.K., Agrawal, R., Wireless and Solar-Powered Multipurpose Robot for Industrial Automation: A Sustainable Solution. *2023 8th International Conference on Communication and Electronics Systems (ICCES)*, Coimbatore, India, pp. 146–151, 2023, doi: 10.1109/ICCES57224.2023.10192614.
9. Sarma, P., Hussain, N., Dixit, S.K., Gupta, A.K., A novel approach of unsupervised feature selection using iterative shrinking and expansion algorithm. *J. Interdiscip. Math.*, 26, 3, 519–530, 2023, DOI: 10.47974/JIM-1678.
10. Kumar, Kalpana, V., Hariram, V., Artificial Intelligence based Health Monitoring System on IoTH platform. *2023 Second International Conference on Augmented Intelligence and Sustainable Systems (ICAISS)*, Trichy, India, pp. 1458–1463, 2023, doi: 10.1109/ICAISS58487.2023.10250460.
11. Pandya, P.M. and Gupta, A.K., Development of object identification model with deep reinforcement learning algorithm. *J. Inf. Optim. Sci.*, 44, 3, 355–367, 2023, DOI: 10.47974/JIOS-1346.
12. Kranthi, M. and Tanguturi, R.C., Design of Intelligent Medical Integrity Authentication and Secure Information for Public Cloud in Hospital Administration. *2023 2nd International Conference on Edge Computing and Applications (ICECAA)*, Namakkal, India, pp. 256–261, 2023, doi: 10.1109/ICECAA58104.2023.10212391.

13. Suryawanshi, V.A. and Chaturvedi, A., Novel Predictive Control and Monitoring System based on IoT for Evaluating Industrial Safety Measures. *IJEER*, 10, 4, 1050–1057, 2022, DOI: 10.37391/IJEER.100448.
14. Premkumar, S., Hussain, N., Chinamuttevi, V.S., A novel RF-SMOTE model to enhance the definite apprehensions for IoT security attacks. *J. Discrete Math. Sci. Cryptogr.*, 26, 3, 861–873, 2023, DOI: 10.47974/JDMSC-1766.
15. Singla, A. and Sharma, N., IoT Group Key Management using Incremental Gaussian Mixture Model. *2022 3rd International Conference on Electronics and Sustainable Communication Systems (ICESC)*, pp. 469–474, 2022, doi: 10.1109/ICESC54411.2022.9885644.
16. Latha, J., Selvakumar, C., Shekhar, R., Chaturvedi, A., Securing networked image transmission using public-key cryptography and identity authentication. *J. Discrete Math. Sci. Cryptogr.*, 26, 3, 779–791, 2023, DOI: 10.47974/JDMSC-1754.
17. Prasad, K.D.V., Kumar, P.S.V.V.S.R., R, S., Ashreetha, B., Performance Analysis of Energy Efficiency and Security Solutions of Internet of Things Protocols. *IJEER*, 11, 2, 442–450, 2023, DOI: 10.37391/IJEER.110226.
18. Mary, P.A. and Begum, A.Y., A Novel IoT Framework and Device Architecture for Efficient Smart city Implementation. *2023 7th International Conference on Trends in Electronics and Informatics (ICOEI)*, Tirunelveli, India, pp. 420–426, 2023, doi: 10.1109/ICOEI56765.2023.10125677.
19. M, S.P., Reddy, A.M., Tanguturi, R., Improved Secure Communication Mechanism for IoT Platform Devices. *2022 International Conference on Smart Generation Computing, Communication and Networking (SMART GENCON)*, Bangalore, India, pp. 1–6, 2022, doi: 10.1109/SMARTGENCON56628.2022.10083714.
20. Kumar, P. and Singh, P., IoT Enabled Smart Lighting System for Smart Cities. *J. Phys. Conf. Ser.*, 2089, 1, 012037, 2021, https://doi.org/10.1088/1742-6596/2089/1/012037.
21. Sharma, A., S, K., Arun, M.R., Priority Queueing Model-Based IoT Middleware for Load Balancing. *2022 6th International Conference on Intelligent Computing and Control Systems (ICICCS)*, pp. 425–430, 2022, doi: 10.1109/ICICCS53718.2022.9788218.
22. De, T., Tanguturi, R.C., Ashreetha, B., A Novel method of Improving Spectrum sensing Management system for CR-IoT Networks. *2023 4th International Conference for Emerging Technology (INCET)*, Belgaum, India, pp. 1–6, 2023, doi: 10.1109/INCET57972.2023.10170314.
23. Lokaj, Z., Srotyr, M., Vanis, M., Broz, J., Mlada, M., C-ITS SIM as a tool for V2X communication and its validity assessment. *2021 Smart City Symposium Prague (SCSP)*, Prague, Czech Republic, pp. 1–5, 2021, doi: 10.1109/SCSP52043.2021.9447399.
24. Rondinone, M., Walter, T., Blokpoel, R., Schindler, J., V2X Communications for Infrastructure-Assisted Automated Driving. *2018 IEEE 19th International Symposium on "A World of Wireless, Mobile and Multimedia Networks"*

(WoWMoM), Chania, Greece, pp. 14–19, 2018, doi: 10.1109/WoWMoM.2018.8449775.

25. Marroquin, A., To, M.A., Azurdia-Meza, C.A., Bolufé, S., A General Overview of Vehicle-to-X (V2X) Beacon-Based Cooperative Vehicular Networks. *2019 IEEE 39th Central America and Panama Convention (CONCAPAN XXXIX)*, Guatemala City, Guatemala, pp. 1–6, 2019, doi: 10.1109/CONCAPANXXXIX47272.2019.8977034.
26. Agbaje, P., Anjum, A., Mitra, A., Oseghale, E., Bloom, G., Olufowobi, H., Survey of Interoperability Challenges in the Internet of Vehicles. *IEEE Trans. Intell. Transp. Syst.*, 23, 12, 22838–22861, Dec. 2022, doi: 10.1109/TITS.2022.3194413.
27. González, E.E., Estrada, Y., Garcia-Roger, D., Monserrat, J.F., Performance Evaluation and Optimal Management of Mode 2 V2X Communications in 5G Networks. *IEEE Access*, 11, 128810–128825, 2023, doi: 10.1109/ACCESS.2023.3333680.
28. He, Y., *et al.*, D2D-V2X-SDN: Taxonomy and Architecture Towards 5G Mobile Communication System. *IEEE Access*, 9, 155507–155525, 2021, doi: 10.1109/ACCESS.2021.3127041.

11

Toward Smarter Streets: Leveraging Machine Learning, 5G, and V2X Communication for Traffic Insights

Smitha A. B.[1]*, Manjunatha Badiger[2], Sumiksha Shetty[1], Chinmaya H.[1], Sanketh C. Naik[1], Sujan R. Arasa[1], Ajay Deepak Lobo[1] and Shreyas K.[1]

[1]*Dept. of Electronics & Communication Engineering, Sahyadri College of Engineering & Management, Adyar, Mangaluru, Karnataka, India*
[2]*Department of VLSI Design and Technology, Nitte (Deemed to be University), NMAM Institute of Technology, Nitte, Udupi, India*

Abstract

Urbanization has intensified complexity, underscoring the critical need for creative traffic management techniques in growing metropolitan areas. In this article, the integration of 5G technology, machine learning (ML), and vehicular-to-everything (V2X) communication for the transformative possibilities is addressed. The study clarifies how they cooperate to rethink frameworks for traffic prediction and management, resulting in improved efficiency, safety, and sustainability for urban transportation systems. The study emphasizes the significant role expected of 5G technology in transforming transportation infrastructure. It highlights the crucial role of V2X connectivity in enabling smooth interaction between vehicles and infrastructure. Vehicles and roadside units, pedestrians, and the network can easily communicate essential information with one another and with one other using V2X communication, enabling adaptive traffic control interventions and dynamic routing strategies. The study emphasizes that in order to maximize the benefits of smart transportation systems, research and development teams must work together to address important issues like privacy, cybersecurity, and sustainability.

***Keywords*:** 5G technology, machine learning, V2X communication, traffic management, smart transportation, urban mobility, cybersecurity, dynamic routing

**Corresponding author*: smitha.ec@sahyadri.edu.in

Rathishchandra R. Gatti and Chandra Singh (eds.) Digital Convergence in Intelligent Mobility Systems, (241–270) © 2025 Scrivener Publishing LLC

11.1 Introduction

The combination of 5G communication and smart vehicles signifies the beginning of a new phase in mobility, where connectivity, automation, and intelligence combine to transform urban transportation. 5G, the fifth-generation cellular network technology, promises transformative capabilities that go beyond conventional communication systems. As an essential technology for facilitating smart city infrastructure, 5G networks play a crucial role in delivering high-speed broadband communication services necessary for transmitting data from sensors to the cloud [1].

Smart vehicles, equipped with sensors, controls, and advanced technology, are spearheading the mobility revolution. They act as central hubs in a massive network where data flows and smart decisions are made. With the lightning-fast speeds, minimal delays, and widespread connectivity of 5G, these smart vehicles act as game changers, reshaping urban transportation [2]. They open up a world of possibilities, making urban mobility safer, more efficient, and more convenient for everyone involved.

The integration of 5G communication in smart vehicles facilitates real-time data transmission, enabling vehicles to communicate seamlessly with each other [3], with traffic management systems, and with pedestrians. This real-time connectivity forms the backbone of advanced driver assistance systems (ADAS), autonomous driving capabilities, and enhanced safety measures. Vehicles can exchange critical information such as traffic conditions, road hazards, and emergency alerts instantaneously, fostering a safer and more efficient transportation ecosystem [4].

Furthermore, 5G provides smart vehicles with improved connections to cloud services, edge computing resources, and Internet of Things (IoT) devices dispersed throughout urban areas. This connectivity facilitates smart decision-making processes fuelled by comprehensive data analysis, enhancing route optimization, energy conservation, and overall vehicle functionality [5]. Smart vehicles integrate seamlessly into a dynamic, interconnected urban framework, playing a vital role in mitigating traffic congestion, reducing emissions, and enhancing the quality of life for urban residents.

11.2 Literature Survey

The article by Gaurav Kumar and Suresh Mikkili [6] provides a thorough examination of vehicle-to-everything (V2X) topologies, focusing on the communication and power flow dynamics between electric vehicles (EVs) and various entities like the grid, homes, buildings, and other vehicles. It delves into integrating EVs into the power grid, discussing the challenges, opportunities, potential applications, and benefits of V2X technology. It covers different V2X communication protocols such as IEEE standards, 3GPP, ISO standards, Wi-Fi, and IoT-based protocols, evaluating their strengths and weaknesses. The article also addresses the adoption challenges like infrastructure complexity and technology availability while highlighting opportunities for improving transportation environmental impact, power system efficiency, and resilience. It underscores V2X's role in bi-directional power flow, enabling EVs to bolster grid stability, and outlines V2X topologies like V2G, V2H, V2B, V2L, and V2V.

The study conducted by Ahmad Alalewi *et al.* [7] on 5G technologies for vehicle-to-everything (V2X) communications focuses on integrating vehicular communication systems with 5G and the associated challenges. It covers various V2X use cases such as safety, non-safety, and infotainment services, along with enabling technologies like network slicing, cloud and edge computing, and artificial intelligence. They also address network management, security, and interoperability challenges. It provides a historical perspective on vehicular communications, the evolution of standards, and the role of different organizations in shaping 5G-V2X's future. Emphasizing 5G's potential to revolutionize vehicular communications with faster connections, lower latency, and higher reliability, the research provides a valuable resource for understanding the current state and future prospects of 5G-V2X technologies in intelligent transport systems and autonomous driving.

A thorough introduction to the 3GPP Release 16 5G NR V2X standard is given in the paper by Alejandro Molina-Galan *et al.* [8], with a focus on sidelink communications in particular, which are crucial for satisfying the demanding requirements of connected and automated driving use cases. The physical layer, resource allocation, QoS management, Uu interface upgrades, mobility management for V2N communications, and coexistence strategies between 5G NR V2X and LTE V2X are all covered. In addition, they examine the system architecture, use cases, and assessment process for 5G NR V2X, offering suggestions for potential improvements for subsequent iterations. The tutorial aims to make the new standard and its characteristics easier to understand in order to evaluate and enhance 5G NR V2X's capabilities and performance. A detailed overview of the 3GPP Release 16 5G NR V2X standard is given, with special attention on sidelink communications, which are essential to meeting the strict criteria of use cases such as automated and connected driving. Along with examining the application cases, system architecture, and assessment process for 5G NR V2X, the research offers suggestions for potential improvements for upcoming iterations.

The development of vehicle-to-everything (V2X) communications is described by Sohan Gyawali *et al.* [9], who highlight the shift from dedicated short-range communications (DSRC) to cellular-based technologies like LTE and 5G. They highlight the motivations for cellular V2X, including enhanced safety, traffic efficiency, and infotainment applications. Additionally, the paper explores the potential of 5G for vehicular communications, which is expected to incorporate technologies like massive MIMO, millimeter waves, and network slicing. These advancements promise to address issues like short communication range and high path loss. They provide a thorough look at current and future cellular-based V2X communications, covering challenges, solutions, and research directions in this evolving field.

In their study, Jordi Casademont *et al.* [10] address challenges and propose solutions for interoperability and security in cooperative intelligent transport systems (C-ITS). They emphasize the importance of multi-radio communication interoperability for seamless vehicle-to-everything (V2X) connectivity among vehicles using different radio technologies like IEEE 802.11p and LTE-V2X. They also emphasize the need for a strong public key infrastructure (PKI) to protect V2X communications from attacks such as GPS spoofing and illegal modification of on-board units (OBUs). The research outlines a C-ITS system architecture incorporating multi-access edge computing (MEC), detailing the functions of roadside units (RSUs), small cells, and PKI servers. It also clarifies procedures for detecting GPS spoofing attacks and managing certificates, emphasizing MEC's role in these tasks. Ultimately, the authors underscore MEC's vital contribution to enhancing secure and interoperable C-ITS, addressing challenges related to multi-radio interoperability, security, system architecture, and efficient utilization, thereby ensuring dependable and effective deployments.

Sibin Mohan *et al.* [11] conducted a study on security and privacy challenges in vehicle-to-everything (V2X) communication systems. They explore the V2X landscape, examining security vulnerabilities and privacy issues arising as vehicles connect with other vehicles, pedestrians, infrastructures, and cloud services. They address possible dangers and ways to launch an attack that can jeopardize the security and effectiveness of intelligent transportation systems. They examine ongoing efforts in standardization and define mechanisms within the V2X domain, identifying gaps in current security solutions and suggesting areas for future research.

It underscores the importance to secure V2X communication for dependable and trustworthy emerging technologies, essential for broadening intelligent vehicular networks. They also categorize misbehavior detection methods by thoroughly analyzing current V2X security solutions and engage in talks regarding initiatives from industry, academia, and government to enhance V2X security.

Saptarshi Ghosh *et al.* [12] offer a thorough architecture for vehicle-to-everything (V2X) communications that enhances intelligent transportation systems and smart city applications using blockchain technology and mobile edge computing (MEC). The proposed architecture aims to ensure the network's robustness, resilience, and reliability. In order to efficiently handle resources and data migration based on service requirements, it provides a three-stage computing service: cloud computing (CC), edge computing (EC), and fog computing (FC). The architecture also integrates a resource allocation algorithm that prioritizes nodes and network technologies according to their usability and physical channel characteristics. It also seeks to increase network resilience by suggesting a blockchain-based transaction service. The article focuses at large-scale IoT data services for driverless automobiles as well as experimental situations with plug-in electric vehicles in smart grid settings.

The article by Robbin Blokpoel *et al.* [13] delves into V2X communications for infrastructure-assisted automated driving. It underscores the significance of cooperative automated vehicles (CAVs) in urban traffic management and the role of road infrastructure in coordinating CAV movements. The design of V2X communications is described in the article, which takes interoperability, backward compatibility, and application needs into consideration. It goes over the use cases and specifications of MAVEN for urban platooning, situational I2V interactions, and integrating vulnerable road users and non-cooperative vehicles. The article provides a functional verification methodology for V2X communication services and ends by emphasizing the potential of MAVEN solutions for industrial use in the future.

The research article by Elyes Ben Hamida *et al.* [14] provides an in-depth examination of vehicular communication standards essential for the progression of intelligent transportation systems (ITS), with a particular focus on autonomous driving. It discusses the evolution from connected vehicles to autonomous vehicles, emphasizing the role of vehicular communication as a cornerstone for deploying advanced ITS applications like platooning and remote vehicle control. The discussion then moves on to the MAC and PHY layers, highlighting initiatives by the automotive sector and research community to create new standards, 5G NR V2X for C-V2X and

IEEE 802.11bd for DSRC, in order to meet the strict latency and reliability requirements of autonomous driving.

In order to ensure standard compliance and achieve interoperability among LTE-V2X devices, Qinglong Xie *et al.* [15] describe the construction of a conformance testing system for the C-V2X standard protocol. They introduce VeTest as the test tool for conducting conformance tests. They address the crucial role of conformance testing for LTE-V2X devices, detailing the creation of a prototype system and the delineation of test suites for message and network layers. The testing platform's effectiveness had been proven across various manufacturers, confirming the precision of the system under test (SUT) and laying the foundation for LTE-V2X device interoperability.

The article authored by Haeyoung Lee *et al.* [16] offers an extensive examination of the advancements and potential implications of 6G technology on V2X communications. In order to support the future generation of linked autonomous vehicles, it emphasizes the need for a more sophisticated and capable V2X network, which promises better user experiences, increased road safety, improved air quality, and a variety of transportation scenarios. They analyze several crucial enabling technologies that are anticipated to revolutionize networking and communication in automobiles, such as terahertz communications, blockchain, and machine learning. Additionally, they go over the difficulties and stages of development of these technologies, focusing especially on machine learning's contribution to the advancement of vehicular networks. In order to stimulate further study in the field of 6G-V2X communications, the research functions as a forward-looking work.

Seilendria Hadiwardoyo *et al.* [17] introduce CAMINO framework, a versatile hybrid connectivity platform designed to support cooperative, connected, and automated mobility (CCAM) services across Europe. In addition to providing integrated cooperative intelligent transport systems (C-ITS) services for real-world testing, this framework seamlessly combines short-range direct and long-range cellular technologies. It also makes it possible to integrate external services via the distributed uniform streaming (DUST) framework and with sensors/actuators in vehicles and infrastructure. The modular architecture of CAMINO makes it possible to dynamically manage a variety of V2X technologies and services, enhancing connectivity and communication among vehicles. The article highlights CAMINO's potential to foster cross-technology vehicular connectivity and contribute to advancements in vehicular communications and CCAM services research.

Gorka Velez *et al.* [18] provide a solution that addresses the challenges of managing the extensive network infrastructure required for intelligent transport systems (ITS) in the context of 5G vehicle-to-everything (V2X) communication. A cognitive network management architecture called CogITS is presented. It uses machine learning to dynamically distribute resources and modify physical layer configurations in response to traffic predictions. In applications like platooning, where cars self-organize to maximize road capacity, this design attempts to improve network latency and optimize control message traffic efficiency in ITS situations. The article emphasizes the need for intelligent network management solutions that can manage the mobility information and complexity of ITS networks, indicating that machine learning-based management holds potential in such scenarios.

In order to improve safety for vulnerable road users (VRUs), Alexandre Santos *et al.*'s study [19] investigates the application of machine learning (ML) in intelligent transportation systems (ITSs). It describes the difficulties in putting safety measures in place for VRUs because of their small size and great agility, which make it harder to predict their behavior. Using stacked unidirectional long short-term memories (LSTMs) on V2X communication data produced by the VEINS simulation framework, the research suggests a collision prediction system for motorcycle riders. The article emphasizes the potential of using ML to forecast accidents and improve road safety for VRUs. They also look at the suggested system's design, which follows the fog computing paradigm, and emphasize how important mobility and low latency are in the implementation of ML systems for ITSs.

In order to improve real-time traffic state prediction, Tianren Wang *et al.* [20] describe the creation of an intelligent transportation system (ITS) that makes use of mobile edge computing (MEC) and vehicle-to-everything (V2X) communication. In order to improve perceptual and computational capabilities, the authors provide a multi-source sensor-based traffic perception system that is incorporated into a V2X network and enhanced by a MEC-assisted architecture. Using roadside testing, they present a novel traffic prediction model that significantly improves prediction accuracy over existing neural network models. The model integrates graph convolutional network (GCN), gated recurrent unit (GRU), and soft-attention mechanism to extract and fuse spatiotemporal features. The research project highlights the value of accurate, real-time traffic state prediction in intricate traffic networks and the ways in which V2X and MEC technologies can help conventional traffic sensors overcome their limitations.

Mostafa Karimzadeh *et al.* [21] introduce a method to improve safety in vehicular networks (V2N) by predicting vehicle paths and sending safety messages efficiently. They suggest using a combination of machine learning and a smart system to forecast where vehicles will go and then send safety alerts to the ones likely to run into danger spots. Their system picks the best way to send messages—either directly between vehicles (V2V) or to infrastructure (V2I)—depending on the connection. The article discusses existing challenges in current methods and proposes an improved approach for estimating traffic flow. Their research introduces a new method for predicting vehicle paths, an advanced early warning system, and an efficient method for transmitting data within vehicle networks.

The paper by Arati Kantu Kale *et al.* [22] focuses on combining vehicle-to-everything (V2X) and artificial intelligence (AI) technology to improve intersection traffic safety. They present the intersection traffic safety framework (ITSF), a system that uses vehicle-to-infrastructure (V2I) connections and machine learning to reduce the probability of crashes at intersections. Among the measures the framework uses to evaluate performance are the end-to-end latency, driver responsiveness to safety alerts, and the penetration rate of V2X-enabled vehicles. The study shows that the ITSF achieves over 98% accuracy in classifying risky cars and dramatically lowers collisions when it reaches a penetration rate of 60% or higher. Because it can reduce crash rates even when some drivers choose to disregard warnings, the system is clearly robust. The article also emphasizes the value of sensors in gathering vehicle state data, stresses the benefits of cellular V2X technology in improving traffic safety, and investigates the potential of infrastructure-based warning systems in CITS.

In their research, Ming Ye *et al.* [23] provide an innovative approach to hybrid car energy management control that makes use of vehicle-to-everything (V2X) communication to predict speed and improve energy efficiency. In order to dynamically modify engine and motor power output based on traffic circumstances, researchers model vehicle speed prediction by integrating intelligent network connectivity technology and deep learning algorithms. The proposed approach shows a 16.04% decrease in CO_2 emissions and a 13.02% improvement in vehicle energy economy over conventional threshold-based control methods using MATLAB/Simulink platform simulations using a plug-in hybrid vehicle model. In order to reduce traffic and automobile emissions in urban areas, their research emphasizes the importance of accurate speed prediction for real-time energy management in hybrid vehicles. This will advance intelligent transportation systems and make it easier for hybrid vehicles to use fuel sustainably and efficiently.

The study conducted by Hongbo Gao *et al.* [24] explores using AI and V2X technology to advance intelligent transport systems (ITS) in autonomous vehicles, focusing on overcoming challenges like uncertain driving conditions and sensor limitations. It suggests using reinforcement learning to share environmental data across V2X autonomous cars, improving efficiency and safety. The research designs and tests a V2X autonomous driving architecture with three subsystems using OpenAI's reinforcement learning framework, demonstrating improved autonomous driving through the integration of environmental data with onboard sensors.

Mingjie Feng *et al.* [25] explore a framework for predicting latency in V2X applications within mobile cloud/edge computing systems, emphasizing the critical need for accurately estimating offloading latency in delay-sensitive tasks for connected and autonomous vehicles (CAVs). This framework uses statistical techniques and machine learning, utilizing substantial latency data that are collected while driving. An LSTM network is employed to predict latency trends, supplemented by a k-medoids classification technique, and the random noise is handled using a statistical method that combines Epanechnikov Kernel and moving average functions.

11.3 5G Technology and Its Role in Transportation

5G networks offer a number of important characteristics and capabilities that distinguish them from earlier generations, marking a substantial advancement in telecommunications technology. Its introduction has a profound impact on data collection, transfer speeds, and connectivity within transportation systems. Real-time gaming, remote surgery, and driverless cars depend on near-instantaneous reaction, which is ensured by its lightning-fast rates and minimal latency [26]. In order to improve the effectiveness, security, and sustainability of transportation networks, 5G makes it easier to deploy intelligent transportation solutions including linked traffic lights, pedestrian detection systems, and intelligent transportation systems (ITS). 5G technology is fundamental in shaping the future of transportation by enabling seamless connectivity, improving safety, and optimizing traffic flow [27]. In order to provide more effective, secure, and environmentally friendly transportation networks, 5G promotes the implementation of smart transportation solutions, such as intelligent transportation systems (ITS), connected traffic signals, and pedestrian detection systems.

The potential of 5G technology in transforming transportation systems is significant, as it can facilitate faster, more reliable, and extensively interconnected networks. Its uses include facilitating the development of autonomous cars and enhancing vehicle-to-vehicle (V2V) and vehicle-to-infrastructure (V2I) communication [28]. This supports the advancement and implementation of advanced driver assistance systems (ADAS) and autonomous vehicles, thereby enhancing road safety and efficiency. Intelligent traffic management technologies, such as adaptive traffic signal control, which modify signal timings in response to real-time traffic information, are also made easier to integrate with 5G [29]. In addition, 5G facilitates the deployment of intelligent transportation solutions, including advanced transportation systems (ATS), pedestrian detection systems, and connected traffic signals, all of which are intended to promote safer, more environmentally friendly, and more effective transportation networks. This enables better monitoring and management of traffic flow, congestion, and road conditions. The impact of 5G on data collection, transfer speeds, and connectivity in transportation systems is profound [30], paving the way for more efficient, safer, and smarter transportation networks.

11.4 Vehicular Communication and V2X Standards

11.4.1 Overview of Vehicular-to-Everything (V2X) Communication Technologies

V2X communication technologies represent an important aspect of modern transportation systems, facilitating the exchange of data among vehicles, roadside infrastructure, pedestrians, and other entities within the vehicular environment. The principal aim of vehicle-to-everything (V2X) communication is to facilitate the real-time sharing of vital information between vehicles [11]; this will ultimately improve traffic efficiency, road safety, and overall effectiveness of transportation. V2X communication relies on wireless communication protocols to enable seamless data exchange. These protocols allow vehicles to broadcast their current status, such as position, speed, acceleration, and heading, to nearby vehicles and infrastructure units [31]. Likewise, vehicles can receive information from other vehicles and infrastructure elements, including traffic signals, road conditions, and hazard warnings. Automobiles are able to minimize dangers and optimize their travel routes by using this two-way information flow to make well-informed decisions and suitable actions.

V2X communication encompasses several key components:

1. **V2V (Vehicle-to-Vehicle) Communication:** Vehicle-to-vehicle (V2V) communication allows direct communication between vehicles that are close to one another. By exchanging information such as speed, position, and trajectory, vehicles can collaborate to avoid collisions, coordinate lane changes, and optimize traffic flow. V2V communication is particularly valuable in scenarios where line-of-sight communication is feasible, such as intersections, highway merges, and dense urban environments [32].
2. **V2I (Vehicle-to-Infrastructure) Communication:** Vehicle-to-infrastructure (V2I) communication refers to communication between moving cars and roadside infrastructure elements such as toll booths, traffic lights, and signs. Vehicles can get updates on road conditions, traffic light timings, and traffic information in real time through vehicle-to-infrastructure (V2I) communication, which enables them to modify their driving behavior. Vehicle-to-infrastructure (V2I) communication (V2I) improves traffic efficiency and makes intelligent transportation systems (ITS) applications possible, like dynamic route guiding and traffic signal optimization [33].
3. **V2P (Vehicle-to-Pedestrian) Communication:** V2P communication enables vehicles to detect and communicate with pedestrians and other vulnerable road users, such as cyclists and scooter riders. Vehicles and pedestrians can identify possible collision hazards and take evasive action to avert accidents by exchanging information about pedestrian positions, motions, and intentions. V2P communication enhances road safety and fosters a more inclusive and pedestrian-friendly transportation environment [34].
4. **V2N (Vehicle-to-Network) Communication:** Vehicle-to-network (V2N) communication entails communication between cars and backend infrastructure, including traffic control centers and cloud servers. Through V2N communication, vehicles can access additional information services, such as real-time traffic updates, weather forecasts, and road incident reports. V2N communication increases the general efficiency of V2X systems and empowers cars to make better decisions [11].

Vehicle-to-everything (V2X) communication technologies are the cornerstone of connected and autonomous vehicle (CAV) systems, allowing cars to communicate with one another and their surroundings instantly. By facilitating the exchange of critical information, V2X communication enhances road safety, reduces traffic congestion, and lays the groundwork for the future of intelligent transportation systems [9].

11.4.2 V2X Communication Standards and Protocols

Vehicular-to-everything (V2X) communication standards and protocols play a critical role in defining the specifications and rules governing communication between vehicles and infrastructure units. These standards enable seamless data sharing and cooperation between linked cars and roadside infrastructure by guaranteeing interoperability, dependability, and security in V2X communication networks [35, 36]. Several standards and protocols have been developed to support V2X communication, each tailored to specific deployment scenarios and technological requirements. Key V2X communication standards and protocols are as follows [37]:

1. **IEEE 802.11p (DSRC 1st Gen):** IEEE 802.11p, also known as wireless access in vehicular environments (WAVE), is one of the earliest standards developed for V2X communication. It operates in the 5.9 GHz dedicated short-range communications (DSRC) band and provides low-latency communication capabilities suitable for safety-critical applications. IEEE 802.11p defines protocols for message exchange, channel access, and security, enabling direct communication between nearby vehicles and infrastructure units.
2. **3GPP Rel13 (LTE D2D):** The 3rd Generation Partnership Project (3GPP) Release 13 introduced support for device-to-device (D2D) communication in long-term evolution (LTE) networks. LTE D2D enables direct communication between LTE-enabled devices without the need for network infrastructure. This mode of communication can be leveraged for V2X applications, allowing vehicles to exchange information directly with each other, bypassing the cellular network infrastructure.
3. **3GPP Rel13 (LTE D2D Enhanced):** Building upon the initial LTE D2D capabilities, 3GPP Release 13 introduced enhancements to LTE D2D communication to support V2X applications more effectively. These enhancements include

improved proximity services, group communication, and resource allocation mechanisms, enabling more efficient and reliable communication between vehicles and infrastructure units.

4. **3GPP Rel14 (LTE V2X):** 3GPP Release 14 expanded the capabilities of LTE networks to support V2X communication more comprehensively. LTE V2X encompasses both direct communication (PC5 interface) between nearby vehicles and infrastructure and network-based communication (Uu interface) through cellular networks. LTE V2X standards define protocols for message exchange, mobility management, and security, ensuring interoperability and compatibility with existing LTE infrastructure.
5. **3GPP Rel15 (5G-NR V2X Phase1):** 3GPP Release 15 introduced the first phase of 5G new radio (NR) standards for V2X communication. 5G-NR V2X Phase 1 builds upon the capabilities of LTE V2X and extends them to leverage the enhanced features of 5G networks, such as higher data rates, lower latency, and improved reliability. 5G-NR V2X Phase 1 standards aim to enhance the performance and scalability of V2X communication in preparation for the widespread deployment of 5G networks.
6. **IEEE 802.11bd (DSRC 2nd Gen):** IEEE 802.11bd, also known as the next-generation DSRC (DSRC 2nd Gen), is a proposed extension of the IEEE 802.11p standard. By adding cutting-edge features including faster data rates, more dependability, and support for new applications, it seeks to improve DSRC's capabilities for V2X communication. IEEE 802.11bd standards are expected to address the evolving requirements of V2X communication systems and support future automotive applications.
7. **3GPP Rel16 (5G-NR V2X Phase2):** 3GPP Release 16 introduces the second phase of 5G-NR standards for V2X communication, further enhancing the capabilities and performance of 5G networks for V2X applications. Massive machine-type communication (mMTC), ultra-reliable low-latency communication (URLLC), and vehicle-to-network-to-vehicle (V2N2V) communication scenarios are just a few of the new use cases and needs that 5G-NR V2X Phase 2 standards seek to solve.

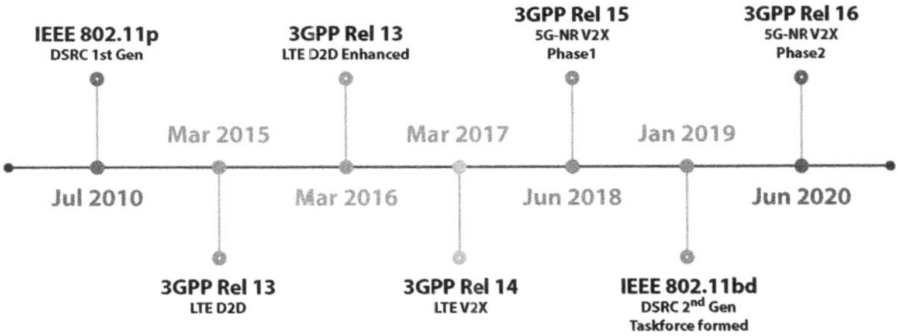

Figure 11.1 V2X communication standard and protocols [16].

Figure 11.1 shows the development stage of the V2X protocol and standards over the years. V2X communication standards and protocols encompass a diverse range of technologies and specifications, each tailored to specific deployment scenarios and technological requirements. These standards are essential for enabling security, dependability, and interoperability in V2X communication systems, opening the door for more interconnected, safer, and effective transportation systems [38].

11.4.3 Importance of Interoperability for Seamless Communication between Vehicles and Infrastructure

Interoperability is essential for enabling seamless communication between vehicles and infrastructure in V2X environments. It ensures that different V2X devices and systems, developed by various manufacturers and deployed in different regions, can effectively exchange information and collaborate to achieve common objectives [39]. Interoperability standards define common communication protocols, message formats, and interface specifications, enabling heterogeneous V2X systems to communicate seamlessly and interoperable across diverse deployment scenarios.

One of the key advantages of interoperability is increased transportation safety and efficiency. Interoperable V2X systems enable cars to interact with each other and with roadside infrastructure units, facilitating cooperative collision prevention, traffic management, and emergency response coordination [40]. For example, interoperable V2X systems allow vehicles from different manufacturers to share real-time traffic information, road hazard warnings, and emergency braking signals, enabling safer and more efficient travel for all road users. Interoperability promotes innovation and competition in the V2X ecosystem by fostering an open and interoperable marketplace for V2X solutions and services [36]. By adhering to common standards and protocols, V2X stakeholders can develop interoperable products and solutions that seamlessly integrate with existing transportation infrastructure and backend systems. This integration provides users with additional flexibility and choice while also encouraging the development of new apps and services that make use of V2X communication capabilities.

Interoperability facilitates regulatory compliance and harmonization of V2X deployments across different geographical regions and jurisdictions. By adopting common interoperability standards, V2X stakeholders can ensure consistency and compatibility in V2X implementations, enabling seamless cross-border communication and cooperation [41]. Interoperability standards also facilitate regulatory certification and testing, ensuring that V2X devices and systems meet specified performance and interoperability requirements. Interoperability is critical for maximizing the promise of V2X communication technologies and realizing the vision of connected and autonomous cars. By enabling seamless communication between vehicles and infrastructure, interoperable V2X systems can enhance road safety, reduce traffic congestion [42], and pave the way for more efficient and sustainable transportation systems.

11.5 Integration of Machine Learning with 5G and V2X Communication

11.5.1 Introduction to Machine Learning Algorithms Used in Traffic Prediction

Machine learning algorithms play an essential role in anticipating traffic flow by utilizing the massive amounts of data provided by current transportation systems. These algorithms, ranging from classical methods like linear regression to sophisticated deep learning models such as convolutional neural networks (CNNs) and recurrent neural networks (RNNs), enable accurate and timely traffic predictions. Classical algorithms like linear regression are used for simple traffic prediction tasks, where historical data is used to model traffic patterns over time [43]. However, for more complex scenarios involving non-linear relationships and temporal dependencies, advanced techniques such as support vector machines (SVMs), decision trees, and ensemble approaches, such as random forests and gradient boosting, are used.

Deep learning models have emerged as powerful tools for traffic prediction [44], especially in scenarios where the data is high dimensional, non-linear, and exhibits complex temporal dynamics. Convolutional neural networks are effective for spatial data analysis, such as predicting traffic congestion based on spatial features like road network topology and geographical information. Recurrent neural networks excel in capturing temporal dependencies in traffic data, making them suitable for predicting traffic flow over time intervals. The type of machine learning method used is determined by the nature of the data, the prediction horizon, processing resources, and the desired level of accuracy. Hybrid approaches that combine multiple algorithms or incorporate domain knowledge alongside machine learning techniques are also prevalent in traffic prediction systems [45].

11.5.2 Overview of Data Sources and Features Used for Training Traffic Prediction Models

Training accurate traffic prediction models relies heavily on diverse and comprehensive data sources. These sources include real-time traffic data acquired by various sensors, like loop detectors, GPS devices, traffic cameras, and V2X communication systems [46]. Also, historical traffic data, weather conditions, road infrastructure details, and socio-economic factors contribute to building robust prediction models.

Key features used in training traffic prediction models are as follows [47]:

1. **Traffic Volume:** Quantifies the number of vehicles passing through a specific location over time.
2. **Traffic Speed:** Measures the velocity of vehicles, indicating congestion levels and traffic fluidity.
3. **Traffic Density:** Reflects the concentration of vehicles per unit length of road, influencing traffic flow dynamics.
4. **Road Network Characteristics:** Includes road type, lane configuration, intersections, and traffic control measures.
5. **Temporal Factors:** The time of day, day of the week, seasonal variations, and special events all have an impact on traffic patterns.
6. **Weather Conditions:** Variables like temperature, precipitation, visibility, and wind speed affect road conditions and driver behavior.

7. **V2X Data:** Information exchanged between vehicles, infrastructure, and other entities in the transportation ecosystem, providing real-time insights into traffic conditions and potential hazards.

Integrating diverse data sources and relevant features enhances the predictive capability of machine learning models, enabling accurate and actionable traffic predictions. Following are the applications and effectiveness of machine learning in traffic prediction [48]:

- A machine learning model can forecast patterns of traffic congestion throughout a city with high accuracy by utilizing GPS traces, historical traffic data, and meteorological data. This helps with traffic management and route optimization.
- To forecast traffic flow, machine learning algorithms use real-time traffic data from sensors placed along roadways. This enables the implementation of dynamic speed limits and lane control by authorities.
- Machine learning algorithms optimize traffic signal timings to reduce congestion and improve traffic flow efficiency by assessing traffic volume, vehicle kinds, and historical trends at crossings.
- By predicting passenger demand using machine learning algorithms on public transportation data, bus and train schedules and resource allocation can be optimized.
- By utilizing event data from events like sporting events, musical performances, or open spaces, machine learning models predict traffic jams and help with traffic control during major occasions.

11.5.3 Challenges and Opportunities in Integrating Machine Learning with 5G and V2X Communication

There are advantages and disadvantages in combining machine learning with 5G and V2X communication [49, 50]. The challenges are as follows:

- Ensuring that data from various sources, such as 5G networks, V2X communications, and conventional traffic sensors, is compatible, consistent, and of high quality.

- Processing architectures that are efficient and scalable for machine learning is necessary when managing massive amounts of data in real time, particularly in environments with dynamic traffic patterns.
- Protecting private, authenticated, and integrity data transmitted across 5G and V2X networks from online attacks.
- Ensuring compatibility between various data formats, machine learning frameworks, and communication protocols to promote easy integration and cooperation.

Outlined next are the opportunities of integrating machine learning with 5G and V2X communication protocols [49]:

- **High-Fidelity Data:** Obtaining real-time, high-fidelity data for more precise and responsive traffic forecasts by utilizing fast, low-latency 5G networks and V2X communications.
- **Edge Computing:** By performing distributed machine learning inference, edge computing capabilities at roadside units and automobiles can reduce latency and improve prediction accuracy.
- **Dynamic Adaptation:** Making use of machine learning models that are adaptable to changing network dynamics, user behavior, and traffic conditions in order to learn and change.
- **Predictive maintenance:** This technique uses machine learning algorithms to anticipate and stop possible malfunctions in traffic management systems, V2X devices, and 5G infrastructure, guaranteeing dependability and ongoing operation.

11.5.4 Potential Applications of Machine Learning in Optimizing Traffic Flow and Management

Through a variety of applications, machine learning has enormous potential to optimize traffic flow and management. Applications show how machine learning can help develop more intelligent, effective, and long-lasting traffic control strategies [51].

- **Dynamic Traffic Signal Control:** Adaptive traffic signal management systems reduce congestion and improve traffic flow by adjusting signal timings based on current traffic circumstances. They do this by using machine learning.

- **Route Optimization:** To provide drivers with the best possible routes that save on travel time and fuel, machine learning algorithms examine past traffic statistics, present road conditions, and user preferences.
- **Traffic Incident Detection:** By identifying and categorizing traffic incidents including collisions, road closures, and abnormalities in traffic, machine learning models allow for quick responses and mitigating actions.
- **Public Transport Optimization:** By improving fleet management, passenger routing, and timetables, predictive models improve the dependability of public transportation and the commuter experience.
- **Predictive Maintenance:** By using machine learning to forecast maintenance requirements, this technique lowers downtime and boosts overall system reliability for communication, transportation, and automotive systems.

11.6 Dynamic Traffic Prediction and Management

11.6.1 Real-Time Data Utilization for Dynamic Traffic Prediction

Utilizing real-time data from 5G and V2X communication systems revolutionizes the accuracy and timeliness of traffic prediction [52]. These systems continuously gather data on vehicle movements, road conditions, and environmental factors, providing transportation authorities with a comprehensive understanding of current traffic patterns. Machine learning algorithms analyze this data to predict future traffic conditions with remarkable precision [45]. Traffic signal timing optimization and vehicle rerouting are two proactive measures that authorities can apply to reduce traffic congestion. These strategies can be forecasted in advance. In addition to improving overall travel efficiency, this proactive approach to traffic management lowers the possibility of delays caused by traffic. These predictions allow transportation administration systems to dynamically alter traffic signal timings, redirect vehicles, and distribute resources in real time to alleviate congestion hotspots and optimize traffic flow [53].

Furthermore, V2X connectivity enables vehicles to communicate data with one another and with infrastructure, delivering useful information about traffic dynamics and potential hazards.

11.6.2 Techniques for Route Optimization and Vehicle Rerouting

Techniques for route optimization and vehicle rerouting leverage real-time traffic predictions to minimize travel times and alleviate congestion. Advanced algorithms consider various factors, including traffic flow, road conditions, and historical data, to dynamically adjust routes for individual vehicles [54]. By rerouting vehicles away from congested areas and toward less congested routes in real time, these techniques optimize the overall flow of traffic. Additionally, these algorithms prioritize efficiency while balancing factors such as distance, travel time, and road capacity. By providing drivers with optimal routes tailored to current traffic conditions, these techniques contribute to a smoother and more efficient transportation network [55].

11.6.3 Machine Learning and V2X in Dynamic Traffic Signal Optimization

Machine learning algorithms play a crucial role in adaptive traffic signal control systems, allowing them to learn and adapt to changing traffic circumstances. These systems utilize ML techniques to analyze vast amounts of real-time traffic data, including vehicle counts, speeds, and congestion patterns [53]. Traffic signal controllers can dynamically modify signal timings based on this data to improve traffic flow and alleviate congestion. Furthermore, ML algorithms can recognize repeating traffic patterns and forecast future traffic conditions, enabling traffic signal control systems to anticipate and respond to probable congestion hotspots. In addition to ML, V2X communication technologies contribute significantly to adaptive traffic signal control [56]. V2X enables vehicles to communicate with each other and with infrastructure, including traffic signal controllers, in real time. This communication allows vehicles to share information about their current positions, speeds, and intended routes, enabling traffic signal controllers to make more informed decisions. Using V2X communication, adaptive traffic signal control systems can improve their responsiveness to changing traffic circumstances, resulting in better traffic flow and shorter travel times.

Adaptive traffic signal control systems use a variety of algorithms to dynamically change traffic signal timings based on real-time data. One common approach is the use of reinforcement learning algorithms, such as Q-learning and deep Q-networks (DQN) [57]. These algorithms enable traffic signal controllers to learn optimal signal timings by iteratively adjusting them based on feedback received from the environment, such as traffic flow and congestion levels. Another strategy involves the use of optimization tools, such as genetic algorithms and particle swarm optimization, to find ideal signal timings that minimize trip times and maximize traffic flow efficiency [58 , 59]. Predictive algorithms, like neural networks and time-series analysis approaches, are also used to forecast future traffic conditions using existing data, allowing for proactive signal timing adjustments before congestion begins.

11.6.4 Benefits of Adaptive Traffic Signal Control in Improving Traffic Flow and Reducing Congestion

Adaptive traffic signal control provides various benefits for increasing traffic flow and reducing congestion. These systems enhance traffic flow at intersections by dynamically altering signal timings in accordance with real-time traffic data, decreasing delays and travel times for cars [60]. Adaptive traffic signal control can help to reduce traffic congestion by efficiently allocating green time to high-volume traffic movements and coordinating signal timings across multiple intersections to facilitate smoother traffic flow along roads. By reducing idling time and stop-and-go traffic patterns, adaptive traffic signal control systems contribute to lower fuel consumption, emissions, and overall environmental impact. So, the implementation of adaptive traffic signal control can lead to more efficient transportation networks, improved mobility, and enhanced quality of life for residents in urban areas [61].

11.6.5 Safety Applications and Collision Avoidance Systems

V2X communication, which combines vehicle-to-vehicle (V2V) and vehicle-to-infrastructure (V2I) communications, together with machine learning techniques, has transformed automobile safety applications. V2X communication allows vehicles to communicate information with each other and with roadside infrastructure, enabling a variety of safety applications [11]. Machine learning algorithms process this data to analyze complex patterns and make predictions, enhancing the effectiveness of safety systems. One of the major safety application facilitated by V2X and machine learning is cooperative collision warning systems. These systems use V2V communication to exchange real-time data about vehicle positions and speeds, enabling vehicles to detect potential collision risks and alert drivers [33]. Furthermore, machine learning algorithms can constantly enhance the accuracy and reliability of these collision warning systems by learning from previous collisions. Additionally, V2X communication and machine learning enable advanced driver assistance systems (ADAS), such as adaptive cruise control and intersection collision warning, which further enhance vehicle safety by assisting drivers in various traffic conditions [62].

The development of collision avoidance systems and lane departure warnings represents a significant key feature in automotive safety technology. Collision avoidance systems utilize a combination of sensors, including radar, lidar, and cameras, to detect potential collision threats in the vehicle [63]. These systems uses algorithms to analyze sensor data, predict collision risks, and initiate timely process, such as automatic emergency braking or steering assistance, to prevent or mitigate collisions. Machine learning improves the efficacy of collision avoidance systems by allowing them to understand complicated patterns in sensor data and accurately distinguish between normal driving circumstances and collision conditions [62]. Furthermore, lane departure warning systems utilize cameras or sensors to monitor the vehicle's position within its lane and provide visual, auditory, or any warnings to alert drivers when unintentional lane departures occur. Machine learning algorithms can refine the performance of lane departure warning systems by learning from various driving scenarios and adapting to individual driver behavior patterns. As a result, collision avoidance systems and lane departure warnings contribute significantly to reducing the frequency of road accidents [64], enhancing overall road safety for drivers, passengers, and pedestrians alike.

11.7 Future Directions and Challenges

11.7.1 Emerging Trends and Future Directions in the Integration of Machine Learning, 5G, and V2X Communication

The convergence of machine learning, 5G technology, and V2X communication has significant potential to influence the trajectory of intelligent transportation systems (ITS) in the future. One emerging trend is the utilization of edge computing capabilities enabled by 5G networks to process vast amounts of data generated by connected vehicles and roadside infrastructure in real time. This facilitates more responsive decision making in traffic management and safety applications, such as dynamic traffic signal control and cooperative collision avoidance. Moreover, machine learning algorithms deployed at the network edge can leverage localized data to optimize traffic flow and enhance situational awareness without relying heavily on centralized cloud resources [65]. Furthermore, advancements in V2X communication standards, such as the evolution toward cellular vehicle-to-everything (C-V2X) technology, promise to enhance the reliability and scalability of communication between vehicles and infrastructure. C-V2X uses the low-latency and high-bandwidth capabilities of 5G networks to enable more effective data transmission and coordination among connected vehicles, paving the way for revolutionary safety and mobility applications in future transportation systems [9].

11.7.2 Addressing Challenges

Despite the great opportunities given by advances in ITS technology, a number of difficulties must be overcome to assure their widespread acceptance and efficacy. Privacy considerations around the collecting and sharing of sensitive vehicle data constitute a significant hurdle in the adoption of V2X communication systems [67]. Robust privacy-preserving mechanisms, such as secure data anonymization and encryption techniques, are essential to protect users' privacy while enabling effective data exchange for traffic management and safety applications [66]. Additionally, cybersecurity threats, such as malicious attacks targeting connected vehicles or roadside infrastructure, underscore the importance of implementing robust security measures, including intrusion detection systems and secure communication protocols, to safeguard against cyber threats and ensure the integrity and reliability of ITS deployments. Furthermore, scalability issues associated with the growing number of connected vehicles and the increasing complexity of ITS applications require scalable architectures and protocols capable of handling large volumes of data and accommodating diverse communication requirements across heterogeneous vehicular networks.

11.7.3 Opportunities for Further Research and Development in the Field of Intelligent Transportation Systems

Intelligent transportation systems provide numerous opportunities for future research and development to address emerging difficulties and unlock new capabilities. One area of study is the development of AI-powered traffic management systems that can adapt to changing traffic circumstances and optimize resource allocation in real time. Additionally, research efforts aimed at advancing the interoperability and standardization of V2X communication protocols can facilitate seamless integration and collaboration among diverse stakeholders in the transportation ecosystem [68]. Furthermore, investigating the potential of emerging technologies like blockchain and edge computing to improve the security, scalability, and resilience of ITS systems is a viable route for future research. By addressing these research priorities and fostering interdisciplinary collaboration, the intelligent transportation systems community can continue to innovate and drive positive societal impacts in the realm of mobility, safety, and sustainability.

11.8 Conclusion

In conclusion, the convergence of machine learning, 5G, and V2X communication represents a transformative force in shaping the future of transportation [69]. These technologies have enormous potential to transform how vehicles interact with one another and with the surrounding infrastructure, paving the way for safer, more efficient, and environmentally friendly transportation systems. Machine learning algorithms enable vehicles and traffic management systems to evaluate massive quantities of data and make intelligent judgments in real time [53], optimizing traffic flow, increasing safety, and improving travelers' overall mobility experiences. The implementation of 5G networks enables smooth communication between connected vehicles and roadside infrastructure, opening up new opportunities for cooperative driving and improved mobility services. Furthermore, V2X communication permits the interchange of crucial information, such as traffic conditions, road dangers, and vehicle trajectories, allowing for proactive interventions and collaborative solutions to reduce congestion and improve road safety [68]. By harnessing the combined power of machine learning, 5G, and V2X communication, transportation stakeholders can realize a future where vehicles are not just connected but intelligent, capable of navigating complex traffic environments autonomously while minimizing environmental impact and maximizing efficiency.

In the future, machine learning, 5G, and V2X communication could have a significant impact on traffic management and prediction. These technologies enable more accurate and granular traffic forecasting, allowing transportation agencies and service providers to anticipate congestion hotspots, optimize route planning, and deploy targeted interventions to alleviate traffic bottlenecks. Machine learning algorithms can examine historical traffic data, weather trends, and real-time sensor inputs to develop predictive models that reflect the dynamic character of traffic flow and forecast future traffic conditions with unparalleled accuracy [48]. Furthermore, 5G networks' low-latency communication capabilities, combined with widespread adoption of V2X communication protocols, allow for real-time data exchange between vehicles and infrastructure, facilitating adaptive traffic signal control, dynamic route guidance, and collaborative traffic management strategies. As a result, transportation stakeholders can leverage these technologies to proactively manage traffic flow, reduce travel times, and enhance the overall efficiency and resilience of transportation networks. Finally, the convergence of machine learning, 5G, and V2X communication ushers in a new era of intelligent transportation systems, fueled by data-driven insights and collaborative decision making to drive continuous innovation and improvement in urban mobility and efficiency.

References

1. Sharma, S., Deivakani, M., Srinivasa Reddy, K., Gnanasekar, A.K., Aparna, G., Key enabling technologies of 5G wireless mobile communication. *J. Phys. Conf. Ser.*, 1817, 1, 012003, IOP Publishing, 2021.
2. Nikitas, A., Michalakopoulou, K., Njoya, E.T., Karampatzakis, D., Artificial intelligence, transport and the smart city: Definitions and dimensions of a new mobility era. *Sustainability*, 12, 7, 2789, 2020.
3. Biswas, A. and Wang, H.-C., Autonomous vehicles enabled by the integration of IoT, edge intelligence, 5G, and blockchain. *Sensors*, 23, 4, 1963, 2023.
4. Abdelkader, G., Elgazzar, K., Khamis, A., Connected vehicles: Technology review, state of the art, challenges and opportunities. *Sensors*, 21, 22, 7712, 2021.
5. Lv, Z. and Shang, W., Impacts of intelligent transportation systems on energy conservation and emission reduction of transport systems: A comprehensive review. *Green Technol. Sustain.*, 1, 1, 100002, 2023.

6. National Institute of Technology Goa and Kumar, G., Critical Review of Vehicle-to-Everything (V2X) Topologies: Communication, Power Flow Characteristics, Challenges, and Opportunities. *CPSS Trans. Power Electron. Appl.*, 9, 1, Mar. 2024, doi: 10.24295/CPSSTPEA.2023.00042.
7. Alalewi, A., Dayoub, I., Cherkaoui, S., On 5G-V2X use cases and enabling technologies: A comprehensive survey. *IEEE Access*, 9, 107710–107737, 2021.
8. Garcia, M.H.C., Molina-Galan, A., Boban, M., Gozalvez, J., Coll-Perales, B., Şahin, T., Kousaridas, A., A tutorial on 5G NR V2X communications. *IEEE Commun. Surv. Tutorials*, 23, 3, 1972–2026, 2021.
9. Gyawali, S., Xu, S., Qian, Y., Hu, R.Q., Challenges and solutions for cellular based V2X communications. *IEEE Commun. Surv. Tutorials*, 23, 1, 222–255, 2020.
10. Casademont, J., Cordero, B., Camps-Mur, D., da Conceição, L.A.M., Lalos, A., Vitale, C., Laoudias, C., Khodashenas, P.S., Multi-radio V2X communications interoperability through a multi-access edge computing (MEC), in: *2020 22nd International Conference on Transparent Optical Networks (ICTON)*, IEEE, pp. 1–4, 2020.
11. Hasan, M., Mohan, S., Shimizu, T., Lu, H., Securing vehicle-to-everything (V2X) communication platforms. *IEEE Trans. Intell. Veh.*, 5, 4, 693–713, 2020.
12. Khan, M.A., Ghosh, S., Busari, S.A., Huq, K.M.S., Dagiuklas, T., Mumtaz, S., Iqbal, M., Rodriguez, J., Robust, resilient and reliable architecture for v2x communications. *IEEE Trans. Intell. Transp. Syst.*, 22, 7, 4414–4430, 2021.
13. Rondinone, M., Walter, T., Blokpoel, R., Schindler, J., V2X communications for infrastructure-assisted automated driving, in: *2018 IEEE 19th International Symposium on "A World of Wireless, Mobile and Multimedia Networks" (WoWMoM)*, IEEE, pp. 14–19, 2018.
14. Zeadally, S., Javed, M.A., Hamida, E.B., Vehicular communications for ITS: Standardization and challenges. *IEEE Commun. Stand. Mag.*, 4, 1, 11–17, 2020.
15. Ge, Y., Xie, Q., Yu, R., Ma, J., Han, Q., Zhang, Q., Design of Conformance Testing System for C-V2X Standard Protocol, in: *2020 IEEE 91st Vehicular Technology Conference (VTC2020-Spring)*, IEEE, pp. 1–5, 2020.
16. Noor-A-Rahim, M., Liu, Z., Lee, H., Khyam, M.O., He, J., Pesch, D., Moessner, K., Saad, W., Vincent Poor, H., 6G for vehicle-to-everything (V2X) communications: Enabling technologies, challenges, and opportunities. *Proc. IEEE*, 110, 6, 712–734, 2022.
17. Naudts, D., Maglogiannis, V., Hadiwardoyo, S., Van Den Akker, D., Vanneste, S., Mercelis, S., Hellinckx, P., Lannoo, B., Marquez-Barja, J., Moerman, I., Vehicular communication management framework: A flexible hybrid connectivity platform for ccam services. *Future Internet*, 13, 3, 81, 2021.
18. Barros, M.T., Velez, G., Arregui, H., Loyo, E., Sharma, K., Mujika, A., Jennings, B., CogITS: cognition-enabled network management for 5G V2X communication. *IET Intel. Transport Syst.*, 14, 3, 182–189, 2020.

19. Ribeiro, B., Nicolau, M.J., Santos, A., Using machine learning on v2x communications data for vru collision prediction. *Sensors*, 23, 3, 1260, 2023.
20. Wang, P., Liu, X., Wang, Y., Wang, T., Zhang, J., Short-term traffic state prediction based on mobile edge computing in V2X communication. *Appl. Sci.*, 11, 23, 11530, 2021.
21. Li, H., Liu, F., Zhao, Z., Karimzadeh, M., Effective safety message dissemination with vehicle trajectory predictions in V2X networks. *Sensors*, 22, 7, 2686, 2022.
22. Shahriar, M.S., Kale, A.K., Chang, K., Enhancing Intersection Traffic Safety Utilizing V2I Communications: Design and Evaluation of Machine Learning Based Framework. *IEEE Access*, 11, 106024–106036, 2023, doi: 10.1109/ACCESS.2023.3319382.
23. Ye, M., Chen, J., Li, X., Ma, K., Liu, Y., Energy management strategy of a hybrid power system based on V2X vehicle speed prediction. *Sensors*, 21, 16, 5370, 2021.
24. Wu, Z., Qiu, K., Gao, H., Driving policies of V2X autonomous vehicles based on reinforcement learning methods. *IET Intel. Transport Syst.*, 14, 5, 331–337, 2020.
25. Zhang, W., Feng, M., Krunz, M., Volos, H., Latency prediction for delay-sensitive v2x applications in mobile cloud/edge computing systems, in: *GLOBECOM 2020-2020 IEEE Global Communications Conference*, IEEE, pp. 1–6, 2020.
26. Kumar, R., Gupta, S.K., Wang, H.-C., Shyamala Kumari, C., Korlam, S.S.V.P., From Efficiency to Sustainability: Exploring the Potential of 6G for a Greener Future. *Sustainability*, 15, 23, 16387, 2023.
27. Attaran, M., The impact of 5G on the evolution of intelligent automation and industry digitization. *J. Ambient Intell. Hum. Comput.*, 14, 5, 5977–5993, 2023.
28. Hakak, S., Gadekallu, T.R., Maddikunta, P.K.R., Ramu, S.P., Parimala, M., De Alwis, C., Liyanage, M., Autonomous Vehicles in 5G and beyond: A Survey. *Veh. Commun.*, 39, 100551, 2023.
29. Aljeri, N. and Boukerche, A., Smart and green mobility management for 5G-enabled vehicular networks. *Trans. Emerging Telecommun. Technol.*, 33, 3, e4054, 2022.
30. Gohar, A. and Nencioni, G., The role of 5G technologies in a smart city: The case for intelligent transportation system. *Sustainability*, 13, 9, 5188, 2021.
31. Jeong, H.H., Shen, Y.C., Jeong, J.P., Oh, T.T., A comprehensive survey on vehicular networking for safe and efficient driving in smart transportation: A focus on systems, protocols, and applications. *Veh. Commun.*, 31, 100349, 2021.
32. Jung, C., Lee, D., Lee, S., Shim, D.H., V2X-communication-aided autonomous driving: System design and experimental validation. *Sensors*, 20, 10, 2903, 2020.

33. Ameen, H.A., Mahamad, A.K., Saon, S., Md Nor, D., Ghazi, K., A review on vehicle to vehicle communication system applications. *Indones. J. Electr. Eng. Comput. Sci.*, 18, 1, 188–198, 2020.
34. Kabil, A., Rabieh, K., Kaleem, F., Azer, M.A., Vehicle to pedestrian systems: Survey, challenges and recent trends. *IEEE Access*, 10, 123981–123994, 2022.
35. Naik, S.C., AH, M.H.A., Lobo, A.R., Sona, S.S., Badiger, M., A Comprehensive Review of Electric Vehicles: A Smart Choice for Environmental Sustainability and Energy Conservation, in: *E-Mobility in Electrical Energy Systems for Sustainability*, pp. 257–273, 2024.
36. Storck, C.R. and Duarte-Figueiredo, F., A survey of 5G technology evolution, standards, and infrastructure associated with vehicle-to-everything communications by internet of vehicles. *IEEE Access*, 8, 117593–117614, 2020.
37. Abdel Hakeem, S.A., Hady, A.A., Kim, H., Current and future developments to improve 5G-NewRadio performance in vehicle-to-everything communications. *Telecommun. Syst.*, 75, 3, 331–353, 2020.
38. Chen, S., Hu, J., Shi, Y., Zhao, L., Li, W., A vision of C-V2X: Technologies, field testing, and challenges with Chinese development. *IEEE Internet Things J.*, 7, 5, 3872–3881, 2020.
39. Zhou, H., Xu, W., Chen, J., Wang, W., Evolutionary V2X technologies toward the Internet of vehicles: Challenges and opportunities. *Proc. IEEE*, 108, 2, 308–323, 2020.
40. Gholamhosseinian, A. and Seitz, J., A comprehensive survey on cooperative intersection management for heterogeneous connected vehicles. *IEEE Access*, 10, 7937–7972, 2022.
41. Sedar, R., Kalalas, C., Vázquez-Gallego, F., Alonso, L., Alonso-Zarate, J., A comprehensive survey of v2x cybersecurity mechanisms and future research paths. *IEEE Open J. Commun. Soc.*, 4, 325–391, 2023.
42. Soto, I., Calderon, M., Amador, O., Urueña, M., A survey on road safety and traffic efficiency vehicular applications based on C-V2X technologies. *Veh. Commun.*, 33, 100428, 2022.
43. Tedjopurnomo, D.A., Bao, Z., Zheng, B., Choudhury, F.M., Qin, A.K., A survey on modern deep neural network for traffic prediction: Trends, methods and challenges. *IEEE Trans. Knowl. Data Eng.*, 34, 4, 1544–1561, 2020.
44. Kashyap, A.A., Raviraj, S., Devarakonda, A., Nayak K, S.R., KV, S., Bhat, S.J., Traffic flow prediction models–A review of deep learning techniques. *Cogent Eng.*, 9, 1, 2010510, 2022.
45. Yin, X., Wu, G., Wei, J., Shen, Y., Qi, H., Yin, B., Deep learning on traffic prediction: Methods, analysis, and future directions. *IEEE Trans. Intell. Transp. Syst.*, 23, 6, 4927–4943, 2021.
46. Olugbade, S., Ojo, S., Imoize, A.L., Isabona, J., Alaba, M.O., A review of artificial intelligence and machine learning for incident detectors in road transport systems. *Math. Comput. Appl.*, 27, 5, 77, 2022.

47. Tahir, M.N., Leviäkangas, P., Katz, M., Connected vehicles: V2V and V2I road weather and traffic communication using cellular technologies. *Sensors*, 22, 3, 1142, 2022.
48. Boukerche, A. and Wang, J., Machine learning-based traffic prediction models for intelligent transportation systems. *Comput. Netw.*, 181, 107530, 2020.
49. Christopoulou, M., Barmpounakis, S., Koumaras, H., Kaloxylos, A., Artificial Intelligence and Machine Learning as key enablers for V2X communications: A comprehensive survey. *Veh. Commun.*, 39, 100569, 2023.
50. Sona, S.S., Lobo, A.R., AH, M.H.A., Naik, S.C., Badiger, M., Sustainable Mobility Revolution: Best Practices and Strategies for Enhanced Energy Efficiency in E-Mobility, in: *E-Mobility in Electrical Energy Systems for Sustainability*, pp. 1–17, IGI Global Scientific Publishing, 2024. doi: 10.4018/979-8-3693-2611-4.ch001.
51. Mao, T., Mihăiță, A.-S., Chen, F., Vu, H.L., Boosted genetic algorithm using machine learning for traffic control optimization. *IEEE Trans. Intell. Transp. Syst.*, 23, 7, 7112–7141, 2021.
52. Alhilal, A.Y., Finley, B., Braud, T., Su, D., Hui, P., Street smart in 5G: Vehicular applications, communication, and computing. *IEEE Access*, 10, 105631–105656, 2022.
53. Nama, M., Nath, A., Bechra, N., Bhatia, J., Tanwar, S., Chaturvedi, M., Sadoun, B., Machine learning-based traffic scheduling techniques for intelligent transportation system: Opportunities and challenges. *Int. J. Commun. Syst.*, 34, 9, e4814, 2021.
54. Jiang, S., Zhang, Y., Liu, R., Jafari, M., Kharbeche, M., Data-driven optimization for dynamic shortest path problem considering traffic safety. *IEEE Trans. Intell. Transp. Syst.*, 23, 10, 18237–18252, 2022.
55. Boukerche, A., Tao, Y., Sun, P., Artificial intelligence-based vehicular traffic flow prediction methods for supporting intelligent transportation systems. *Comput. Netw.*, 182, 107484, 2020.
56. Lu, Q., Jung, H., Kim, K.-D., Optimization-based approach for resilient connected and autonomous intersection crossing traffic control under V2X communication. *IEEE Trans. Intell. Veh.*, 7, 2, 354–367, 2021.
57. Wang, H., Yuan, Y., Yang, X.T., Zhao, T., Liu, Y., Deep Q learning-based traffic signal control algorithms: Model development and evaluation with field data. *J. Intell. Transp. Syst.*, 27, 3, 314–334, 2023.
58. Shaikh, P.W., El-Abd, M., Khanafer, M., Gao, K., A review on swarm intelligence and evolutionary algorithms for solving the traffic signal control problem. *IEEE Trans. Intell. Transp. Syst.*, 23, 1, 48–63, 2020.
59. Singh, C., Shetty, S.C.N., Badiger, M., Nischitha, A Study on Connected Cars–V2V Communication, in: *Modeling and Optimization of Optical Communication Networks*, pp. 251–265, 2023.
60. Maadi, S., Stein, S., Hong, J., Murray-Smith, R., Real-time adaptive traffic signal control in a connected and automated vehicle environment: optimisation

of signal planning with reinforcement learning under vehicle speed guidance. *Sensors*, 22, 19, 7501, 2022.
61. Paiva, S., Ahad, M.A., Tripathi, G., Feroz, N., Casalino, G., Enabling technologies for urban smart mobility: Recent trends, opportunities and challenges. *Sensors*, 21, 6, 2143, 2021.
62. Fu, Y., Li, C., Yu, F.R., Luan, T.H., Zhang, Y., A survey of driving safety with sensing, vehicular communications, and artificial intelligence-based collision avoidance. *IEEE Trans. Intell. Transp. Syst.*, 23, 7, 6142–6163, 2021.
63. Rammohan, A., Chavhan, S., Chidambaram, R.K., Manisaran, N., Pavan Kumar, K.V., Automotive Collision Avoidance System: A Review, in: *Virtual and Augmented Reality for Automobile Industry: Innovation Vision and Applications*, pp. 1–19, 2022.
64. Tan, H., Zhao, F., Hao, H., Liu, Z., Evidence for the crash avoidance effectiveness of intelligent and connected vehicle technologies. *Int. J. Environ. Res. Public Health*, 18, 17, 9228, 2021.
65. Chen, C., Liu, B., Wan, S., Qiao, P., Pei, Q., An edge traffic flow detection scheme based on deep learning in an intelligent transportation system. *IEEE Trans. Intell. Transp. Syst.*, 22, 3, 1840–1852, 2020.
66. Shen, X.S., Huang, C., Liu, D., Xue, L., Zhuang, W., Sun, R., Ying, B., Data management for future wireless networks: Architecture, privacy preservation, and regulation. *IEEE Netw.*, 35, 1, 8–15, 2021.
67. Ghosal, A. and Conti, M., Security issues and challenges in V2X: A survey. *Comput. Netw.*, 169, 107093, 2020.
68. Ravi, D.K. and Arunachalam, R., Revolutionizing Intelligent Transportation Systems with Cellular Vehicle-to-Everything (C-V2X) technology: Current trends, use cases, emerging technologies, standardization bodies, industry analytics and future directions. *Veh. Commun.*, 43, 100638, Oct. 2023, doi: 10.1016/j.vehcom.2023.100638.
69. Fallgren, M., Dillinger, M., Mahmoodi, T., Svensson, T., Wiley, J. (Eds.), *Cellular V2X for connected automated driving*, vol. 270, Wiley, Hoboken, NJ, USA, 2021.

12

Empowering Healthcare through Mobility as a Service: A Comprehensive Review

Manjunatha Badiger[1]*, Thrisha B.[2], Kshithij H. S.[2], Sathwik M. S.[2] and Rakshitha N.[2]

[1]*Department of VLSI Design and Technology, Nitte (Deemed to be University), NMAM Institute of Technology, Nitte, Udupi, India*
[2]*Department of ECE, Sahyadri College of Engineering & Management, Mangaluru, Adyar, India*

Abstract

The nature and effects of MaaS in improving the accessibility of healthcare systems are discussed in this chapter using the launch of 24/7 low-cost generic medicine dispensers. The chapter starts with the problem of offering affordable healthcare for the world population, focusing on the countries where access to essential medicines is still a question. The chapter then introduces MaaS as a crucial new connectivity solution for enhancing healthcare. The focus of this discourse will be on the low-cost generic medicine dispensers, which are open throughout to respond to the needs of the patients at a cheaper cost than retail outlets. These dispensers, when incorporated into the system's MaaS platforms, form a proper, efficient, and economical dispensing system that has the potential to transform the health sector. The chapter also discusses the technology used in these dispensers, the general regulations and infrastructure required for their deployment, and the possible barriers to their large-scale application. Additionally, the chapter examines how these systems affect citizens' access to healthcare, the efficiency of health economic systems, and the impact of social equity on the environment. Finally, it briefly discusses future developments in dispensers and their generalization in the context of MaaS for healthcare. Finally, based on the findings of the chapter, some suggestions are outlined that could be implemented by policymakers, healthcare practitioners, and technology creators to make the most of this innovative model. All in all, this chapter is intended to stress the importance of MaaS and low-cost medicine dispensers for improving the existing equity and sustainability of healthcare.

**Corresponding author*: badiger_manju@yahoo.com

Rathishchandra R. Gatti and Chandra Singh (eds.) Digital Convergence in Intelligent Mobility Systems, (271–292) © 2025 Scrivener Publishing LLC

Keywords: MaaS, low-cost, medicine dispensers, generic medicines, dispensers, medical infrastructure, digital health solutions, innovations

12.1 Introduction

While access to healthcare is considered a human right, on the ground, it is still an unrealized dream in so many ways for most people of the world, not least as regards access to essential medicines. This disparity in health access has roots reaching deep into socioeconomic, geographical, and infrastructural challenges. Health infrastructure and access to advanced medical technology might be assured in high-income countries, but increasingly prohibitive medicine costs present an insurmountable obstacle. Prescription drugs are noted to be among those services difficult to pay for, even by those who have insurance. The financial burden most often results in non-compliance with prescribed treatment programs and the advancement of conditions that are otherwise supposed to be manageable, thus leading to a considerable increase in hospitalization and a higher overall health expenditure. The problem is altogether different in low- and middle-income countries. Other than medicine's affordability, there are issues with its availability and access. Health facilities are usually concentrated in urban areas and, therefore, beyond the reach of many rural communities. Some of these regions have few and far-flung pharmacies; their supply chains are also frequently disrupted due to logistical problems like poor infrastructure, political instability, or even natural disasters. The operating hours of such pharmacies are rather short, which is dangerous, especially when emergencies occur at night or when workers fail to visit a pharmacy in time due to long working hours. The lack of access to medicines on a 24/7 basis exacerbates health inequity, particularly among the most vulnerable populations: the elderly, the chronically sick, and those from remote and less privileged parts of the world [1].

Inequities in healthcare utilization can have a truly vicious cycle of consequences, including worse health outcomes and higher costs of healthcare. Those who do not receive essential medications in a timely manner are more likely to experience complications from health problems and need costlier medical intervention. Lack of access to such medicines at affordable prices may also contribute to the use of inferior or counterfeited drugs, which play a large role in patient safety. These call for scalable and innovative solutions that could bridge gaps in health access and make medicines accessible, available, and affordable to all, regardless of geographical location or socio-economic status. Such technologies must, however, be framed within an overall context of healthcare delivery, new technology integration, and community-based interventions—together with policy reforms—with the objective of reducing disparity and improving health outcomes.

Mobility as a Service (MaaS) is one of these new, innovative concepts that are going to shake the very foundations of a number of industries, health included. Initially designed to make urban transportation easy, MaaS joined different modes of transportation—public transportation, car sharing, and bicycle rental—along with a number of other services under one umbrella that a customer could access from his digital interface. It enables the user to plan, book, and pay for any transport mode in one application. The ultimate spirit of MaaS is to make transportation user-centered, convenient, efficient, and at affordable costs, meeting the specific needs of the users. Though still at a nascent stage, the concept of MaaS is finding applications beyond transport, presenting revolutionary solutions to areas where access and convenience are of essence, such as healthcare [2]. The most useful implementations of MaaS in healthcare will probably be with 24/7, low-cost generic medicine dispensers. Such automated dispensers can be placed in easy-to-reach areas, such as near hospitals or clinics, or in areas where the community is underserved, for around-the-clock access to necessary medications. With the integration of mobile technology, the dispensers will be able to give real-time medication availability and prescription verification remotely and also guide users through the process in an easy manner. This kind of integration will make not only access to medication easier but also ensure that the right medication is provided as per the prescription, hence minimizing the risk of a prescription error. Moreover, such automated dispensers will release the pressure from community pharmacies and emergency services by making the medication supplies more decentralized. This enables healthcare professionals to spend more time on complicated cases, which are more critical to them, while ensuring that patients get easy and quick access to their drugs. Given the evolution that health systems continue to experience globally, there is sufficient merit for MaaS concepts such as these dispensers to be integrated into practice and be pivotal in efforts to advance access to essential medicines, improve patient outcomes, and ultimately ensure that people take responsibility for their health. This could help toward less health disparity, lower healthcare expenditure, and improved efficiency overall in the global healthcare delivery system [3].

12.2 Mobility as a Service (MaaS) in Healthcare

MaaS, also known as Mobility as a Service, is a relatively new paradigm of transportation that will combine and utilize multiple modes of transportation services as one easily accessible service. In the healthcare sector, MaaS becomes an essential part in making sure that patients are able to access the facilities and services accordingly. Combined with public and private transport, as well as ride-sharing services and even non-emergency transportation for patients, MaaS provides increased patient satisfaction through diversity and dependability of transport to the healthcare provider. Hence, by integrating real-time data of transport services through digital platforms and on-demand services, a patient can be able to plan, book, and even pay for transport to his or her appointment without facing any challenge in mobility or even the availability of transport.

12.2.1 Overview of Healthcare Access Challenges

Issues of healthcare access present themselves greatly in remote and rural fringes of a region where either health facilities are scarce or when these places are hard to get to. Such places can quite often be very far-traveled for basic healthcare, leading to late diagnosis and treatment. In addition to that, the limited number of health workers available at that time further compounds the situation, leaving many without timely access to care. City centers are daunting enough with crowded conditions as it is; the long waits already take their toll while the overburdened hospitals and resources at capacity make life difficult for city dwellers to gain access to appropriate care when they need it most. Most importantly, care comes at a cost, and it blocks access both in the city and the countryside. Most cases are blocked since the costs are extremely high concerning what's paid by patients and long-term insurance, and the treatments themselves are expensive. The burdens put on patients' basic lives due to poverty further threaten their access to timely treatment, which ends up causing worse health status. In addition, people who do not have complete insurance find it tough to deal with healthcare workers language and communication, mainly foreigners or those with low literacy skills. Mistakes in verbal diagnosis of ailments, plans of treatment, and instructions about drugs lead to improper care and further deterioration of health. These and many other challenges have resulted in the deplorable state of resources in health facilities; old equipment, inadequate ration of staff workers, and drugs impinge upon the quality and availability of care. The issue becomes very acute in periphery areas where hospitals do not even have much infrastructure to provide comprehensive services. Equally, the chances to access healthcare are greatly impeded by environmental threats and climate change. The very same environmental hazards and climate changes that turn into health problems are in fact making it considerably difficult to gain access to healthcare. Natural disasters, extreme weather conditions, and pollution lead to health problems but also destroy health-related infrastructure. With their growing trend, this leads to a higher vulnerability of communities in disease outbreaks or health-related crisis situations. Another major access barrier to healthcare is emergencies, both natural and human-made. During emergency situations such as pandemics or natural disasters, the demand for healthcare services can be so high that delivering care in a timely fashion could prove to be challenging. Moreover, emergencies of this sort actually force the hand and bring home just how much systems to cope with changes in demand are a must. In the end, this spans from geographic barriers to financial restrictions of resources and environmental concerns, which add layers upon layers that will further complicate any attempts at equality in health for all [4].

12.2.2 Enhancing Medical Access with Mobility as a Service

MaaS in healthcare would be the evolution of how patients access medical services. This is one of the single largest obstacles to getting timely care. MaaS can unite all forms of transportation, from public transit to ride-sharing and even non-emergency medical options, on a single platform that makes it simple for patients or providers to plan, book, and pay for journeys. This is particularly beneficial in rural areas or underserved communities where it may have little to no transport, if any. An app will have the ability to give live updates of the most efficient route and mode of transportation, hence easing a patient's decision on how best they can reach health facilities in time. Moreover, besides improving access for patients with geographic or mobility constraints, MaaS can ease transportation concerns in urban settings. Traditional means of transport are often undependable or too time-consuming in most urban centers where crowding presents a problem; all these situations mean missed appointments and delayed care. This is what the MaaS model entails: the wide varieties of travel choices within a single system take away much of the stress and logistical discomforts associated with navigating through urban congestion. This benefits not only the patients but also the healthcare providers, as more regular attendance to the appointments with medical specialists usually means better health outcomes and lessened strain on emergency services from preventable health crises [5]. More importantly, MaaS in healthcare will be in a position to support special populations, such as elderly or disabled persons, with services catering to their needs. This means that MaaS platforms can organize non-emergency medical transportation that is adapted for wheelchairs or other medical equipment and thus allow such patients to receive the care they need without further complications. Therefore, MaaS decreases the overall cost of healthcare because it reduces missed appointments, allows for increased precautionary care, and optimizes health resource utilization. Facilitating transportation to increase access to medical services for the patients themselves, MaaS relieves transportation burdens, making it a cornerstone to improving access and efficiency in healthcare. MaaS for health is quite an exciting prospect; it may hold one of the major keys to improvement, especially in transport barriers to access to medical services. MaaS simplifies how one would get to healthcare by aggregating options for public transit, rideshare, and medical transport on a single platform. This is particularly helpful for patients that may be in rural or underserved areas where transportation options might be at a minimum and, therefore, ease the burden of attending the medical appointment. MaaS, in simple terms, increases efficiency in health services through better organization in the area of transport by providing real-time information on the best routes and options that will prevent missed or delayed appointments. MaaS has given these urban settings flexibility in that congestion and overloading of the public transport means delay in the visits. By integrating various modes of transport, the patients are guaranteed reliability without stress and wastage of time navigating the busy cities. This improves health outcomes as both the patient and healthcare provider benefit. It will reduce pressures on emergency services that could otherwise be called upon to deal with an avoidable health crisis because of a lack of care. MaaS can support efficient use of healthcare resources by making sure patients can attend on time and thereby make better use of medical personnel and facilities. Moreover, there would also be a targeting of Maas toward a special population, if needed, for the elderly, disabled, and people with chronic diseases. The customized transportation options would consider needs around wheelchair accessibility, mobility aids, or other medical equipment so that the most vulnerable populations have no further complications in accessing healthcare services. For chronic conditions that necessitate frequent doctor and hospital visits, MaaS would make quite some difference in ensuring continuity of care. It will be very easy for them to access transportation, which makes it more likely that the patients will adhere to their treatment schedule and have better long-term health. The MaaS platforms also provide data on transportation trends of the patients and arrival rates at appointments to healthcare providers. These data would offer insights that could be used in identifying transportation gaps in access where targeted intervention needs to take place to improve service delivery. In instances of any emergencies or crises-like situations, whether it be a pandemic or natural disaster, MaaS can arrange needed transportation for both patients and medical workers alike, ensuring access to services. This will also allow for better resource planning and the flexibility that health systems require to make timely responses toward routine care and those that are of utmost importance. Overall, MaaS bears the potential to enhance not only healthcare access but also efficiency, equity, and resilience in health systems [6].

12.3 Low-Cost Generic Medicine Dispensers

Low-cost generic medicine dispensers reinforce the health sector since they tackle huge problems, which are affordability and availability. In several regions, especially the rural ones or the ones served by few suppliers, lack of access to essential medicines is one of the concerns. High prices of brand-name medications and few pharmacy outlets make it impossible for people to access the drugs they need. These dispensers are designed to store and dispense prescription medications that the general population can take out any time and any day at a lower price than what is offered across the pharmacy counters. Even the expiry of the normal working hours would not inhibit patients from getting the drugs they need, as they could get the appropriate dispensers strategically positioned at public transport shelters. This is particularly important for patients who would otherwise be compelled to make a long journey or wait a long time just to fill their prescriptions [7]. Both high-tech and easy to operate for users, these types of dispensers utilize advanced technology. Fitted with secured storage systems, these machines guarantee that the medicines are stored at their optimum temperature and humidity, thus maintaining their usefulness. Core technical adeptness versus usability in the dispensers is minimized in order that users from different ages and skill abilities would not have a hard time operating them. Most times, the patient has to scan a prescription or a code before the prescription is issued to them through the machine. The process is made as quick and easy as possible in order to discourage patients from any forms of access barriers. This emphasis on how the dispensers should be designed to enhance the ease of usage is important to ensure that they can be used in different places without any hindrances. The real-time inventory tracking system is one of the notable attributes of these dispensers. Such technology makes it possible to check for the level of stock in the machine at any time and thus guarantees that capsules that would be urgent are never out. In case some stock levels begin to deplete, the system notifies the supply chain management system, which can then organize for purchasing some more. Such situations as where a patient has to look for a dispenser only to discover that it is empty due to poor logistics support have been eliminated. Furthermore, this system also aids in making the supply chain less efficient, minimizing wastage, and ensuring the availability of necessary medicines at the required location. Including these dispensers on the MaaS platform enhances their effectiveness. By assimilating the dispensers into the wider transportation system, healthcare contractors ensure that medicines can be delivered, even in the remote areas, without any delays. For instance, public transport plus private vehicles arranged by a MaaS platform could deliver the medicines to the rural dispenser. Such integration enhances the efficiency of medication delivery and lowers overall expenditure on the system, making it sustainable. It is this perfect combination of technology and new-age logistics that enables the healthcare accessibility impact of such dispensers to be felt as far as possible [8]. One more aspect of inexpensive generic medicine dispensing devices that is worthy of note is their potential to improve patients' adherence and education. Due to inadequate education or the lack of professionals available, patients in the countryside or in the try-in areas face additional difficulty not only in getting treatment but also in how it should be taken. These dispensers can have digital screens installed, where the instruction is given in several languages so that patients' correct intake of the medication is ensured. For instance, this could mean that the dispenser has instructions as to how one should take the medication, when it should be taken, and what are the side effects, if any. This feature is probably the most important in areas with a lack of health practitioners and hence no professional guidance for the patients. Besides, such dispensers can be interfaced with health monitoring systems for constant patient care support. For example, they may be set up to remind patients of their prescription refills, follow up on their medication compliance, or even measure their wellness indicators using connected gadgets. If a patient's health data suggests that he/she requires a dose change or appointment with the doctor, the dispenser may notify either the healthcare personnel or the client at once. By doing so, it helps patients to take medicines on time and, at the same time, enables them to ensure better overall health, thus reducing hospitalizations and improving long-term survival rates. Finally, these dispensers can also be very useful in situations of a public health emergency, say, during outbreaks or in the wake of disasters. Indeed, in such cases where facilities for healthcare may otherwise be lacking due to a collapse of those facilities or other reasons, these dispensers may offer basic drugs and medical items in a dependable way. Their rapid acquisition would help the deployment in the affected areas so that the communities have necessary medicines even in emergencies. This versatility is beneficial to both the normal delivery of healthcare services and occurrences of the need for medical care, which exposes their sufficiency beyond just drug distribution [9].

12.4 Regulatory and Infrastructure Considerations

Successful implementation of 24/7 inexpensive over the counter medicine dispensers lies in the ability to overcome regulatory complexities and secure adequate infrastructural support. There are major differences in how drug sale and distribution is structured in the different regions; thus, dispensers are required to abide by local regulations which govern the dispensing of pharmaceuticals, handling and protection of data, as well as protection of consumers. For example, dispensers should follow some internal procedures to ensure prescription verification, and these may require interfacing with existent EHR systems to verify patient prescription history and dispensing records. Furthermore, legal requirements tend to require the dispensers to observe proper storage requirements which affect the stability of the products within the containers such as humidity and temperature range. In terms of infrastructure, these dispensers require high-speed Internet for sending and receiving transactions, making payments, and constant power which may require solar and battery backup. Meeting these compliance and infrastructural requirements means working with government agencies, healthcare organizations, and service providers, and the creation of clear-cut guidelines for the installation and exploitation of the dispensers in different settings [10].

12.4.1 Challenges and Solutions

Although it is feasible to have low-cost generic medicine dispensers around the clock and within Maas frameworks, it presents several problems including technological barriers, logistical barriers, and societal barriers. One of the major problems is the technological assurance of the dispensers with regard to availability, especially in developing countries where power and Internet services are unreliable. Solutions such as solar power, offline ability, and other auxiliary systems can improve the performance of the dispenser under such conditions. Supply chain management of the dispensers comes as a logistical challenge because constant availability of the medication hinges on good inventory strategy and management practices. Employing demand forecasting and stock level optimization through data analytics will help avoid stock outages and also cut down on wastage. Another problem lies in revitalizing public perception as well as securing users' approval, both of which are essential toward a higher penetration level. This could be attained via user education, engagement of the community, and providing reassurance with regard to safety and efficiency of the dispensers. Doing such will not only prepare their deployment but also avert their future abandonment [11].

12.4.2 Strategic Partnerships and Stakeholder Engagement

Successful implementation strategies for low-cost generic medicine dispensers rely heavily on strategic partnerships and stakeholder engagement. A coalition of healthcare providers, technology companies, government bodies, and community organizations will ease the process of deploying and scaling dispensers. In particular, public–private partnerships provide necessary financial resources, technical expertise, and regulatory support to overcome initial deployment barriers. By engaging local communities and patient advocacy groups early in the process, trust is built, enabling dispensers to be designed and operated with users' needs at heart. Internally integrating dispenser technologies into workflows of healthcare providers and pharmacists enhances the effectiveness of such systems. Continuous stakeholder engagement through feedback loops and iterative design are essential double-edged swords that help address emerging challenges while improving services indefinitely. This implies that by facilitating collaborations between various sectors' actors who share similar goals, implementation strategies become more resilient, adaptable, and responsive to ongoing changes in the face of changing healthcare environments.

12.4.3 Funding and Sustainability Models

Funding is crucial for the long-term success of 24/7 affordable generic drug vending machines, which must also have sustainable business models. It can come from various sources like government grants, private investments, and international aid organizations working to improve global health access. Different models can be explored for financial sustainability like subscription services, pay-per-use fees, or partnerships with drug manufacturers. Also, the financial burden could be reduced and operational costs spread evenly through cost-sharing arrangements between public health systems and private entities. Other possible revenue streams that can support dispenser operations include leveraging advertising space on dispensers or providing data insights that may interest pharmaceutical companies. Furthermore, a robust maintenance and support structure must also be implemented since ongoing operational costs have to be taken care of in the sustainability plan. Therefore, by developing holistic funding as well as sustainability strategies, stakeholders can ensure that these dispensers remain a viable solution to enhance healthcare access over time [12].

12.4.4 Technology Integration and Digital Connectivity

Low-cost implementation of medicine dispensers depends on merging them with health IT systems and having a strong Internet connection. It involves linking these dispensers with electronic health record systems (EHRs) and pharmacy management systems, which helps to check prescription authenticity, monitor stock levels, and update in real time. Internet connectivity through the provision of reliable networks or cellular networks is necessary, especially in remote areas where it is hard to get connected. To make it easy for customers to pay through mobile phones or insurance platforms, there is the use of cloud-based platforms, thus making them more scalable and tracking easier since one will have a central point of managing all the machines at different points in time. Because of this technological advancement, patients from various communities receive their medications promptly whenever necessary [13].

12.4.5 User Education, Community Engagement, and Security Measures

To build confidence and encourage widespread adoption of these dispensers, user education and community involvement should be the key goals in the implementation. For instance, workshops, informational campaigns, and on-site demonstrations can help users and healthcare providers learn more about the dispensers. In addition to this, collaborating with local community leaders and patient advocacy organizations can create even more trust. Nevertheless, it is necessary to have tight security and privacy measures so as to ensure that patient data remains safe while the dispensing process remains intact. Among such measures are encryption, secure authentication, and observing data protection regulations which are aimed at protecting sensitive information. Addressing these concerns helps not only in improving user confidence but also in ensuring that the dispensers offer a secure reliable way for obtaining healthcare easily [14].

12.5 Assessing Impact: Benefits to Healthcare, Economy, and Society

Availability around the clock of low-priced generic drug dispensers integrated with Mobility as a Service (MaaS) platforms is of great advantages in areas such as healthcare, economy, and society. In healthcare for instance, these dispensers aid in medication adherence because they provide unfailing access to essential medications, hence managing chronic illnesses like diabetes, hypertension, and asthma better. This minimizes emergency interventions and hospitalizations, hence easing pressure on healthcare systems. Well, apart from this, they also offer cost savings economically by reducing expensive brand-name drugs going on top of these costs arising out of untreated conditions. Additionally, they support local economies by generating employment opportunities related to dispenser maintenance, logistics, and support services. People living in remote or undeserved areas can enjoy an improved quality of life due to enhanced access to medications. These dispensers empower people to stay proactive about their health through reducing long-distance travels to pharmacies, which increases productivity and reduces absenteeism, thereby creating a healthier community overall. Furthermore, the dispensers may help close health equity gaps, thus availing medicines needed by every person irrespective of the level of wealth he/she possesses [15].

12.5.1 Environmental Considerations

The evaluation of 24/7 low-cost generic medicine dispensers is heavily reliant on environmental sustainability. In particular, it is critical that these dispensers be powered by solar panels, as they offer a low-carbon alternative to traditional pharmacy models. They help in reducing the environmental impact associated with pharmaceutical supply chains by minimizing the need for frequent deliveries and packaging. Furthermore, waste prevention involved in medication due to integration of advanced inventory management systems helps in controlling drug wastage by accurate prediction of demand and stocking levels. This way, expired or excess drugs are not disposed of, which might harm the environment if not managed well. Furthermore, localizing access to medications through this type of dispenser has reduced patients' need to travel long distances, thus reducing greenhouse gas emissions associated with transportation. Besides, there is an increase in digitization that leads to less paper use and smoothens logistics, making this product environmentally friendly. While healthcare systems give more emphasis on sustainability measures, there is no doubt that adopting such dispensaries shall greatly minimize the overall sector's ecological footprints.

12.5.2 Improved Public Health Outcomes

There is a potential for these dispensers to enhance public health outcomes at a large scale due to their ability to improve access of affordable medications. They eliminate one of the significant obstacles that prevent people from getting medical help by making sure that vital drugs are available in both rural and urban areas. These drugs can manage chronic diseases which require constant taking of medicines because they stop disease progression, lessen complications, and hence decrease death rates. Moreover, during times of public health emergencies such as pandemics or natural disasters, these dispensers can be very important for ensuring the availability of drugs, hence promoting community resilience and stability. Their independent and ongoing operation provides a dependable source of essential medicines when normal health services fail to function in emergencies, therefore making them a reliable option during crisis situations [16].

12.5.3 Enhanced Data Analytics and Health Insights

Another important effect of these dispensers is the possibility of better data analysis and more profound health comprehension. Connected to digital health platforms, these dispensers can gather crucial information on how people use medicines, how often they take them correctly, and fluctuations in demand. Such information helps in the formulation of public health strategies, identification of healthcare access gaps, and more targeted interventions. For instance, health authorities may track disease spread using dispenser data, manage drug supplies effectively, and ensure that the delivery of healthcare is optimized in real time. This approach to healthcare is grounded on data hence it is more responsive and adaptive hence meets the needs of diverse population groups better. Furthermore, insights from dispenser usage can facilitate ongoing healthcare research aimed at identifying trends, evaluating the impact of interventions and consequently enhancing health outcomes at a broader level [17].

12.6 Future Perspective Empowering Healthcare MAAS to Support Healthcare

MaaS improves healthcare benefits by facilitating access to the services. For individuals living in rural or deprived areas, MaaS offers consistent and effective means of transportation to seek medical attention. This increased access to delivery helps anxious patients get the necessary medical assistance on time, which plays a big role in preventing worsening of existing illnesses. Similarly, the need is met for arranging and sharing tactics within the community limits where individual patients miss appointments because of transport issues. In addition, the availability of MaaS offers further enhanced support of care coordination, as it incorporates transport and healthcare appointment management coordination. This in turn enables a better organization of various appointments requiring the different healthcare service providers. MaaS can also help in lowering expenditure within the healthcare system since it will reduce initial visits for urgent care when patients fail to show up for medical appointments, and it will also reduce the patient transportation costs. By offering persistent means of transportation, MaaS enables patients to follow through treatments and care more effectively [18]. MaaS enhances profit by creating additional productivity and cutting down transport expenses. People do not need to commute or travel more than required, leading to a situation where they spend a minimum amount on traveling and higher levels on economic output. The introduction of MaaS results in the creation of jobs in areas such as telecommunications, transportation, and others, including but not limited to software development and customer service. Besides that, MaaS is getting people and businesses to places more subtly and cheaply than ever with the use of efficient and cost-effective travel solutions. For example, pooled travel offers cost-effective services such as carpooling and ride-sharing, which results in a decrease in the number of personal vehicle owners; thus, expenses on maintenance, fuel, and insurance are reduced. Additionally, by facilitating greater access to shops and attractions, the new technology is a factor in the growth of local economies, which in essence boosts tourism and permits the cities to develop new markets by means of investments [19]. MaaS definitely improves the societal aspect through creating better accessibility, less traffic congestion, and strengthening sustainability.

It therefore makes the reach of vital services easier for various groups of people, such as those who are not mobile or those who have limited financial means. Thus incorporating integrated transport alternatives, MaaS guarantees that every person can get near the essential services required for healthcare, education, and employment without much problem. MaaS, on the other hand, takes care of traffic congestion problems on roads, routes, and shared mobility solutions, which finally gives smooth and shorter travel times. This in turn results in the enhancement of urban life quality through the elimination of travel-induced stress as well. The resulting effect on the environment is thereby minimized. Through the endorsement of public transit, electric vehicles, and other sustainable alternatives, Mobility as a Service (MaaS) encourages environmental protection, minimization of emissions, and improvement of air quality, respectively. Social equity is one of the major benefits of MaaS, as it provides people transportation services at reasonable rates that bridge the gap between different socio-economic groups. By promoting this, MaaS brings communities together and increases the accessibility of local services and activities, thus helping to develop social bonds and inclusiveness of the community in daily life. Moreover, the cutting-edge technology incorporated into MaaS not only creates technological developments but also makes urban areas smarter and friendlier to the environment, which in turn helps the society level.

12.6.1 Environmental Considerations

Mobility as a Service (MaaS) has a tremendous environmental value because it makes transportation more and more sustainable and has a smaller ecological footprint. The main benefit of MaaS is in its ability to decrease emissions. Through the use of shared and public transportation options, MaaS cuts down on cars on the road. This drop in vehicle usage means that there are fewer greenhouse gases and air pollutants, which are very important in the fight against climate change and the improvement of air quality. In addition, MaaS platforms frequently develop their services by electrifying transportation and using other alternative fuels. This is essentially a shift from conventional gasoline- and diesel-powered vehicles to vehicles that are cleaner and support the transition to renewable energy sources. The transport sector switches to greener technologies such as electric vehicles (EVs) and promotes eco-friendly transportation options. In turn, this fosters the gradual phase-out of fossil fuels. MaaS, moreover, makes the best use of the resources by boosting transportation network function efficiency. By means of intelligent routing and scheduling, MaaS gets the ideal travel distance, which affects the consumption of fuel and the environmental impact of the production, maintenance, and disposal of a vehicle. The use of such efficient resource management leads to transportation's overall carbon footprint reduction. Moreover, Mobility as a Service contributes to less congestion on the roads. Through the provision of intelligent transport systems and the utilization of shared mobility, MaaS contributes to reduce idling times and improve traffic flow. The effect of this reduction in congestion is not only the decrease of fuel consumption and emissions but also the reduction of noise pollution and the provision of an urban environment more capable of pleasantness. The environmental benefits of MaaS are also connected to town planning. Through transportation planning and the land utilization and infrastructure development, MaaS stands for compact, walkable communities. This is the way of life that encourages living patterns that are more sustainable, and as a result, it minimizes the need for long-distance travels. Therefore, this not only contributes to the healthier urban environment but also promotes the environmentally friendly urban environment. MaaS platforms also produce transportation pattern data that is useful in locating the spots emitting high pollution and consequently coming up with targeted actions to address environmental problems. Such an approach utilizing data makes it possible for the adoption of transportation policies and practices based on more reliable information, which in turn results in the further improvement of the environmental effects of MaaS. Furthermore, the prevalence of MaaS will be lessened by fewer high-capacity parking spaces being taken up and new eco-friendly spaces evolving in place of parking facilities. More and more countries are participating in the initiative of shared mobility; thus, the prospects of parking spaces in rich areas turning to green spaces are brighter. In addition to that, by decreasing the hard surfaces, we were able to reduce the water that goes out of the system and, at the same time, promote the health of the local ecosystems. MaaS enables other forms of active transportation, such as biking and walking, and then integrates these into the services. Promotion of active transportation contributes to decreasing dependence on motor vehicles and reducing emissions, along with maintaining good public health. Overall, MaaS gives a great deal to a more sustainable and environmentally friendly transportation system aligned with the broader goals of reduction in ecological impact and enhancement in urban quality of life [20].

12.7 Cost Reduction and Efficiency in Healthcare Delivery

The combination of Mobility as a Service (MaaS) and low-cost generic medicine dispensers marks a progressive development in healthcare accessibility and equity. It is evident from the foregoing that these innovations can go a long way in solving some of the perennial problems bedeviling global health, especially in neglected and remote regions. Such dispensers that permit constant access to cheap prescriptions ought to make healthcare delivery more effective, especially for those who cannot traditionally seek such care. The capacity to position these dispensers in ideal places means that even geographical or economic factors will not limit access to the key medicines [21]. Nonetheless, conclusive reasons may be given for carrying out these systems, even when certain obstacles are present. Changes in the laws are necessary in order to permit the use of automated dispensers, and additional resources are needed in order to provide electricity and Internet access, more so in rural areas. Governments, healthcare practitioners, and technology manufacturers should work hand in hand in solving these problems. Given the right kind of assistance, however, these challenges can be dealt with, making it possible to introduce these systems on a large scale and derive as many health benefits as possible. In terms of the future, the use of low-cost generic medicine dispensers, likely in conjunction with MaaS platforms, will be profound. Such systems provide a reasonable and easily implementable paradigm to enhance healthcare accessibility and efficiency. By eliminating the need for conventional pharmacies and optimizing the supply of medicines, they can actually bring down the cost of healthcare along with its reach. Moreover, as civilization advances, more upgrades can be anticipated in this area, e.g., general inventory systems run by AI or supply chains secured by blockchains that would make these systems more effective and secure [22]. To sum up, there is a great advantage offered by the combination of MaaS and low-cost generic medicine vending in terms of increasing healthcare access. Such strategies address both the issue of cost and the issue of reaching out to patients, which have been a barrier to global health initiatives for a long time. In this case, such innovations should not be avoided but encouraged, and their application should be such that all people, regardless of their geographical or economic position, will benefit. This way, better changes will reveal better and more cost-effective options for healthcare provision, making health services available to all but, most importantly, improving healthcare outcomes for everyone. Innovation in the healthcare delivery model is not only limited to the implementation of decentralized low-cost generic medicine dispensers but also extends to include Mobility as a Service (MaaS), which highlights the opportunity of improving health equity at a global stage. However, one element that remains to be fully unpacked is how these systems could act as adjuncts to healthcare strategies based on the collection of such data. Since health data on medication dispensing, demographics, and overall health is collected in an anonymized manner, such systems self-generate evidence on the changing health landscape to which they will respond. This data will help governments and healthcare facilities predict what interventions are necessary, whom to target with these interventions more efficiently, and even wade off barriers that impede access to healthcare. Further, it is important to examine how the regarded systems can increase community trust in healthcare systems. In a number of underprivileged targets, there tends to be disbelief or lack of trust in formal healthcare systems because of the tendency to neglect or perform poorly [23]. These dispensers of medicines provide a designed solution that fosters trust through responsible medicine provision, which is a great step for a patient claiming to be taken care of by the health system. This can gradually promote further adherence and utilization of other services within the healthcare system, including, but not limited to, primary and secondary prevention of diseases and complications. Last but not least, the environmental sustainability of these systems is still an under-researched area. Surely, there has been an effort to extend healthcare services to all, but this could also entail the root cause analysis and optimal system designs of these dispensers and their supply chains in ways that are ecologically sustainable. For instance, powering the dispensers with renewable energy, routing deliveries so as to minimize emissions, or making the dispensers out of greener materials could practically help in reducing their negative impacts on the environment. Many healthcare practitioners today embrace the concepts of development and reorganization of the healthcare system; therefore, the inclusion of these factors during the design and the practical use of these low-cost generic medicine dispensers could easily change the paradigm of delivering intensive and sustainable healthcare.

References

1. Deng, S., Huang, L., Hu, D., Zhao, J.L., Wu, Z., Mobility-Enabled Service Selection for Composite Services. *IEEE Trans. Serv. Comput.*, 9, 3, 394–407, 1 May-June 2016, doi: 10.1109/TSC.2014.2365799.

2. Barreto, L., Amaral, A., Baltazar, S., Mobility as a Service (MaaS) in rural regions: An overview. *2018 International Conference on Intelligent Systems (IS)*, Funchal, Portugal, pp. 856–860, 2018, doi: 10.1109/IS.2018.8710455.
3. Rothkrantz, L., Applications of Mobility as a Service (MaaS) in a city. *2024 Smart City Symposium Prague (SCSP)*, Prague, Czech Republic, pp. 1–6, 2024, doi: 10.1109/SCSP61506.2024.10552679.
4. Algayar, S.M.S., Goga, N., Hassoon, I.A., Almalchy, M.T.Q., Medical Social Media Systems - Implementation of the Android Application. *2019 11th International Conference on Electronics, Computers and Artificial Intelligence (ECAI)*, Pitesti, Romania, pp. 1–6, 2019, doi: 10.1109/ECAI46879.2019.9042155.
5. Yelaldi, M.B., *et al.*, Fuzzy-based Health Monitoring and Voice Assistance Featured Autonomous Elderly Care Service Robot. *2021 Innovations in Intelligent Systems and Applications Conference (ASYU)*, Elazig, Turkey, pp. 1–6, 2021, doi: 10.1109/ASYU52992.2021.9598966.
6. Valchkova, N., Zahariev, R., Raykov, P., Cvetkov, V., Methodology for Designing a Collaborative Mobile Service Robot based on Criteria for Researching its Functional Capabilities. *2023 International Conference on Engineering and Emerging Technologies (ICEET)*, Istanbul, Turkiye, pp. 1–6, 2023, doi: 10.1109/ICEET60227.2023.10525820.
7. Caliolio, M.H., Frias, J., Paglinawan, C., Integration of a Smart Medicine Container with Medicine Sorting using YOLOv4 and OCR. *2022 13th International Conference on Computing Communication and Networking Technologies (ICCCNT)*, Kharagpur, India, pp. 1–6, 2022, doi: 10.1109/ICCCNT54827.2022.9984526.
8. Patil, C.H., Lightwala, N., Sherdiwala, M., Vibhute, A.D., Naik, S.A., Mali, S.M., An IoT based Smart Medicine Dispenser Model for Healthcare. *2022 IEEE World Conference on Applied Intelligence and Computing (AIC)*, Sonbhadra, India, pp. 391–395, 2022, doi: 10.1109/AIC55036.2022.9848934.
9. Shanthini, M., Vedhavarshini, U., Prem, N., Gouri, K., Roshan, V.S., Reena Josephine, S.S., Design and Implementation of IoT based Automatic Medicine Dispenser for Patients. *2023 3rd International Conference on Innovative Mechanisms for Industry Applications (ICIMIA)*, Bengaluru, India, pp. 24–28, 2023, doi: 10.1109/ICIMIA60377.2023.10426176.
10. Garg, R., Bhatt, I., Eashwer, K., Jindal, S.K., Experimental Design and Implementation of RFID based Clinical Medicine Dispenser. *2022 1st International Conference on the Paradigm Shifts in Communication, Embedded Systems, Machine Learning and Signal Processing (PCEMS)*, Nagpur, India, pp. 33–36, 2022, doi: 10.1109/PCEMS55161.2022.9807886.
11. Prajwal, K.T., Likhitha Sai, G., Kumar Dhan, D., Kumar, C.M., Pramanik, P., Design and Development of an Intelligent Medicine Dispenser. *2023 7th International Conference on Electronics, Communication and Aerospace Technology (ICECA)*, Coimbatore, India, pp. 1860–1864, 2023, doi: 10.1109/ICECA58529.2023.10394720.

12. Athish, M., Solomon, E., Indumathi, R., Manoj Prasath, T., Vinodhini, R., Online Doctor Consultation and Automatic Medicine Dispensers in Primary Health Care Centres Using Machine Learning. *2024 International Conference on Advances in Data Engineering and Intelligent Computing Systems (ADICS)*, Chennai, India, pp. 1–5, 2024, doi: 10.1109/ADICS58448.2024.10533555.
13. Achammal, S.R., *et al.*, Development of Smart Automatic Drug Dispenser for Elderly and Disabled People. *2024 International Conference on Science Technology Engineering and Management (ICSTEM)*, Coimbatore, India, pp. 1–5, 2024, doi: 10.1109/ICSTEM61137.2024.10560887.
14. Rahman, M.M., Aktar, R., Dey, S.K., Design and Implementation of a Low-Cost Automated Medicine Dispenser. *2022 International Conference on Advancement in Electrical and Electronic Engineering (ICAEEE)*, Gazipur, Bangladesh, pp. 1–6, 2022, doi: 10.1109/ICAEEE54957.2022.9836380.
15. Kumar, S.K., Manimegalai, R., Rajeswari, A., Deekshita, R., Dhineshkumar, M., Manikandan, G., A Literature Review: Performance Evaluation of Wearable system with Pill Dispenser Box for Post Covid Elderly Patients. *2021 3rd International Conference on Advances in Computing, Communication Control and Networking (ICAC3N)*, Greater Noida, India, pp. 2008–2014, 2021, doi: 10.1109/ICAC3N53548.2021.9725733.
16. Joshitha, K.L., Aravind, E., Akash, S., Suveka, S., Harsha Vardhan, J., Siddeshwar, S.A., Design and Development of AI based QR Enabled Pharmaceutical Dispenser. *2024 International Conference on Communication, Computing and Internet of Things (IC3IoT)*, Chennai, India, pp. 1–6, 2024, doi: 10.1109/IC3IoT60841.2024.10550325.
17. Hassan, N., Gaur, A., Jadaun, Y., Bhasney, A., IoT-Enabled Medicine Dispenser for Pills and Liquid Medication. *2024 2nd International Conference on Advancement in Computation & Computer Technologies (InCACCT)*, Gharuan, India, pp. 905–910, 2024, doi: 10.1109/InCACCT61598.2024.10550973.
18. Raisa, F.F., Orthy, N.T., Nibir, M.I.S., Faysal, H.M., Huda, A.S.N., Improving Healthcare through an IoT Based Automated Medication Dispenser. *2023 26th International Conference on Computer and Information Technology (ICCIT)*, Cox's Bazar, Bangladesh, pp. 1–6, 2023, doi: 10.1109/ICCIT60459.2023.10441103.
19. Jittrapirom, P., Marchau, V., Heijden, R., Meurs, H., Future implementation of mobility as a service (MaaS): Results of an international Delphi study. *Travel Behav. Soc.*, 21, 281–294, 2018, 10.1016/j.tbs.2018.12.004.
20. Kriswardhana, W. and Esztergár-Kiss, D., A systematic literature review of Mobility as a Service: Examining the socio-technical factors in MaaS adoption and bundling packages. *Travel Behav. Soc.*, 31, 232–243, 2023, ISSN 2214367X, https://doi.org/10.1016/j.tbs.2022.12.007.
21. Saboor, A., Coene, S., Vinogradov, E., Tanghe, E., Joseph, W., Pollin, S., Elevating the future of mobility UAV-enabled Intelligent Transportation Systems, 10.36227/techrxiv.16826743, 2021.

22. Zhang, Y. and Kamargianni, M., A review on the factors influencing the adoption of new mobility technologies and services: autonomous vehicle, drone, micromobility and mobility as a service. *Transp. Rev.*, 43, 1–23, 2022, 10.1080/01441647.2022.2119297.
23. Shekar, P.K.V., Sanil, P.R., Shetty, S.S., U, S., Badiger, M., Smart Driver Warning and Alert System using Visual Features. *2023 7th International Conference on Trends in Electronics and Informatics (ICOEI)*, Tirunelveli, India, pp. 1603–1607, 2023, doi: 10.1109/ICOEI56765.2023.10125651.
24. Badiger, M., A, S.R., Singh, C., C, M.F., Kumara, V., Naik, S.C., Dynamic and Static Wireless Charging of EVs Using Solar Energy. *2024 IEEE International Conference on Distributed Computing, VLSI, Electrical Circuits and Robotics (DISCOVER)*, Mangalore, India, pp. 220–224, 2024, doi: 10.1109/DISCOVER62353.2024.10750556.

13

An Enhanced Sustainable Mobility as a Service Based on 5G Network for Human-Centric Mobile Network in Smart City

Senthil G. A.[1]*, R. Prabha[2], D. Roopa[3] and S. Sridevi[4]

[1]*Department of Information Technology, Agni College of Technology, Chennai, India*
[2]*Department of Electronics and Communication Engineering, Sri Sai Ram Institute of Technology, Chennai, India*
[3]*Department of Computer Science and Engineering, Sri Sai Ram Institute of Technology, Chennai, India*
[4]*Department of Computer Science and Engineering, Vels Institute of Science, Technology and Advanced Studies, Chennai, India*

Abstract

Smart cities, propelled by swift urbanization and ecological apprehensions, endeavor to discover inventive approaches to ecological mobility. This study suggests a better viable Mobility as a Service (MaaS) paradigm that utilizes 5G networks to support human-centric wireless networks in urban areas. The system integrates multiple modes of transport alternatives, real-time traffic management, and personalized transportation services to revolutionize urban mobility by utilizing ultra-fast interaction, minimal latency, and widespread device compatibility of 5G. This lays the foundation for an ecologically conscious, human-centered, and resilient future for public transportation, one in which residents of technologically advanced towns have seamless, customized, and eco-friendly transport experiences—using slicing of networks, computing at the edge, and communication via V2X to integrate 5G infrastructure to MaaS technologies and urban smart city ecosystems. The proposed system presents a range of intermodal choices with price changes, immediate reservations, and smooth intermodal transfers determined by customer preferences and updated information. The incorporation of 5G technology facilitates a revolutionary shift in urban transportation by providing

**Corresponding author*: senthilga@gmail.com

Rathishchandra R. Gatti and Chandra Singh (eds.) Digital Convergence in Intelligent Mobility Systems, (293–314) © 2025 Scrivener Publishing LLC

fast and low-latency connections, allowing real-time data sharing among users, infrastructure, and vehicles. The research optimizing mobility services, MaaS, raises public transportation systems' general effectiveness, security, and long-term viability. With 5G connectivity enabling instantaneous interaction between equipment and vehicles, MaaS automatically controls traffic patterns to minimize wait times and reduce traffic. Mobility options that are context-aware and personalized are offered by the MaaS platform, which keeps the demands of the end users in mind. The model uses extensive statistical analysis to learn about user behavior, patterns of traffic, and impacts on the environment. These understandings enable transportation agencies and planning professionals to make well-informed decisions that further optimize the metropolitan mobility environment.

Keywords: 5G network, communication network, human-centric mobile network, Internet of Things (IoT), Quality of Service (QoS), Mobility as a Service (MaaS), mobility analysis, smart city

13.1 Introduction

Mobility as a Service (MaaS) is a disruptive method of accessibility that emphasizes incorporating diverse forms of transit into a single, easy-to-use platform. This idea is centered on online apps that allow individuals to effortlessly plan, schedule, and purchase multipurpose excursions that include public transportation, sharing rides, sharing bikes, and other choices [1]. MaaS stresses a seamless and linked travel experience, emphasizing multimodal connection and effective payment methods. Biodiversity is a major priority, promoting the adoption of environmentally friendly methods of transportation and helping to decrease automobile congestion and pollution. Finally, MaaS aspires to provide users with an increasingly adaptable, environmentally friendly, and cost-effective method of traversing urbanized surroundings, decreasing reliance upon private automobiles as shown in Figure 13.1.

The combination of Mobility as a Service (MaaS) and 5G networks represents a paradigm shift regarding city mobility. The implementation of 5G technology dramatically improves MaaS potential by providing high-speed communication with reduced delay. Mobility service allows for real-time communication, including quick updates on transit alternatives and congestion, leading to an increasingly proactive and efficient system. The integrated approach of 5G and MaaS enhances the customer experience by providing continuous accessibility to rich multimedia, actual time routing, and interactive features. Furthermore, 5G enables the incorporation of the Internet of Things (IoT), resulting in improved monitoring,

Figure 13.1 MaaS and its application.

administration, or improvement of public transportation. The technology's edge computing capability is useful in analyzing information closer to the source, enabling immediate analysis for routing optimization and traffic control. 5G improves automotive interaction and the use of augmented reality and virtual reality, resulting in safer and more engaging transportation experiences [2]. Furthermore, 5G's sophisticated security capabilities secure sensitive data inside MaaS systems, hence increasing user confidence and adhering to privacy requirements. Overall, the combination of Mobility as a Service and 5G wireless networks transforms urban mobility, providing an increasingly linked together, efficient, and highly advanced mobility scene [3].

13.1.1 Objective and Benefits

The main objective of 5G network integration for a more sustainable development and Mobility as a Service (MaaS) over communication network creates an unprecedented change in urban mobility, focused on environmentally friendly procedures and increased connection. The implementation of 5G technology promotes sustainable MaaS by delivering real-time information analysis, enabling route optimization, congestion reduction, and system efficiency in general. High-speed, low-latency 5G connection allows for seamless incorporation of a variety of green mobility modes into MaaS systems, including electric automobiles, bikes, and public transit.

This collaboration enables users to engage in ecologically responsible travel decisions, resulting in lower carbon emissions and better air quality. The combined effect of 5G's ability for enormous Internet of Things (IoT) integration and green MaaS practices helps in smart transportation planning, boosting collaborative mobility, and increasing the use of renewable energy sources [4].

The benefits of rising usage of Mobility as a Service (MaaS) via a 5G network result in a complex ecological effect, potentially cutting automobile emissions via transportation sharing and other variable congestion control but also offering issues such as greater consumption of energy and technical issues with the environment. Societally, MaaS improves accessibility while raising challenges like the digital divide and possible employment relocation, necessitating equitable layout and strong regulations. In terms of economy, MaaS provides prospects for expansion, new enterprises, and greater tax income; nevertheless, challenges involve disturbances in existing industries and infrastructure expenditures. Strategic expenditures in environmentally friendly procedures, laws, and technological incentives are critical for combining positive outcomes and reducing problems, promoting a more equitable and productive socioeconomic environment [5]. Figure 13.2 shows the model of MaaS from the customer's point of view. Visitors can get current details on the many forms of conveyance available, such as transportation, mass transit, and small-scale mobility services. By taking advantage of 5G's minimal latency abilities, MaaS improves mobility in city security by facilitating prompt reaction times for preventing

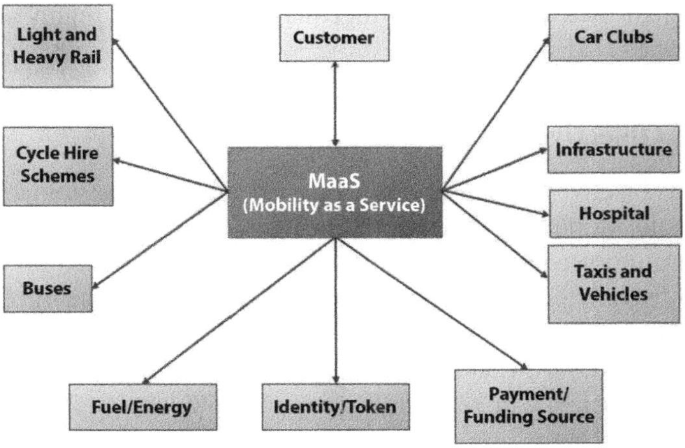

Figure 13.2 MaaS working model.

accidents, coordinating medical care, and facilitating interaction among people and cars.

13.2 Proposed Enhanced MaaS Framework

13.2.1 System Architecture

The proposed framework's design generally includes multiple interrelated parts and layers to provide effortless and effective mobility solutions. A user interfaces with the MaaS system via a user-friendly interface, typically a mobile app or a website. This interface lets users schedule, publish, and pay for their trips. The system uses algorithms to plan the best route according to user choices, real-time data on traffic, and existing transit alternatives. Users may book multiple means of transportation, such as public transportation, ride-sharing services, bike sharing, and auto rentals, using the website. The platform collects statistics from various transportation providers, including timetables, costs, and immediate fashion GPS coordinates. Standardized APIs enable the MaaS infrastructure to communicate with various transportation suppliers [6].

The technology secures payments using integrated payment channels, allowing customers to make payments for their travels. Users acquire e-tickets or electronic cards for their preferred forms of transportation. Secured authentication for user's measures is currently in place to protect the confidentiality of user accounts. Through the MaaS system, individuals can control their account details, choices, and payment data. For tailored services, a database contains the profiles of users, preferences, and past data. Transactions, reservations, and payment data are recorded for audits and analytics. The system retrieves and evaluates data to enhance the quality of service, customer experience, and transit offerings.

The technology interfaces with a variety of mobility transportation service providers, tele-communications, forming and managing relationships as shown in Figure 13.3. It establishes contracts with transit suppliers for data exchange, accessibility, and level of service. It also applies encryption technologies to secure client data and banking transactions and follows local and regional rules on confidentiality of data, protection, and logistics. The technology keeps consumers aware of their journey's progress, modifications, and important updates and provides interaction with client assistance tools for problem solving and help. Users can submit comments on their experiences, which helps to improve the service. They are allowed to assess modes of transportation, assisting fellow passengers in their decisions [7].

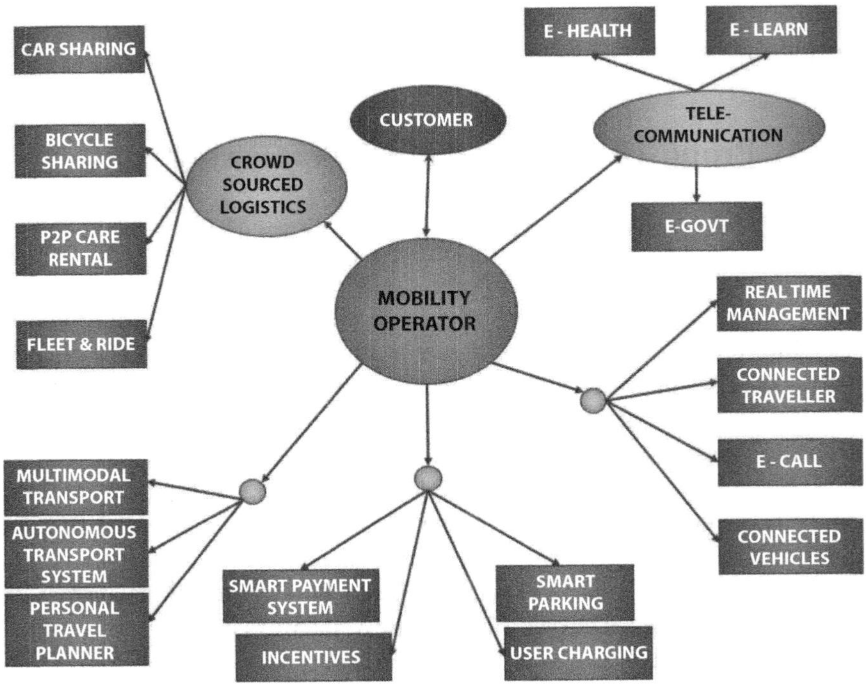

Figure 13.3 Proposed MaaS framework.

13.2.2 Service Components

A trip planner is a key component of a MaaS architecture, allowing users to easily explore and assess various travel alternatives across several modes of transportation. Users may get detailed information about public transportation, bikes, car sharing, and other modes of transportation by entering their starting point, destination, and chosen method of transportation. Real-time data on delays, transportation accessibility, and changes in schedules improve decision making, allowing users to maximize their journey paths in response to changing circumstances. Furthermore, the built-in booking ticketing capability improves the public experience by allowing people to buy tickets and reserve automobiles directly from the MaaS platform. This integrated approach removes the requirement for several applications or ticket machines, resulting in a smooth and efficient solution for route planning and execution [8].

MaaS systems have a significant ability to integrate and effortlessly link with transit systems, combining timetables and live information between buses, trains, and subways. The addition of micro-mobility transportation services like bicycle sharing, scooter sharing, and sharing cars expands travel possibilities, particularly for short journeys and first/last-mile connections. Furthermore, platforms incorporate prominent taxi services such as online vehicle booking Uber and Lyft, giving consumers a wide selection of immediate travel options. The financial and billing aspects of MaaS improve the client's experience by providing an integrated payment system that allows customers to pay for several travel alternatives using one account and wallet. Some MaaS systems also provide membership plans for monthly or annual subscriptions, which provide customers with unlimited or subsidized trips on certain modes of transport.

According to client preferences, transportation times, and real-time information, the system can provide the most effective and comfortable travel alternatives for every journey. The platform may integrate several means of transportation to find the quickest and most cost-effective path for a multi-destination trip. MaaS systems should be enabled for all individuals, including people with impairments, by providing capabilities like voice navigating, speech-to-text interfaces, and wheelchair-accessible vehicles. Some MaaS systems encourage sustainable travel options by emphasizing low-emission automobiles, promoting biking and walking, and offering ecological impact calculators for various transport alternatives [9]. The comparison of existing components and components used in the MaaS is shown in Figure 13.4.

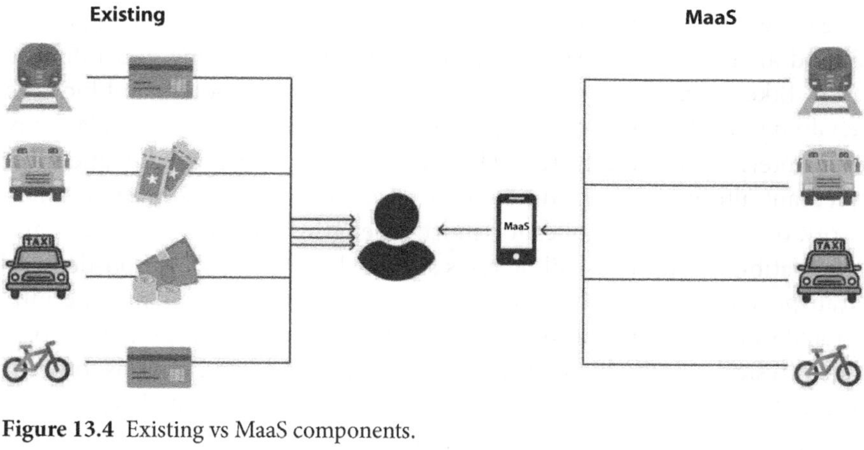

Figure 13.4 Existing vs MaaS components.

13.2.3 Human-Centric Design

Incorporating human-centered design (HCD) concepts into Mobility as a Service (MaaS) systems leads to several benefits, including greater customer acceptance and pleasure. By emphasizing clarity, simplicity, and usability, HCD guarantees that MaaS systems are simple to comprehend, browse, and use, resulting in great user experiences. This strategy includes boosting accessibility and inclusion, taking into consideration varied user requirements and skills, and making MaaS platforms available to everyone, including people with impairments or low technological knowledge. Additionally, the use of HCD principles improves safety and confidence in the MaaS system.

Human-centered design (HCD) integrated with Mobility as a Service (MaaS) includes several critical techniques that promote user-centricity and general platform success. User demands and pain areas may be deeply understood by extensive user research, which includes methods such as survey responses and interviews. The rapid development process of HCD entails continual testing and modification of models to actual consumers at every phase, assuring that the result corresponds with user expectations. Graphic design and UI/UX (user interface/user experience) design are concerned with designing displays that are both visually beautiful and intuitive, hence reducing the cognitive burden for users [10].

13.2.4 Mobility Analysis

MaaS incorporates real-time timetables, live monitoring, and reservation systems for public transportation, allowing customers to effortlessly organize and reserve multi-modal journeys. In coastal municipalities or island areas, MaaS systems might integrate ferry ticketing and information. Bike sharing and scooter sharing offer rented scooters and bicycles, enabling first/last-mile connectivity or brief city journeys. MaaS platforms may interface with e-bike rental businesses, providing a speedier and more pleasant alternative to traditional bicycles. There is accessibility to a network of rented automobiles for short or lengthy excursions. There is also compatibility with cab-hailing apps such as Uber and Lyft for on-demand transportation alternatives. In some areas, traditional taxis may be integrated into the MaaS platform to provide full coverage. MaaS may encourage physical activity by identifying pedestrian and bicycle paths, offering estimates on travel times, and integrating fitness tracker data [11]. Various levels of mobility analysis are shown in Figure 13.5.

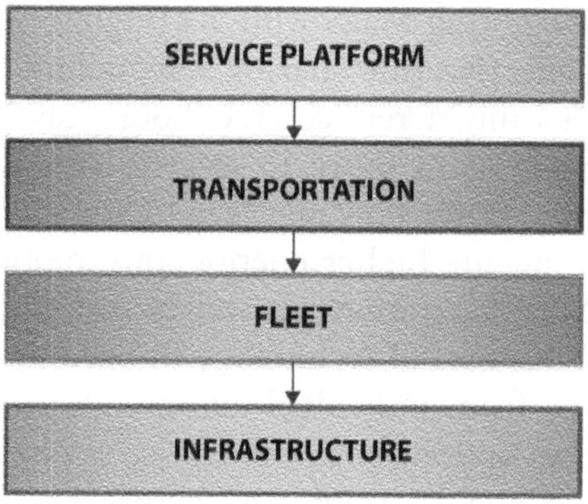

Figure 13.5 Levels in mobility analysis.

13.3 Sustainability Analysis

The three aspects of sustainability are shown in Figure 13.6. Environmental sustainability may lead to social sustainability by generating jobs in the green economy. Social sustainability may contribute to economic sustainability by producing a more stable and productive labor force. By investing in clean technology, you may achieve economic and environmental sustainability.

13.3.1 Environmental Impact

The environmental effect of increased Mobility as a Service (MaaS) on a 5G network is a complex interplay of possible advantages and disadvantages.

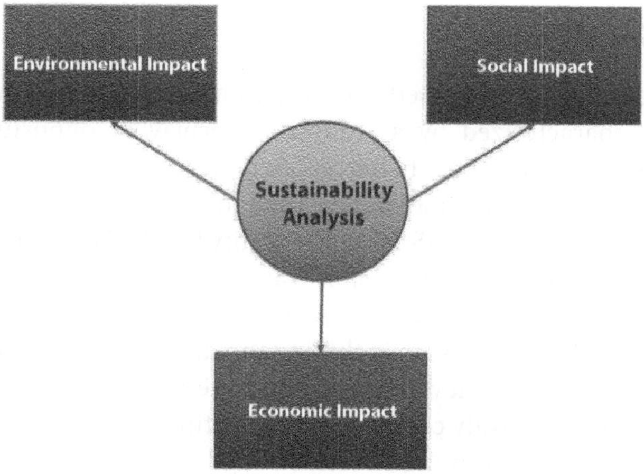

Figure 13.6 Sustainability analysis.

On the plus side, integrating MaaS with 5G might result in lower vehicle emissions through effective ride sharing, carpooling, and dynamic traffic management. This might reduce greenhouse gas emissions, improve air quality, and encourage a move to electric cars within MaaS fleets. Additionally, improved traffic flow may lead to fuel savings. However, possible disadvantages include higher energy consumption connected with 5G networks and MaaS operations, as well as environmental issues over the fabrication and disposal of technology utilized in these systems. The transfer of emissions from individual automobiles to larger vehicles or power plants is also an option.

The total impact will be determined by factors such as particular implementation tactics, government legislation, the utilization of renewable energy sources, and continual improvements in energy-efficient technology. To optimize the good environmental results of increased MaaS over a 5G network, a balance must be struck between technical innovation and sustainable behaviors [12]. The environmental effects of increased Mobility as a Service (MaaS) on the network using 5G are determined by particular applications and laws, with regulations from the government playing an important role in encouraging environmentally friendly procedures and reducing negative consequences. Using energy from renewable sources to power either 5G systems or MaaS operations has been recognized as critical to optimizing environmental advantages. Furthermore, continuous development and research into cost-effective 5G technology and green car manufacture are viewed as critical to further reducing the entire environmental footprint. Taking a comprehensive approach is encouraged, embracing both possible advantages and risks.

13.3.2 Social Impact

The societal effect of increased Mobility as a Service (MaaS) upon a 5G network is characterized by a complex interplay of opportunities and problems. On the plus side, better accessibility and mobility may help a wide range of people by removing barriers to work, education, and social involvement. Enhanced MaaS offers the ability to alleviate social inequities by offering inexpensive and accessible transportation choices, encouraging community development, and improving safety with features such as real-time tracking. However, issues including the digital gap, possible employment displacement, privacy concerns, and the potential danger of social isolation must be carefully considered. Navigating these issues necessitates inclusive design, skill training efforts, strong laws, and active community participation to guarantee that improved MaaS contributes to good social transformation by emphasizing accessibility, equity, and well-being [13].

The societal ramifications of growing Mobility as a Service (MaaS) include worries about the digital gap, potential employment displacement, privacy difficulties, and the possibility of social isolation. Uneven access to MaaS platforms may worsen existing gaps, particularly among individuals with limited skills, technology, or financial resources. Automation in transportation, a critical component of MaaS, raises concerns about job loss and worker rights. Extensive data collecting on MaaS platforms causes privacy issues. Overreliance on digital networks may lead to social isolation, particularly among vulnerable people [14]. To solve these problems, a holistic strategy is required, which includes inclusive design for accessibility, digital literacy campaigns, strong data security rules, and active community participation to guarantee that MaaS positively contributes to social transformation.

13.3.3 Economic Impact

The economic impact of increased Mobility as a Service (MaaS) on a 5G network is complex, with both possible benefits and downsides. On the bright side, MaaS has the potential to boost economic activity by creating new business possibilities, enhancing efficiency, and producing savings through reduced automobile ownership. Enhanced logistical and supply chains, as well as increased tourist and leisure expenditure, all help to drive economic growth. The growth of new enterprises and services related to MaaS generates more tax income for governments. However, obstacles include the possible disruption of current transportation industries, disparate distribution of economic advantages, significant infrastructure and technological expenditures, and cybersecurity issues [15].

To maximize advantages while mitigating negatives, intentional expenditures in sustainable infrastructure, appropriate laws, adoption and innovation incentives, and comprehensive training programs are required. By taking a proactive and equitable approach, stakeholders may realize the economic benefits of expanded MaaS on the 5G network, resulting in an increasingly efficient, viable, and inclusive socioeconomic landscape. Enhanced Mobility as a Service (MaaS) over a 5G network creates a complicated commercial picture. Traditional transportation industries may face disruptions, perhaps resulting in employment losses. The distribution of economic rewards from MaaS may be uneven, exacerbating socioeconomic disparities. Significant expenditures in 5G infrastructure and MaaS technologies create financial issues for governments and enterprises.

Furthermore, cybersecurity threats linked with MaaS platforms and 5G infrastructure necessitate close monitoring [16].

13.4 Challenges and Solutions

The challenges and solutions of the implementation of MaaS are shown in Figure 13.7, which explains the key challenges and solutions for MaaS on 5G networks like technical challenges, social and regulatory, quality of service, critical infrastructure, and communication and bandwidth challenges, which are discussed in the next sections.

13.4.1 Technological Challenges

Ultra-reliable low-latency communication (uRLLC) is critical for Mobility as a Service (MaaS), which depends on real-time information sharing to optimize planning routes, vehicular cooperation, and other critical aspects. The ability of 5G networks to handle large amounts of information at minimal delays and turbulence is critical for the seamless functioning of MaaS. In congested metropolitan settings, significant network capacity is required to handle the rising volume of information related to MaaS operations.

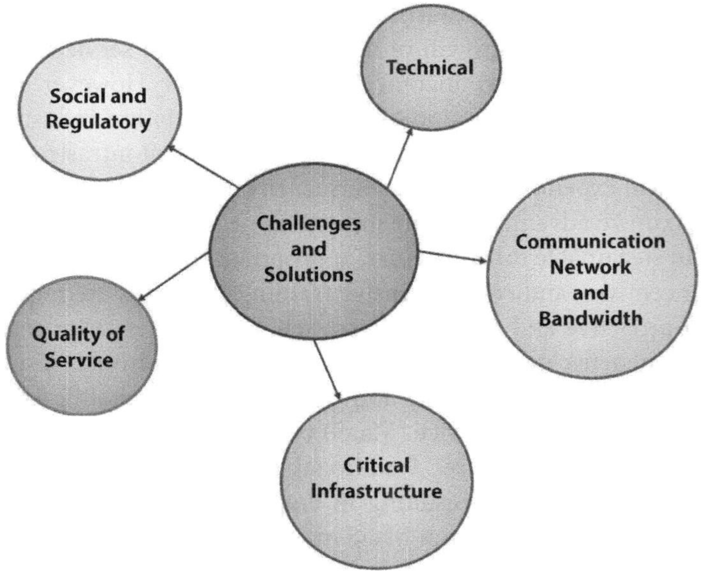

Figure 13.7 Challenges and solutions faced in implementing MaaS.

In contrast, in rural locations, broader network coverage is critical to provide consistent MaaS accessibility over bigger geographical areas. These methods provide dynamic resource allocation, which improves network performance and ensures that MaaS operations have enough bandwidth and responsiveness to deliver services efficiently.

Within Mobility as a Service (MaaS), integrating vehicle-to-everything (V2X) communication is critical for assuring safety and efficient traffic management. This includes developing communication linkages between automobiles, infrastructure, and people. To accomplish flawless MaaS processes, building strong V2X standards and assuring compatibility with various manufacturers' systems are critical. Considering the threat of safety risks provided by fraudulent assaults, cybersecurity in linked automobiles has emerged as an important issue. Though not an imminent requirement for basic MaaS performance, the introduction of autonomous driving technologies has significant promise. However, implementing dependable and secure autonomous vehicles necessitates continual development, research, and rigorous validation methods to ensure their efficacy and fulfillment of safety requirements [17].

Under the framework of Mobility as a Service (MaaS), proper data management is critical for improving operations and protecting user data. Big data integration and analytics are critical because MaaS solutions collect vast amounts of statistical information on patterns of travel, delays, and user activity. Effective integration, analysis, and effective security measures are required to obtain important insights while protecting the data of users. MaaS must be standardized and interoperable to work properly. Standardized norms for data exchange and communication across systems and suppliers of services are required to give consumers a smooth and unified experience. To balance innovation with user privacy, strong data protection legislation and tools for user management of their data are required.

13.4.2 Communication Network and Bandwidth

In the world of Mobility as a Service (MaaS), the dependability and efficacy of 5G networks are critical for smooth operations. Network slicing and virtualization in 5G provide customized resources to MaaS apps, assuring peak performance despite fluctuating bandwidth requirements. To alleviate risks, high availability, and redundancy expenditures are required, which protect against network disruptions that might jeopardize MaaS operations and safety. The extensive coverage and capacity of 5G networks become critical in catering to MaaS operations in a variety of contexts, from urban to rural. Finally, comprehensive cybersecurity measures are required to guard against future assaults while maintaining the security and stability of 5G networks that enable MaaS operations [18].

High bandwidth abilities are required to manage this data flood adequately. Given MaaS's fluctuating traffic patterns, which include significant demand in high-traffic times and decreased usage over off-peak periods, flexible bandwidth allocation strategies maximize resource utilization. This guarantees sufficient connectivity during peak periods while avoiding resource waste during low-demand hours [19]. This enables the seamless functioning of critical operations including rescue efforts while successfully regulating total network traffic. To meet the expected exponential rise in MaaS utilization and data collection, safeguarding is required. Networks must be flexible and adaptive to meet future capacity demands while also incorporating growing technical breakthroughs, enabling MaaS systems' continual development and performance.

13.4.3 Enabling Critical Infrastructures

The combined use of Mobility as a Service (MaaS) services with multiple infrastructure aspects helps create a more environmentally friendly and effective transportation system. Smart grids provide flexible electricity management, optimize electric car charging stations, and eventually power self-driving automobiles using green energy resources. Telecommunications facilities, particularly strong broadband networks, and mobile phone tower deployments are critical for maintaining MaaS's smooth functioning, especially in high-traffic locations, since 5G network efficiency is directly related to this. Traffic management systems are critical because they allow for real-time data interchange and dynamic optimization, which leads to reduced delays, better traffic flow, and increased safety [20]. Combining MaaS with emergency response systems improves reaction speed and cooperation for accidents or crises, maybe preserving lives and reducing damage.

The system helps to reduce delay and improve information handling performance for dependent-on-time MaaS activities, which is especially beneficial to applications like autonomous car routing and catastrophe coordination. The incorporation of Internet of Things (IoT) devices into essential infrastructure and linked cars produces real-time data on characteristics that include flow of traffic, highway conditions, and energy usage. MaaS solutions use analytics to optimize operations and make more informed decisions. As vital infrastructures grow more linked, strong cybersecurity safeguards and privacy regulations are required.

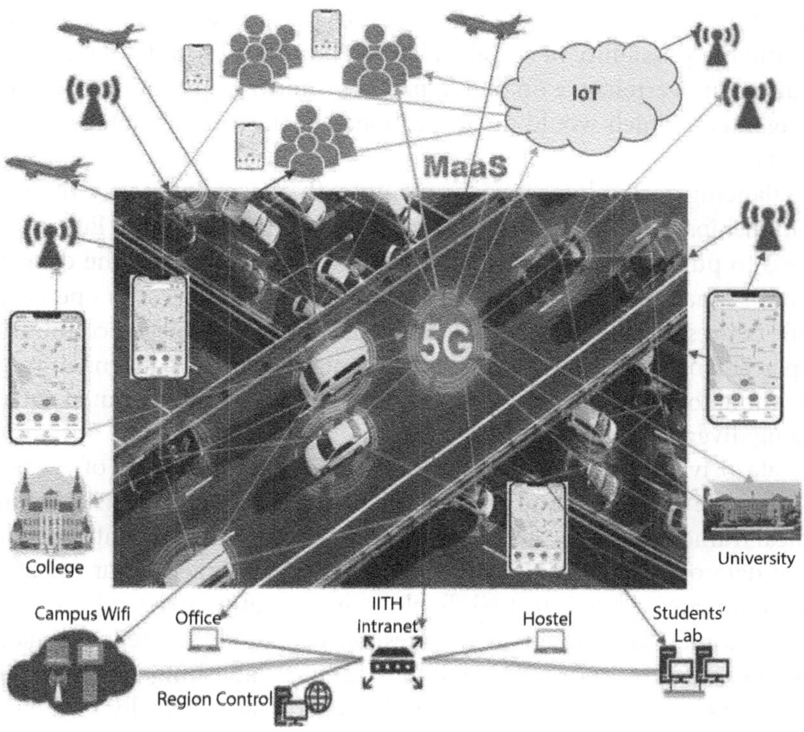

Figure 13.8 Critical infrastructure of the MaaS network with 5G network communication.

These methods protect against possible cyberattacks while also ensuring the confidentiality and safety of private data, emphasizing the significance of cyberattacks in the smooth and secure operation of MaaS [21]. Figure 13.8 shows the critical infrastructure of the MaaS network with 5G network communication.

13.4.4 Social and Regulatory Challenges

The digital gap and accessibility issues may prevent vulnerable communities from realizing the benefits of Mobility as a Service (MaaS) owing to uneven access to technology and low digital literacy levels. To remedy this, efforts must be made to close the gap and enable equitable access to MaaS platforms. Job displacement and labor problems come from transportation automation, such as the deployment of self-driving cars or optimal scheduling, which may result in job losses in conventional industries [30]. Implementing reskilling programs and social safety nets is critical for mitigating the impact on the workforce. Concerns have been raised concerning the possibility of social isolation and mental health concerns as a result of an overreliance on digital platforms for transportation and social engagement, which would disproportionately affect disadvantaged populations [22].

Balancing technology improvements with the maintenance of social relationships is critical for a comprehensive MaaS strategy. Equity and access to public areas are essential factors in MaaS growth. The development of MaaS platforms ought to focus on equitable access to open areas while addressing potential issues that include underprivileged community displacement caused by the process of gent or shifts in patterns of transportation, to make sure the positive effects of MaaS are distributed equally among diverse populations [29].

Data privacy and security are critical in the development of Mobility as a Service (MaaS), mandating stringent data protection legislation and ethical frameworks to protect user privacy and prevent exploitation of personal data obtained via MaaS platforms [23]. The linked nature of MaaS systems creates cybersecurity difficulties, necessitating strict cybersecurity measures and well-defined incident response methods to safeguard against possible assaults and vulnerabilities [27]. Establishing unambiguous frameworks for safety and responsibility is critical, especially in the case of incidents involving self-driving vehicles or complicated MaaS systems. Clarity in these areas helps to define duty and accountability [28].

13.4.5 Quality of Service

Quality of service (QoS) is an important feature of increased Mobility as a Service (MaaS) over 5G networks because it ensures that diverse MaaS apps obtain the necessary degree of efficiency and agility. In data prioritization, QoS techniques filter data traffic, giving priority to crucial MaaS applications like emergency response and self-driving car communication. This assures that certain apps obtain exclusive connectivity and immediate processing, even in the event of network congestion [26]. As regards latency management, low latency is critical in MaaS applications, particularly those involving autonomous cars and emergency response. QoS techniques aid in the management and minimization of latency, assuring that data is delivered and analyzed with minimal delay, hence improving the reactivity and security of MaaS operations [24]. The architectural flow of QoS in 5G networks is explained in Figure 13.9.

Quality of service (QoS) refers to a collection of systems and techniques that provide a certain degree of effectiveness, dependability, and efficacy

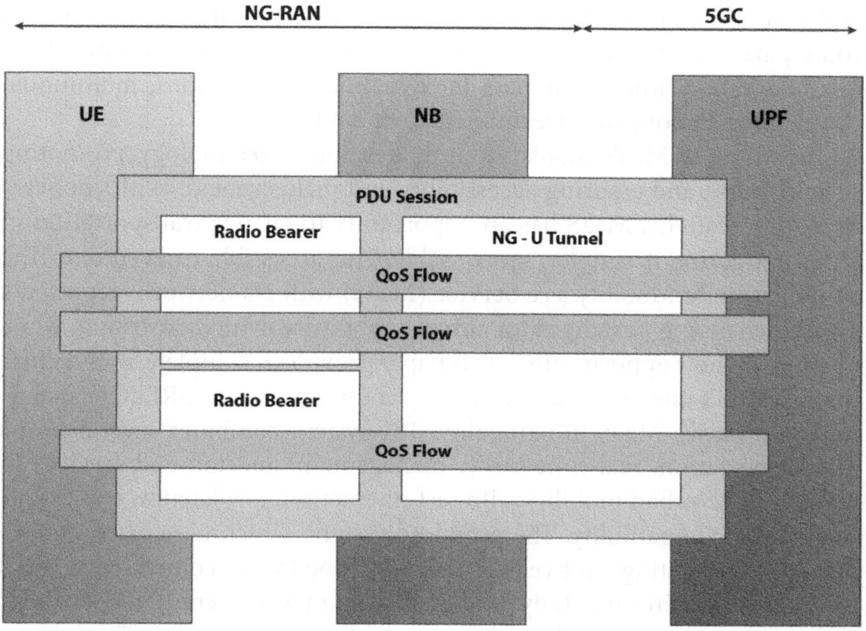

Figure 13.9 QoS flow architecture on 5G network.

in transferring data and network operations. It entails overseeing many components of the data communication process to satisfy specific service needs and user expectations. QoS key components include guaranteeing adequate bandwidth to avoid congestion, reducing latency over real-time applications, lowering jitter for maintaining uninterrupted information flow, preventing packet loss while maintaining the confidentiality of data, ensuring reliability under changing system conditions, and permitting prioritization of certain kinds of flow for priority consideration [31]. Overall, QoS plays an important role in managing network resources and improving customer service across a wide range of services and apps [25].

13.5 Conclusion

In a country where Mobility as a Service (MaaS) combines a variety of transport alternatives into a multi-platform, giving customers easy access to several forms of mobility. Real-time planning and ticketing are incorporated into public transportation systems such as railways, buses, subways, and tramways. Micro-mobility services, including bicycle sharing and scooter sharing, provide easy first- and final-mile connections. Car sharing and ride sharing, as well as regular automobiles, walking, and cycling routes, are available modes of transportation. Key features include effortless integration, immediate data for dynamic modifications, multimodal travel optimization, and streamlined payment methods.

The future of MaaS entails adopting developing technology, promoting sustainability, and assuring accessibility and inclusiveness. With cooperation and creativity, MaaS has an opportunity to change transportation in cities, rendering it simpler, more viable, and accessible to everyone. The combination of Mobility as a Service (MaaS) with 5G networks represents a game-changing paradigm for urban mobility, solving constraints while opening up new opportunities. This paper provides a complete architecture that uses 5G's ultra-reliable low latency communication (uRLLC) capabilities to improve MaaS functionality. The system combines several forms of transportation, real-time traffic management, and tailored services to revolutionize urban mobility with fast interaction, low latency, and extensive device compatibility. The proposed system, which uses network slicing, edge computing, and vehicle-to-everything (V2X) connectivity, seeks to build an environmentally responsible, human-centered, and resilient future for public transit. By enhancing mobility services, MaaS increases the overall efficacy, safety, and long-term viability of public transit. The integration of 5G enables immediate communication and real-time data exchange across users and infrastructure.

Environmental, social, and economic effects are critical issues in the deployment of MaaS over 5G. While integration has the potential to cut emissions, increase accessibility, and spur economic growth, careful planning and legislation are required to address issues such as the digital divide, job displacement, and cybersecurity concerns. Sustainable behaviors, energy-efficient technology, and regulatory frameworks are critical to maximizing the beneficial environmental and economic implications of MaaS. Finally, the suggested framework envisions a future in which MaaS, driven by 5G networks, offers users smooth, customized, and environmentally responsible transportation options. By embracing technology breakthroughs, promoting inclusion, and tackling regulatory constraints, the collaboration between MaaS and 5G has the potential to transform urban transportation, resulting in smarter, greener, and more accessible cities.

13.6 Future Work

We enhance the focus of future work on how electric Mobility-as-a-Service (eMaaS) opens up opportunities to expand community awareness of related areas of mobility growth, including vehicles, batteries, electrical infrastructure for charging, and a variety of auxiliary services. Empowering the revolution Mobility as a Service (MaaS) promotes human-centered rural development. Accessibility to public transit in remote areas is a major challenge. Rural mobility is a global crisis that requires rapid solutions. This paper examines the expansion of Mobility as a Service (MaaS) in rural development, drawing on sustainable research analysis.

References

1. Yano, H., *et al.*, A MaaS System Architecture for Inducing Users to Solve Social Issues. *IEEE 11th Global Conference on Consumer Electronics (GCCE)*, Osaka, Japan, pp. 87–88, 2022, doi: 10.1109/GCCE56475.2022.10014159.
2. Williams, B., Potential Problems Hindering the Instantiation of MaaS, in: *Automated Vehicles and MaaS: Removing the Barriers*, pp. 87–93, IEEE, 2021, doi: 10.1002/9781119765394.ch7.
3. Williams, B., Potential Solutions to Instantiate AVs and MaaS: Managed Optimisation Architecture for Transportation (MOAT), in: *Automated Vehicles and MaaS: Removing the Barriers*, pp. 211–224, IEEE, 2021, doi: 10.1002/9781119765394.ch11.
4. Karo-Karo, G.F.M., Harumnanda, M.S.A., Lim, C., Investigating Multiple Malware as a Service (MaaS): Analysis and Prevention Techniques. *IEEE International Conference on Cryptography, Informatics, and Cybersecurity (ICoCICs)*, Bogor, Indonesia, pp. 270–274, 2023, doi: 10.1109/ICoCICs58778.2023.10277515.
5. Kao, Y.-L., Wang, Y.-W., Su, Y.-W., Exploring Incentives for Mobility as a Service (MaaS) Usage Intentions. *5th International Conference on Computer Communication and the Internet (ICCCI)*, Fujisawa, Japan, pp. 52–55, 2023, doi: 10.1109/ICCCI59363.2023.10210153.
6. Wei, Z. and Zhenglian, H., Host computer software design of MAA hydrolysis reaction based on WinCC configuration software. *Chinese Control and Decision Conference (CCDC)*, Yinchuan, China, pp. 1185–1189, 2016, doi: 10.1109/CCDC.2016.7531163.
7. Kriswardhana, W. and Esztergár-Kiss, D., Cluster Analysis of User Preferences related to MaaS Aspects. *8th International Conference on Models and Technologies for Intelligent Transportation Systems (MT-ITS)*, Nice, France, pp. 1–6, 2023, doi: 10.1109/MT-ITS56129.2023.10241445.
8. Zheng, L., Xu, W., Wei, W., A Method to Elicit User Needs of MaaS Based on Activity Theory. *IEEE 7th International Conference on Intelligent Transportation Engineering (ICITE)*, Beijing, China, pp. 562–567, 2022, doi: 10.1109/ICITE56321.2022.10101462.

9. Campolo, C., Cuzzocrea, D., Genovese, G., Iera, A., Molinaro, A., An OMA Lightweight M2M-compliant MEC Framework to Track Multimodal Commuters for MaaS Applications. *IEEE/ACM 23rd International Symposium on Distributed Simulation and Real Time Applications (DS-RT)*, Cosenza, Italy, pp. 1–8, 2019, doi: 10.1109/DS-RT47707.2019.8958677.
10. Jagyasi, B.G., Chander, D., Merchant, S.N., Desai, U.B., Dey, B.K., MAAS: Multibit Adaptive Aggregation Scheme for wireless sensor networks. *2008 International Conference on Telecommunications*, St. Petersburg, Russia, pp. 1–7, 2008, doi: 10.1109/ICTEL.2008.4652672.
11. Nangraj, S.S., Abbasi, S., Pathan, M., Sindhoo, A., Method as a Service (MaaS) cloud computing solution for usability and interoperability of methods. *4th IEEE International Conference on Engineering Technologies and Applied Sciences (ICETAS)*, Salmabad, Bahrain, pp. 1–6, 2017, doi: 10.1109/ICETAS.2017.8277897.
12. Rekoputra, N.M., Harwahyu, R., Sari, R.F., Performance study of OpenAirInterface 5G System on the Cloud Platform Managed by Juju Orchestration. *International Seminar on Research of Information Technology and Intelligent Systems (ISRITI)*, Yogyakarta, Indonesia, pp. 211–216, 2019, doi: 10.1109/ISRITI48646.2019.9034647.
13. Sergeev, V.A., Bolkhovskaya, O.V., Maltsev, A.A., A Practical Approach to Hybrid Beamforming for 5G Wi-Fi Systems. *2021 Wave Electronics and its Application in Information and Telecommunication Systems (WECONF)*, St. Petersburg, Russia, pp. 1–9, 2021, doi: 10.1109/WECONF51603.2021.9470612.
14. Chandrasekaran, G., Wang, N., Hassanpour, M., Xu, M., Tafazolli, R., Mobility as a Service (MaaS): A D2D-Based Information-Centric Network Architecture for Edge-Controlled Content Distribution. *IEEE Access*, 6, 2110–2129, 2018, doi: 10.1109/ACCESS.2017.2781736.
15. Fujita, Y., Kuwahara, M., Ueda, E., MaaS Blender: Integration of Mobility Simulators for Mobility as a Service Evaluation. *IEEE Access*, 11, 105105–105114, 2023, doi: 10.1109/ACCESS.2023.3319079.
16. Ayuba, Y., Supangkat, S.H., Wibowo, S.S., Mobility as a Service: A Problems and Research Opportunities. *2023 10th International Conference on ICT for Smart Society (ICISS)*, Bandung, Indonesia, pp. 1–7, 2023, doi: 10.1109/ICISS59129.2023.10292068.
17. Wang, J., Exploiting Mobility Prediction for Dependable Service Composition in Wireless Mobile Ad Hoc Networks. *IEEE Trans. Serv. Comput.*, 4, 1, 44–55, 2011, doi: 10.1109/TSC.2010.46.
18. Khadraoui, D. and Feltus, C., Development of Build–MaaS Architecture, a Mobility-as-a-Service platform for the Construction Sector. *6th International Conference on Information and Computer Technologies (ICICT)*, Raleigh, NC, USA, pp. 156–161, 2023, doi: 10.1109/ICICT58900.2023.00033.

19. Barreto, L., Amaral, A., Baltazar, S., Mobility as a Service (MaaS) in rural regions: An overview. *2018 International Conference on Intelligent Systems (IS)*, Funchal, Portugal, pp. 856–860, 2018, doi: 10.1109/IS.2018.8710455.
20. Wagan, A.A. and Jung, L.T., An efficient distributed mobility management scheme for network mobility. *3rd International Conference on Computer and Information Sciences (ICCOINS)*, Kuala Lumpur, Malaysia, pp. 270–275, 2016, doi: 10.1109/ICCOINS.2016.7783226.
21. Hata, M., Soylu, M., Izumi, S., Abe, T., Suganuma, T., Design of SDN based end-to-end routing over multiple domains for mobility management. *13th International Conference on Network and Service Management (CNSM)*, Tokyo, Japan, pp. 1–4, 2017, doi: 10.23919/CNSM.2017.8256056.
22. Kong, X., *et al.*, Mobility Dataset Generation for Vehicular Social Networks Based on Floating Car Data. *IEEE Trans. Veh. Technol.*, 67, 5, 3874–3886, 2018, doi: 10.1109/TVT.2017.2788441.
23. Zhu, X., *et al.*, Traffic simulation and impact analysis for alternative mobility services in the city of Shenzhen. *Ninth International Conference on Advanced Cloud and Big Data (CBD)*, Xi'an, China, pp. 70–76, 2022, doi: 10.1109/CBD54617.2021.00021.
24. Giesecke, R., Surakka, T., Hakonen, M., Conceptualising Mobility as a Service. *Eleventh International Conference on Ecological Vehicles and Renewable Energies (EVER)*, Monte Carlo, Monaco, pp. 1–11, 2016, doi: 10.1109/EVER.2016.7476443.
25. Bai, O. and Wei, J., Governing knowledge mobility in service innovation network for innovation performance: The interplay of relational and contractual governance modes. *IEEE Technology & Engineering Management Conference (TEMSCON)*, Santa Clara, CA, pp. 32–39, 2017, doi: 10.1109/TEMSCON.2017.7998350.
26. Raaza, A. and Kumar, N., Internet of Things Energy Efficient Cluster-Based Routing Using Hybrid Particle Swarm Optimization for Wireless Sensor Network. *Wireless Pers. Commun.*, 122, 3, 2603–2619, 2021, https://doi.org/10.1007/s11277-021-09015-9.
27. Prabha, R., Senthil, G.A., Suganthi, S., Cluster head based secure routing using optimized dual-discriminator conditional generative adversarial network in wireless ad-hoc networks. *Peer-to-Peer Netw. Appl.*, 27, 8, 5207–5215, 2023, https://doi.org/10.1007/s12083-023-01545-2.
28. Senthil, G.A., Prabha, R., Pomalar, A., Leela Jancy, P., Rinthya, M., Convergence of Cloud and Fog Computing for Security Enhancement. *Fifth International Conference on I-SMAC (IoT in Social, Mobile, Analytics and Cloud) (I-SMAC)*, IEEE, pp. 1–6, 2021, DOI: 10.1109/I-SMAC52330.2021.9640872.
29. Prabha, R., Senthil, G.A., Sangeetha, S.K.B., Suganthi, S.U., Roopa, D., Broadband Wireless Network Era in Wireless Communication–Routing Theory and Practices, in: *Modeling and Optimization of Optical Communication Networks*, p. 267, 2023.

30. Prabha, R., Senthil, G.A., Sangeetha, S.K.B., Suganthi, S.U., Roopa, D., Network Routing and Its Real-Time Practice in Broadband Wireless Networks, *Resource Management in Advanced Wireless Networks*, pp. 99–112, Wiley online library, 2023, https://doi.org/10.1002/9781119827603.ch5.
31. Thiyagesan, M., Irfan, B., Raman, R., Ponnarasi, N., Ramakrishnan, P., 5G geological data for seismic inversion data detection based on wide-angle reflection wave technology, in: *Volume 1: Proceedings of the International Conference on Artificial Intelligence, Blockchain, Computing and Security (ICABCS), Gr. Noida, UP, India*, vol. 1, pp. 640–644, CRC Press, 2023.

14

Design and Development of Foldable Electric Vehicle

Akshay S. Bhat*, Puneeth H. S., P. Aniketh Solanki, Karthik P., Prajwal K. Kalal and Manoj S.

Department of Mechanical Engineering, Vidyavardhaka College of Engineering, Mysore, Karnataka, India

Abstract

The foldable electric vehicle (FEV) market is an emerging segment in the automotive industry, driven by the necessity for sustainable transportation solutions and advancements in battery technology, motor power, and fold mechanisms. There are in fact multiple categories available in this industry, such as hover boards and stand-up scooters, appealing to consumers of all ages for short trips, leisure, and transit requirements. Age-based segmentation of the market identifies a large percentage of customers as being those between the ages of 15 to 50. The foldable electric vehicle in this context can provide a range of 12–15 kilometers with a 420W battery capacity and has a 350W BLDC motor that can move 20–25 kph and support a total load of about 200 kg at the most. Legal and regulatory aspects unique to the FEV market are taken into consideration.

Keywords: Electric vehicle design, compact mobility solution, sustainable transportation, foldable EV innovation, lightweight vehicle design, modular vehicle engineering

14.1 Introduction

The concept of developing foldable EVs has existed several years ago similar to the development of new technologies and techniques in developing foldable gadgets as well as consumer's preference for portable compact and

**Corresponding author*: akkshaybhhat@gmail.com

Rathishchandra R. Gatti and Chandra Singh (eds.) Digital Convergence in Intelligent Mobility Systems, (315–330) © 2025 Scrivener Publishing LLC

sustainable means of transportation. These vehicles respond to the issues of traffic and environmental impacts that are characteristic of urban transport and at the same time manage to successfully implement the advantages of electric power along with the convenience of foldability. The old bicycle popular in the early 20th century was the collapsible bicycles, and as such, the general concept of a folding mode of transport was brought to light. This mechanism made it fold into the compact form, and such design was welcome among sometimes bike commuters in congested city areas. Alas, not electric in their original conception, these baby models set out the course for further progress in transport of persons in their portable modes [1, 2].

The use of electric motors on foldable vehicles began at the end of the twentieth century mainly due to the development of batteries and increased realization of the impact to the environment. Electric bikes were the first to be developed in the industry; the type that is pedal assisted and comes with an electric motor. That such bicycles can be folded was another plus, especially as they could easily be stored in flats and offices of the commuters. Folding electric bicycles were gradually introduced to the market in the early 2000s especially in the densely populated metropolitan areas where space and traffic jam were critical issues. These vehicles provided a partially environmentally friendly solution to autos and public transportation means [3, 4].

The type and implementation of folding electric bicycles are initiated by the battery performance. Scientists and engineers of the manufacturers began to apply lighter forms of metals and more effective electric motors to enhance the functionality and beauty of such electric autos. The mid 2010s saw the emergence of electric bicycles which are foldable and ideal for the commercial commuter as they are convenient, environmentally friendly, and cheaper to operate than gasoline-powered automobiles. Electric vehicles are not limited to bicycles; other types of folding electric vehicles include electric scooters and mopeds. These compact foldable scooters were the other category of Zhejiang geographical fame for use in commuting and leisure in cities. The portable and electric scooters have only gained popularity when battery technology and the efficiency of the motor were improved [5, 6].

Manufacturers have additionally focused on integrating smart technology and conjunction elements that improve the user experience and convenience. Looking forward, the future of folding electric vehicles looks good as battery efficiency, materials science, and design evolve. These vehicles will be significant in solving urban mobility problems like congestion and air pollution. Their small footprint and sustainability make them suitable for people and cities for sustainable mobility solutions [7, 8].

Bicycles and scooters that fold up have long been in vogue. People from flat metropolitan areas in Berlin, Hamburg, and Cologne utilize light folding vehicles as an alternative to walking or riding a bike without having to travel far from their homes, site of business, factory floor, or railroad station. Electric folding vehicles often look similar to their unassisted counterparts. They weigh a little bit more, but it's a worthy compromise for that bit of boost. Whether you're looking for something to take on the public transport and ride the rest of the way to reach the destination, or you live somewhere with little storage space and need a compact bike, there's likely a folder for you in our list of the best. In general, folding electric vehicles are a great urban companion, particularly in flatter areas, but that doesn't mean they're not good for quick leisure rides on country lanes too [9, 10].

Currently, it's not required to enforce legal speed restrictions on Asian-made (large and inexpensive) and Swiss-made (small and expensive) vehicles at a maximum speed of 25 km/h. Foldable electric vehicles reduce the risk of theft or damage. Overall, the main benefits of folding vehicles are portability, storage, convenience, flexibility, and security. This vehicle is easy to transport and use. With this as an idea, we are attempting to modernize the foldable electric vehicle by reducing the cost of the electric vehicle. We have designed the product which consists of less weight and low cost and still serves the purpose, competitive to the vehicles in the market [11].

14.2 Problem Formulation

Mobility at large and compact places like urban traffic, shop floor, warehouse, or campus, where standard vehicles are not feasible in addition to impractical use, are always a concern. So, a solution is needed to overcome this gap in mobility. This project aims to address the enhancement by developing an efficient and affordable electric vehicle. This solution will provide a sustainable alternative to traditional commuting and give a new perspective and approach with regard to transportation, creating a foldable electric bike for industry shop floor, warehouse, and large campus, making short-distance travel quicker and more accessible.

A few significant issues are addressed by our project:

- Urban Mobility Alternative: Foldable electric vehicles are an excellent option for urban commuters with limited storage space and several modes of transportation.
- Last-Mile Connectivity: The problem is solved by foldable electric vehicles, as they are a portable resource and are environmentally efficient when it comes to short haulage, thus relieving the pressure of motor vehicles in terms of mobility.
- Storage and Portability: Those who have limited space where they dwell or where they work may be privileged to use foldable electric vehicles. For easy storage in people's homes, various workplaces, or other public places, their folding shape is usable.
- Multimodal Transportation: These bikes are light and can be folded and unfolded very fast; hence, they can harbor easily with many means of transport like buses, trains, or even cars.
- Tourism and Recreation: "Traditional commuters, new visitors and recreational riders are starting to turn their attention to foldable e-bikes." They are the most suitable for assessing new territories because they are portable; it does not need enormous bike stands or moving large groups of bicycles.

14.3 Methodology and Material

Cutting-edge engineering, materials science, and design ideas must be merged to produce a folding electric vehicle to create in turn a tiny and portable transportation solution. Although there aren't many well-known folding electric vehicles on the road yet, the concept is in accord with the growing trend of electric mobility and small-space urban transportation.

- Purpose and Requirements: Who will use the foldable electric vehicle? What are the technical specifications? Weight, speed, and range.
- Concept Design: What is the folding mechanism: vertical, half-fold, or other? How to include the folding mechanism into the outside design?

- Material Selection: Select lightweight materials for the body and frame to provide portability without sacrificing structural integrity.
- Electric Powertrain: Install a tiny, efficient battery and motor. Optimize energy storage to ensure weight and range balance.
- Foldable Parts: Create foldable components such as handlebars, wheels, and frames. Folding and unfolding require no additional equipment and are simple to do.
- User Interface and Controls: Hence, there is a simple user interface control, and the driver has full control of the automobile. Think of smart characteristics.
- Safety Mechanisms: Ensure that measures are put in place to avoid folding/unfolding by accident as is practiced in normal electric cars.
- Testing and Iteration: Design a practical model of the folding electric car and perform various tests on it. Collect feedback and implement improvements based on the observation to increase work efficiency.
- Regulatory Compliance: Thus, in the case with a person, it means the identification of the vehicle that is sufficient to provide necessary safety and establish traffic laws.
- Production Strategies and Marketing: Devise a schedule on a large scale of production. Evaluate a commercial plan to make the foldable electric car ready for sale.

14.3.1 Material Selection Process

- Mechanical Properties: Assess its elasticity, ability to stand tough conditions, strength, and fatigue. Reflect on how some of these attributes meet the application requirements, so the material should stand the loads and conditions expected of it.
- Chemical Compatibility: Determine some aspects of its performance such as its resistance to chemicals and corrosion and other factors in the environment. To predict the service life and performance of a material used in application, it is compulsory that the reactions the material has to chemicals on contact are well understood.
- Material Costs: Usually, look at the nature of the material that is being used, how it is being processed, and additional

treatments or coating applied to the material. How to assess the needs for the best possible performance with minimum spending is something that allows enhancing the factor of the project's economic viability.

- Manufacturability and Processing: Assess the material for its workability, that is, how easily this material can be processed in fabrication. The properties that have to be taken into account are formability, machinability, and applicability to ordinary production processes. This optimizes the production lines and ensures that the material is transformed to the final product in the right manner and in the shortest time possible.

Some examples of such materials are the steel and the alloys, the plastic elastomers, aluminum alloys, polymer composites, rubber, and foams.

14.3.2 Working

The vehicle has an electric propulsion system that moves it to around 25 mph backed by a hub motor of that potential. The battery backup is expected to operate with a range of 12–15 kilometers. The handle's neck portion is where the vehicle's folding characteristic is seen. The handle could be completely folded, with the presence of a height adjustment system for better comfort of the rider. This helps the vehicle to be more compact and still provide the required features to the rider.

The folding mechanism utilizes a latch-like mechanism that keeps the handle in place. Once the locket is removed, the vehicle is folded and reattached to prevent its unfolding.

Users can conveniently fold and unfold their vehicle because of their compact design, which also makes them storable in limited locations or on public transportation. Because of their performance and portability, foldable electric vehicles lead the way in the new urban commuting scenario.

14.3.3 Electrical Components

The electrical components that play an essential role in the development of our electric vehicles are as follows:

a) Hub Motor

Hub motors are typically brushless direct current (BLDC) motors, which have an edge over conventional direct current (DC) motors; they avoid transmission loss as they are directly mounted on the wheels of a vehicle. The hub motor is also known as wheel motor or wheel hub drive and is characterized by the integration of power, transmission, and braking device into the wheel hub.

There is an electronic braking system in the hub motor; when throttle response is cut off, the electronic brake is actuated.

A hub motor is an electric motor that is integrated directly into a vehicle's wheel hub. In this arrangement, the motor powers the wheel directly, eliminating the need for an additional transmission system.

Hub motors have two primary varieties: in-wheel motors and mid-mounted motors.

- ➢ Advantages of Hub Motors:
  - Simple Mechanism: Hub motors eliminate mechanical complexity and possible causes of failure by dealing with the requirement for an intricate transmission system.
  - Efficiency: By driving the wheels directly, hub motors can achieve great efficiency without the losses found in conventional drivetrains.
  - Regenerative Braking: This feature, which increases overall economy and extends the vehicle's range, is supported by a large number of hub motors. Regenerative braking operates via converting mechanical energy back to electrical energy during braking.
  - Space Utilization: In allowing an extra space in the vehicle, in-wheel motors allow more creative and flexible designs.

b) Battery

Lead acid batteries are only currently used in such electric vehicles to supplement the battery loads as these batteries are high powered, inexpensive, safe, and reliable. These batteries have a greater amount of safety and are able to offer enough backup for our vehicle keeping in mind the cost-effective nature of the battery.

- ➢ Properties of Batteries:
  - Energy Density: It's a crucial factor in choosing batteries for electric vehicles. It symbolizes the quantity of energy a battery can store in a given volume or weight. Higher energy density allows for a larger driving range while maintaining battery size and weight. High energy density

materials or devices are required for efficient batteries. Battery packs and energy storage technologies have applications for holding more energy in less area.

- Range and Charging: An electric vehicle's range is defined by its battery capacity. Larger capacity batteries often provide greater driving ranges. Charging time is also a crucial factor. The reason for enhancements to fast changing technology is to reduce the time necessary.
- Battery Management System (BMS): It is vital to monitor and manage various kinds of battery-related challenges; for example, a battery management system has to maintain the lid on and control an array of factors, including temperature, voltage, and battery status. It promotes battery life, performance optimization, and safety.
- Lifecycle: As regards the cost and ecological impact of electric vehicles over the long term, the battery's longevity has a considerable effect. To extend the life of batteries, manufacturers are conducting research and development.
- Price: The expense of an electric vehicle's batteries has a significant influence on the vehicle's overall worth. Continuous research and development aims to bring down the expense of battery production, which will in turn bring down the worth of electric vehicles.
- Heat Management: The performance and lifespan of batteries can be influenced by heat. To remove heat and maintain optimal operating temperatures, thermal heat management systems are implemented.

c) Electronic Control Unit

An E-vehicle controller is a component that links all electrical sections of the vehicle together. It connects things like the battery, motor, throttle, display, pedal assist, and various sensors. It can manage the overall functioning of the vehicle.

The electronic control unit is important for the management and control of the electric powertrain of the vehicle. The control unit is in charge of making sure the battery, electric motor, and other related parts operate effectively and safely.

It connects things like the battery, motor, throttle, display, pedal assist, and various sensors. It can manage the overall functioning of the bike.

- Functions of ECU: The engine control unit (ECU) is a vital aspect of contemporary autos because it handles and regulates a variety of engine and associated system operations. Through sensors and actuators, the electronic control unit collects data regarding the vehicle's operating conditions and modifies engine parameters as necessary. The engine control unit operates the following primary functions:
  - Motor Control: The speed, torque, and rotational of the electric motor's direction are all controlled by the control unit. It transforms battery-powered DC electricity into AC power for the motor and modifies the output in response to input from the driver and vehicle parameters.
  - Battery Management: The battery management system assists in monitoring the battery's condition, including its life and consumption, cycles of recharging and charging, and the wear and tear that the battery experiences from these cycles.
  - Charging Control: The control unit manages the charging process for electric vehicles that use rechargeable batteries. To ensure that the battery is charged safely and effectively, it regulates the charging voltage and current.
  - Control of Temperature: The electric motor and the battery are two of the many components whose temperatures are tracked and managed by a control unit system. To keep things running at their best and avoid overheating, proper thermal management is essential.
  - Power Distribution: The electronic control unit keeps check to ensure that the various vehicle systems, including the motor, the cooling and heating systems, and the auxiliary components, get the right amount of electrical power.

d) Electrical Power Assisted Folding Vehicle

A foldable electric vehicle is designed to be portable and lightweight, making storage and transit easier. These electric vehicle models are perfect for urban transportation, shop floors, and other tight spaces. Its ability to be folded, often at the frame, folding handle, and removable seat, is its defining feature. This reduces the vehicle's size, resulting in easier carrying and storing. Additionally, the foldable vehicle has a rechargeable battery and an integrated electric motor. The detailed design draft of foldable electric vehicle is shown in Figure 14.1. Also, the isometric view and side view of detailed design are shown in Figures 14.2 and 14.3 respectively.

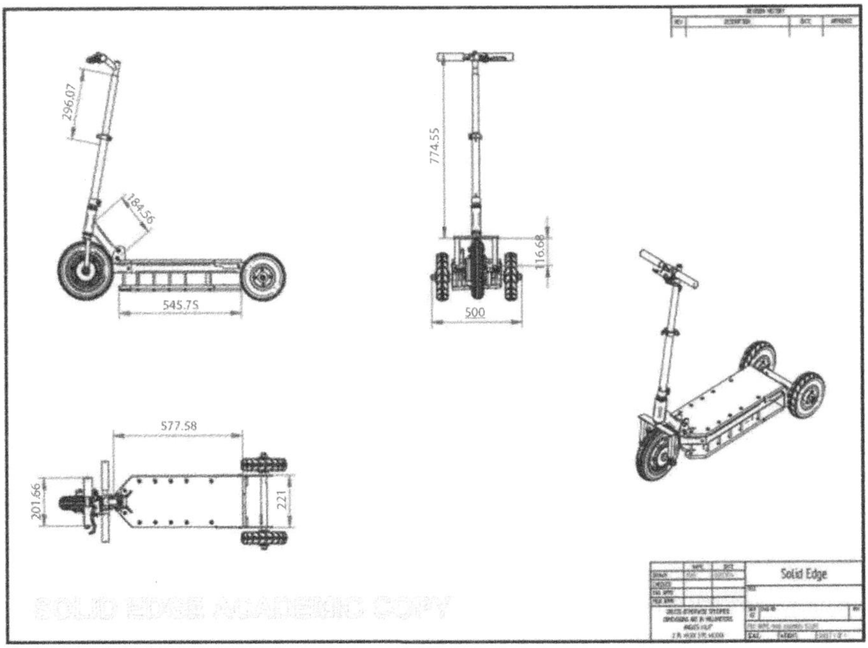

Figure 14.1 Detailed design draft of foldable electric vehicle.

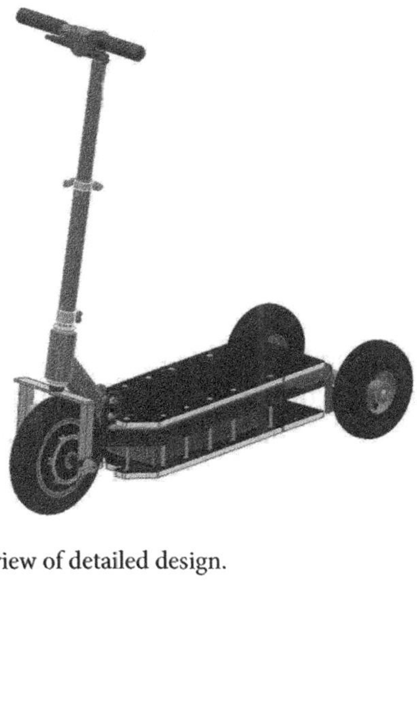

Figure 14.2 Isometric view of detailed design.

Figure 14.3 Side view of detailed design.

Foldable electric bikes are easy to carry about and ideal for city riding. The drum brake mechanism is commonly used in electric bikes and other small vehicles, including this design. High-power lead acid batteries are well known for their inexpensive cost, safety, and reliability.

Electrical power assisted folding vehicles (EPAFVs) offer an exciting future for urban personal mobility. There are a few things to be aware of:

- Technology
  - Better Batteries: A greater amount of energy in batteries and longevity means more range and efficiency for EPAFVs. They'll be more useful for regular commutes because a single charge may be used more effectively.
  - Compact and Lighter Design: This is because the new-generation frames will benefit from material science technology such as carbon fiber/composite and excessive grade plastic. This will address the problem of storage, especially in the urban areas, while on the other hand, carrying and storage of EPAFVs will become easy especially when folded.
  - Intelligent Power Management: New EPAFVs could possibly involve aspects of smart power management, the use of which is dictated by the customer's preference and the territory. Some of examples are regenerative braking and smart charging.

- Features and Design:
  - User Experience and Foldability: Successive EPAFVs will thus be expected to fold in a more stylish manner and be easy to handle, while on the other hand, it must be able to open fully in the shortest time possible. A boot and storage that citizens of the crowded city would find very convenient and safe for their non-violent confrontation.
  - Smart Integration: They will be fashionable and practical to have built-in GPS, which will have an application interface for the search and choice of a route and potentially semi- or fully automated for parking spaces and/or narrow streets.

- Market and Consumer
  - Urban Mobility: EPAFVs will be utilized in the urban milieu to replace conventional cars for first and second mile mobility. Consequently, it can be implemented in the present transport system, hence alleviating over-crowded transport and pollutant prone units.
  - Customization: When it comes to the market demand, the producer is likely to have more in terms of designs, battery capacity, and other probable features that may include storage space or covers.

- Environmental Impact
  - Emissions Reduction: Therefore, EPAFVs shall play a key role in cutting the city's air pollution, especially when they are rechargeable and do not emit any pollutants to the atmosphere and also decrease greenhouse gas emissions. This is in regard to the sustainable development goals and the provisions on climate change as embraced under the world policies.
  - Lifecycle: Because of EPAFVs, there will be an increase in the deterioration of the ecology; thus, there will be the need for the production and use of environment-friendly batteries and components and also battery and component recycling services.

- Challenges
  - Infrastructure: Urban charging extensions to the infrastructure will be required to facilitate widespread EPAFV use. This consists of charging stations in ideal places like workplaces, residential areas, and public spaces.

- Regulatory Framework: Policymakers have to adapt regulations to EPAFVs, including safety criteria for folding mechanisms, roadworthiness, and user licensing requirements.

14.4 Static Analysis

Static analysis is carried on the base frame, as it carries the most amount of the total vehicle loading and is to be the less durable component of the design. Static analysis focuses on the base frame in vehicle design because it bears the majority of the weight and is fragile. This study focuses on structural integrity under static loads, which ensures that the frame can withstand the stress induced by the vehicle's weight and external forces. As the foundational component, the base frame bears the majority of the vehicle's load, making it critical to identify and correct any problems. Engineers can effectively reinforce the frame to meet safety and performance requirements by attentively analyzing its design and materials. Therefore, the analysis is carried out on the base frame. The results are described below (Figures 14.4 and 14.5).

The investigation was conducted using SolidWorks, a popular program in the industry today. SolidWorks provides a wide range of capabilities in a single tool which benefit the users well; therefore, both modeling and analysis were done with the help of this software. The meshing technique employs 6501 tetrahedral elements, which include the sum of 13121 nodes. Each element measured around 1.10786 cm and featured a tolerance of 0.0553931 cm. The maximum aspect ratio obtained from the Ansys

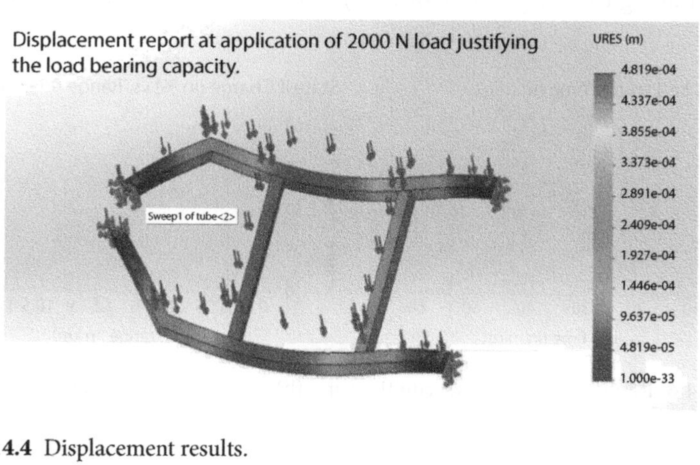

Figure 14.4 Displacement results.

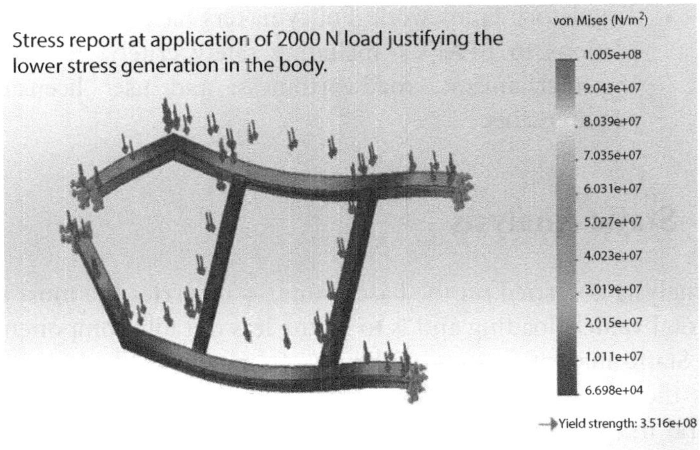

Figure 14.5 Stress results.

findings is 21.774, which indicates the divergence of a mesh element from having all sides of equal length.

The report clearly describes whether the design is consistent with future work that must be completed in accordance with the schedule. Therefore, it is significant to ensure that the project's outcomes are accurately assessed, preventing any additional complications.

14.5 Results

The two graphs in Figure 14.6 justify the vehicle's reliability and accuracy by comparing the range, state of charge, and run time of the vehicle.

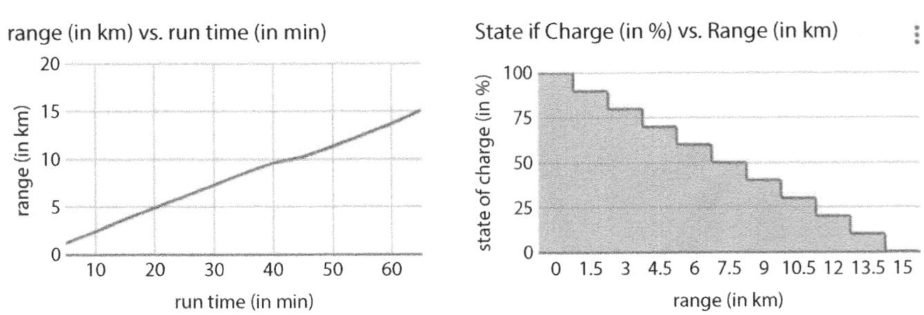

Figure 14.6 Results of (a) range vs. run time and (b) state of charge vs. range.

As we can see from the graph, there was a constant increase, indicating that the growth in the range is progressive as the run duration increases. When it comes to range, the longer the vehicle operates, the farther it travels. However, as we all know, if the charge in the battery is depleted, it will ultimately stop, and the graph shows that after traveling around 15 kilometers, the battery charge was depleted, and the vehicle must be recharged for the next journey.

On the contrary, the state of charge deteriorates with vehicle use. Figure 14.6 depicts a slow and constant step decline in the battery's charging in relation to the vehicle's driving range. The graph depicts the approximate charged condition of the vehicle's battery for the given range of kilometers driven.

Note: The graphs above are a theoretical portrayal of the practical outcomes that are shown for better comprehension, rather than the theoretical results.

14.6 Conclusion

A foldable electric vehicle is an interesting proposal in the automotive industry. It provides solutions for issues like vehicle theft and damage by being compact and portable, scarcity of parking spaces in urban areas like metropolitan cities (like Delhi, Mumbai, Kolkata, Chennai, and many more), and providing a faster mode of transport for a limited cost. It also encourages people to use public transport that can increase the quality of living in urban as well as rural areas, as it helps target lower emissions of pollution on an overall count. Its ability to be rider friendly and customizable makes it an attractive option for the target audience of the age group between teens to old age and backed by its powerful machinery and energy pack filling up other points in the blank. It is an environmentally friendly vehicle that has the ability to charge with solar energy at parking stations (if stations are equipped with the facility) and runs on electricity. The vehicle incorporates a lead acid battery, keeping the vehicle ready to go, and a powerful hub motor integrated with drum brakes that serves its purpose. Many more characteristics are to be included as well, like regenerative braking, navigation system, music and audio system, and so on, which can be incorporated in the current model. Furthermore, employing rechargeable batteries extends the life of the vehicle. Overall, this is believed to be an extraordinary vehicle for the current period and urban travel.

References

1. Zirn, O., Strobel, O., Norkauer, A., TrottiElec – ultraleichter E-Kick Roller für geschlosseneWegekettenimurbanenVerkehr. *AALE 2014*, OTHRegensburg.
2. Foldable Electrified Ultralight Vehicles on Public Walkways for Sustainable Traffic Chains. Avestia Publishing, *Int. J. Civ. Infrastruct. (IJCI)*, 1, 1–8, 2018, ISSN: 2563-8084, DOI: 10.11159/ijci.2018.001.
3. Innovation Design of Folding Bicycle Based on Triz Theory. *Proceedings of the MATRIZ TRIZ fest 2016 International Conference*, Beijing, China, July 28-30, 2016.
4. Baldrati, F., Chaks, L., Dallacasa, E., Frizziero, L., QFD and SDE applied to design of a new non-electric folding vehicle, Alma Mater Studiorum University of Bologna, Department of Architecture, Viale.
5. Zirn, O. and Rüther, M., Foldable Electrified Ultralight Vehicles as Key Components for Sustainable Traffic Chains. *5th International Energy and Sustainability Conference 2016*, IEEE Xplore, DOI: 10.1109/IESC.2016.75.
6. Karkera, T. and Singh, C., Autonomous bot using machine learning and computer vision. *SN Comput. Sci.*, *2*, 4, 251, 2021.
7. Soans, R.V., Hegde, A., Singh, C., Kumar, A., Object tracking robot using adaptive color thresholding, in: *2017 2nd international conference on communication and electronics systems (ICCES)*, 2017, October, IEEE, pp. 790–793.
8. Gatti, R.R., Singh, C., Agrawal, R., Serrao, F.J. (Eds.), *Self-Powered Cyber Physical Systems*, John Wiley & Sons, Hoboken, USA, 2023.
9. Singh, C., Shetty, S.C., Badiger, M., Nischitha, A Study on Connected Cars–V2V Communication, in: *Modeling and Optimization of Optical Communication Networks*, pp. 251–265, 2023.
10. Singh, C. and Gatti, R., *Drone applications for industry 5.0*, IGI Global, Hershey, USA, 2024.
11. Gatti, R. and Singh, C., *Shaping the Future of Automation With Cloud-Enhanced Robotics*, IGI Global, Hershey, USA, 2024.

15

Design and Development of Ultrasonic Assisted Collision Detection and Blind-Spot Reduction

Puneeth H. S.*, Akshay S. Bhat, Bhavani A., Lalit V., Sathyarjun A. B. and Vishnu K. J.

Department of Mechanical Engineering, Vidyavardhaka College of Engineering Mysore, Karnataka, India

Abstract

The project demonstrates that the findings of the survey indicate that 50% of accidents involve two-wheeler drivers; hence, two-wheeler safety is crucial. When nearby vehicles are within the driver's braking distance, we are attempting to regulate the vehicle's speed in order to prevent collisions and improve safety for two-wheelers. In the case of both IC engine vehicles and electric vehicles, this is accomplished via long-range sensors, a motor controller, and the ECU. In our project, we aim to regulate the DC motor speed, which is crucial for vehicle speed in both internal combustion engine and electric vehicle scenarios. When implementing for internal combustion engines, we have to control the speed of the DC motor in the throttle body by controlling the power supply from the battery, which lowers the angle at which the butterfly valve opens; the input from the sensors are also considered to reduce the vehicle's speed. In the case of electric vehicles, we must adjust the motor speed by managing the battery's power flow in response to the sensor input. In addition, we are attempting to use head-up displays by eliminating the traditional designs to improve rearward visibility so that drivers can monitor oncoming vehicles without having to turn around. This might lessen the number of collisions that happen as a result of unseen vehicles in blind zones, particularly while changing lanes, lowering the chance of crashes. Integrating both systems in two-wheelers improves driver safety and provides a comfortable driving experience.

**Corresponding author*: puneeth.hs@vvce.ac.in

Rathishchandra R. Gatti and Chandra Singh (eds.) Digital Convergence in Intelligent Mobility Systems, (331–346) © 2025 Scrivener Publishing LLC

***Keywords*:** Ultrasonic collision detection, blind-spot reduction, advanced driver assistance systems (ADAS), vehicle safety technology, collision avoidance systems, ultrasonic sensors in vehicles, blind-spot monitoring, intelligent vehicle safety

15.1 Introduction

The risk of severe collisions is increased, according to a recent survey, when drivers exceed authorized speed limits while failing to recognize potential hazards. In order to promote a harmonious atmosphere and prevent collisions, the Indian Law Commission has issued guidelines pertaining to the reduction of velocity in congested regions. Despite this, existing approaches remain ineffective in mitigating collisions resulting from negligent driving. Any motorized vehicle is required to have speed control [1].

Accidental incidents increased by 11.9% in 2022 compared to 2021, resulting in an aggregate increase of 9.4% in fatalities and 15.3% in injuries. Road accidents were 72.3%, fatalities were 71.2%, and injuries accounted for 72.8%. This demonstrates the critical need for an automatic speed reduction system in vehicles. The accident rate is reduced when a vehicle's braking distance shortens in tandem with a drop in speed [2].

Globally, India has the highest number of registered two-wheelers in 2020, totaling 32.63 crores. The world's second-largest manufacturer and producer of two-wheelers, India, has seen an accelerated expansion in recent years due to fuel-efficient technology and the introduction of electric cycles and scooters. Electric components, including chargers, controllers, BLDC motors, and DC–DC converters, are essential for the future of personal mobility with electric cycles and scooters [3].

Two-wheelers are common due to their fuel efficiency, affordability, and simplicity of steering on tiny, irregular streets. However, two-wheeler collisions are much riskier than those involving automobiles, as drivers are not protected by any safety apparatus. Determining the blind spot region of scooters is critical, as these regions can be a major contributor to collisions between motorcycles and other vehicles [4].

Experienced drivers examine their side and rearview reflectors around five times more often than novice drivers, and 1.5 times more often while changing lanes than less experienced drivers. Head-up displays, first used in fighter aircraft, enable pilots to focus without continuously gazing down at the equipment, enhancing driving safety by reducing irritation and delay caused by constant eye focus [5].

When fighter jets first employed head-up displays, vital information was shown on a clear glass screen in front of the aircraft, allowing pilots to focus without constantly looking down at the equipment. It appeared in cars for the first time a few years ago. The head-up display device allows drivers to keep their heads up and keep an eye on the data and display on the instrument without having to look down. By reducing the discomfort and delay caused by needing to continuously shift eye focus, it improves driving safety [6].

Prior to delving into the methodology of our project, the following provides a concise overview of the elements that are integral to its operation:

15.1.1 Head-Up Display

A two-wheeled vehicle's performance improves when the driver has access to transparent display devices that provide real-time rearview visibility. It allows the driver view of both approaching traffic and the vehicles in front of him. There is a reduction in the time it takes the driver to check both mirrors. In contrast to traditional displays that are mounted on the dashboard of vehicles, these displays are positioned so that the driver can quickly examine them since they are head-up displays [7, 8].

The first head-up displays have been observed on fighter aircraft. Head-up displays are becoming more and more widespread in car-mounted objects since they debuted a few years ago. Head-up displays improve driving safety by eliminating the need for drivers to look down to check the instrument's display and data, allowing drivers to maintain an elevated head position, slowing the rapid changes in the external environment between head-down and head-up, and reducing the discomfort and delay associated with constantly adjusting their line of sight. Even though these systems have just lately begun to appear in our automobiles, a significant change in the industry is scheduled to occur as a result of falling technological costs. Distracted driving is becoming more important as law enforcement concentrates its efforts on drivers who are not paying attention to the road [9, 10].

15.1.2 Elements That Control IC Engine Vehicles' Speed

15.1.2.1 Electronic Control Unit

The electronic engine control unit (ECU) is the primary controller of the engine management system. It regulates fuel injection, ignition, air intake, and fuel delivery. This control unit allows it to integrate vehicle and gearbox functions as well as manage the exhaust system. The ECU manages a wide range of powertrain topologies, including gasoline, diesel, CNG, ethanol, hybrid, and fuel cell systems. An engine control unit and an electronic control unit have vast applications and are the key components in all the automobiles [11, 12]. The name "powertrain control module" (PCM) is responsible for managing both engine and transmission.

15.1.2.2 Sensors Operated by ECU

(a) Position Sensors
- Crankshaft location sensor (CKP)
- Throttle position sensor (TPS)
- Airflow sensors
- Mass air flow (MAF)

(b) Pressure Sensors
- Manifold absolute pressure (MAP) sensor
- Fuel pressure sensor
- Temperature sensors
- Intake air temperature (IAT) sensor
- Engine coolant temperature (ECT) sensor
- Air–fuel ratios, emissions, etc.
- Oxygen sensor (O_2)
- Knock sensor

15.1.2.3 Air–Fuel Ratio

The air–fuel ratio (AFR) is the proportion of fuel to oxygen during combustion. In an internal combustion engine, the stoichiometric AFR is around 14.7:1, i.e. 14.7 kilograms of oxygen utilizes 1 kg of propellant. The minimum AFR is 6:1, while the maximum is 20:1. A lean mixture has a ratio higher than the stoichiometric ratio, while a rich mixture has a ratio lesser than the stoichiometric ratio. In modern automobiles, based on information from sensors, the powertrain control module (PCM) modulates the air–fuel mixture.

In internal combustion engines, the air–fuel ratio (AF or AFR) is the ratio between the mass of air (ma) to the mass of fuel (mf). Internal combustion engines operate closer to ideal AFR levels, making the AFR ratio both ideal and realistic. The equivalency air–fuel ratio, lambda (λ), is the ratio of the actual AFR to the ideal/stoichiometric AFR [13].

15.1.2.4 Air–Fuel Ratio and Engine Performance

The engine's power and fuel consumption are significantly influenced by the air–fuel ratio. The lowest fuel consumption for a gasoline engine is achieved with a lean AFR. The primary reason is that there is sufficient oxygen available to burn the fuel totally, providing mechanical work. However, rich air–fuel combinations offer the maximum power production.

The system's ability to function depends on the lambda (oxygen) sensor. This sensor provides information to the engine's electronic control unit (ECU), which counts the oxygen molecules in exhaust fumes. The oxygen sensor reading is utilized by the gasoline engine ECU to decide how much fuel mass to inject to keep the air–fuel ratio around the stoichiometric level ($\lambda = 1.00$).

15.1.2.5 Throttle Body

Electronic throttle control (ETC), also known as throttle-by-wire or e-gas, is a technology that attaches the accelerator lever to the throttle, enabling a more efficient driving experience. The ETC system comprises of an accelerator pedal module, an electric motor-operated throttle valve (ETB), and a powertrain or engine control module (PCM). The ECM is an embedded system that calculates the required throttle position based on various sensors, such as accelerator pedal position sensors, engine speed sensors, and cruise control switches. The throttle body, a mechanical component of the ETC, is used to inject more gasoline as more air enters the engine. Throttle bodies are typically operated electronically, but they still have TPS and MAP sensor inputs.

15.1.3 Components Associated with the Vehicle Speed in EVs

Electric scooters are powered by a battery, which impacts their performance and range on a charge. The engine is equally essential, and the quality and quantity of the power source substantially impact speed, torque, and hill ascending ability. The motor and batteries are connected via electric lines, and throttles are affixed for simple operation. The controller component enables the rider to regulate their performance, with instructions displayed on a screen and controls used to manipulate the brake and the throttle.

Modern motorcycles usually have motors integrated into the wheels, doing away with the need for a transmission. That provides the designation of the motors that are mounted in the tire axles. Stronger scooters sometimes have two motors, one for each tire. The scooter's most apparent characteristic is its wheels.

15.1.3.1 Throttle

Electric scooters use a throttle to regulate the scooter's speed. Throttles direct the scooter to accelerate at a specific speed. When the potentiometer is compressed, the controller transmits a signal to the controller, which then gives the motor more power. The pressure used determines the speed of the vehicle. Throttles are beneficial for various velocities, riding on rough surfaces, and extending battery life.

15.1.3.2 Motor

The electric scooter's motor, which transforms electrical energy into mechanical motion, is its central component. It is often brushless and manufactured with dependability and efficiency in mind. The scooter can move because of the motor's capacity. It is in control of accelerating and halting the wheels. The scooter's intended application determines the motor's size and capability. Scooters with high performance levels feature large motors that provide more torque and speed. The scooter's functionality is directly impacted by its motor capacity. The motor is connected to the wheels via a drivetrain. When engaged, the operator can choose to propel the vehicle forward or backward by rotating the wheels. The motor's speed and power output are controlled by the electronic speed controllers.

15.1.3.3 Controller

On electric scooters, controllers function as the connection between the motor, the battery, and the throttle and brake levers. When the toggle is pressed, a signal is sent to the controller via the cables. The controller then instructs the battery to release the appropriate amount of power for the motor. As soon as the scooter's electric brakes eliminate power, the motor will cease rotating.

Our goals are as follows:

- To construct a two-wheeler motor speed controller prototype that will improve the driver's hold on the two-wheelers and optimize the braking distance, which will lower the likelihood of a collision

- To construct and integrate a head-up display device into two-wheelers and eradicate blind spots, providing drivers a real-time rear view by minimizing the amount of time they spend distractedly gazing in the traditional mirrors

These devices can be incorporated into vehicles with internal combustion engines and those with battery power.

15.2 Problem Formulation

According to our research and observation, we have identified safety concerns for two-wheeler drivers. They are as follows:

15.2.1 Integration of Head-Up Display

As we know, in India, the number of two-wheeler drivers is more compared to any other automobile drivers. Prior to shifting lanes, the motorist must invest time examining both mirrors. Many of these locations are blind areas, which cause vehicles to drive into each other without realizing, resulting in collision. The accident rate is very significant in the case of two-wheeler drivers; their safety has been our concern. Our objective is to reduce the risk of accidents in two-wheeler drivers by incorporation of head-up displays.

15.2.2 Vehicle Speed Controller

The accident rate is also high in the case of two-wheeled vehicles; their safety has been our concern. When a two-wheeler approaches another vehicle or barrier, it takes the viewer around three to six seconds to observe and respond. The vehicle would have travelled 1/3 of the distance by this reaction time. As the vehicle approaches an obstacle or another vehicle, the likelihood of a collision increases, and the stopping distance increases in proportion to the speed of the vehicle. Our objective is to reduce the risk of accidents in two-wheeler drivers by incorporation of motor speed controllers.

To address these issues, we are implementing measures such as head-up displays and electronic motor speed controllers to enhance safety and reduce collision risks.

15.3 Methodology

Throttle systems in IC engines and electric vehicles regulate power delivery, enhancing efficiency and performance. Head-up displays enhance safety, demonstrating advanced technologies. Construction involves careful component selection for seamless functionality and optimal performance.

15.3.1 Components Used

- E-bike DC motor
- E-bike motor controller
- Battery
- Throttle unit
- Ultrasonic sensor
- Speed controller
- Servo motor
- Coupler
- Display unit (LCD)
- Car DVD-based motherboard

15.3.2 Construction and Working

The drive circuit of the system is represented in Figure 15.1 and its construction is established as mentioned below.

(a) Selecting the Bicycle:
  - Selection of a bicycle that was in good shape and could accommodate the necessary parts

(b) Addition of Components:
  - Positioning and securing the free wheel adapter on the hub
  - Insertion of additional free wheel after removing the back wheel

(c) Mounting the Motor:
  - Identification of motor mounting position on frame
  - Utilization of mounting plates or brackets and then welding of the motor and frame together

(d) Connecting Components:
  - Establishment of the appropriate chain length required to connect the free wheel and motor

- Alignment of the chain by properly placing and adjusting it on the motor and free wheel sprockets
- Connection of the battery pack to the speed controller, which is coupled with the servo motor
- The speed controller is coupled with the servo motor, which is controlled by the Arduino Uno microcontroller.
- The Arduino Uno microcontroller takes input from the ultrasonic sensor.

(e) Setting up the Transparent Display:
- Choose a front-tech car DVD-based motherboard with additional capabilities.
- Install the motherboard and connect it to the mirror LCD display.
- Test the functionality of the display to ensure it works properly.

(f) Installing the Backup Camera System:
- Connection of the DVD player-based motherboard to a camera installed at the back of the vehicle
- Identification of the best position for the camera to reduce blind spots effectively

(g) Motor Controller Selection:
- Selection of 24V motor controller by taking into consideration the several controllers available like 24V, 36V, and 48V motor controllers that are on the market, due to compatibility with speed controllers limited to 24V
- Selection of a compatible battery and motor for the 24V motor controller
- Opting for a speed controller which is capable of handling up to 24V to adjust resistance and regulate power to the motor efficiently

In general, an electric vehicle (EV) operates by turning on the electrical system, attaching the motor to the controller, transferring energy from the battery to the motor via the controller, and regulating the speed using the throttle. The electrical system is triggered by turning on the key, which permits electricity to travel from the battery to other elements. The controller, which regulates the passage of current from the battery to the motor, is powered by the primary battery cell. The driver may regulate the speed of the vehicle by modulating the throttle, which modifies the quantity of electricity sent to the motor. Circuit diagram is depicted in Figure 15.1.

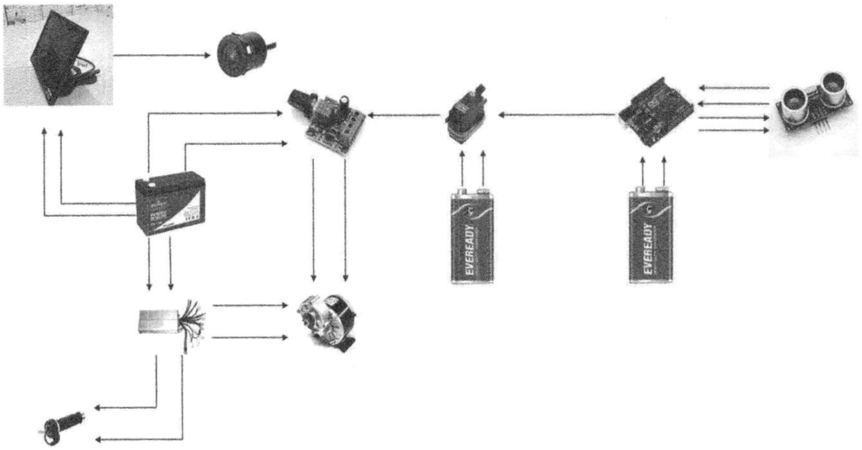

Figure 15.1 Circuit connections.

To ensure safety during setup, the speed modulating circuit requires numerous phases. First, the vehicle's electrical system is turned off, and the motor is disconnected from its controller. The switch is then flipped on, and jumper wires are connected to complete the circuit. An ultrasonic sensor detects obstructions and delivers the length of the signal to an Arduino UNO microcontroller. The Arduino UNO examines the time data and computes the distance to the barrier.

The Arduino UNO is fuelled by a 9V battery, so it can operate independently of the vehicle's electrical system. The Arduino UNO calculates the appropriate angle of rotation for the servo motor depending on the determined distance. The servo motor is mechanically connected to the speed controller via a coupler, allowing it to alter the speed controller's parameters.

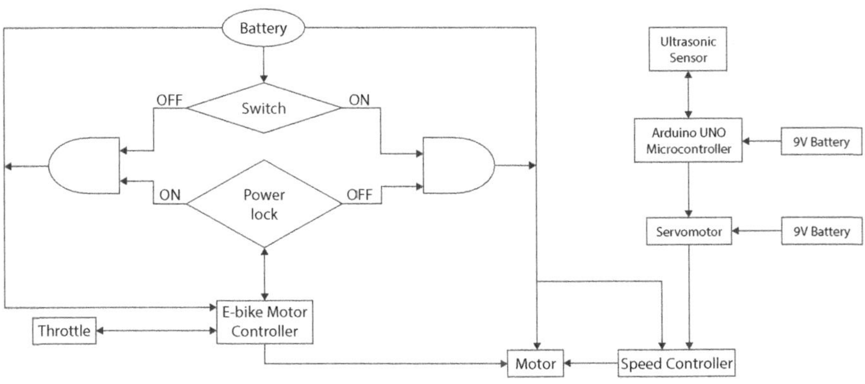

Figure 15.2 EV with speed controller circuit block diagram.

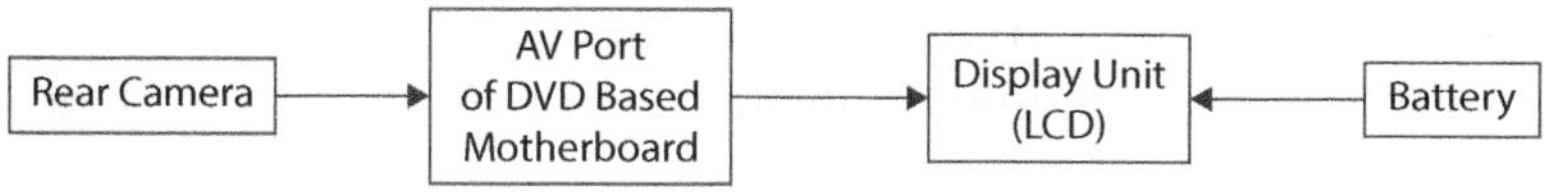

Figure 15.3 Display unit block diagram.

The decision making is followed as per the controller circuit block diagram represented in Figure 15.2.

The speed controller, which is powered by a 24V battery, regulates the motor's RPM (revolutions per minute). The servo motor modifies the speed controller's resistance and, as a result, modifies the motor's RPM when the Arduino UNO sends signals to it depending on the distance of obstacles.

The display device in this system is powered by a 24V battery, which provides the required electrical energy. It receives signals from a camera device linked to the motherboard's audio–video interface, which displays video footage of the vehicle's rear perspective. The display unit then interprets these signals and presents the video feed gathered by the camera unit on the screen. This design provides the driver visual aid by displaying the video data collected by the camera device. The display unit's functionality maintains the driver's safety throughout the procedure. The funtional block diagram of the display unit is represented in Figure 15.3.

15.4 Scope of the Project

To address the high accident rates among two-wheeler drivers in India, we can improvise and incorporate our project in IC engine vehicles and electric vehicles. The implementation could be as follows:

15.4.1 Implementation in IC Engines

Throttle Body Butterfly Valve Control for Combustion Engines

- The throttle body butterfly valve regulates air flow, air–fuel mixture, engine power, and speed.
- The proximity sensor generates sound waves and measures the time it takes for waves to travel through an obstruction and return.
- The throttle body actuator modulates the voltage of the butterfly valve based on distance data from the proximity sensor.
- The vehicle's speed is managed by altering the voltage supply to attain the required motor speed.

- The DC motor affixed to the throttle body rotates in response to voltage variations, influencing the butterfly valve's range of rotation.
- The throttle impacts the air–fuel mixture, optimizing engine power and speed and varying the air–fuel ratio or volumetric efficiency based on the distance of the obstacle.
- The ECU employs an ultrasonic sensor to measure the distance between the vehicle in front and itself, and then adjusts the voltage supply to accomplish the necessary motor speed.
- This method can optimize the vehicle's speed in accordance with the necessary braking distance and will contribute to the increase in fuel efficiency.
- If the ECU cannot be regulated directly, as ECU specifications and controls vary from vehicle to vehicle, an external controller can be used to reduce volumetric fuel efficiency.

15.4.2 Implementation in Electric Vehicle

Voltage Control and Throttle Body for Electric Vehicles

- The throttle body regulates current flow to the DC motor, a component of the electric powertrain.
- The controller modifies and governs the voltage provided to the DC motor by the data received by the ultrasonic sensor which is in turn used to calculate the distance of the approaching vehicle, as the motor's speed is directly correlated with the voltage.
- The speed control system monitors the vehicle's speed and modifies the voltage of the DC motor by regulating the throttle body's position.
- The controller examines the data collected by ultrasonic sensor and then regulates the voltage supply to the DC motor via throttle body, modulating the DC motor's RPM.
- The system's dynamic operation guarantees that the vehicle maintains speed and adjusts to traveling conditions or terrain changes by constantly changing the voltage based on real-time data from the ultrasonic sensor.

15.4.3 Head-Up Display

Head-up Displays for Motorcyclists

- Rider awareness is increased by a head-up display that provides real-time information about their surroundings. This reduces blind spots and enhances overall safety.
- Rearview information on a head-up display reduces distractions by allowing motorcyclists to concentrate on the road ahead while keeping a watch on the traffic behind them.
- With real-time rearview information right in front of them, motorcyclists may make better educated judgments while executing maneuvers like turning or changing lanes.
- In situations when traffic is heavy, this might be really useful.

15.5 Results and Discussions

15.5.1 Results

Figures 15.4(a) and 15.4(b) demonstrate that, in accordance with the results of our experiment, the speed of the vehicle and the motor's RPM were successfully decreased through the implementation of a speed controller.

15.5.2 Discussions

- The quality and transparency of head-up displays could potentially be improved with the use of appropriate materials and suitable electronic systems.
- With the aid of proper and compatible electronics, the motor can be directly integrated to the speed controller circuit, thereby eliminating the transition from EV to speed controller.
- It is possible to reduce the frequency of changing 9V batteries by using an appropriate auxiliary battery that can power the servo motor and microcontroller for an extended period of time.

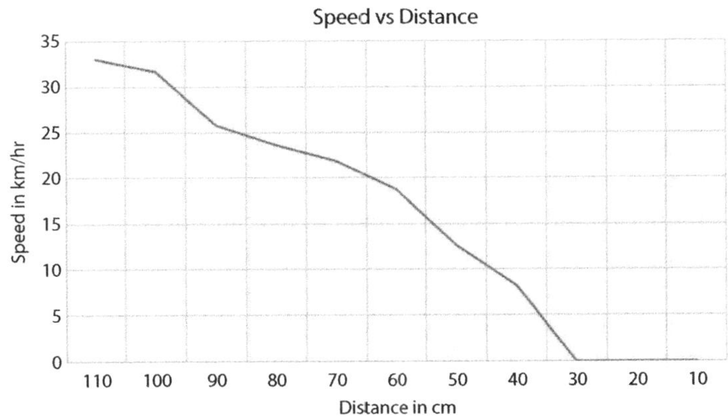

(**a**) Speed vs Distance

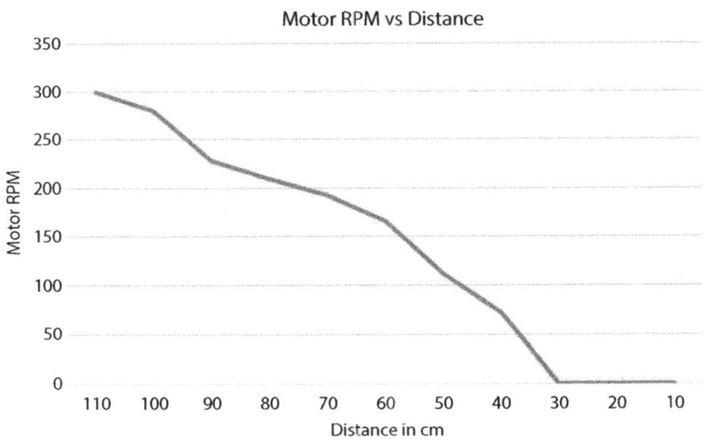

(**b**) Motor RPM vs Distance

Figure 15.4 Depiction of (a) vehicle's speed and (b) motor RPM as per the distance data.

15.6 Conclusion

In conclusion, it is possible to state that the addition of the motor speed controllers and the HUD technology are a considerable enhancement in two-wheeler drivers' safety especially in regions like the densely populated India where two-wheeled vehicles are widely used. All these innovations are directed toward the increase in the probability of the general safety on the roads and decrease of probability of accidents with the help of settlements of critical problems such as reaction time and blind zones.

Head-up displays ensure that rearview information is displayed in real time, hence minimizing distractions while at the same time allowing motorcyclists to have ample time to analyze their surrounding environment. Quick decisions have to be made in order to ensure safety within driving conditions; these include traffic congestion, changing lanes, and overtaking, among others. It is especially helpful in such points of use.

Furthermore, the utilization of motor speed controllers optimizes vehicle control and deceleration distance, thereby significantly decreasing the probability of collisions by improving the driver's capacity to react effectively to other vehicles or obstacles on the road.

As these technologies are versatile, they enable their implementation in both internal combustion engineered vehicles and electric vehicles, irrespective of the driving conditions. These technologies combined will effectively lessen the number of accidents in two-wheelers on the road as they quickly react to approaching vehicles or any other road barriers. In densely populated regions like India, we believe this is the need of the hour. As a result, this technology can efficiently contribute to increasing two-wheeler safety.

References

1. Hashim, M.S., Hamati, A.A., Mohd Hafzi, M.I., Shahriman, A.B., Ismail, A.H., Azmi, M.S., Zuradzman, M.R., Harun, A., Kamarrudin, N.S., Ibrahim, I., Faizi, M.K., Saad, M.A., Rojan, M.A., Determination of blind spot zone for Motorcycles. *IOP Conf. Ser.: Mater. Sci. Eng.*, 670, 1, 012075, 2019, Https://doi.org/10.1088/1757-899x/670/1/012075.
2. Mekata, Y., Ohtsubo, T., Matsuba, Y., Sugawara, D., Matsuda, M., Nakanishi, M., Effects of placing a CMS monitor to present side and rear view at the driver-centred position on drivers' rearward visual behaviour, cognitive load, and mental stress. *Int. J. Automot. Eng.*, 13, 4, 196–205, 2022, Https://doi.org/10.20485/jsaeijae.13.4_196.
3. Mao, Y., The design of car head-up display system. *IOP Conf. Ser.*, 729, 1, 012025, 2020, Https://doi.org/10.1088/1757-899x/729/1/012025.
4. Stamenković, Z., Tittelbach-Helmrich, K., Domke, J., Lorchner-Gerdaus, C., Anders, J., Sark, V., Masson, É., Sira, N., Rear view camera system for car driving assistance. *Proc. 28th International Conference On Microelectronics (MIEL 2012)*, Niš, Serbia, 13-16 MAY, 2012, Https://doi.org/10.1109/miel.2012.6222882.
5. Uyulan, Ç. and Arslan, E., Sliding Mode-based Traction Control System Design for Electric Scooter BLDCM through Field-Oriented Vector Control

Approach. *DEÜ FMD*, 25, 74, 433–450, 2023, Https://doi.org/10.20944/preprints202210.0274.v1.
6. Sharma, H., Tripathi, M., Kumar, A., Gaur, M.S., Embedded assistive stick for visually impaired persons, in: *Proc. 9th Int. Conf. Comput., Commun. Netw. Technol. (ICCCNT)*, pp. 1–6, Jul. 2018, doi: 10.1109/ICCCNT.2018.8493707.
7. Jarraya, S.K., Al-Shehri, W.S., Ali, M.S., Deep multilayer perceptron-based obstacle classification method from partial visual information: Application to the assistance of visually impaired people. *IEEE Access*, 8, 26612–26622, 2020, doi: 10.1109/ACCESS.2020.2970979.
8. Karkera, T. and Singh, C., Autonomous bot using machine learning and computer vision. *SN Comput. Sci.*, *2*, 4, 251, 2021.
9. Soans, R.V., Hegde, A., Singh, C., Kumar, A., Object tracking robot using adaptive color thresholding, in: *2017 2nd international conference on communication and electronics systems (ICCES)*, IEEE, pp. 790–793, 2017, October.
10. Gatti, R.R., Singh, C., Agrawal, R., Serrao, F.J. (Eds.), *Self-Powered Cyber Physical Systems*, John Wiley & Sons, Hoboken, USA, 2023.
11. Singh, C., Shetty, S.C., Badiger, M., Nischitha, A Study on Connected Cars–V2V Communication, in: *Modeling and Optimization of Optical Communication Networks*, pp. 251–265, 2023.
12. Singh, C. and Gatti, R., *Drone applications for industry 5.0*, IGI Global, Hershey, USA, 2024.
13. Gatti, R. and Singh, C., *Shaping the Future of Automation With Cloud-Enhanced Robotics*, IGI Global, Hershey, USA, 2024.

16

Voting Classifier-Based Machine Learning Technique for the Prediction of the Traffic Flow for the Intelligent Transportation System

Sandeep Kumar Hegde[1]*, Rajalaxmi Hegde[1] and Thangavel Murugan[2]

[1]*Department of Computer Science and Engineering, NMAM Institute of Technology, NITTE (Deemed to be University), Nitte, Karnataka, India*
[2]*Department of Information Systems & Security, College of Information Technology, United Arab Emirates University, AI Ain, Abu Dhabi, UAE*

Abstract
A vital function of the intelligent transportation system is traffic flow prediction. This is an exact forecast of the amount of traffic in a certain location on a given day in the future. The study of traffic forecasting helps to lessen traffic while promoting more affordable, safe, and efficient forms of transportation. Although conventional models rely on shallow networks, the number of vehicles has increased exponentially in recent years, making these standard machine learning methods unsuitable for the present situations. The proposed research presents a voting classifier-based machine learning algorithm (ML) that combines many ML techniques, including random forest, naive Bayes, logistic regression, and SVM. The experimental findings demonstrate that, in comparison to the conventional methods, the suggested voting classifier achieved greater accuracy and precision rate.

Keywords: Traffic prediction, voting classifier, machine learning, intelligent transportation system, random forest

**Corresponding author*: sandeep.hegdey@gmail.com

Rathishchandra R. Gatti and Chandra Singh (eds.) Digital Convergence in Intelligent Mobility Systems, (347–362) © 2025 Scrivener Publishing LLC

16.1 Introduction

Traffic congestion and pollution have grown to be serious problems as cities expand and more cars are driven. Thankfully, a lot of work has been put into creating intelligent transportation systems and doing research to address these issues during the past several years. Data science has gained relevance because it makes it possible to extract information, identify patterns, and derive insights from data for well-informed decision making [1]. As a subject that facilitates knowledge extraction, pattern recognition, and data-driven insights for informed decision making, data science has gained prominence in recent years. The rise in the population and the number of cars on the road have led to a variety of other difficulties, including a rise in fuel consumption, air and noise pollution, accidents, health concerns connected to stress, and time spent in traffic. Intelligent vehicle technologies that can efficiently manage and regulate traffic are therefore desperately needed [2]. These networks are essential to individual commuters as well as the local administration. By using traffic data for efficient decision making and traffic control, intelligent transport systems significantly contribute to the transformation of the transport sector [3]. Traffic congestion is one of India's biggest problems. The situation is extremely bad in a number of the country's largest cities. For instance, congested roads are a continual reminder of the terrible condition of the resort. There is no incentive for automobiles to use the roads correctly as they are routinely underpaid, which leads to traffic gridlock every time the need exceeds capacity. Two strategies that have been put out to lessen traffic through monetary rewards and disincentives are street estimation and interstate privatization. Unusual parkway occurrences like accidents or construction could reduce the route's capacity and create traffic bottlenecks. While a variety of transport modes may be impacted by congestion, most tactics concentrated on obstructing traffic on open roadways. Every moving vehicle coming to a stop for a lengthy period of time is likely to cause traffic congestion [4]. When they come across obstacles, drivers may get confused or even angry. When it comes to numbers, a clog is typically regarded to be the quantity of cars that travel through a stream or a certain area in a given amount of time. One prevalent traffic concern is poor highway condition brought on by increased traffic. The ridiculous traffic that results from people using private vehicles so frequently degrades the natural aspects of city streets. This usually leads to ongoing traffic problems. Our lives are now more clever, useful, and productive thanks to the innovative solutions brought forth by the Internet of Things. Smart cities are a few examples of these solutions. The intelligent transportation system (ITS), which has been incorporated into several applications to enhance mobility and transportation, is the foundation of smart cities. ITS seeks to address a variety of traffic-related problems, including congestion. In an effort to increase the precision of traffic flow estimates, new frameworks and models have been created quickly recently, coinciding with the development of machine learning techniques. In the transportation sector, traffic forecasting is an essential responsibility [5]. It has a big impact on traffic legislation and route planning, but it may also have a big impact on how roads are built. 1.35 million road traffic deaths were reported in 2016, according to the World Health Organization's (WHO) 2018 assessment of the state of road safety worldwide. As a result, studies on traffic forecasting are helpful in reducing traffic and guaranteeing more economical, safe travel [6].

One of the primary uses of ITS is traffic prediction, which seeks to precisely forecast the volume of traffic on a particular route in the future. Traffic prediction using machine learning algorithms has been quite successful in the last several years. By being able to identify trends in traffic data, machine learning algorithms may be able to more accurately predict traffic conditions and increase the effectiveness of transportation. Before machine learning-based traffic forecast gets more accurate, a number of issues still need to be resolved. The enormous amount of data needed to train the machine learning models is one of the primary obstacles. High-quality, historical, real-time data that include outside factors like weather, events, and road closures must be included. The intricate traffic patterns, which might vary depending on the day of the week, location, time of day, and season, provide another difficulty. Therefore, choosing the right ML model and features is essential to producing correct predictions. Neural networks, SVM, decision trees, and regression models are some of the machine learning methods utilized in traffic forecasting. Regression models may be used to simulate the link between traffic flow and other factors, such the weather and time of day. This study looked into supervised ensemble approaches for creating forecasting models for traffic jams on roads. In machine learning, ensemble techniques are used to strengthen many classifiers and enhance their overall performance. The primary goal of ensemble methods is to outperform base learners, which are more conventional machine learning techniques [7]. Recently, ensemble approaches have demonstrated greater performance in the realm of road traffic congestion. The goal of this work is to create an ensemble learning model utilizing a real-world road traffic flow dataset in order to assess the detrimental effects of traffic congestion, which can result in delays and a high rate of collisions on the roads, among other things. This study, which uses a real-life road traffic flow dataset from Kaggle repository, has the following primary goals:

(i) To use appropriate strategy to handle missing values and overfitting and underfitting of the model
(ii) To balance the data considered for training model using SMOTE algorithm
(iii) To accurately predict the traffic flow for the intelligent transportation system by building the voting classifier-based machine learning model using a combination of machine learning algorithms
(iv) To evaluate the predictive ability of the implemented model using the various state-of-the-art metrics

16.2 Literature Review

Numerous studies on advanced machine learning approaches have been conducted in the past with the goal of anticipating traffic. Nevertheless, due to the size of the dataset, the majority of these models' performance is still lacking because they employ shallow machine learning models. A framework for a smart traffic control system and an effective technique for identifying traffic congestion were suggested in [8]. The author of the research suggests a real-time video processing technique based on traffic volume statistics. Camera video clips are subjected to object recognition analysis in order to calculate the traffic density. The estimated vehicle density is compared with the densities of the other lanes on the route in order to efficiently manage the traffic signal. The technique makes use of RFID sensors to ensure law enforcement. Thus, any vehicle that disobeys traffic laws may be promptly pulled over. An upgrade on the current manual transportation control system is the aim of this study. Data is collected using an apparatus known as an infrared sensor. These sensors tell an embedded system how many automobiles are travelling by counting them. The red and green signal timings are predicted by the system using this data. This article also discussed the automated traffic control system, which has set times for red and green lights. In [9], a novel hybrid machine learning-based approach for forecasting vehicle traffic flow was introduced. Two original, reasonably priced methods were used for this project. While hardware aid was used in the creation of one of the approaches, it was not used in the other. It counts the number of cars on each route using computer vision. Based on the number of automobiles, the system calculates the proper length for green signals and the duration for red signals. The existing fixed-time, predefined traffic system may be replaced with a dynamically controlled one with the aid of this fully computerized technology. A hybrid machine learning framework was implemented in [10] for the study and performance modeling of a traffic forecasting system. This research provides a unique strategy to anticipate vehicle traffic flow and generate accurate traffic predictions by utilizing a hybrid machine learning-based methodology. The suggested approach improves traffic flow prediction by combining two machine learning techniques: Xtreme Machine Learning and the Long Short-Term Memory (LSTM) network. The system integrates weather, event, and road closure data from the past and present. The recommended course of action may be utilized to enhance traffic management, reduce congestion, and increase the overall efficacy of the transportation network. Deep learning algorithms were used to classify network traffic [11]. To do this, preparing network traffic resulted in the creation of several packet-based datasets. To classify network traffic, convolutional neural networks (CNN) and residual networks (ResNet) were also used [12]. Five deep learning models were trained using these strategies. Using the recall factor of CNN and ResNet deep learning models, the performance of packet-based datasets in network traffic categorization was assessed. The results showed how well deep learning models worked for classifying network traffic. Network traffic was categorized using a brand-new semi-supervised learning approach [13]. The suggested approach was predicated on a unique label propagation mechanism and the x-means clustering algorithm. The classification accuracy of the proposed technique was assessed in this study using the Moore dataset. An 85% classification accuracy was obtained using the suggested method. In [14] a novel pattern-matching real-time traffic classification system was proposed. This method matched the characteristics of the real-time network traffic using pattern matching. The suggested method yielded a classification accuracy of 89%. This outcome showed how effective this method is at learning network traffic classifiers with partially labeled data. In the near future, a semi-supervised feature selection method will be employed to enhance the suggested strategy.

Furthermore, the program's implementation efficiency was significantly enhanced by the use of the parallel computing structure known as Spark and the distributed messaging technology known as Kafka [15]. The results of the tests showed that the suggested strategy did well in terms of accuracy. Various supervised algorithms were analyzed to address the problem of Internet traffic categorization [16]. The feature subset was chosen using a feature set that had 266 features. There were only eight characteristics chosen from the provided subset. The feature selection method had decreased the amount of calculation time needed for the framework's training.

PSO technique was employed to enhance the network classification algorithms that are already in use [17]. The semi-supervision learning technique has also been established in this study. This method resolved the time and efficiency problems. With supervised learning, these problems could not be disregarded. In addition, a framework for classifying network traffic was created to improve the current algorithm [18]. According to the obtained test results, the PSO-optimized KNN algorithm demonstrated a faster rate of convergence than the KNN method. A classification strategy based on ensemble feature selection was suggested in [19]. The suggested method increased the large-scale unbalanced network traffic's categorization efficiency. The frequency matrix was produced using many data sets and a supervised machine learning method. It has been mentioned that dataset support may be used to choose the ideal feature set. The effectiveness of the ensemble feature selection strategy was tested in this work using the dataset provided by Moore of Cambridge. The results of the tests demonstrated the unique method's superiority over a general supervised machine learning algorithm. The C4.5 decision tree is a widely used supervised classifier [20]. Network traffic classification was the primary use for this classifier. Nevertheless, this classifier's performance decreased as the number of data increased. An open source cloud computing technology was the Hadoop platform. This strategy performed well with large amounts of data. Therefore, handling huge data was the primary use of this method. Compared to the C4.5 methods, the new algorithm was easier to understand. The recommended method was similar to the Hadoop architecture. This technique was called the C4.5 decision tree algorithm. The test results demonstrated that the modified approach not only ran quicker but also improved computation accuracy.

A redundant window-based optimal feature subset finding method for feature selection was proposed in [21]. The feature selection process has been carried out using the proposed algorithm. Finding pertinent characteristics was the suggested algorithm's primary goal. The feature reduction method was applied in this study to get rid of the unnecessary features. The technique had integrated Window redundancy with a parallel computing framework called Spark. This phenomenon significantly increased the algorithm's efficiency. The results of the tests showed that the accuracy and scalability of the suggested method were good. The suggested method increased feature selection and traffic classification's implementation efficiency. For machine learning models, there are several categorization techniques that are based on various viewpoints. Furthermore, research [10] shows that linear regression models work well. The forecasting technique offered by the authors combines time correlation coefficients with linear regression. Road network spatiotemporal relationships are the subject of linear regression, which may also be used to forecast future events. Each model was integrated with many traffic data, including upstream, current traffic, and historical average.

Tree-based technique, integrated stepwise variable selection, and linear regression are used in [22]. The authors worked around the intersection problem by using cross-validation (CV). According to [23], the k-nearest neighbor (KNN) model is a data-driven, non-parametric regression technique. The KNN model uses the K data to predict the value of the next period by finding the k-nearest neighbors who share the current variable value. In addition, the proposed study identified four primary challenges that need to be addressed: (i) choosing a suitable state vector, (ii) determining a distance measure, (iii) creating a prediction, and (iv) keeping up with the prospective neighbor information. In [24], the traffic flow was predicted at various intervals of prediction using the KNN model. To improve the K nearest neighbors selection process, this work [25] employed the correlation coefficient distance as the distance metric to find the better related neighbors. In [26], a MapReduce-based KNN was employed to forecast traffic flow. Additionally, the authors used distance weighted voting to lessen the effect of K's amount. The literature has assessed a wide range of strategies. The SVM model served as the foundation for the live traffic estimate system in [24]. However, SVM finds it difficult to manage a network problem when there is a lot of traffic. Additionally, grid search necessitates a significantly larger initial outlay of funds in order to ascertain the appropriate hyper-parameters in contrast to KNN or regression models [27].

16.3 Methodology

The primary goal of the proposed research is to estimate traffic flow using a machine learning model based on voting classifiers. An ML technique called a voting classifier makes predictions about a class or output depending on which class has the highest probability of becoming the output. It gains experience by being trained on a variety of models. In the suggested article, vote classifier is developed by applying ML techniques: random forest, naive Bayes, logistic regression, and SVM. The dataset obtained from the Kaggle repository is used to conduct the experimental research. In its initial state, the dataset could have included undesired features, noise, and outliers. In order to eliminate outliers and unnecessary characteristics from the dataset, the gathered dataset will be preprocessed. The interquartile range (IQR) notion is used to remove the dataset's outliers. Z score normalization is used to normalize the entire dataset. The dataset is subjected to a correlation analysis to see whether there is a relationship between traffic volume and a certain day or time of day. The voting classifier-based machine learning model's architectural design is displayed in Figure 16.1.

The architectural diagram for the work being proposed is shown in Figure 16.1. In the proposed work, the dataset is imposed on the voting classifier-based machine learning model in order to use the predictability of various machine learning methods, as was covered in the previous section. Exploratory data analysis is done as part of the data preparation to determine how the different elements of the dataset relate to one another. An unbalanced dataset increases the likelihood that the ML model will produce biased prediction results by taking majority class into account. In order to avoid the class imbalance issue, the dataset is balanced by applying the synthetic minority over sampling technique (SMOTE) algorithm. In the proposed work, the issue of model overfitting or underfitting is handled by performing the 10 fold cross validation technique. The proposed

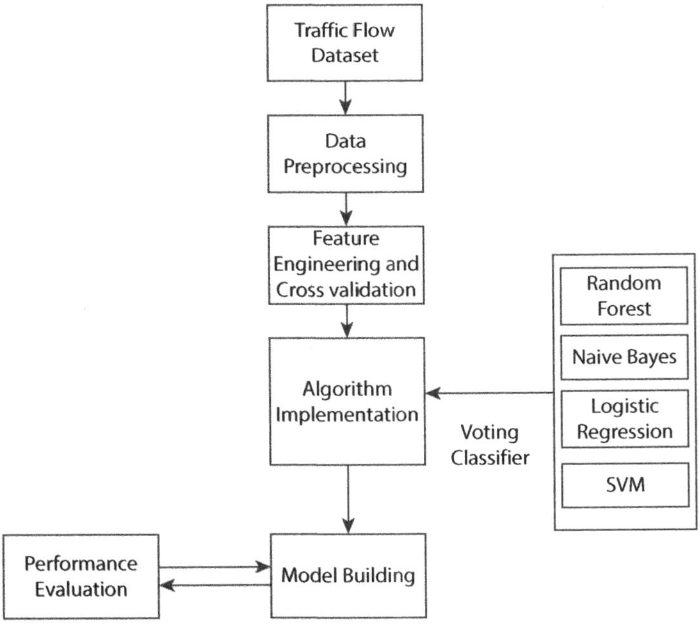

Figure 16.1 Proposed architecture diagram.

work filtered essential features from the dataset using genetic algorithm (GA). The genetic algorithm is heuristic based algorithm which is inspired by the evolution theory of nature. The considered dataset is initially imposed on the GA. The GA will apply crossover and mutation operations on the features of the dataset to generate offspring, so moving on to the next generation. The method selects those features who are most suitable to be the most likely to procreate into the next generation, much like natural selection. The features extracted by the GA will be further applied on the proposed ML algorithm. The predictive ability of the proposed model is validated using various metrics such as ROC, true positive rate, true negative rate, confusion matrix, recall, F1 rate, accuracy, and precision. The experimental investigation revealed that the proposed approach attained a higher accuracy rate in predicting the traffic compared to traditional approaches. The section below discusses about the experimental results obtained through the proposed approach.

16.4 Experimental Results

By merging the predictive ability of several independent classifiers, the ensemble voting classifier is formed that raises the overall prediction accuracy of the ML model. An ensemble voting classifier undergoes training on a dataset of traffic situations utilizing a variety of input elements, including traffic flow measurements, weather information, and time of day, in order to anticipate traffic.

To determine the association between the data, exploratory data analysis is done on the dataset, as was covered in the section above as a first step.

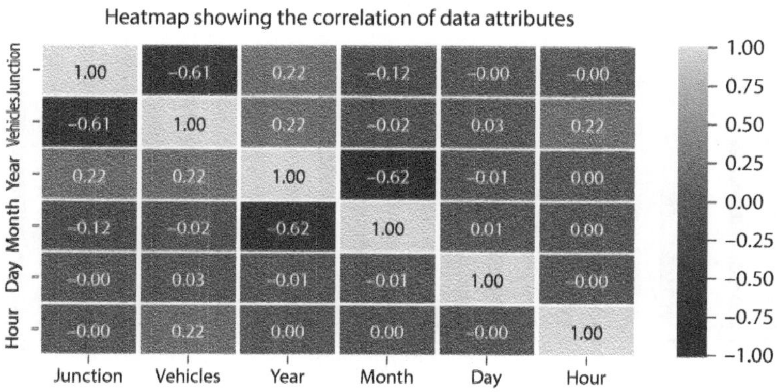

Figure 16.2 Correlational analysis on considered dataset.

Figure 16.2 shows the correlation analysis among the various features considered in the dataset. The average traffic analysis by day of the week is shown in Figure 16.3. The statistic indicates that there will be greater traffic during the weekdays than on the weekends.

The hourly study of average traffic is shown in Figure 16.4. The number suggests that there will be higher traffic in the morning from 10 to 12 and in the evening from 7 to 8 hours of the clock.

Figure 16.5 shows the traffic volume over time. According to the image, average traffic increased throughout the course of the year. Compared to the present, there was less traffic in 2015.

The average traffic volume based on different trends is shown in Figure 16.6. The aforementioned chart shows that traffic peaks during seasonal periods, whereas traffic decreases during off-season periods. Additionally, this data study shows that between 2015 and 2017, there were more automobiles on the road.

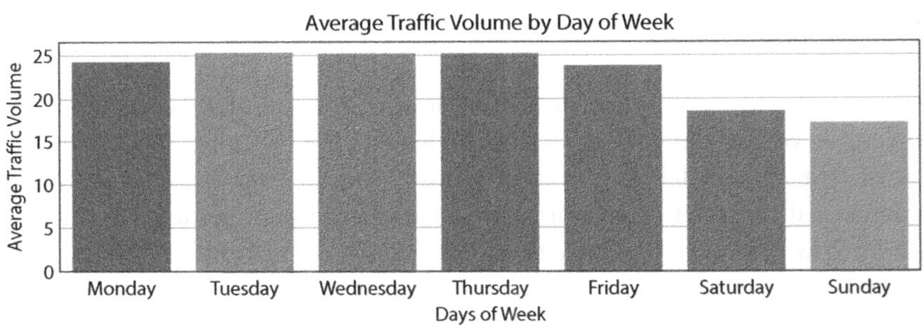

Figure 16.3 Exploratory analysis on average volume of traffic during day of week.

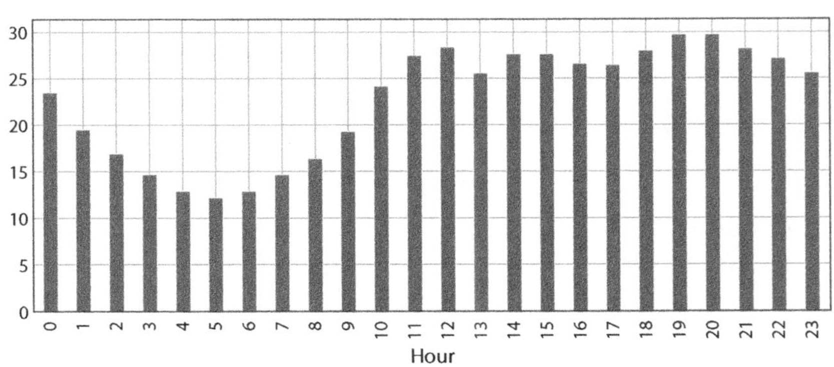

Figure 16.4 Exploratory analysis on average volume of traffic by hour.

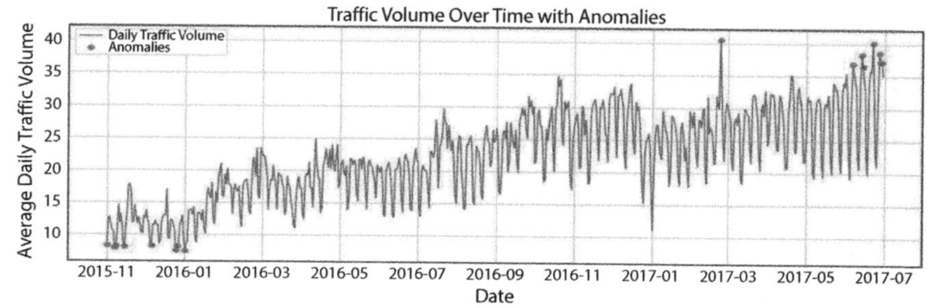

Figure 16.5 Exploratory analysis on average volume of traffic analysis over period of time.

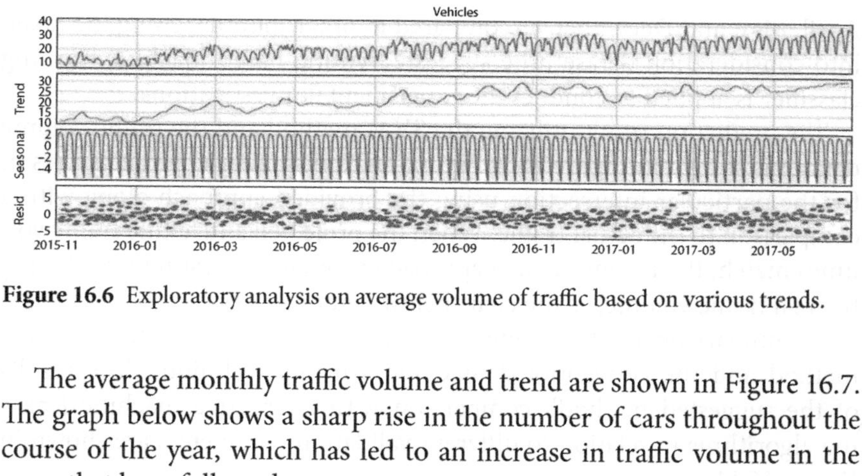

Figure 16.6 Exploratory analysis on average volume of traffic based on various trends.

The average monthly traffic volume and trend are shown in Figure 16.7. The graph below shows a sharp rise in the number of cars throughout the course of the year, which has led to an increase in traffic volume in the years that have followed.

The examination of monthly traffic volume in relation to the average number of cars is shown in Figure 16.8. The figure below shows that there is an increase in traffic volume throughout the holiday season, specifically in

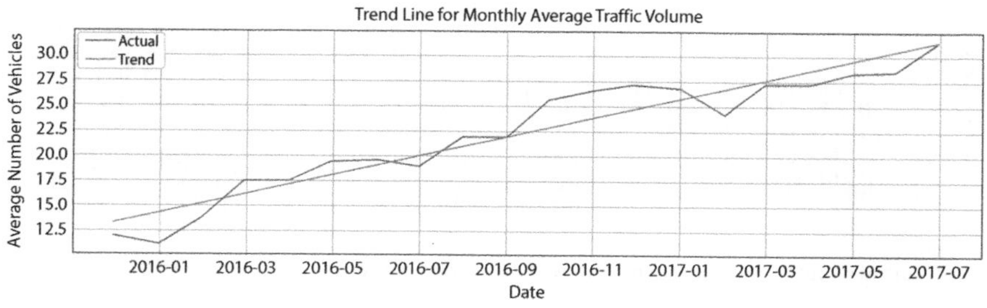

Figure 16.7 Exploratory analysis on average number of vehicles and traffic volume trend.

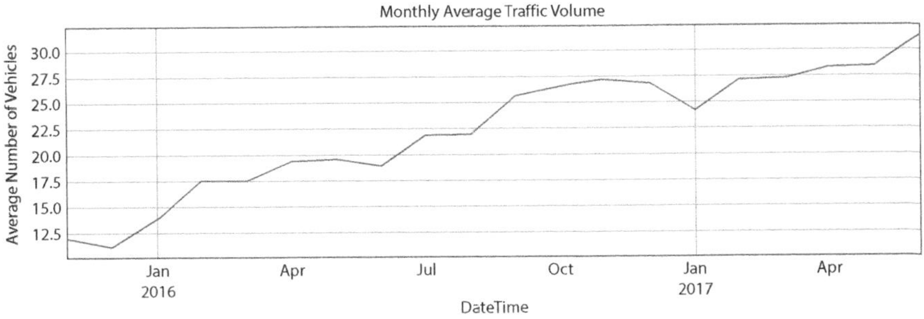

Figure 16.8 Exploratory analysis on average number of vehicles and month wise traffic analysis.

April, May, and December, as compared to other months. Using the taken into consideration dataset, the suggested voting-based machine learning classifier is applied to conduct the experimental investigations.

The prediction result utilizing the SVM method and the traffic volume dataset is shown in Figure 16.9. Figure 16.10 displays the projected result for the particular intersection using the provided approach along with a comparison to the actual traffic. When the projected and actual traffic volumes match, the recommended approach is often successful in predicting the real traffic volume, as the chart below demonstrates.

A comparison is also made between the outcome of the suggested method and the conventional machine learning technique. The results of the suggested method's comparison with alternative machine learning algorithms in relation to different validation parameters are shown in Figure 16.11.

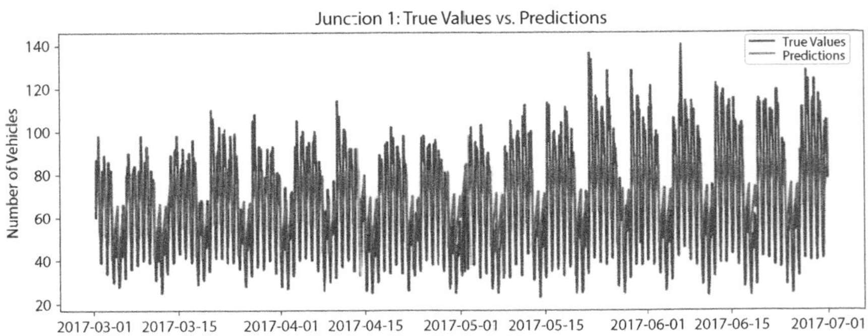

Figure 16.9 Result analysis on true value versus predictions on Junction 1 using SVM model.

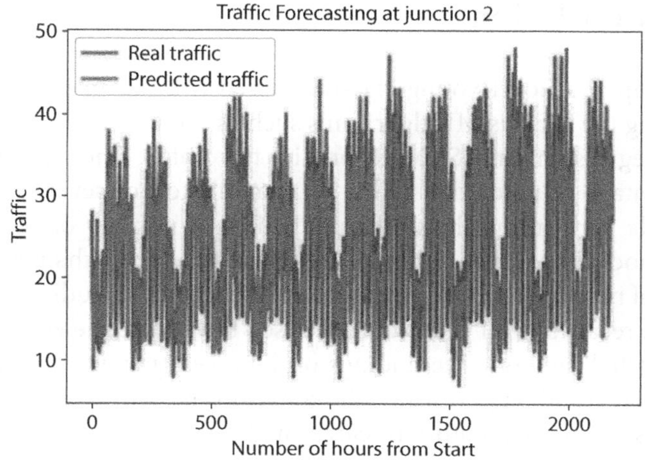

Figure 16.10 Result analysis on real traffic versus predicted traffic.

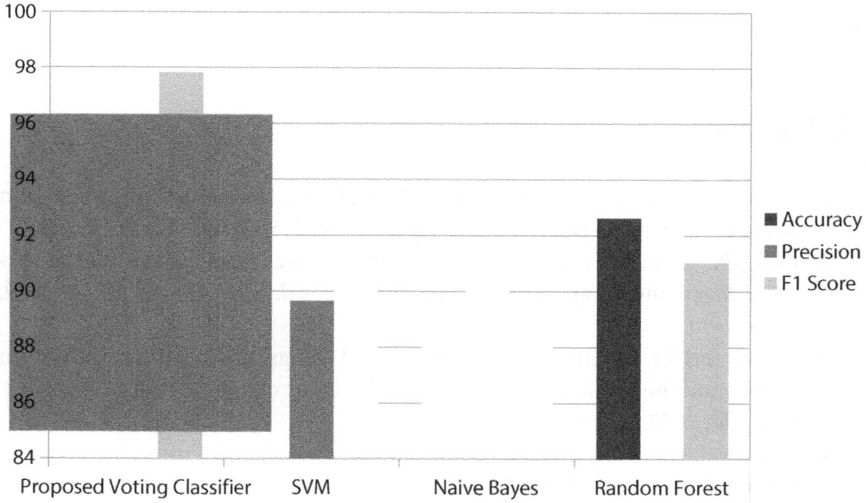

Figure 16.11 Comparison of prediction result with machine learning algorithms.

It can be concluded from Figure 16.11 that the proposed voting classifier achieved higher results in terms of various validation parameters such as accuracy, F1 score, and precision rate. So it can be concluded that the proposed approach can be applied successfully in predicting the traffic volume compared to the traditional ML approaches.

16.5 Conclusion

In this paper, a novel voting classifier-based ML has been proposed by combining the various ML algorithms such as random forest, naive Bayes, logistic regression, and SVM to predict the traffic. The algorithm took the advantage of predictive ability of combination of several ML classifiers while performing the traffic prediction. A number of conventional ML methods are used to compare the suggested approach's performance. A range of machine learning performance indicators, including prediction, accuracy, recall, and F1 score, are also used to validate the effectiveness of the suggested method. The findings of the investigation indicate that the suggested method outperformed the conventional ML algorithms in terms of the desired results. Future research might look at approaches for identifying and classifying various traffic occurrences (such as accidents, road closures, and construction) using voting classifiers trained on historical incident data. Furthermore, the classifier might be utilized to recommend relevant responses or interventions based on the nature and severity of the occurrence.

References

1. Hossin, M.A., *et al.*, Big Data-Driven Public Policy Decisions: Transformation Toward Smart Governance. *SAGE Open*, 13, 4, 21582440231215123, 2023.
2. Deng, X., *et al.*, A review of 6G autonomous intelligent transportation systems: Mechanisms, applications and challenges. *J. Syst. Archit.*, 142, 102929, 2023.
3. Liu, C. and Ke, L., Cloud assisted Internet of things intelligent transportation system and the traffic control system in the smart city. *J. Control Decis.*, 10, 2, 174–187, 2023.
4. Bhardwaj, A., *et al.*, Understanding sudden traffic jams: From emergence to impact. *Dev. Eng.*, 8, 1001055, 2023.
5. Gamel, S.A., *et al.*, Exploring the effects of pandemics on transportation through correlations and deep learning techniques. *Multimed. Tools Appl.*, 83, 1–22, 2023.
6. Torbaghan, M.E., *et al.*, Understanding the potential of emerging digital technologies for improving road safety. *Accid. Anal. Prev.*, 166, 1065435, 2022.
7. Ganaie, M.A., *et al.*, Ensemble deep learning: A review. *Eng. Appl. Artif. Intell.*, 115, 1051515, 2022.

8. Kumar, N., *et al.*, Deep reinforcement learning-based traffic light scheduling framework for sdn-enabled smart transportation system. *IEEE Trans. Intell. Transp. Syst.*, 23, 3, 2411–2421, 2021.
9. Wang, Z., *et al.*, An improved hybrid highway traffic flow prediction model based on machine learning. *Sustainability*, 12, 20, 8298, 2020.
10. Boukerche, A. and Wang, J., Machine learning-based traffic prediction models for intelligent transportation systems. *Comput. Netw.*, 181, 107530, 2020.
11. Azhar, A., *et al.*, Detection and prediction of traffic accidents using deep learning techniques. *Cluster Comput.*, 26, 1, 477–493, 2023.
12. Ma, X., *et al.*, EETC: An extended encrypted traffic classification algorithm based on variant resnet network. *Comput. Secur.*, 128, 1031755, 2023.
13. Jin, Z., *et al.*, A federated semi-supervised learning approach for network traffic classification. *Int. J. Netw. Manage.*, 33, 3, e2222, 2023.
14. Shanmugavel, A.B., *et al.*, A Novel Ensemble Based Reduced Overfitting Model with Convolutional Neural Network for Traffic Sign Recognition System. *Electronics*, 12, 4, 926, 2023.
15. Hajji, T., *et al.*, Optimizations of Distributed Computing Processes on Apache Spark Platform. *IAENG Int. J. Comput. Sci.*, 50, 2, 422–434, 2023.
16. Liu, W., *et al.*, Multiclass imbalanced and concept drift network traffic classification framework based on online active learning. *Eng. Appl. Artif. Intell.*, 117, 1056075, 2023.
17. Redhu, P. and Kumar, K., Short-term traffic flow prediction based on optimized deep learning neural network: PSO-Bi-LSTM. *Physica A*, 625, 129001, 2023.
18. Asha, A., *et al.*, Optimized RNN-based performance prediction of IoT and WSN-oriented smart city application using improved honey badger algorithm. *Measurement*, 210, 1125055, 2023.
19. Dai, G., Tang, J., Luo, W., Short-term traffic flow prediction: An ensemble machine learning approach. *Alexandria Eng. J.*, 74, 467–480, 2023.
20. Cherfi, A., Nouira, K., Ferchichi, A., MC4. 5 decision tree algorithm: an improved use of continuous attributes. *Int. J. Comput. Intell. Stud.*, 9, 1–2, 4–17, 2020.
21. Rajakani, M., Kavitha, R.J., Ramachandran, A., Adaptive Window Based 3-D Feature Selection for Multispectral Image Classification Using Firefly Algorithm. *Comput. Syst. Sci. Eng.*, 44, 1, 265–280, 2023.
22. Moumen, I., Abouchabaka, J., Rafalia, N., Adaptive traffic lights based on traffic flow prediction using machine learning models. *Int. J. Electr. Comput. Eng. (IJECE)*, 13, 5, 5813–5823, 2023.
23. Ali, A., *et al.*, A k-nearest neighbours based ensemble via optimal model selection for regression. *IEEE Access*, 8, 132095–1321055, 2020.
24. Toan, T.D. and Truong, V.-H., Support vector machine for short-term traffic flow prediction and improvement of its model training using nearest neighbor approach. *Transp. Res. Rec.*, 2675, 4, 362–373, 2021.

25. Cunningham, P. and Delany, S.J., k-Nearest neighbour classifiers-A Tutorial. *ACM Comput. Surv. (CSUR)*, 54, 6, 1–25, 2021.
26. Wang, J., Vehicular Traffic Flow Prediction Model Using Machine Learning-Based Model, Diss., Université d'Ottawa/University of Ottawa, 2021.
27. Yang, L. and Shami, A., On hyperparameter optimization of machine learning algorithms: Theory and practice. *Neurocomputing*, 415, 295–316, 2020.

17

Influence of Feature Selection Techniques for Social Media Data Analysis (Text and Image)

Aruna Bajpai* **and Yogesh Kumar Gupta**

Department of Computer Science, Banasthali Vidyapith, Jaipur, Rajasthan, India

Abstract

Social media is a web application where a significant amount of data has contributed by the users. Therefore, social media has been used in various data-driven application developments. The data available on social media can be images, text, or video. Additionally, their processing needs different approaches to be utilized. In this paper, we are providing three main contributions (1) conducting a survey on social media-based research in recent years (2) providing an overview of different feature selection techniques used for processing the different formats of data i.e. text and images (3) conducting an experimental evaluation of feature selection techniques and their effectiveness on processing the social media content. In order to analyze the text feature selection techniques we consider Word Count Vectorizer, TF-IDF, Word2vector, POS Tagging, and Bi-gram. Similarly, for image-based feature analysis, we involve the Sobal operator, LBP, and a combination of Sobal and LBP, and Sobal, LBP, and Color feature. The experiments are conducted on two popular datasets obtained from Kaggle for social media-based images and text. Additionally for classifying the extracted features from the datasets are utilized an artificial neural network for training and validation. Based on the experimental results we found that for classifying the social media text the TF-IDF-based features are far superior to other implemented feature selection approaches on unknown samples. Additionally for image-based classification, the combination of edge, color, and texture features is providing more accurate results.

***Keywords*:** Feature selection, image and text classification, machine learning, social media, social media text classification, social media image classification

**Corresponding author*: arunabajpai20@gmail.com

Rathishchandra R. Gatti and Chandra Singh (eds.) Digital Convergence in Intelligent Mobility Systems, (363–378) © 2025 Scrivener Publishing LLC

17.1 Introduction

Social media is one of the popular and new sources of user-generated data. Therefore the social media data will have significant dimensions of opportunities. In social media, data may contain text, images, or video for sharing information. Using social media data we can develop different kinds of applications, which will provide ease and assistance in our daily lives. In such a kind of application development, machine learning technology has played an essential role. In automated data analysis using machine learning algorithms the data preparation is an important step, which involves data pre-processing and feature selection techniques.

In this context, we are motivated to explore the techniques for extracting features from social media text and image data. However, the process of feature selection can be different for the different formats of data but the machine learning technique will be the same. Therefore, using the feature selection technique we need to transform the data in such a manner that the data will be easily accepted and processed by the machine learning algorithms. In this paper, we include the study of different feature selection techniques for extracting meaningful insights from text data as well as image data. Additionally, we also utilize these features with the popular machine learning algorithm namely artificial neural network for training and validation. Finally, the performance of the feature selection techniques is measured and compared to identify the appropriate technique for utilization in future work.

17.2 Literature Review

Social media is a platform for user-based data generation; this data can be used in serving a number of applications. However, there are a number of issues exist related to social media content analysis, among them data heterogeneity, Validity of contents, and Credibility of information sources are major. In order to design an effective and accurate machine learning model for solving these issues we need a new solution strategy, which may able to deal with heterogeneous data, identify the validity of contents, and analyze the credibility of information sources. Table 17.1 shows the list of considered research articles. Table highlights key research area, results, dataset used and algorithms.

In this context, we aimed to employ machine learning techniques for solving the mentioned issues. Therefore, in this section, we present a review of recent development using social media content analysis. In this

Table 17.1 Literature summary.

No.	Research direction	Offers	Results	Data set	Algorithms
1	Identifying fake profiles on Facebook	Survey of 500 users, A prototype	98% Accuracy	Facebook	Bayesian classifier
2	On fake profile detection	A survey of the latest technical work	NA	NA	NA
3	How fake identities created and withstand aggressive and bigoted dialogs	Sociotechnical and conversational practices that offers new styles	How hate is created and distributed	11 Danish Facebook pages	Investigation of text posts, about, comments and images
4	Fake accounts to detect and deactivate them	Deep learning model to classify accounts	93.63% Accuracy	Instagram	Deep Learning
5	Considering 'distrust of digital politics'	Movement coalitions and explores media conflicts	Technology can be used as political tool	Digital media	Theoretical
6	Classifying hate speech from unpleasant semantic	Crowd-sourced lexicon to collect hate keywords	Classification of hate speech from offensive	Twitter	Multi-class classifier
7	Hate speech posted to social media	Examine origins of free speech and overview in US, Jurisprudence for imposing limitations	Real-world examples, addressed when limitations are appropriate	Facebook	NA
8	Spreading hate speech	Assumed that social media contains higher amount of hate speeches; also tests ideas to deal hate speech to avoid political talk	(a) Social media hate speech is very high (b) relationship among hate speech and political talk	Survey performed on U.S. Elections	Theoretical analysis

(*Continued*)

Table 17.1 Literature summary. (*Continued*)

No.	Research direction	Offers	Results	Data set	Algorithms
9	Social media hate dialog recognition	Analyze ML algorithms for deciding in social media hate dialog	Reviewed such as ensemble and deep learning for finding gaps and challenges	NA	Inform users with steps of hate speech detection, weakness, and strengths
10	Explore technique to prevent spread of Hate dialogs in social platforms	Hate dialog identification to the quarantining the hate dialogs	Provides a balance of freedom of expression and censorship	Facebook, Twitter, and Google	Law enforcement
11	Early disease outbreaks prediction and monitoring	Review trends, and ML based text classification used by surveillance systems	24% Studies focused on influenza; 64% used Twitter as data source	Twitter data	SVM (33%) is most used ML algorithm for text classification
12	Disaster from social media posts	ML pipeline to uncover disaster corresponding to different locations	Mapping of events with time and space with high accuracy	Data set of Twitter for 2017 Hurricane	Named Entity, fusion, BERT, graph-clustering
13	Disaster management suffer from high temporal lags and spatial resolution	Social media data evaluation for finding disaster footprints	Earthquake is accurately identified	Analyze social media	ML techniques
14	Social media is introducing new method of violence and aggression	ML techniques to deal with social media aggressive conduct	Issues, challenges, and new research directions		

(*Continued*)

Table 17.1 Literature summary. (*Continued*)

No.	Research direction	Offers	Results	Data set	Algorithms
15	Cyber risk is increasing with the progress of digital economic activity	Model which is utilizing big data analytics and ML to identify the cyber risks	The accuracy rate of 96.73%	CVE and Twitter	Artificial neural network (ANN)
16	Understand behavior and favorites of buyers	Forecast buyers decision	Indicating WEKA performs better		WEKA
17	Using large amount of unstructured data simulating actionable insights	Utilizing ML for producing actionable insights	Outlooks and philosophy to improve social platform		
18	Identify contagious illnesses by analyzing social platforms data	Contagious illnesses is defined as a catching bug	Precision 0.77, recall 0.68, and F1 score 0.724	Twitter data Aug 2012-May 2013	Unsupervised sentiment analysis model
19	Discover the polarity in Arabic content	Applied ML on social media data to recover orientation	Review the popular tools	Twitter	SVM and K-Mean
20	Use of Social media to identify emergency help during disaster	Tweets are categorizing into disaster type	F1 scores of over 0.86	Tweets during Hurricane Houston	CNN, SVM, and MLP on a unigrams and POS
21	Customers review about a firm	Developed a two-stage system to deal with customer review	Binary classifier provides accurate results	Binary classification	Social media review dataset

(*Continued*)

Table 17.1 Literature summary. (*Continued*)

No.	Research direction	Offers	Results	Data set	Algorithms
22	Offensive language identification from Urdu and Roman text	Perform abusive language detection	Accuracy for Urdu 96.2% and for Roman Urdu 91.4%	Large dataset with Urdu comments	NB, SVM, IBK, JRip, CNN, LSTM, BLSTM, CLSTM
23	Fake news	-	False headlines are perceived less accurate	Facebook and others	Theoretical analysis
24	Fake news	Plans to use in Facebook and other to deal with false news	Rumors had higher shares than verified news	Zika based news	-
25	Fake news	Understand health-related rumors	99.4% accuracy	Fake posts	Logistic classifier
26	Fake news	Fake news Popularity in light of communication	Online belief, self-expose, missing out fear, and fake news sharing	1022 social media users data	Social comparison, rational psychology, communication, and self-determination
27	Fake news sharing behavior	Examines links of social media wrong use	Potential to differentiate false news	Datasets measuring users trust level	Comparative analysis over profile features
28	Detecting fake news	Correlation between profiles and fake news	-	-	-

review, we have involved 28 research papers, which are based on machine learning is depicted in Table 17.1 and social media data. These articles are describing the different applications for identifying fake news, fake profiles, disease outbreak detection, and disaster management. In this review, we found that social media data is much useful and has an appropriate combination with machine learning techniques to serve humans. It is also found the diverse set of information needs a specific kind of methodology to deal with the challenge, not a single method can able to solve all the kinds of problems related to the data analysis. Therefore we need to explore the different techniques which are dedicated to utilizing the different formats of data and can be utilized with machine learning techniques.

17.3 Proposed Work

In this section, we provide an overview of the different feature selection techniques which can be utilized with social media data analysis for image and text data.

17.3.1 Text Feature Analysis

The text is mostly available in an unstructured manner; therefore the handling of text requires an additional process to make use of the machine learning algorithms. Therefore, before utilizing the machine learning algorithm with the text data we need to preprocess steps and feature selection techniques for transforming the data from an unstructured format to a structured format. In this section, we are discussing some text feature selection techniques which are frequently utilized in text analysis.

Word Count Vectorizer: The Word Count Vectorizer (WCV) is used to convert text documents into sparse matrix representations based on the token count. If we do not provide a dictionary additionally and use the WCV as the default setting then the number of features will be equal to the size of the total token found by analyzing the text documents.
Term Frequency–Inverse Document Frequency (TF-IDF): This method is very similar to WCV, which transforms raw documents into TF-IDF features. This method includes a more refined matrix based on weighted tokens in the feature set. Therefore we have the ability to refine the features more as compared to WCV.
Word2vector: That method is frequently used with deep learning-based models for preparing the word embedding mapping for selecting the features from the row text document. The method contains the tokenization, mapping, and then sequencing for preparing the word embedding vector.
POS tagging: The POS tagging is a part of the NLTK library for converting the text sentences into the part of speech sequence. This vector contains the count of different parts of speech tags as the feature set.
Bi-gram: The word "Bi" represent the number two, in the similar ways a bigram is a variant of text feature n-gram with n=2. Therefore, a bigram is a sequence of two words, appeared in documents. The frequency of each bigram of the string is considered as the text feature for text classification task.

17.3.2 Image Feature Analysis

The images are the graphical representations of the pixel values captured through the sensors from the real world. In social media, a significant amount of images are also used for sharing information. In order to analyze the image-based data we need to extract the features from image data, which minimizes the computational resource requirements as well as improves the classification ability. There are some essential feature selection approaches, which are discussed in this section.

Sobel operator: This method is simple to use, and efficient way for edge feature extraction. There are two types of operators or kernels (horizontal and vertical) for extracting edges. Both the operators are trying to find the complete curves from the given image. These operators are including a 3×3 matrix and used to perform convolution with the images to identify the edges. The matrix used in Sobel based processing is given in Figure 17.1.

The given kernels in Figure 17.1 are convoluted with the images to get edges (vertically and/or horizontally). The outcome of first kernel results G_x and second kernels results G_y as separate computations. But, we can also combine both the components to calculate final magnitude as:

$$|G| = \sqrt{Gx^2 + Gy^2}$$

It is also computed using:

$$|G| = |Gx| + |Gy|$$

−1	0	+1
−2	0	+2
−1	0	+1

G_x

+1	+2	+1
0	0	0
−1	−2	−1

G_y

Figure 17.1 Sobel kernels.

The edge degree or slop is measured as angle by using:

$$\theta = \arctan\left(\frac{Gy}{Gx}\right)$$

Local Binary Pattern (LBP): The textures feature of an image is extracted by using the neighbor pixel analysis using:

$$LBP_{P,R} = \sum_{P=0}^{P=1} s\left(g_p - g_e\right)2^P$$

$$s(x) = \begin{cases} 0\; x \geq 0 \\ 1\; x < 0 \end{cases}$$

where central pixel is given by g_e and neighbours pixels are denoted using g_p, number of neighbor pixels are P and radius is given by R. In this condition, for an image initial position (0, 0), the neighbor pixel g_p coordinates is given by:

$$\left(Rcos\left(\frac{2\pi p}{P}\right), Psin\left(\frac{2\pi P}{P}\right)\right)$$

For an image size I*J, LBP of each pixel is calculated as histogram and represented in form of:

$$H(k) = \sum_{i=1}^{I}\sum_{J=1}^{j} f\left(LBP_{p,r}(i,j),k\right), k \in [0,k]$$

$$f(x,y) = \begin{cases} 1\; x = y \\ 0\; otherwise \end{cases}$$

where, K is the highest value. The number of bitwise changes U is calculated as:

$$U\left(LBP_{P,R}\right)=\left|s\left(g_{p-1}-g_{e}\right)-s\left(g_{0}-g_{e}\right)\right|+\sum_{p=1}^{p-1}\left|s\left(g_{p}-g_{e}\right)-s\left(g_{p-1}-g_{e}\right)\right|$$

Static LBP means, it has small change ($U \leq 2$) in the center pixel neighbors. The transformation between $LBP_{P,R}$ to $LBP_{P,R}^{u2}$ has P*(P-1) +3 outputs. It is processed using a lookup table, which has 2^{P} components, and can be given as:

$$LBP_{P,r}^{riu2}=\begin{cases}\sum_{p=0}^{p-1} s\left(g_{p}-g_{e}\right) ifU\left(LBP_{P,R}\right)\leq 2\\ P+1\, otherwise\end{cases}$$

The mapping from $LBP_{P,R}$ to $LBP_{P,R}^{u2}$ which has P+2 distinct output values.

Sobal and LBP: The two different features extracted by using the Sobel operator and local binary pattern are stacked to gather for constructing this feature set. Thus the dataset has a dimension of (image size * 2) because the LBP and the Sobal are used with the gray scale images. The prepared feature set is further used with the ANN algorithm for training and validation.

Sobal, LBP, and Color: In this feature set, we utilize the LBP and the Sobal-based features as well as the image color feature are also associated with the feature vector. Therefore the feature set has the dimension of (Image Size * 5).

After implementing the different feature selection techniques of text and image data. Next, we can utilize machine learning algorithm for performing classification task. In this presented work, the aim is to compare the effectiveness of different text and image feature selection techniques. Therefore, we are utilizing the ANN algorithm. The implemented ANN model is a back-propagation neural network configuration. The configured ANN algorithm is used for training with the extracted text and image features. Additionally, after training the machine learning algorithm can be used for performing the classification of unknown data samples. In this section, we provide an overview of different approaches to feature selection, which are used for text and image data analysis. The next section provides the evaluation of the implemented feature selection techniques over the classification accuracy.

17.4 Results Analysis

In order to know which feature extraction technique is effective and appropriate for accurate text and image data classification, a set of experiment have been carry out. For conducting the experiments, we have identified and considered two different datasets obtained from Kaggle. The first dataset is used for hate speech detection using text posts, and the second dataset is used for sentiment analysis using images. Both datasets are processed using the described feature selection techniques and then a common ANN classifier is developed for classifying the features. There are two main parameters are measured in terms of accuracy and loss. The accuracy of a machine learning algorithm indicates the correctness of classification. That can be measured using the following formula:

$$Accuracy = \frac{Correctly\ Classified\ Samples}{Total\ Samples}$$

Additionally, the loss is not measured in terms of percentage but used to know the quality of training. That is a heuristic process which helps to minimize the error in prediction. In this presented work the binary cross entropy is considered as the loss function. Both the parameters are measured for training as well as validation of the algorithm and feature combination. Figure 17.2 shows the performance of feature selection approaches based on image classification.

Additionally Figure 17.3 shows the performance of text classification features. In both diagrams, the X axis contains the number of the training cycle (epoch) used and the Y axis is used for demonstrating the obtained accuracy and loss values. The accuracy can be defined as the amount of correctly classified instances over the total samples provided for classification. That is measured in terms of percentage (%). On the

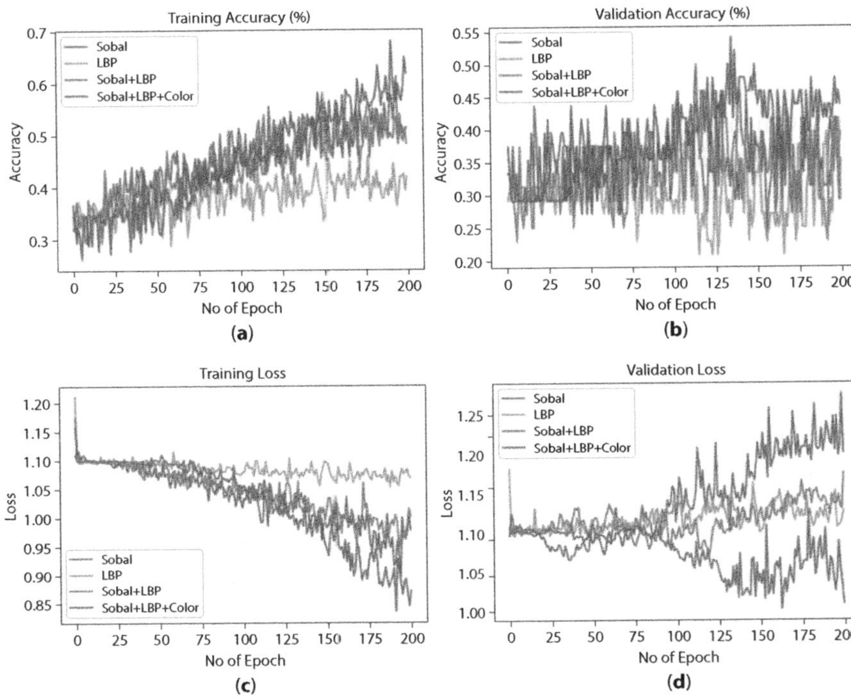

Figure 17.2 Performance of the feature selection techniques for classifying image data in terms of (a) training accuracy, (b) validation accuracy, (c) training loss, and (d) validation loss.

other hand, the loss is a heuristic function, which is used to estimate the distance between the current solution and desired solution. Figure 17.2(a) and Figure 17.3(a) show the training accuracy of the feature selection techniques for image and text respectively. Additionally, Figure 17.2(b) and Figure 17.3(b) show the validation accuracy of the feature selection techniques. Similarly, Figure 17.2(c) and Figure 17.3(c) show the training loss and Figure 17.2(d) and Figure 17.3(d) show the validation loss of the models. Based on the results obtained we found for image classification the combination of all the features Sobal, LBP and color-based feature provides higher classification accuracy for both training and validation. On the other hand for text classification during training word count Vectorizer provides higher classification accuracy but for validation, TF-IDF-based features provide higher accuracy. The similar reflection we can see on the calculated loss.

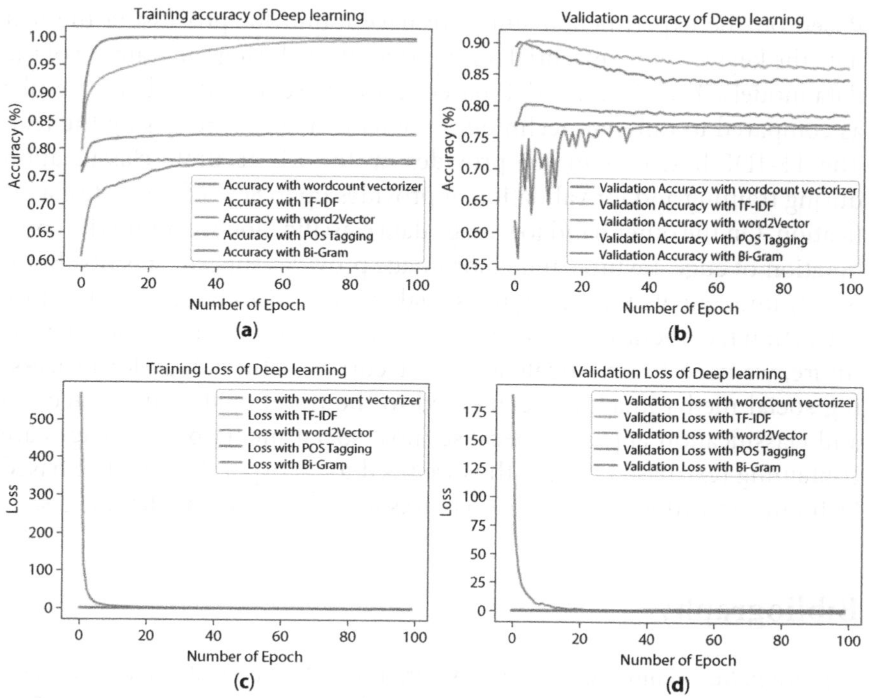

Figure 17.3 Performance of text feature extraction techniques in terms of (a) training accuracy, (b) validation accuracy, (c) training loss, and (d) validation loss.

17.5 Conclusions

Social media is one of the great sources of information. It is being utilized in various kinds of application development. Social media will contribute the data in different formats which are suitable for a range of applications. In this paper, we are contributing in three main parts first we provide a review of the recent development using social media data and machine learning techniques. Based on the survey we have identified the different algorithms used, datasets, and the key issues and challenges.

Among the different research issues the different formats of data processing are one of the key issues in developing a common framework. Therefore, in this presented work, we have studied different feature selection techniques which are utilized for selecting features from the image and text data. Further, an experimental study has been carried out for classifying different kinds of features selected from text and image data formats.

Based on the experimental study we have found for processing the text data the keywords are essential for incorporating during the training of the data models. Therefore TF-IDF-based features are providing better results as compared to different techniques implemented for processing the text. The TF-IDF-based technique provides up to 98% accurate classification during training and for validation, it provides up to 86% of accurate classification. On the other hand for image data classification we found the combination of edge, texture, and color image provides superior results. But it is very unfortunate for classifying social media images the classical feature extraction techniques are not providing effective results. Therefore, in near future, we need to investigate a more accurate methodology for processing social media images as compared to the traditional feature selection and classification approach because most social media-based images are containing text-based images thus we need to incorporate the OCR-based technique to extract appropriate features form the social media images.

Bibliography

1. Sami, M., Memon, S., Baloch, J., Mehran, S.B., An Automated Framework for finding Fake Accounts on Facebook. *Int. J. Adv. Stud. Comput. Sci. Eng.*, 7, 2, 8–16, 2018.
2. Ramalingam, D. and Chinnaiah, V., Fake profile detection techniques in large-scale online social networks: A comprehensive review. *Comput. Electr. Eng.*, 65, 1–13, 2017.
3. Farkasa, J., Schouc, J., Neumayer, C., Platformed antagonism: racist discourses on fake Muslim Facebook pages. *Crit. Discourse Stud.*, Taylor & Francis Group, 15, 5, 463–480, 2018.
4. Kesharwani, M., Kumari, S., Niranjan, V., Detecting Fake Social Media Account Using Deep Neural Networking. *Int. Res. J. Eng. Technol.*, 08, 07, 1191–1197, 2021.
5. Rone, J., Fake profiles, trolls, and digital paranoia: digital media practices in breaking the Indignados movement. *Social Mov. Stud.*, Taylor & Francis Group, 21, 1–2, 25–41, 2022.
6. Davidson, T., Warmsley, D., Macy, M., Weber, I., Automated Hate Speech Detection and the Problem of Offensive Language. *Proceedings of the Eleventh International AAAI Conference on Web and Social Media*, 2017.
7. Guiora, A. and Park, E.A., Hate Speech on Social Media. *Philosophia*, 45, 3, 957–971, 2017.
8. Barnidge, M., Kim, B., Sherrill, L.A., Luknard, Ž., Zhanga, J., Perceived exposure to and avoidance of hate speech in various communication settings. *Telemat. Inf.*, 44, 101263, 2019.

9. Mullah, N.S. and Zainon, W.M.N.W., Advances in Machine Learning Algorithms for Hate Speech Detection in Social Media: A Review. *IEEE*, 9, 88364–88376, 2021.
10. Ullmann, S. and Tomalin, M., Quarantining online hate speech: technical and ethical perspectives. *Ethics Inf. Technol.*, Springer, 22, 69–80, 2020.
11. Gupta, A. and Katarya, R., Social media based surveillance systems for healthcare using machine learning: A systematic review. *J. Biomed. Inf.*, Elsevier, 108, 103500, 2020.
12. Fan, C., Wu, F., Mostafavi, A., A Hybrid Machine Learning Pipeline for Automated Mapping of Events and Locations From Social Media in Disasters. *IEEE*, 8, 10478–10490, 2020.
13. Resch, B., Usländer, F., Havas, C., Combining machine-learning topic models and spatiotemporal analysis of social media data for disaster footprint and damage assessment. *Cartogr. Geogr. Inf. Sci.*, Taylor & Francis Group, 45, 4, 362–376, 2018.
14. Al-garadi, M.A., Hussain, M.R., Khan, N., Murtaza, G., Nweke, H.F., Ali, I., Mujtaba, G., Chiroma, H., Khattak, H.A., Gani, A., Predicting Cyberbullying on Social Media in the Big Data Era Using Machine Learning Algorithms: Review of Literature and Open Challenges. *IEEE*, 7, 2169–3536, 2019.
15. Subroto, A. and Apriyana, A., Cyber risk prediction through social media big data analytics and statistical machine learning. *J. Big Data*, Springer, 6, 50, 2019.
16. Arasu, B.S., Backia Seelan, B.J., Thamaraiselvan, N., A machine learning-based approach to enhancing social media marketing. *Comput. Electr. Eng.*, Elsevier, 86, 106723, 2020.
17. Adikari, A., Burnett, D., Sedera, D., de Silva, D., Alahakoon, D., Value co-creation for open innovation: An evidence-based study of the data driven paradigm of social media using machine learning. *Int. J. Inf. Manage. Data Insights*, Elsevier, 1, 100022, 2021.
18. Lim, S., Tucker, C.S., Kumar, S., An unsupervised machine learning model for discovering latent infectious diseases using social media data. *J. Biomed. Inf.*, Elsevier, 66, 82–94, 2017.
19. Kanan, T., Sadaqa, O., Aldajeh, A., Alshwabka, H., AL-dolime, W., AlZu'b, S., Elbes, M., Hawashin, B., Alia, M.A., A Review of Natural Language Processing and Machine Learning Tools Used to Analyze Arabic Social Media. *Jordan International Joint Conference on Electrical Engineering and Information Technology IEEE*, 2019.
20. Devaraj, A., Murthy, D., Dontula, A., Machine-learning methods for identifying social media-based requests for urgent help during hurricanes. *Int. J. Disaster Risk Reduct.*, Elsevier, 51, 101757, 2020.
21. Marquez, J.L.J., Carrasco, I.G., Cuadrado, J.L.L., Mezcua, B.R., Towards a big data framework for analyzing social media content. *Int. J. Inf. Manage.*, Elsevier, 44, 1–12, 2019.

22. Akhter, M.P., Jiangbin, Z., Naqvi, I.R., Majeed, M.A., Zia, T., Abusive language detection from social media comments using conventional machine learning and deep learning approaches. *Multimed. Syst.*, Springer, 28, 1925–1940, 2022.
23. Clayton, K., Blair, S., Busam, J.A., Forstner, S., Glance, J., Green, G., Kawata, A., Kovvuri, A., Martin, J., Morgan, E., Sandhu, M., Sang, R., Bright, R.S., Welch, A.T., Wolf, A.G., Zhou, A., Nyhan, B., Real Solutions for Fake News? Measuring the Effectiveness of General Warnings and Fact Check Tags in Reducing Belief in False Stories on Social Media. *Political Behav.*, Springer, 42, 1073–1095, 2020.
24. Sommariva, S., Vamos, C., Mantzarlis, A., Đào, L.U.L., Tyson, D.M., Spreading the (Fake) News: Exploring Health Messages on Social Media and the Implications for Health Professionals Using a Case Study. *Am. J. Health Educ.*, Taylor & Francis Group, 49, 4, 1–10, 2018.
25. Aldwairi, M. and Alwahedi, A., Detecting Fake News in Social Media Networks. *Procedia Comput. Sci.*, Elsevier, 141, 215–222, 2018.
26. Talwar, S., Dhir, A., Kaur, P., Zafar, N., Alrasheedy, M., Why do people share fake news? Associations between the dark side of social media use and fake news sharing behavior. *J. Retail. Consum. Serv.*, Elsevier, 51, 72–82, 2019.
27. Shu, K., Wang, S., Liu, H., Understanding User Profiles on Social Media for Fake News Detection. *Conference: FakeMM'18 Workshop*, 2018.
28. Babu, N.V., Kanaga, E.G.M., Sentiment Analysis in Social Media Data for Depression Detection Using Artifcial Intelligence: A Review. *SN Comput. Sci.*, 3, 74, 2022.

About the Editors

Dr. Rathishchandra R. Gatti

Dr. Rathishchandra R. Gatti is currently a researcher in the field of self-powered systems, energy harvesting, and wave energy and also working as a Professor, Department of Mechanical and Robotics Engineering, Sahyadri College of Engineering & Management, Mangaluru, Visvesvaraya Technological University, Belagavi, India. Prior to his role, he has worked as Research Academic and IP Analyst at Curtin University, Australia; NPI program manager at General Electric; Design Engineering roles at Meritor Automotive; SVI; and Rapsri. He pursued his B.E. in Mechanical Engineering from NITK Suratkal, MBA from IGNOU, PG Diploma in Global Strategic Management from ICFAI, and PhD from Curtin University, Perth, Australia. His PhD work "Spatially varying multi-degree-of-freedom electro-magnetic energy harvesting" was funded by an Australian Post Graduate Award fellowship by the Australian Federal Government for PG students of exceptional research potential. During his PhD, he also pursued Graduate Certificate in Research Commercialization funded by GCRC fellowship from Commonwealth Australia. His awards during his tenure at GE IIC include the following: Management Award from GE India Innovation Centre for efficient execution of NPI projects, GE APPLAUSE Award for patented Retrofit LV Switchgear, GE Centre of Excellence Contribution Award, and a Micro Innovation Award from GE India Innovation Centre. His current projects include point absorber wave energy generator, which is funded by VGST, Government of India, and automated robotic welding TIG and MIG funded by KCTU, Government of Karnataka State. His previous funded projects include "Design, fabrication and characterization of cantilever based *in vitro* body energy harvester using piezoelectric composites" funded by INUP, GoI; "Affordable hybrid solar-mechanical powered agricultural dryer" funded by TRIP-VGST; and about 3 KSCST student projects. During his tenure at GE, he has worked on industrial R&D projects that include Zero Energy Home and Lexus Panel, which are relevant to early-stage smart grids (2004–2008). He has 4 international patents—1 US Patent, 1 Mexican Patent, 1 Canadian

Patent commercialized at GE, and 1 Indian Patent (filed) at SCEM. He has around 13 publications to his credit. He is a reviewer of *IEEE Transactions on Magnetics, Journal of Mechanical Systems and Signal Processing*, and *Walailak Journal of Science and Technology*.

Mr. Chandra Singh

Mr. Chandra Singh has been working as Assistant Professor at NMAM Institute of Technology, Nitte (Deemed to be University). He has 6+ years of experience in academics, research, and administration. He is currently pursuing PhD in Optical Communication from Visvesvaraya Technological University. He has obtained M. Tech and B.E. from NMAM Institute of Technology, Nitte, and Srinivas School of Engineering, Mukka, Mangaluru, respectively. He has received best project awards during his engineering and Masters also. Prof. Chandra Singh has published 9 books, 15 book chapters, and more than 15 research articles in reputed peer-reviewed national and international journals, presented around 10 papers in national and international conferences, and attended more than 20 conferences, seminars, and workshops. He has been granted/awarded 4 international patents and 6 Indian patents. He was awarded with 4 best paper awards from conferences conducted by institutes of repute. He has been awarded HackerRank Topper twice for Python & Advanced CPP conducted by VIT, Chennai FDP organized under IIT Bombay Spoken Tutorial under Pandith Madan Mohan Malaviya National Mission on Teachers and Teaching and NMEICT funded by MHRD, Government of India. He has also emerged as one of the toppers of a Java quiz held at FDP organized by VIT, Chennai. He has also received several best guide awards for guiding noteworthy projects from various authorities of central and state government. He has served as TPC/PC member for IEEE DISCOVER 2023, CASE 2022, ICMIAC 2022, DTIS 2021, DPPR 2021, ICSC 2019, MRCN 2020, SPTM 2020, and ICCCIS-2021. He has also served as reviewer for IEEE DISCOVER 2018, ICSC 2019, MRCN 2020, and SPTM 2021. His areas of interest are optical networking and communication, wireless communication, IoT machine learning, robotics, and CPS.

Index

Also of Interest

Check out these other related titles from Scrivener Publishing

Urban Transportation Systems: Sustainability and Future Development, By Kundan Meshram, ISBN: 9781394228249. Written and edited by a team of experts in the field, this exciting new volume covers the most up-to-date advances, theories, and practical applications for non-motorized transportation (NMT) systems, geographic information system-based transportation systems, and signal processing for urban transportation systems.

AI for Autonomous Vehicles: The Future of Driverless Technology, Edited by Sathiyaraj Rajendran, Munish Sabharwal, Yu-Chen Hu, Rajesh Kumar Dhanaraj, and Balamurugan Balusamy, ISBN: 9781119847465. This title presents the research prospects and security challenges present in the exciting new field of autonomous vehicles by comprehensively introducing advanced concepts of artificial intelligence (AI) in driverless technology.

SMART GRIDS FOR SMART CITIES VOLUME 1, Edited by O.V. Gnana Swathika, K. Karthikeyan, and Sanjeevikumar Padmanaban, ISBN: 9781119872078. Written and edited by a team of experts in the field, this first volume in a two-volume set focuses on an interdisciplinary perspective on the financial, environmental, and other benefits of smart grid technologies and solutions for smart cities.

SMART GRIDS FOR SMART CITIES VOLUME 2: Real-Time Applications in Smart Cities, Edited by O.V. Gnana Swathika, K. Karthikeyan, and Sanjeevikumar Padmanaban, ISBN: 9781394215874. Written and edited by a team of experts in the field, this second volume in a two-volume set focuses on an interdisciplinary perspective on the financial, environmental, and other benefits of smart grid technologies and solutions for smart cities.

INTEGRATED GREEN ENERGY SOLUTIONS VOLUME 1, Edited by Milind Shrinivas Dangate, W. S. Sampath, O. V. Gnana Swathika, and Sanjeevikumar Padmanaban, ISBN: 9781119847434. This first volume in a two-volume set presents the state of the art for the concepts, practical applications, and future of renewable energy and how to move closer to true sustainability.

INTEGRATED GREEN ENERGY SOLUTIONS VOLUME 2, Edited by Milind Shrinivas Dangate, W. S. Sampath, O. V. Gnana Swathika, and Sanjeevikumar Padmanaban, ISBN: 9781394193660. This second volume in a two-volume set continues to present the state of the art for the concepts, practical applications, and future of renewable energy and how to move closer to true sustainability.

MODERN AUTOMOTIVE ELECTRICAL SYSTEMS: Theory and Applications, Edited by Pedram Asef, Sanjeevikumar Padmanaban, and Andrew Lapthorn, ISBN: 1119801047. Presenting the concepts and advances of modern automotive electrical systems, this volume, written and edited by a global team of experts, also goes into the practical applications for the engineer, student, and other industry professionals.

INTELLIGENT GREEN TECHNOLOGIES FOR SMART CITIES, Edited by Suman Lata Tripathi, Souvik Ganguli, Abhishek Kumar, and Tengiz Magradze, ISBN: 9781119816065. Presenting the concepts and fundamentals of smart cities and developing "green" technologies, this volume, written and edited by a global team of experts, also goes into the practical applications that can be utilized across multiple disciplines and industries, for both the engineer and the student.

DESIGN AND DEVELOPMENT OF EFFICIENT ENERGY SYSTEMS, Edited by Suman Lata Tripathi, Dushyant Kumar Singh, Sanjeevikumar Padmanaban, and P. Raja, ISBN: 9781119761631. Covering the concepts and fundamentals of efficient energy systems, this volume, written and edited by a global team of experts, also goes into the practical applications that can be utilized across multiple industries, for both the engineer and the student.

Green Energy: Solar Energy, Photovoltaics, and Smart Cities, Edited by Suman Lata Tripathi and Sanjeevikumar Padmanaban, ISBN: 9781119760764. Covering the concepts and fundamentals of green energy, this volume, written and edited by a global team of experts, also goes into the practical applications that can be utilized across multiple industries, for both the engineer and the student.

HYDROGEN ELECTRICAL VEHICLES, Edited by Mehmet Sankir and Nurdan Demirci Sankir, ISBN: 9781394166381. Hydrogen electrical vehicles are an essential component of the "Green New Deal" and this book covers cutting-edge technologies designed for fuel-cell-powered cars.

PAVEMENT ASSET MANAGEMENT, By Ralph Haas, W.R. Hudson, and Lynne Cowe Falls, ISBN: 9781119038702. Whether you are new to managing pavement assets or a seasoned practitioner, this book provides the most up-to-date information in the field on the history, technology, practice and look ahead.

Printed and bound by CPI Group (UK) Ltd, Croydon, CR0 4YY
17/09/2026
14964261-0005